Dignity and International Human Rights Law

The Punta del Este Declaration, and this book dedicated to elaborating upon it, is devoted to exploring the ways that human dignity for everyone everywhere can be a useful tool in helping to address the challenges and strains facing human rights in the world today.

In 2018, an initiative was instigated to revitalize the human rights project by way of engaging the notion of human dignity. This resulted in the Punta Del Este Declaration on Human Dignity for Everyone Everywhere (Punta Del Este Declaration), a declaration co-authored by over 30 human rights experts from all over the world. The Punta Del Este Declaration simplifies and brings coherence to the concept of human dignity in 10 brief statements that capture the many dimensions and aspects of human dignity and the practical ways that human dignity is useful in the promotion of human rights. This book provides an overview of how the notion of human dignity has been used to strengthen human rights. It discusses how human dignity plays many different roles in human rights discourse and has the force to revitalize the human rights project; it is the foundational principle upon which the human rights project is built. But it is also the telos, or end goal, of human rights. At the same time, it is an important evaluative mechanism for assessing how well a country is doing in the implementation of human rights.

The book will be a valuable resource for all those working in the areas of International Human Rights Law, Legal Philosophy, and Law and Religion.

Brett G. Scharffs is the Rex E. Lee Chair and Professor of Law; Director, International Center for Law and Religion Studies, Brigham Young University, USA.

Ewelina U. Ochab is a human rights advocate, author and co-founder of the Coalition for Genocide Response.

ICLARS Series on Law and Religion

The *ICLARS Series on Law and Religion* is a new series designed to provide a forum for the rapidly expanding field of research in law and religion. The series is published in association with the International Consortium for Law and Religion Studies, an international network of scholars and experts of law and religion founded in 2007 with the aim of providing a place where information, data and opinions can easily be exchanged among members and made available to the broader scientific community. The series aims to become a primary source for students and scholars while presenting authors with a valuable means to reach a wide and growing readership.

Series Editors:
Silvio Ferrari, University of Milan, Italy, Russell Sandberg, Cardiff University, UK, Pieter Coertzen, University of Stellenbosch, South Africa, W. Cole Durham, Jr., Brigham Young University, USA, and Tahir Mahmood, Amity International University, India

Other titles in this series:

Law, Religion, and Freedom
Conceptualizing a Common Right
Edited by W. Cole Durham, Jr., Javier Martínez-Torrón, and Donlu Thayer

Dignity and International Human Rights Law
An Introduction to the Punta del Este Declaration on Human Dignity for Everyone Everywhere
Brett G. Scharffs and Ewelina U. Ochab

Law, State and Religion in Bosnia and Herzegovina
Nedim Begović and Emir Kovačević

For more information about this series, please visit:
www.routledge.com/ICLARS-Series-on-Law-and-Religion/book-series/ICLARS

Dignity and International Human Rights Law

An Introduction to the Punta del Este Declaration on Human Dignity for Everyone Everywhere

Brett G. Scharffs and Ewelina U. Ochab

Routledge
Taylor & Francis Group
LONDON AND NEW YORK

First published 2022
by Routledge
2 Park Square, Milton Park, Abingdon, Oxon OX14 4RN

and by Routledge
605 Third Avenue, New York, NY 10158

Routledge is an imprint of the Taylor & Francis Group, an informa business

British Library Cataloguing-in-Publication Data
A catalogue record for this book is available from the British Library

Library of Congress Cataloging-in-Publication Data
Names: Scharffs, Brett G., author. | Ochab, Ewelina U., author.
Title: Dignity and international human rights law : an introduction to the Punta del Este Declaration on Human Dignity for everyone everywhere / edited by Brett Scharffs and Ewelina U. Ochab.
Description: Abingdon, Oxon ; New York, NY : Routledge, 2021. |
Series: Iclars series on law and religion | Includes bibliographical references and index.
Identifiers: LCCN 2021016738 (print) | LCCN 2021016739 (ebook) |
ISBN 9781032074580 (hardback) | ISBN 9781003207030 (paperback) |
ISBN 9781032074627 (ebook)
Subjects: LCSH: Respect for persons--Law and legislation. | Punta del Este Declaration on Human Dignity for Everyone Everywhere. | United Nations. General Assembly. Universal Declaration of Human Rights.
Classification: LCC K3249 .S33 2021 (print) | LCC K3249 (ebook) |
DDC 341.4/8--dc23
LC record available at https://lccn.loc.gov/2021016738
LC ebook record available at https://lccn.loc.gov/2021016739

ISBN: 978-1-032-07458-0 (hbk)
ISBN: 978-1-032-07462-7 (pbk)
ISBN: 978-1-003-20703-0 (ebk)

DOI: 10.4324/9781003207030

Typeset in Galliard
by Taylor & Francis Books

Dedicated to wonderful experts and friends taken from us too early – Norberto Padilla and Juan Marin Vives – and to all who continue to struggle to have their human rights recognized, affirmed and protected.

Contents

Acknowledgments xv
Foreword by Ján Figel' xvi

Introduction 1

1 Seventy years after the Universal Declaration of Human Rights: Towards strengthening the protection of human rights 9

Introduction 9
The rationale for the Punta del Este Declaration: human rights in the world today 11
Universality of human rights 12
Implementation and application of human rights 13
Understanding human rights 16
Implementing human rights 16
Monitoring and enforcing human rights 21
Human dignity for everyone everywhere 24
The "Human Dignity for Everyone Everywhere" project 25
What the Punta del Este Declaration is not 28
Conclusions 35

2 An introduction to the Punta del Este Declaration and its Preamble 36

Introduction 36
Expanded explanation of the Declaration's title 36
Preliminary consideration: human dignity "of" and "for" everyone everywhere 36
Expanded explanation of the Declaration's Preamble 38
The "whereas" clauses 38

The "recalling" clauses 44
The "recognizing" clauses 54
The "emphasizing" clauses 60
The "believing" clauses 62
The "hoping" clause 63
Expanded explanation of the reaffirmation of the initial declaration of the UDHR 64
A common standard of achievement 64
For all peoples and all nations 65
For every individual and every organ of society 65
Keeping the Declaration constantly in mind 67
Striving through teaching and education 68
By progressive measures 69
Local, national, and international 70
Securing their universal and effective recognition and observance 71
Conclusion 72

3 Article 1: Foundation, objective, and criterion 73

a. The inherent human dignity of all people and the importance of respecting, promoting, and protecting human dignity for everyone everywhere is the foundational principle and the key objective or goal of human rights 73
Foundational principle 74
The aim or end of human rights 75
b. Human dignity for everyone everywhere is an invaluable criterion for evaluating laws, policies, and government actions for how well they accord with human rights standards 76
c. Protecting, promoting, and guaranteeing respect for the human dignity of everyone is a fundamental obligation of states, governments, and other public bodies, whether local, regional, national, or international 80
d. Promoting human dignity is also a responsibility of all sectors of society, and each of us as human beings 81
e. Promoting human dignity is the key to protecting the equal and inalienable rights of all members of the human family, and remains the foundation of freedom, justice, and peace in the world 83

4 Article 2: Generating agreement and building common understanding 86

a. The inherent dignity of every human being was the key idea that helped generate agreement and a common understanding at the time of the adoption of the UDHR about human rights of all people, in spite of diversity and deep differences, notwithstanding divergent political and legal systems 86

b. Human dignity for everyone everywhere is valuable as a point of departure for exploring and understanding the meaning of human rights 105

c. Human dignity for everyone everywhere is a basis for finding common ground regarding human rights and consensus about their content and meaning 107

d. Dignity provides an approach to building bridges between various normative justifications of human rights, including those with religious and secular theoretical groundings 116

e. Respecting human dignity for everyone everywhere facilitates discussions on different conceptions of shared values 122

f. Human dignity is a broad concept that nevertheless invites in-depth reflection within different traditions and perspectives 123

g. Human dignity for all reminds us that human rights are universal, inalienable, indivisible, interdependent, and interrelated 124

Universal 125

Inalienable 125

Indivisible 126

Interdependent 126

Interrelated 126

5 Article 3: Defining and specifying human rights 127

a. Dignity is an essential part of what it means to be human 127

Definitions of human dignity 127

Dignity as status 129

Human dignity as worth 132

Dignity in international and domestic law 134

Treaties 135

The Convention on the Rights of the Child 137

Domestic laws 140

Agreement about core definition 140

Human dignity is broader than human rights 142

b. Respect for human dignity for everyone everywhere helps us define and understand the meaning and scope of all human rights 144
Defining and understanding the rights of conscience 144
c. Focusing concretely and in actual situations on human dignity and its implications for particular human rights claims can help identify the specific content of these rights as well as how we understand human dignity itself 148
Human dignity and the rights of enemy combatants 149
Flexible universalism and different social, political, legal, and economic contexts 151

6 Article 4: Duties and responsibilities 152

a. Human dignity for everyone everywhere emphasizes the concept in the UDHR that rights include accompanying obligations and responsibilities, not just of states but also of all human beings with respect to the rights of others 152
Distortions of a rights-first (or rights-only) approach to human rights 154
The UDHR on rights and duties 155
The conceptual connections between rights and duties 156
Not every interest creates a right 159
Not every right will be immediately realized 160
Human dignity for everyone everywhere: implications for rights and duties 162
The duty of the state: duty to protect 163
Consequences of exaggerating the state's duties regarding human rights 165
The duty of others: duty to respect and promote 166
Other rights instruments on the relationship between rights and duties 166
b. Dignity is a status shared by every human being, and the emphasis on everyone and everywhere makes it clear that rights are characterized by reciprocity and involve corresponding duties 167
The duty of others: duty to respect and promote 168
My duty to others 168
My duty to myself 169
c. Everyone should be concerned not only with his or her own dignity and rights but with the dignity and rights of every human being 170
Rights as shields or spears 170
Overreliance on courts for defining and vindicating rights 171
Respecting ourselves 171

Respecting others 171
Human dignity and freedom 171
d. Nonetheless, human dignity is not diminished on the ground that persons are not fulfilling their responsibilities to the state and others 172
Human rights are not conditional upon people fulfilling their responsibilities 172
Basic human rights and human dignity exist without conditions or prerequisites 173
The state has obligations to respect and protect the dignity of those who violate their duties 173
Acting in a dignified manner is not a prerequisite to having human dignity or human rights 174

7 Article 5: Education 175

a. Recognition of human dignity is a vital basis for teaching and education 175
b. Human rights education is of importance to promoting respect for the equal dignity of everyone 176
The UN Declaration on Human Rights Education and Training 177
World Program for Human Rights Education 179
Sustainable Development Goals 179
c. Human rights education is essential for sustaining dignity and human rights into the future 182
d. Equal access to education is a crucial aspect of respecting human dignity 182

8 Article 6: Seeking common ground 184

a. Focusing on human dignity for everyone everywhere encourages people to search for ways to find common ground regarding competing claims 184
Religious freedom and non-discrimination 184
Ordinary exceptions to non-discrimination provisions 187
b. Focusing on human dignity for everyone everywhere encourages people to move beyond exclusively legal mechanisms for harmonizing, implementing, and mutually vindicating human rights and finding solutions to conflicts 188
Informal accommodations of conscience 188

9 Article 7: Implementing and realizing human rights in legislation 193

a. Recognition of human dignity for everyone everywhere is a foundational principle of law and is central to developing and protecting human rights in law and policy 193

Human dignity and the specification of human rights 193

Human dignity in law as a response to dictatorship or severe injustice 194

Human dignity in the German Basic Law 195

Human dignity in other legal systems 197

Is dignity too vague to be useful? 201

Dignity as the foundational value of the social order 202

Human dignity may have different meanings in different legal systems 203

The implications of treating dignity as an absolute right 203

Other uses of dignity as a constitutional principle 204

Dignity as a principle in adjudication 205

b. The richness of the concept of dignity resists exhaustive definition, but it encourages the pursuit of optimum mutual vindication where conflicting rights and values are involved 209

Human dignity's upward lift 209

Mutual vindication of dignity 209

c. Human dignity is critical for moving beyond exclusively thinking in terms of balancing and trade-offs of rights and interests 210

10 Article 8: Reconciliation and adjudication 212

a. Recognition of human dignity for everyone everywhere is an important constitutional and legal principle for reconciling and adjudicating competing human rights claims, as well as claims between human rights and other important national and societal interests 212

b. Mutual vindication of rights may be possible in adjudication and may be further facilitated if all involved focus on respecting the human dignity of everyone 213

c. When mutual vindication of rights is not possible, dignity for all can help us to delineate the scope of rights, to set the boundaries of permissible restrictions on the exercise of rights and freedoms, and to seek to bring into fair balance competing rights claims 215

d. Respect for dignity plays an important role not only in formal adjudication but also in mediation or other forms of alternative dispute resolution 216

11 Article 9: Potential difficulties involving competing human rights claims 218

a. Respecting the human dignity of everyone everywhere supports effective human rights advocacy 218
b. Recognizing the universal and reciprocal character of human dignity is a corrective to positions claiming rights for some but not for others 220
Human dignity and dignitary harms 221
Human dignity and identity politics 221
c. It helps to diffuse the hostility that is often associated with human rights controversies and to foster constructive dialogue. It also helps mitigate the distortion, avoidance, and selective recognition of human dignity 222
Distortion and avoidance of human rights 222
Instrumentalization of human rights 223
Depoliticizing human rights 225

12 Article 10: Most egregious and most feasible 226

a. Human dignity for everyone everywhere reminds us to work toward the elimination of the most egregious abuses of the human rights of individuals and groups, including genocide, crimes against humanity, war crimes, and other atrocities 226
Egregious abuses of human dignity 227
Human dignity and the road to "final solution" 227
Contemporary genocides 228
b. Human dignity for everyone everywhere reminds us to protect those human beings most at-risk of human rights violations 229
c. At the same time, it encourages efforts to respond to problems that may be amenable to practical and feasible solutions 231
Conclusion 231

13 Conclusions and the way forward 232

Introduction 232
How should the Punta del Este Declaration be used? 232
The Human Dignity for Everyone Everywhere approach 234
Strengthening human rights mechanisms 235

Appendix A: The Punta del Este Declaration on Human Dignity for Everyone Everywhere 237

Appendix B: African perspectives on human dignity for everyone everywhere: An endorsement and elaboration of the Punta del Este Declaration on Dignity for Everyone Everywhere 242
Bibliography 247
Index 262

Acknowledgments

The authors would like to acknowledge contributions of the many who helped with the work around the Punta del Este Declaration of Human Dignity for Everyone Everywhere and on this manuscript. This book wouldn't have been possible without their invaluable assistance.

We also would like to thank 2019 fellows Sara Plater, Madison Moss, Rachel Whipple, Miranda Cherkas, and Gabriell Sabalones, and 2020 fellows Brock Mason and Chery Yang who provided research assistance.

We are grateful to Jane Wise for her language editing and proofreading.

We would like to thank the International Center for Law and Religion Studies (ICLRS) at BYU Law School for accommodating some of the research that went into the manuscript.

We express our gratitude to the convenors of the Punta Del Este Conference, namely, Carmen Asiaín Pereira, Heiner Bielefeldt, W. Cole Durham, Jr., Ján Figel', Tahir Mahmood, Alberto Melloni, Dicky Sofjan, Renáta Uitz, and Robin Fretwell Wilson.

Foreword by Ján Figel'

Human dignity and fraternity: roots and fruits of human rights universality

Religion has been with humankind from the beginning of history helping to build personal relationships and communities (*religare*). Faith served to inspire, to strengthen spiritual life, and to guide the human person. But religion has been frequently abused in the quest for power and supremacy, and to subdue others. We have seen repetitive waves of persecution and mass atrocities, the latest ones in Sri Lanka, New Zealand, Burkina Faso, and Nigeria. Peace and peaceful cohabitation of different people, communities, and cultures are based on justice. Justice for all. The core of modern justice is defined by fundamental human rights. And human dignity is a foundational principle of all human rights.

Why do we need to emphasize dignity? Because we need to defend principles of justice against religious and other types of fundamentalism, ideological and totalitarian oppression, and ethical relativism. We witness opposition to the universality of fundamental human rights, divisions among countries and nations on human rights, and the refusal or questioning of these rights in times of migration crises. If there is a point of convergence and consent between religious humanists and secular humanists, it is human dignity as a base of each person's undeniable and inalienable rights. Dignity is a privileged way to correctly address issues of freedom and equality in society.

Human dignity is the common denominator of the three monotheistic religions. All Abrahamic traditions consider that religious freedom is rooted in the dignity of the human person. It is their common denominator, from the past and for the future.

In Judaism, the notion of Human Dignity (*medabèr 'al kavod*) is a key concern. In the first place, human dignity stems from a person's resemblance to God in the story of Genesis. An important question then is to interpret whether dignity is in the likeness of the divine. Or, if there is a dignity that is intrinsic to human nature and that is sourced without reference to transcendence? A vast question, indeed. Other references underline the importance of dignity in Judaism. This dignity granted to humans gives freedom but also demands responsibility and creativity.

In Christianity, human dignity is equally central. Let me share this quote:

> A sense of the dignity of the human person has been impressing itself more and more deeply on the consciousness of contemporary [men and women], and the demand is increasingly made that men [and women] should act on their judgment, enjoying and making use of responsible freedom, not driven by coercion but motivated by a sense of duty.

This is the first paragraph of *Dignitatis Humanae* of 1965, the Declaration on Religious Freedom made by the Second Vatican Council. It speaks to all of us today. "The Council further declares that the right to religious freedom has its foundation in the very dignity of the human person."

In Islam, human dignity (*karamah*) is an important and well-established principle. The very foundation of the dignity of women and men is that they have been endowed with reason and freedom of belief, opinion, and expression. As a result, no one has the right to judge people for their faith or persecute and discriminate against them on religious or ethnic grounds or wage war against someone because of their beliefs. The right to dignity is a key part of the Beirut Declaration on Religious Freedom (Makassed Philanthropic Islamic Association, June 20, 2015). This is a powerful and clear text reminding us of the Quranic roots of this freedom. The importance of human beings and dignity in the Quran is established since "the angels are asked to bow down to Adam."

Therefore, major faith traditions affirm a commitment to upholding the dignity and the equal worth of all human beings, women and men. It is often forgotten that the Universal Declaration of Human Rights is based on and derived from values common to major religions.

Three dimensions of human dignity

Human dignity can be articulated in three dimensions, which are critical for a positive change in the human rights climate: Me – Thee – We. They need to be brought together.

Human dignity concerns me. My specificity is my uniqueness. In common with every person, past, present, and future billions, I am unique. And from this uniqueness, I draw my dignity and project my specificity. This is something original that nobody can ever replicate or replace. It is a specific and unique contribution to my fellow human beings. If this originality, authenticity, and uniqueness is not "revealed," is not "fulfilled," it will be lost. My own dignity causes me to interpret the world, make choices, and interact with others, according to my conscience, my reason, and my convictions. To do so I need to exercise all my freedoms: freedom of thought, of expression, of action.

Human dignity is not limited to my freedom. It includes the freedom of the other. It invites me to exercise tolerance and to define my limits, to respect the other. There is of course also an imperative of equity and equality and therefore of justice. It is certainly not a coincidence that Plato, in his *Republic*, gives such a central place to justice, presenting it as mortal perfection. It is not abstract. Plato delineates it in concrete terms: "to render to each one his due, this is the fact of justice." It contributes directly and centrally to living together in the city.

Human dignity is a responsibility that must be shouldered. If dignity gives rise to rights, it also implies duties and responsibilities. These responsibilities are not fixed or static, but must be developed and exercised, and maintained through time. Also, human dignity is not only an individual responsibility. Since I am part of the community, dignity has also a collective, a social, or societal dimension. The "religious social responsibility" in particular is that of seeking the "common good." For their part, religious actors need to contribute to the strengthening of social cohesion and justice in society.

Consequently, we need to rediscover the old notion of the "common good" coined in the 13th century by Thomas Aquinas. *Bonum communae* was a decisive objective for Schuman, Adenauer, and de Gasperi, when they launched the unparalleled project of European integration. This notion has the advantage of summarizing the principles and objectives set out in the European Treaties (solidarity, subsidiarity, proportionality). However, it seems again the most relevant ethical and political vision to face the most burning issues we need to address today in the world.

Let me add some references to the European Union, as the first-ever EU Special Envoy on Freedom of Religion or Belief.

(1) Any contribution that the EU seeks to make to the cause of freedom of religion or belief must be constructive and promoted through a rights-based approach and cooperation. Not teaching, not preaching, but sharing.

We are here to listen, to engage, but also to learn. To play host to each other. It is only through "shared hospitality" that we can live together without divisions and conflicts, united in diversity. The alternative is to give in to the temptations of populism, nationalism, and violent extremism.

(2) Attention to youth and education is a prerequisite for fruitful hospitality. Schools, universities, and textbooks play a major role in the presentation of the other. There is dignity of difference, says Jeffrey Sachs.[1] We are all different in identity, but we are all equal in dignity! Europe and the world have had to learn the importance of education to peace and reconciliation. Robert Schuman[2] believed that the "detoxification" of history textbooks, on both sides, was one of the first necessities of peace. This is *conditio sine qua non* for Israeli–Palestinian peaceful coexistence. Pope Francis in his Al-Azhar address (April 2017) made education a top priority; education could become, he said, "wisdom for life if it draws out of men and women the best of themselves, is centered on human dignity, fosters a sense of identity, and overcomes temptations to rigidity and closed-mindedness."

1 Professor of economics and Director of the Center for Sustainable Development at Columbia University.

2 A Luxembourg-born French statesman regarded as one of the founding fathers of European unity.

Finally, the European Union attaches to human dignity the primary position in the Charter of Fundamental Rights of the Union (Title 1, Article 1).

The Abu Dhabi Declaration: Document on Human Fraternity for world peace and living together (February 2019) starts with "Human beings equal in rights, duties, and dignity ..." Equal dignity gives each of us a place within one human family, one humanity. Therefore, in line with the UDHR, a spirit of sisterhood and brotherhood is our duty and right. To be treated as brothers and sisters and to treat others as brothers and sisters. The concept of dignity is basic to the reason and logic behind the universality of human rights. Dignity is the root/source of inalienable and undeniable rights of each person. The universality of human rights is implicit in the logical character of fundamental human rights. And fraternity is the fruit of this conviction. Dignity is the root and fraternity is the fruit of these roots. One, equal dignity calls for one, equal fraternity. This represents one humanity and universality of humankind.

Human dignity, the universality of rights, and the duty or privilege of the fraternity are interrelated, indivisible – like roots, trees, and fruits. Without equal dignity, how could we speak about universality, the oneness of humankind, and the demands of fraternity? Individual human dignity entered global constitutional history in a small country – Ireland, in 1937. But after the drama of World War II, we can find it in many modern constitutions – those of Federal Germany and India for example, but also in the UN Charter and Universal Declaration of Human Rights. To bear more and better fruits of this universal, humane approach to our conflicted world, we must cultivate this notion: the understanding and promotion of human dignity for all. We all need to nurture cultures of human dignity.

Let me conclude by reflecting on the Declaration on Human Dignity for Everyone Everywhere, adopted in December 2018, in Punta del Este, Uruguay. By issuing the Punta del Este Declaration, its signatories wish to respect and protect the human dignity of every human person as to its innate worth. And to make an even stronger and active commitment, they subscribe to "human dignity for everyone everywhere." Dignity is described here as the foundational principle, criterion, and key objective of human rights.

Despite the achievements of the landmark document that the Universal Declaration still represents, we need a positive change in the human rights climate. The Punta del Este Declaration appears as an active step to trigger this transformation throughout the ongoing UDHR jubilee year and beyond. In other words, it is an invitation to the global community for an enriching conversation about "dignity for everyone everywhere." The Declaration is a commitment to tapping the inspirational potential of the notion of human dignity and to promote cultures of human dignity. Economy and security are necessities like daily bread. But culture gives sense to our lives and to our living together, gives meaning to our relations. While economy and security are the roots, culture is the flowering.

There are many commendable initiatives on peaceful coexistence, from Morocco, Jordan, Bahrain, UAE, the Vatican, and Al Azhar.

Therefore, it is time to move onwards and upwards together, to do more, and to do it better. Every community and country must move forward. Change comes from words to deeds to habits forming character, impacting culture, and destiny. A culture of human dignity for all is the opposite of ignorance and stands against intolerance, indifference, and fear. The 21st century can be an era of hope, replacing the past century of divisions, manipulative propaganda, violence, and genocides. We must stand up to our promise: NEVER AGAIN will there be a genocide. We must learn how to live (not just to exist) in diversity. Special attention must be given to young people: working with youth, for youth, through youth, and finding a peaceful future for the MENA region, for the Israeli–Palestinian conflict, for a democratic Pakistan, for peace and real development in the ACP countries.

Respect for human dignity starts with respect of FoRB, i.e., freedom of thought, conscience, and religion. My hope is for a renewed, strong commitment to human dignity culture. Thank you very much for your attention, cooperation, and support.

Ján Figel', Special Envoy for Promotion of Freedom of Religion outside the EU, National Press Club, Washington D.C., July 15, 2019, at the side event conference to the 2nd Ministerial Summit on Advancing Religious Freedom

Introduction

The project culminating in the Punta del Este Declaration began with an anecdote. In January 2018, Ján Figel', the EU Special Envoy for Freedom of Religion and Belief, had come to visit Cole Durham and Brett Scharffs at the International Center for Law and Religion Studies at BYU Law School. They met to discuss what might be done to commemorate the 70th anniversary of the adoption of the Universal Declaration of Human Rights, which took place on December 10, 1948.

As they spoke about marking and honoring this anniversary, the conversation turned to what the fundamental, foundational principles are that undergird the human rights project. Ján shared a story about an experience he had as EU Special Envoy when he reached out to the government of Pakistan to try and set up a meeting to discuss the situation of religious minorities in Pakistan, who often face not only discrimination and mistreatment but hostility and persecution because of their religious identity and beliefs. Ján Figel' suggested to the Pakistani government to meet to talk about human dignity rather than human rights and religious persecution, topics that are often considered to be a way to criticize the government rather than engage in a constructive dialogue. As he described it, the conversation went something like this.

> "Hello, Pakistan, this is Ján Figel', EU Special Envoy for Freedom of Religion and Belief Outside the EU and I'd like to come to visit."

This, he said, with a smile, was met with a long silence. Eventually, the voice on the other side of the phone said, somewhat suspiciously, "What do you want to talk about?"

> "Human dignity," Ján responded. "I'd like to come to talk about how human dignity is important, and how protecting human dignity for all people, at all times, and all places is important."

This was followed by another long pause. Eventually, the Pakistani government official responded, with a more open tone of voice – "Ah, human dignity. That is an important principle for Muslims. It is an important idea in the Holy Koran – *karama*. God granted Adam dignity. Why don't you come and we can talk."

DOI: 10.4324/9781003207030-1

This led, Ján noted, to a series of meetings with successively more senior and influential government officials in Pakistan. It helped lay the groundwork for building trust and establishing relationships that made it possible to talk about difficult human rights issues, including freedom of religion or belief. It was not a magic wand that ended human rights problems in Pakistan, but it was a concept that helped build bridges of communication and understanding.

This story led to several days of brainstorming about various ways that human dignity is helpful in human rights discourse. Ján noted an interesting feature of human dignity – which ultimately made its way into Article 1 of the Punta del Este Declaration. Human dignity plays many different roles in human rights discourse. It is in an important sense the *foundational principle* upon which the human rights project is built. But it is also the *telos*, or *end goal*, of human rights. At the same time, it is an important *evaluative mechanism* for assessing how well a country is doing in the implementation of human rights.

As we began talking about the many ways that human dignity has been, and could even more effectively become a tool for promoting human rights, our notepads were quickly filled with a list of perhaps 20 different ways that human dignity is practically useful in promoting and protecting human rights.

At that meeting, we decided to help organize a series of conferences during 2018 for exploring various dimensions of human dignity, with the goal of holding a conference at the end of the year to adopt a joint voice declaration that would commemorate the 70th anniversary of the adoption of the Universal Declaration of Human Rights (UDHR), celebrating its recognition of human dignity at the core of the panoply of human rights and recommitting to protecting it for everyone everywhere.

Over the year as we studied and explored human dignity from a variety of perspectives, the list of the ways that human dignity had been or could be useful as a tool in the human rights project proliferated. In time, the list of the uses of human dignity grew to include more than 40 related, but distinguishable ideas. This list included many different dimensions of dignity, including the following:

- Human dignity is the foundational principle of human rights.
- Human dignity is the telos, or end goal, of human rights.
- Human dignity is a metric that can be used to assess human rights performance.
- Human dignity has played an important role in forming, guiding, and sustaining consensus on core human rights.
- Human dignity remains important in a world that is highly polarized and pluralistic.
- Human dignity was recognized as one of the foundational principles in the preamble of the Charter of the United Nations.
- Human dignity is recognized in the first sentence of the preamble of the UDHR.
- Human dignity is also recognized in the first article of the UDHR.

- It was grave violations of human dignity that provided much of the impetus for the nations of the world adopting the UDHR.
- National and local laws alone are not adequate to protect human dignity; it should be emphasized as a principle of international law as well.
- Despite their differences, the drafters of the UDHR, and the nations they represented, rallied around the idea of human dignity as a basic principle for promoting freedom, justice, and peace in the world.
- The UDHR, in turn, has served as the foundational document for many other important human rights instruments, including international treaties, regional human rights instruments, and constitutions and laws in many parts of the world.
- Human dignity is an extremely generative concept, inviting many different conceptions and understandings.
- Although human dignity is sometimes criticized as being too abstract or general to be useful, in fact like many important fundamental legal principles such as freedom, equality, justice, and nondiscrimination, it has been used in a variety of ways in legal instruments.
- Human dignity as a counterpart to human identity helps us focus on not only the many ways that we are different as human beings but what we have in common as well.
- Human dignity reminds us of the importance for human beings of the right to find and define meaning and purpose in their own lives.
- Human dignity points us towards respecting pluralism and differences among people and groups.
- Human dignity helps us think beyond rights, and beyond ourselves, to focus on others, as well as our obligations to others.
- Violations of human dignity, including severe violations, continue today as well, including in wars and other armed conflicts, in genocides, crimes against humanity, war crimes, and the global crises concerning refugees, migrants, asylum seekers, and human trafficking.
- Human dignity helps counter the tendency for human rights to be fragmented, eroded, or neglected.
- Human dignity for everyone everywhere reminds us of the problems that arise when the interests or rights of one group or individual are placed ahead of those of other groups or individuals.
- There are many different theories of human dignity, some emphasizing status, other inherent value or worth, and other standards of behavior.
- Violations of human dignity are something important that warrant appropriate redress.
- Human dignity is a concept that can help us find common ground and build bridges.
- Human dignity can help us understand other important legal and moral concepts such as justice, freedom, and equality.
- Human dignity can help with the implementation of human rights.

- Human dignity can help adjudicate conflicts between human rights, or between human rights and other important state interests.
- Human dignity can help reduce the divisiveness of human rights discourse.
- Human dignity reminds us that human rights must be read and realized together.

Many of these ideas made their way into the preliminary clauses of the Punta del Este Declaration. As we've noted, it is important to recognize that human dignity is not a "magic wand" that will resolve all human rights violations, solve all human rights controversies, or guarantee a world where human rights for all are recognized, promoted, and protected. But we believe it is uniquely powerful and versatile as a tool to facilitate building the human rights edifice.

After the process of expansion in identifying the many dimensions and uses of dignity, the drafters of the Punta del Este Declaration attempted a second process of trying to simplify and bring coherence to the concept of human dignity. In a way that was analogous to the process of the UDHR being transformed from a "laundry list" of rights into a coherent architecture of 30 brief articles, our goal became to summarize and focus the many uses of human dignity into 10 brief statements that would hopefully capture the many dimensions and aspects of dignity. Each of these articles would have a primary theme, and each would, in turn, identify variations on that theme – all the while focusing on practical ways that human dignity is useful in human rights discourse, and can be a tool helpful in furthering the work of the human rights project.

To summarize, each article of the Punta del Este Declaration identifies practical and useful dimensions of human dignity as an important tool in the human rights toolbox. In time, the metaphor of the Swiss army knife also became powerfully resonant: human dignity turns out to be a tool with many uses.

Article 1 – Foundation, objective, and criterion

- Human dignity for everyone everywhere is the foundational principle of human rights.
- Human dignity reminds us of why it is important to respect, promote, and protect human rights.
- Human dignity for everyone is the key objective or goal of human rights.
- Human dignity for everyone is also an invaluable criterion for evaluating laws, policies, and government actions to assess how well they accord with human rights.
- Protecting human dignity is a fundamental obligation of governments at all levels, including states, governments, and other public bodies, whether local, regional, national, or international.
- Promoting human dignity is also a responsibility of all sectors of society, including civil society, business, and religious groups.
- Promoting human dignity is also a responsibility of all of us as human beings.

- Promoting and protecting human dignity is key to promoting the equal and inalienable rights of all human beings.
- As recognized in the preamble of the UDHR, human dignity remains the foundation of freedom, justice, and peace in the world.

Article 2 – Generating agreement and building common understanding

- Human dignity was the key idea that helped generate agreement and common understanding at the time of the drafting and adoption of the UDHR.
- Human dignity was appealing to diverse and different groups.
- Human dignity was appealing across political and legal systems.
- Human dignity was an important point of departure for exploring and understanding the meaning of human rights.
- Human dignity helped establish common ground for human rights.
- Human dignity helped establish agreement about the content and meaning of human rights.
- Human dignity helps build bridges across various normative justifications of human rights.
- Human dignity helped build bridges between religious and non-religious theoretical groundings for human rights.
- Human dignity is a concept with many conceptions of a shared value.
- Human dignity invites in-depth examination of our traditions and perspectives.
- Human dignity reminds us that human rights are universal.
- Human dignity reminds us that human rights are inalienable.
- Human dignity reminds us that human rights are indivisible.
- Human dignity reminds us that human rights are interdependent.
- Human dignity reminds us that human rights are interrelated.

Article 3 – Defining and specifying human rights

- Dignity is an essential part of what it means to be human.
- Respect for human dignity for everyone everywhere helps us define and understand the meaning and scope of human rights.
- Focusing concretely and in actual situations on human dignity and its implications for particular human rights claims can help identify the specific content of these rights.
- Focusing on specific human rights helps us understand dignity better.

Article 4 – Duties and responsibilities

- Human dignity for everyone everywhere emphasizes that rights include accompanying duties, obligations, and responsibilities.
- Human dignity reminds us that duties and responsibilities regarding human rights accrue not only to states but to all human beings.

- Dignity is a status shared by every human being.
- The emphasis on "everyone" and "everywhere" makes it clear that rights involve corresponding duties.
- Human dignity reminds us that all of us should be concerned not only with our dignity and rights but the dignity and rights of every person.
- Human dignity is not diminished when people fail to fulfill their responsibilities to the state and others.
- Our dignity may be especially important when we violate the law or fail to fulfill our responsibilities to the state and others.

Article 5 – Education

- Human dignity is an important foundational principle of education and teaching.
- Human dignity is also important as a foundational principle for human rights education.
- Human rights education is important for promoting respect for the equal dignity of everyone.
- Human rights education is important for sustaining dignity and human rights into the future.
- Equal access to education is a crucial aspect of respecting human dignity.

Article 6 – Seeking common ground

- Today as well, focusing on human dignity for everyone everywhere encourages us to search for ways to find common ground regarding human rights.
- Focusing on human dignity for everyone can help us navigate competing human rights complaints.
- Focusing on human dignity for all helps us move beyond exclusively legal mechanisms for addressing human rights claims.
- Focusing on human dignity for all can help us find solutions to conflicts, including conflicts involving human rights.

Article 7 – Implementing and realizing human rights in legislation

- Human dignity is a foundational principle of law.
- Human dignity is central to developing and protecting human rights in legislation and policymaking.
- Human dignity resists precise definition, but it encourages the pursuit of mutually vindicating multiple rights and values.
- Human dignity helps us move beyond thinking exclusively in terms of balancing and tradeoffs when thinking about rights and interests.

Article 8 – Reconciliation and adjudication

- Human dignity for all is an important principle of constitutional law and other foundational legal provisions.

- Human dignity is an important principle for adjudicating human rights claims.
- Human dignity is important in adjudicating claims involving more than one person's human rights.
- Human dignity is also helpful in adjudicating claims between human rights and other national and societal interests.
- Although adjudication often does not do a good job of mutually vindicating rights and interests, it is more likely to happen if courts focus on respecting the human dignity of everyone involved in a conflict.
- When mutual vindication of rights is not possible, dignity for all can help judges set the boundaries for acceptable limitations on the exercise of rights and freedoms.
- Human dignity can help bring into fair balance competing rights claims.
- Respect for human dignity is important not only in formal adjudication of rights, but also in alternative dispute mechanisms such as mediation, restorative justice, and alternative dispute resolution.

Article 9 – Potential difficulties involving competing human rights claims

- Human dignity can be especially helpful in facilitating effective and responsible human rights advocacy.
- Respecting the human dignity of all people involved in a human rights conflict can facilitate effective human rights advocacy.
- Recognizing the universal and reciprocal character of human dignity is a corrective to positions claiming rights for some but not for others.
- Human dignity for everyone everywhere is an important corrective to the excesses of identity politics.
- Focusing on the human dignity of all can reduce hostilities that often accompany human rights controversies and help foster constructive dialogue.
- Focusing on the dignity of all can help mitigate the distortion of human rights that can take place when the dignity or rights of only some people or groups are taken into account.
- Focusing on the dignity of all can help address situations where governments or officials want to avoid their responsibilities with regards to human rights.
- Human dignity of all can also help address the problem of selective recognition of human dignity.

Article 10 – Most egregious violations of human rights and opportunities for improvement

- Human dignity for everyone everywhere reminds us to work toward the elimination of the most egregious abuses of the human rights of individuals and groups, including genocide, crimes against humanity, war crimes, and other atrocities.
- Human dignity of all also reminds us to protect those human beings who are most weak and vulnerable or otherwise at risk of human rights violations.

- Human dignity also encourages efforts to respond to problems that might be especially amenable to improvement.

One of the primary purposes of the Punta del Este Declaration, and in turn of this book, is to recognize the many ways that human dignity is practically useful as a tool that can facilitate in building and maintaining the human rights project. Since the adoption of the UDHR, the human rights project has taken on many dimensions, with international and regional treaties, in constitutions and other fundamental laws, and perhaps most importantly in the creation of constitutional cultures that are mindful of and respectful of fundamental human rights. At the same time, we are acutely aware that the human rights project is subject to serious challenges and strains. The Punta del Este Declaration, and this book devoted to elaborating upon it, is also devoted to exploring the ways that human dignity for everyone everywhere can be a useful tool in helping in addressing the challenges and strains facing human rights in the world today.[1]

1 The "Human Dignity for Everyone Everywhere" project and its aims are spelled out below in subsequent chapters.

1 Seventy years after the Universal Declaration of Human Rights

Towards strengthening the protection of human rights

Introduction

On a cold December night in Paris in 1948, the UN General Assembly unanimously adopted the Universal Declaration of Human Rights (UDHR), formally proclaiming to the world a new conception of human rights founded on the central idea of human dignity for everyone everywhere.[1]

The first paragraph of the Preamble to the UDHR sets the stage:

> Whereas recognition of the inherent dignity and of the equal and inalienable rights of all members of the human family is the foundation of freedom, justice, and peace in the world.[2]

Human dignity is identified as the "foundation" of freedom, justice, and peace in the world with the shadows of World War II still looming long. The countries of the world came together to declare that if we want a world where freedom is respected, where justice is implemented, and where peace is realized, that world will be built upon a foundation of human dignity for everyone everywhere. The "equal and inalienable rights of all members of the human family" will be realized when human dignity for everyone everywhere is realized.

The centrality of the idea of human dignity for everyone everywhere is also evident in Article 1 of the UDHR, which states:

> All human beings are born free and equal in dignity and rights. They are endowed with reason and conscience and should act towards one another in a spirit of brotherhood.[3]

1 UN General Assembly Resolution 217 (III) A, Universal Declaration of Human Rights (Dec. 10, 1948). (Later cited as the UDHR.)
2 *Id.*
3 *Id.*

DOI: 10.4324/9781003207030-2

Although there are many ways in which we differ as human beings, we are all born equal in dignity and rights.[4] The inclusion of this phrase presumes that "freedom and equal dignity are what every human being is due, whether or not he or she is accorded them."[5]

One important aspect of the human rights revolution is that human rights are recognized as a birthright of all people – not gifts bestowed by states.[6] Rather, individuals possess inherent dignity, and the human dignity of every person is to be recognized and respected by all. Thus, the task for states is not to give or bestow dignity upon people or even to accept that all human beings possess human dignity. Rather, the state's obligation is to recognize, respect, and protect the human dignity of all human beings.[7]

This simple idea – human dignity for everyone everywhere – is the central idea of human rights.[8] The UDHR was a consensus document that articulated time-

4 During the Third Committee's drafting of the UDHR, France's representative, Salymon Grumbach, supported this language in Article 1 because it demonstrated that "all representatives agreed that inequality did, in face exist, but that the statement "All human beings are born free and equal..." meant that the right to freedom and equality was inherent from the moment of birth." Tore Lindholm, "Article 1" in Gudmundur Alfredsson and Asbjørn Eide (eds.), *The Universal Declaration of Human Rights: A Common Standard of Achievement* (Martinus Nijhoff Publishers, 1999) 42, 59. (Later cited as Lindholm (1999)).

5 Lindholm (1999) 42, 59

6 For example, Morsink articulated his theory that "all human rights ... are inherent in the person on account of her birth into the human family. I therefore think the human person per se, and not just as a citizen of some country or other, has these rights." Johannes Morsink, *The Universal Declaration of Human Rights and the Challenge of Religion* (University of Missouri Press: Columbia, MO, 2017) 283. He further added that "Together the drafting fragments comprising these three words ['inherent', 'inalienable', and 'born'] add up to what I shall call the inherence view of human rights. This is the view that human rights in here in people as such; people have these moral rights because of their membership in the human family, not because of any external force or agency." *Id.*, 290.

7 Tollefsen emphasized that "the State has an obligation to protect individual or collective freedom of action and use of resources ... The State has an obligation to refrain from interfering in the self-provision efforts of individuals and groups, and it must also protect people from being deprived of their means of subsistence by others." Christopher Tollefsen, "The Dignity of Marriage" in Christopher McCrudden (ed.), *Understanding Human Dignity* (Oxford University Press: Oxford, 2013) 483, 485. For example, in Germany, to create a clear connection between "inner and outer freedom" (*inner freedom* referring to the "freedom from compulsion to act against one's convictions ... an attribute ... distinguish[ing] humans from other creatures), Article 1 of the German Basic Law was written in 1949 to include the state's responsibilities in human dignity: "The dignity of man is inviolable. To respect it and to protect it is the duty of all state authority." Christoph Goos, "Restoring Human Dignity in Post-Nazi Germany" in Christopher McCrudden (ed.), *Understanding Human Dignity* (Oxford University Press: Oxford, 2013) 79, 86–89.

8 Ján Figel', "Freedom of religion or belief is a litmus test of civil and political rights" (April 21, 2019). Available at: https://www.janfigel.eu/single-post/2019/04/21/Freedom-of-religion-or-belief-is-a-litmus-test-of-civil-and-political-rights; Ján Figel', "Freedom of Faith a 'Litmus Test' for All Human Rights" (April 28, 2019). Available

honored and widely-recognized rights and duties.[9] Upon the 70th anniversary of the UDHR, the time has come to explore and reassert the central place of this core idea. It is time to articulate a set of principles that explain the many ways that the idea of human dignity for everyone everywhere can help with the promotion, recognition, implementation, and realization of human rights for all people in all places. The Punta del Este Declaration emphasizes the practical ways that human dignity for everyone everywhere is a useful concept that can do considerable work relating to human rights.

This chapter scrutinizes the background and rationale for the Punta del Este Declaration while focusing on the UDHR, engaging with the events leading to the UDHR, the UDHR itself, and the subsequent 70 years. The chapter then elaborates on the events that have led to the Punta del Este Declaration and the process of its conception, drafting, and adoption. The chapter concludes by focusing on the significance of the Punta del Este Declaration by explaining what the document is not.

The rationale for the Punta del Este Declaration: human rights in the world today

December 10, 2018, marked the 70th anniversary of the adoption of the UDHR. As we look ahead to the next decade, it is important to explore and reiterate the fundamental concepts and ideas that motivated and illuminated the human rights project.

at: https://europe.upf.org/what-we-do/conferences/ilc/315-2018/vienna-4-2018/session-1/573-freedom-of-faith-a-litmus-test-for-all-human-rights.

9 Prior to voting on the adoption of the UDHR, the UN General Assembly polled member state representatives for their support for individual articles of the UDHR. There were some abstentions and votes against specific articles; however, 23 of the 30 articles were unanimously supported and when it came time for voting on the document as a whole, 48 nation representatives voted in favor of the UDHR's adoption, with only 8 abstentions and not a single vote against its adoption. The strong support for the UDHR's adoption warranted the framers' victorious claim of the document's universality. Mary Ann Glendon, *A World Made New: Eleanor Roosevelt and the Universal Declaration of Human Rights* (Random House: New York, 2001) 169–71 (Later cited as Glendon (2001)). The UDHR's universality was achieved in part by originating from rights that were already acknowledged in legal systems throughout the world. In writing the initial UDHR draft, John Humphrey researched material offered to the UN by various governments and groups; drafters collected central values from documents such as England's Magna Carta, the American Declaration of Independence, and the French Declaration of 1789 and expounded upon them to articulate the fundamental freedoms the UDHR describes. Glendon (2001) 48–49, 173. Ultimately, "[a]fter canvassing sources from North and South, East and West" and including input from representatives of 18 different countries, the drafters "found a core of principles so basic that no nation would wish openly to disavow them. They wove those principles into a unified document that quickly displaced all antecedents as the principal model for the rights instruments in force in the world today." *Id.*, xvii, 32.

By some measures, the human rights project has been a remarkable success. The UDHR is a landmark document that proclaimed basic rights belong to everyone: "the inalienable rights which everyone is inherently entitled to as a human being – regardless of race, color, religion, sex, language, political opinion, national or social origin, property, birth, or another status."[10] It was the direct response to the heinous crimes perpetrated by the Nazis and a much-needed affirmation of human rights and human dignity for everyone everywhere.

The UDHR is as important now as it was in 1948, even though the circumstances (in many places) have changed. The rights enshrined in the UDHR empower us all. Indeed, over the past 70 years, significant progress has been made to ensure that the UDHR is universally accepted and recognized as the primary document on human rights. The very fact that the UDHR, as a declaration, is not legally enforceable, should not hinder its implementation. The UDHR, as a part of the international customary law, is a set of basic principles that inform the implementation of all human rights. However, the issue of its implementation leaves much to be desired.

The key to ensuring that the UDHR does not lose its significance but continues to empower and allow human rights to flourish is to go back to basics and affirm human dignity for everyone everywhere. The universality of the UDHR is often diminished by the fact that its protected rights are only guaranteed for some people and only in some parts of the world. Such an approach means that these rights are not seen as universal. Affirming human dignity for everyone everywhere means that it would not be possible to deny anyone their rights. The focus on human dignity for everyone everywhere may facilitate the universality of human rights.

Indeed, at the time of drafting the UDHR, the concept of human dignity played a crucial role in transcending differences and reaching consensus. Now more than ever we need to find ways to invoke this core concept to find solutions for the ever-present failures to guarantee and protect human rights for all.

Universality of human rights

A general recognition that human rights are important is evident by the numerous international[11] and regional[12] instruments that have been created to strengthen

10 UN Human Rights, Human Rights Day Message. See: https://www.un.org/en/observances/human-rights-day.

11 For example: the International Convention on the Elimination of all forms of Racial Discrimination (ICERD), the International Covenant on Civil and Political Rights (ICCPR), the International Covenant on Economic, Social, and Cultural Rights (ICESCR), the Convention on the Elimination of All Forms of Discrimination against Women (CEDAW), the Convention against Torture and Other Cruel, Inhuman or Degrading Treatment or Punishment (CAT), the Convention on the Rights of the Child (CRC),the International Convention on the Protection of the Rights of All Migrant Workers and Members of Their Families (ICRMW), the International Convention for the Protection from Enforced Disappearance (CED), the Convention on the Rights of Persons with Disabilities (CRPD).

12 For example: the American Convention on Human Rights (1969), the Additional Protocol to the American Convention on Human Rights in the Area of Economic,

the protection of various human rights. As we know too well, however, this does not mean that human rights are universally implemented, applied, and understood.

Implementation and application of human rights

Human rights remain uneven in their implementation and application. In some quarters, human rights are controversial, sometimes subject to withering criticism. Some view human rights as western constructs[13] that do not apply universally, despite the language of human rights being present in virtually all the world's constitutions, especially those (the overwhelming majority) adopted after World War II.[14] For example, among others, in the 1990s, Singapore's Lee Kuan Yew, at the time the Prime Minister of Singapore, proposed the concept of "Asian values" to argue that Asian cultures are significantly different from western cultures and hence should be exempt from human rights considerations.[15] Among others, the Iranian government has objected to the implementation of the UDHR, arguing that "the UDHR represented a secular interpretation of the Judeo-Christian tradition which could not be implemented by Muslims."[16] Indeed, Mr. Rajaie-Khorassani, the Iranian representative to the UN, elaborated this position, stating that:

> the concept of human rights was not limited to the [UDHR]. Man was of divine origin and human dignity could not be reduced to a series of secular norms [...] certain concepts contained in the [UDHR] needed to be revised. [Iran] recognized no authority or power but that of Almighty God and no legal tradition apart from Islamic law. As his delegation had already stated at the thirty-sixth session of the General Assembly, conventions, declarations, and resolutions or decisions of international organizations, which were contrary to Islam had no validity in the Islamic Republic of Iran. [...] The

Social and Cultural Rights (Protocol of San Salvador) (1988), the African Charter on Human Rights and Peoples' Rights (1981), the African Charter on the Rights and Welfare of the Child (1990), the Protocol to the African Charter on Human and Peoples' Rights on the Rights of Women in Africa (2003), the European Convention for the Protection of Human Rights and Fundamental Freedoms (1950), the European Social Charter (1961), the Revised European Social Charter (1996).

13 Adamantia Pollis and Peter Schwab, "Human Rights: A Western Construct with Limited Applicability" in Christine M. Koggle (ed.), *Moral and Political Theory* (Broadview Press, 2006) 60.

14 Joshua Cohen, "Minimalism about Human Rights: The Most We Can Hope For?" (2004) 12 *Journal of Political Philosophy* 190–213; Allen Buchanan, "Human Rights and the Legitimacy of the International Order" (2008) *Legal Theory* 42.

15 For example, Lee Kuan Yew, "Asian Values Did Not Cause The Meltdown" (1998) 15 *New Perspectives Quarterly* 12: 32–34. See also: Joakim Öjendal and Hans Antlöv, "Asian Values and Its Political Consequences: Is Cambodia the First Domino?" (1998) 11 *The Pacific Review* 4: 525–40, 527; Francis Fukuyama, "Asian Values and the Asian crisis" (1998) 105 *Commentary* 2: 23–27, 23.

16 David Littman, 'Universal Human Rights and "Human Rights in Islam"' (1999) *Midstream*.

> [UDHR], which represented a secular understanding of the Judeo-Christian tradition, could not be implemented by Muslims and did not accord with the system of values recognized by the Islamic Republic of Iran; his country would therefore not hesitate to violate its provisions, since it had to choose between violating the divine law of the country and violating secular conventions.[17]

Similarly, some scholars have questioned the universality of human rights enshrined in the UDHR, and especially taking into consideration Islamic tradition.[18] For example, Ann Elizabeth Mayer, Associate Professor of Legal Studies at the Wharton School of the University of Pennsylvania, claims that "Islamic schemes do not offer protection for what international law deems fundamental rights."[19] Reza Afshari, Professor of History at Peace University, while recognizing the notion of human in the Islamic tradition, notes the difference in the way Muslim thinkers approach the issue, stating that "they make no clear distinction between human rights in the modern nation-state and human rights in Islam. When a right is recognized in Islam, it is often an ethical and spiritual assertion … when a right is recognized in a state, it is fundamental entitlement."[20]

Furthermore, some human rights experts have questioned universality, noting the interest in human rights that comes from developing countries including those still under colonial occupation and from non-western thinkers and voices.[21] Among others, Mary Ann Glendon spoke of "universality [being] under siege."[22] Indeed, she has noted that it is easy to over- ascribe universality of human rights:

> No one has yet improved on the answer of the UNESCO[23] philosophers: Where basic human values are concerned, cultural diversity has been exaggerated. The group found, after consulting with Confucian, Hindu, Muslim, and European thinkers, that a core of fundamental principles was widely

17 See: Summary record of the 65th meeting, 3rd Committee, held on Friday, 7 December 1984, New York, General Assembly, 39th session. UN Doc. A/C.3/39/SR.65, paras. 91–95.

18 Riffat Hassan, "Are Human Rights Compatible with Islam? The Issue of the Rights of Women in Muslim Communities". Available at: https://www.iemed.org/documents/novesrealitats/Strawson/a.pdf; Raimundo Panikkar and Arvind Sharma, *Human Rights as a Western Concept?* (DK Print World, 2007); Jacqueline Langwith (ed.), *Human rights* (Greenhaven Press: Detroit, MI, 2008).

19 As Mayer suggests, "Islamic schemes do not offer protection for what international law deems fundamental rights." Ann Elizabeth Mayer, *Islam and Human Rights: Tradition and Politics* (Routledge, 1999) 186.

20 Reza Afshari, "An Essay on Islamic Cultural Relativism in the Discourse of Human Rights" (1994) 16 *Human Rights Quarterly* 235, 250.

21 See for example: Lynda S. Bell, Andrew J. Nathan and Ilan Peleg, "Introduction: Culture and Rights" in Lynda S. Bell, Andrew J. Nathan, and Ilan Peleg (eds.), *Negotiating Culture and Human Rights.* (Columbia University Press: New York, 2001) 7.

22 Glendon (2001) 221.

23 UNESCO, 4th General Conference (November 1949) 258–59.

shared in countries that had not yet adopted rights instruments and in cultures that had not embraced the language of rights. Their survey persuaded them that basic human rights rest on "common convictions," even though those convictions "are stated in terms of different philosophic principles and on the background of divergent political and economic systems."[24]

Similarly, Alison Renteln, Professor of Political Science, Anthropology, Law, and Public Policy at the University of California questions the universality, stating that:

> There was in the 1940s and there remains today some question about the degree to which the "Universal" Declaration of Human Rights truly reflects "universal" values. Doubts were not laid to rest on December 10, 1948, with the consequence that the credibility of this potentially revolutionary document has been enveloped in controversy … What remains to be determined is the extent to which the UDHR is, in fact, based on values shared by all systems.[25]

Alasdair MacIntyre, Notre Dame University philosopher, is suspicious of moral ideas that are not rooted in human history – He dismisses all accounts of rights because there are no self-evident moral truths in general.[26] As he claims:

> The best reason for asserting so bluntly that there are no such rights is indeed of precisely the same type as the best reason which we possess for asserting that there are no witches and the best reason which we possess for asserting that there are no unicorns: every attempt to give good reasons for believing that there are such rights has failed. The eighteenth-century philosophical defenders of natural rights sometimes suggest that the assertions which state that men possess them are self-evident truths; but we know that there are no self-evident truths. Twentieth-century moral philosophers have sometimes appealed to their and our intuitions; but one of the things that we ought to have learned from the history of moral philosophy is that the introduction of the word "intuition" by a moral philosopher is always a signal that something has gone badly wrong with an argument. In the United Nations declaration on human rights of 1949 [sic] what has since become the normal UN practice

24 Glendon (2001) 222.
25 Alison Dundes Renteln, *International Human Rights: Universalism versus Relativism* (Sage: Newbury Park, CA, 1990) 32.
26 MacIntyre further adds that: "Such sets of rules only come into existence at particular historical periods under particular social circumstances. They are in no way universal features of the human condition. Gewinh readily acknowledges that expressions such as 'a right' in English and cognate terms in English and other languages only appeared at a relatively late point in the history of the language toward the close of the Middle Ages. But he argues that the existence of such expressions is not a necessary condition for the embodiment of the concept of a right in forms of human behavior; and in this at least he is clearly right." Alasdair MacIntyre, *After Virtue: A Study in Moral Theory* (University of Notre Dame Press: Notre Dame, IN, 1981) 67.

of not giving good reasons for any assertions whatsoever is followed with great rigor.[27]

Understanding human rights

Furthermore, apart from not being a universal concept, there are also different views about the specific content of human rights. For example, Allen Buchanan, Professor of Law and Philosophy at Duke University, emphasized that there are serious disagreements about the specific content of even the most basic human rights, differences that are rooted in different cultural views.[28] Buchanan states that this approach is not justified anymore and challenges it.[29] He notes that,

> When international legal institutions authorize military interventions, prosecute state leaders for war crimes, or judge states or governments to be illegitimate, they justify such actions by appealing to the special status of certain norms. These norms are thought to be capable of grounding enforcement efforts and legitimacy assessment *because they are human-rights norms*, norms that identify rights that all human individuals have, independently of whether their own government acknowledges them. Only such universal rights could justify the kinds of restraints on sovereignty and even on the self-determination of democratic peoples that the international legal order now attempts to impose. So when international legal institutions justify their most important and controversial functions by appeals to human rights, the rights they appeal to not only must be justifiable; they must be justifiable as human-rights norms. For this justification to succeed, it must include a credible response to a perennial challenge to the very idea of human rights: the parochialism objection, according to which *what are called human rights are not really universal in the sense of being rights of all individuals but instead merely reflect (1) an arbitrarily restricted set of moral values; or (2) an arbitrary ranking of certain moral values.*[30]

This understanding of human rights as fundamental protections that are universal and intrinsic provides for a basis of ensuring their implementation, independently of whether they are recognized in the state.

Implementing human rights

Human rights are also implemented through many national constitutions, statutes, ordinances, and judicial decisions. As Mary Ann Glendon notes, support of the

27 *Id.*, 69.
28 Allen Buchanan, "Human Rights and the Legitimacy of the International Order" (2008) *Legal Theory* 41.
29 *Id.*, 40.
30 *Id.*

UDHR and its universal quality has been strengthened since its adoption "by endorsements from most of the nations that were not present at its creation."[31] The widespread, continued support of the UDHR by the majority of nations reinforces the idea that

> [r]epresentatives of diverse religious and cultural traditions might be unable to reach agreement on the requirements of human dignity … But this did not prevent the attainment of practical agreement on dignity and rights. Through practical reason, it was possible to reach common practical ideas that led to "the affirmation of a single body of beliefs *for guidance in action.*"[32]

First, specific references to the UDHR have been made in at least 18 nations' constitutions across the globe. Second, a large portion of the world's countries has shown support for documents based on the UDHR, with 173 parties to the International Covenant on Civil and Political Rights and 171 parties to the International Covenant for Economic, Social, and Cultural Rights. Third, 171 countries "affirmed by consensus their commitment to the purposes and principles contained in the Charter of the United Nations and the Universal Declaration of Human Rights" at the 1993 Vienna Conference on Human Rights.[33]

As Mary Ann Glendon notes, "[t]hough the Declaration as such is not binding, most of its rights had already received a significant degree of recognition by 1948 in the constitutions of many nations, if not in their practices. Since that time, most of its rights have been incorporated into the domestic legal systems of most countries."[34]

Nihal Jayawickrama, former Professor of Law at the University of Hong Kong, notes that "no fewer than 90 national constitutions drawn up since 1948 contain statements of fundamental rights which, where they do not faithfully reproduce the provisions of the Universal Declaration, are at least inspired by it."[35] Indeed, several constitutions make explicit reference to the UDHR[36], for example, the constitutions of Afghanistan,[37]

31 Glendon (2001) 228.

32 David Hollenbach, "Experience and History, Practical Reason and Faith" in Christopher McCrudden (ed.), *Understanding Human Dignity* (Oxford University Press: Oxford, 2013) 123, 132.

33 Glendon (2011) 228.

34 Mary Ann Glendon, "The Rule of Law in the Universal Declaration of Human Rights" (2004) 2 *Nw U J Int'l Hum Rts* 1, 5.

35 Nihal Jayawickrama, "Hong Kong and the International Protection of Human Rights" in Raymond Wicks (ed.), *Human Rights in Hong Kong* (Oxford University Press: Hong Kong, 1992) 25.

36 Hurst Hannum, "The UDHR in National and International Law" (1995) *Health and Human Rights* 151.

37 Article 7 states: "The state shall observe the United Nations Charter, inter-state agreements, as well as international treaties to which Afghanistan has joined, and the Universal Declaration of Human Rights. The state shall prevent all kinds of terrorist activities, cultivation and smuggling of narcotics, and production and use of intoxicants."

Benin,[38] Bosnia-Herzegovina,[39] Burkina Faso,[40] Burundi,[41] Cambodia,[42] Chad,[43] Comoros,[44] Côte d'Ivoire,[45] Equatorial Guinea,[46] Ethiopia (draft 1994 Constitution),[47]

38 Article 40: "The State has the duty to assure the diffusion and the teaching of the Constitution, of the Universal Declaration of Human Rights of 1948, of the African Charter on Human and Peoples' Rights of 1981 as well as all of the international instruments duly ratified and relative to Human Rights."

39 The Preamble states "Inspired by the Universal Declaration of Human Rights, the International Covenants on Civil and Political Rights and on Economic, Social and Cultural Rights, and the Declaration on the Rights of Persons Belonging to National or Ethnic, Religious and Linguistic Minorities, as well as other human rights instruments."

40 The Preamble indicates that "subscribing to the Universal Declaration of the Rights of Man of 1948 and to the international instruments concerning economic, political, social and cultural problems."

41 Article 19: "The rights and duties proclaimed and guaranteed, between others, by the Universal Declaration of Human Rights, the International Pacts related to human rights, the African Charter of human and community rights, the Convention on the elimination of all forms of discrimination at towards women and the Convention related to children's rights are an integral part of the Constitution of the Republic of Burundi."

42 Article 31: "The Kingdom of Cambodia recognizes and respects human rights as enshrined in the United Nations Charter, the Universal Declaration of Human Rights and all the treaties and conventions related to human rights, women's rights and children's rights."

43 In the Preamble: "Reaffirm our commitment to the principles of the Rights of Man as defined by the Charter of the United Nations of 1945, the Universal Declaration of the Rights of Man of 1948 and the African Charter of the Rights of Man and of Peoples of 1981."

44 In the Preamble: "to emphasize their commitment to the principles and fundamental rights defined by the Charter of the United Nations, by the Charter of the Organization of African Unity, by the Pact of the League of Arab States, by the Universal Declaration of Human Rights and by the African Charter on Human and Peoples' Rights, as well as by the international conventions, particularly those relating to children and women rights."

45 In the Preamble: "Reaffirm our determination to build a Rule of Law in which human rights, public freedoms, human dignity, justice and good governance as defined in the international legal instruments to which the Côte d'Ivoire is a party, in particular the United Nations Charter of 1945, the Universal Declaration of Human Rights of 1948, the African Charter on Human and Peoples' Rights of 1981 and its supplementary protocols, the Constitutive Act of the African Union of 2001, are promoted, protected and guaranteed."

46 In the Preamble: "Firmly supported by the principles of social justice and solemnly reaffirmed by the rights and liberties of men defined in the Universal Declaration of Human Rights of October 10, 1948."

47 Article 13(2): "The fundamental rights and freedoms specified in this Chapter shall be interpreted in a manner conforming to the principles of the Universal Declaration of Human Rights, International Covenants on Human Rights and international instruments adopted by Ethiopia."

Gabon,[48] Mali,[49] Mauritania,[50] Nicaragua,[51] Niger,[52] Portugal,[53] Romania,[54] Sao Tome and Principe,[55] Senegal,[56] Spain,[57] and Togo.[58] Other constitutions have been

48 In the Preamble: "Affirm solemnly its attachment to human rights and to fundamental liberties that result from the Declaration of the Rights of Man and the Citizen of 1789 and from the Universal Declaration of Human Rights of 1948, consecrated by the African Charter of the Rights of Man and the Rights of Peoples of 1981, and by the National Charter of Liberties of 1990."

49 In the Preamble: "subscribe to the Universal Declaration of the Rights of Man of December 10, 1948 and to the African Charter of the Rights of Man and People of June 27, 1981."

50 In the Preamble: "Strong from its spiritual values and from the radiation of its civilization, it also proclaims, solemnly, its attachment to Islam and to the principles of democracy as they have been defined by the Universal Declaration of the Rights of Man of 10 December 1948 and by the African Charter of the Rights of Man and of Peoples of 28 June 1981 as well as in the other international conventions to which Mauritania has subscribed."

51 Article 46: "All persons in the national territory shall enjoy State protection and recognition of the rights inherent to the human person, as well as unrestricted respect, promotion and protection of those human rights, and the full applicability of the rights set forth in the Universal Declaration of Human Rights; in the American Declaration of the Rights and Duties of Man; in the International Pact of Economic, Social and Cultural Rights; in the International Pact of Civil and Political Rights of the United Nations; and in the American Convention of Human Rights of the Organization of American States."

52 In the Preamble: "Proclaim our attachment to the principles of pluralist democracy and of human rights as defined by the Universal Declaration of Human Rights of 1948, the International Pact Relative to Civil and Political rights of 1966, the International Pact Relative to the Economic, Social and Cultural Rights of 1966, and by the African Charter of the Rights of Man and of Peoples of 1981."

53 Article 16(2): "The provisions of this Constitution and of laws concerning fundamental rights shall be interpreted and construed in accordance with the Universal Declaration of Human Rights."

54 Article 20(1): "Constitutional provisions concerning the citizens' rights and liberties shall be interpreted and enforced in conformity with the Universal Declaration of Human Rights, with the covenants and other treaties Romania is a party to."

55 Article 12(2): "The Democratic Republic of Sao Tome and Principe proclaims its adherence to the Universal Declaration of the Rights of Man and to its principles and objectives of the Organization of African Unity and of the United Nations Organization."

56 In the Preamble: affirm "their adhesion to the Declaration of the Rights of Man and of the Citizen of 1789 and to the international instruments adopted by the Organization of the United Nations and the Organization of African Unity, notably the Universal Declaration of the Rights of Man of 10 December 1948, the Convention on the Elimination of All Forms of Discrimination with Regard to Women of 18 December 1979, the Convention relative to the Rights of the Child of 20 November 1989 and the African Charter of the Rights of Man and of Peoples of 27 June 1981."

57 Article 10(2): "Provisions relating to the fundamental rights and liberties recognized by the Constitution shall be construed in conformity with the Universal Declaration of Human Rights and international treaties and agreements thereon ratified by Spain."

58 Article 50: "The rights and duties, stated in the Universal Declaration of the Rights of Man and in the international instruments relative to the Rights of Man, ratified by Togo, are an integral part of this Constitution."

inspired by the UDHR, for example, the constitutions of St. Vincent and the Grenadines, Kazakhstan, the European Constitution, India, Chad, Zimbabwe, Chile, and many more.

For example, in the German constitution, human dignity is an absolute right.[59] Human dignity is

> the supreme value of the German constitution. It [views] human dignity as the spirit and the essence of the entire constitution; it is the epicenter of the constitutional structure; it is the primary principle governing all part of the Constitution.[60]

Influenced by the German usage, the European Union Charter of Fundamental Rights "also devotes its first article to guaranteeing human dignity, described as 'inviolable', before proceeding to an extensive series of other rights."[61] In Title I of this Charter, the European Union "enshrines human dignity" and enumerates what it believes are the vital elements of preserving dignity.[62] The South African Constitution creates a unique usage of human dignity as

> both a founding value and a discrete right in the Bill of Rights ... It was the Constitutional Court that declared, in its decision outlawing the death penalty that dignity played a larger role than merely as a right: it was also the value on which the new democracy was founded .... Dignity thus operates ... as a foundational value that informs the interpretation of all other rights; and as a fully justiciable right.[63]

Furthermore, as Jack Goldsmith, Professor of Law at Harvard University, explains, several parts of the UDHR are regarded as part of customary international law.[64]

59 Gerald L. Neuman, "Discourses of Dignity" in Christopher McCrudden (ed.), *Understanding Human Dignity* (Oxford University Press: Oxford, 2013) 631, 641.
60 Aharon Barak, "The Constitutional Value and the Constitutional Right" in Christopher McCrudden (ed.), *Understanding Human Dignity* (Oxford University Press: Oxford, 2013) 361, 369.
61 Gerald L. Neuman, "Discourses of Dignity" in Christopher McCrudden (ed.), *Understanding Human Dignity* (Oxford University Press: Oxford, 2013) 631, 641.
62 Catherine Dupré, "Constructing the Meaning of Human Dignity" in Christopher McCrudden (ed.), *Understanding Human Dignity* (Oxford University Press: Oxford, 2013) 113, 114.
63 Edwin Cameron, "Moral Citizenship and Constitutional Protection" in Christopher McCrudden (ed.), *Understanding Human Dignity* (Oxford University Press: Oxford, 2013) 467, 474. See also: Erin E. Goodsell, "Constitution, Custom, and Creed: Balancing Human Rights Concerns with Cultural and Religious Freedom in Today's South Africa" (2007) 21 *BYU Journal of Public Law* 111.
64 Jack Goldsmith, "International Human Rights Law and the United States Double Standard" (1998) I *Green Bag* 365, 366, 371 (1998). "The customary international law of human rights is thought to include many of the rights in the Universal Declaration, as well as rights like freedom from slavery and torture and the right to democratic government."

As Charles Malik noted, "whenever the question of human rights has arisen throughout the world, the appeal has been far more to the Declaration than to the covenants."[65] However, as Hurst Hannum emphasizes, "the mere recitation of norms may not necessarily reflect an honest intention to adhere to them. In addition, hortatory constitutional references may be of little value if they are not judicially enforceable."[66]

Care must be taken to not approach human rights in an overly abstract or theoretical way, which could lead to backtracking on progress relating to understanding human rights over the 70 intervening years since the adoption of the UDHR.

Some states marginalize, distort, or exploit human rights as a way of avoiding their obligations to promote and protect the human dignity of those within their jurisdiction. Human rights must not become a vehicle for abuse by authorities. For example, in the last decade, there have been at least two clear cases of genocidal atrocities, one perpetrated by the Burmese military (as authorized or allowed by the Burmese government) against the Rohingya Muslims in Rakhine State, Myanmar, and one perpetrated by Daesh against religious minorities in Syria and Iraq. In both cases, the perpetrators targeted religious (numeric) minorities for annihilation, not only denying their right to freedom of religion or belief but first and foremost, their right to life, among other fundamental rights. In both cases, the targeted minorities were not afforded the protection of human rights that resulted in them being vulnerable to such atrocities.

Monitoring and enforcing human rights

The international system has taken great strides in recognizing and articulating human rights. International and regional human rights bodies and courts have helped define and implement human rights. Nonetheless, the mechanisms for monitoring human rights have different enforcement powers that ultimately limit their ability to be effective oversight mechanisms. Even where human rights are implemented and applied, it is crucial that human rights are monitored and where they are violated, that steps be taken to rectify these violations.

David Luban, Professor of Law and Philosophy at Georgetown University, claims that the human rights project is failing because human rights cases cannot be adjudicated, whether because of jurisdictional or political reasons.[67] Put simply, if human rights are not adequately implemented, very often there will be no entity that could enforce any human rights claims. The fact that the majority of human

65 Charles Malik, "1948 – The Drafting of the Universal Declaration of Human Rights" (1986) *U.N. Bull. Hum. Rts.* 97.

66 Hurst Hannum, "The Status of the Universal Declaration of Human Rights in National and International Law" (1995) 25 *Georgia Journal of International and Comparative Law* 312.

67 David Luban, "Human Rights Pragmatism and Human Dignity" in Rowan Cruft, S. Matthew Liao, and Massimo Renzo (eds.), *Philosophical Foundations of Human Rights* (Oxford University Press: Oxford, 2005) 7.

rights instruments are without legal remedies he called the "enforcement deficit,"[68] meaning that the human rights project remains more theoretical than an empirical reality and dependent on non-legal avenues without the same legal force.[69] This is a significant concern that makes the whole human rights project a promise yet to be fulfilled. For example, UN mechanisms are quite toothless when it comes to enforcing human rights protections. The UN Human Rights Committee, responsible for human rights observance within the UN mechanisms, lacks enforcement powers.[70] Similarly, the UN Universal Periodic Review, despite conducting a regular and in-depth review of the human rights and their implementation by the states, effectively can only shame but not more than that.[71] Over the years, the UN has established several ad-hoc mechanisms to investigate human rights abuses, although with mixed results. For example, the UN Security Council established several international ad-hoc tribunals, namely, the International Criminal Tribunal for Rwanda (ICTR)[72] and the International Criminal Tribunal for the Former Yugoslavia (ICTY),[73] both to prosecute some of the most egregious human rights violations amounting to genocide. Despite having achieved some results, the mechanisms have been widely criticized for securing only a few prosecutions, and for being slow and expensive.[74] The negative legacy of the ad-hoc mechanism (but also the establishment of the first international permanent criminal court, the International Criminal Court (the ICC), that was meant to take over the burden of dealing with international crimes from the UN Security Council) has resulted in general reluctance to initiate similar mechanisms.[75]

Other UN bodies have also undertaken to establish ad-hoc mechanisms to focus on human rights violations in various parts of the world. Among others, the UN Human Rights Council established the International Independent Commission of Inquiry on the Syrian Arab Republic (IICoISAR),[76] the Fact-Finding Mission on Myanmar,[77] and the Commission of Inquiry on Human Rights in the Democratic

68 *Id.*, 7.
69 Robert F. Drinan, *The Mobilization of Shame: A World View of Human Rights* (Yale University Press: New Haven, CT, 2001).
70 See: Emilie M. Hafner-Burton and Kiyoteru Tsutsui, "Human Rights in a Globalizing World: The Paradox of Empty Promises" (2005) 110 *American Journal of Sociology* 1373.
71 See for example: Hillel Neuer, "South Africa at the UN: Your Freedom and Mine" (December 9, 2007) *Sunday Times of South Africa*. Available: http://blog.unwatch.org/?p=78.
72 UN Security Council Res. 955, U.N. Doc S/RES/955 (November 8, 1994)
73 UN Security Council Res. 808, U.N. Doc. S/RES/808/ (Feb. 22, 1993).
74 See: Catherine Cisse, "The International Tribunals for the Former Yugoslavia and Rwanda: Some Elements of Comparison" (1997) 7 *Transnational Law and Contemporary Problems* 103; David Wippman, "The Cost of International Justice" (2006) 100 *American Journal of International Law* 861.
75 Stuart Ford, "Complexity and Efficiency at International Criminal Courts" (2014) 29 *Emory International Law Review*.
76 UN Human Rights Council Resolution S-17/1 (August 22, 2011).
77 UN Human Rights Council Resolution 34/22 (March 24, 2017).

People's Republic of Korea (CoIDPRK).[78] The mechanisms have been credited for being effective in collecting evidence of human rights violations in these countries. However, the mechanisms have not been followed by effective mechanisms for ensuring justice for the victims. Indeed, although the CoIDPRK made a finding of crimes against humanity, the crimes remain unprosecuted.

Other international mechanisms tasked with human rights enforcement are also weak and unable to deliver the intended results. Often the mechanisms are unable to do their job in the first place as they are "treaty-bound" and dependent on states' voluntary acceptance of these treaties. For example, only 20 out of 35 states have accepted the jurisdiction of the Inter-American Court of Human Rights.[79] Similarly, the African Court of Human Rights lacks mandatory jurisdiction, limiting its effectiveness even though under Article 3 it has the titular power to adjudicate violations of treaties other than its foundational charter, the African Charter.[80]

Some international mechanisms have been more successful. For example, the Court of Justice of the European Union has been gaining significance in adjudicating human rights claims under the EU Charter of Fundamental Rights. NYU Law Professor, Grainne de Burca, has even argued for expanding its mandate to further build on its successes.[81] Most noteworthy, the European Court of Human Rights (the ECtHR) merits particular attention as it is the only human rights court in the world that has robust enforcement powers. Once a state becomes a party to the European Convention on Human Rights (the ECHR), the state is bound to adhere to its provisions, and any violation of its provisions may result in adjudication by the ECtHR (if all requirements for triggering the ECtHR jurisdiction are fulfilled). All parties to the ECHR are then bound by the judgments of the ECtHR, even if the judgments were not made against them.[82]

The ICC, the only international permanent court, is treaty-bound and hence does not have territorial jurisdiction over situations in countries that are not parties to its foundational treaty, the Rome Statute (apart from a few exceptions where

78 UN Human Rights Council Resolution 22/13 (March 21, 2013).

79 Argentina, Barbados, Bolivia, Brazil, Chile, Colombia, Costa Rica, Dominican Republic, Ecuador, El Salvador, Guatemala, Haiti, Honduras, Mexico, Nicaragua, Panama, Paraguay, Peru, Suriname, and Uruguay.

80 See: Protocol to the African Charter on Human and Peoples' Rights on the Establishment of an African Court on Human and Peoples' Rights, June 10, 1998, Organization of African Unity, 3, 7; Yakaré-Oulé (Nani) Jansen Reventlow and Rosa Curling, "The Unique Jurisdiction of the African Court on Human and Peoples' Rights: Protection of Human Rights Beyond the African Charter" (2019) 33 *Emory International Law Review*.

81 Grainne de Búrca, "After the EU Charter of Fundamental Rights: The Court of Justice as a Human Rights Adjudicator?" (2013) 20 *Maastricht Journal of European and Comparative Law*, 168–184.

82 Eckart Klein, "Should the Binding Effect of the Judgments of the ECtHR be Extended?" in P. Mahoney et al. (eds.), *Protecting Human Rights: The European Perspective* (Carl Heymanns: Cologne, 2000) 708; Elisabeth Lambert-Abdelgawad, *The Execution of Judgments of the European Court of Human Rights* (Council of Europe Publishing: Strasbourg, 2002).

the jurisdiction can be imposed[83]). As a consequence, the ICC often cannot act even in the face of dire human rights violations amounting to international crimes.

Human dignity for everyone everywhere

The distinctive contribution of the Punta del Este Declaration on Human Dignity for Everyone Everywhere (Punta del Este Declaration) is that it focuses on the many ways the idea of human dignity can be useful in the human rights context. The purpose of the Punta del Este Declaration is not to provide an authoritative definition of dignity, but rather to identify and elucidate some of the remarkable ways that the concept of human dignity can respond to many of the challenges facing human rights.

The goal is for each Article in the Punta del Este Declaration to be brief, clear, accessible, ecumenical, and to illustrate how we can move human rights discourse beyond zero-sum game understandings of human rights conflicts. Each of these Articles can be explored in greater depth, which is one of the primary purposes of this analysis.

The project culminating in the Punta del Este Declaration seeks to articulate a deeper understanding of the ways the foundational human rights idea, human dignity for everyone everywhere, can facilitate a deeper understanding of human rights, help achieve the objectives of human rights, and be used for evaluating how well a country is doing in protecting human rights.[84]

The idea of human dignity for everyone everywhere can assist in finding common ground among different conceptions of human rights,[85] can help build bridges between human rights and other worldviews, can help define and specify human rights,[86] and can help focus our minds on duties as well as rights.[87] The idea of human dignity for everyone everywhere is also a powerful basis for teaching and education about human rights[88] and can help find common ground regarding competing claims.[89] It also helps us move beyond exclusively legal mechanisms for harmonizing, implementing, and mutually vindicating human rights and finding solutions to conflicts.[90]

As a principle of law, human dignity for everyone everywhere is central to developing and protecting human rights in law and policy. It can help devise legislative solutions to human rights problems.[91] It is also an important constitutional

83 See Article 13(b) of the Rome Statute stating that: "(b) A situation in which one or more of such crimes appears to have been committed is referred to the Prosecutor by the Security Council acting under Chapter VII of the Charter of the United Nations."
84 See Punta del Este Declaration, Article 1, Appendix A.
85 See Punta del Este Declaration, Article 2.
86 See Punta del Este Declaration, Article 3.
87 See Punta del Este Declaration, Article 4.
88 See Punta del Este Declaration, Article 5.
89 See Punta del Este Declaration, Article 6.
90 See Punta del Este Declaration, Article 6.
91 See Punta del Este Declaration, Article 7.

and legal principle for reconciling and adjudicating competing human rights claims, as well as claims between human rights and other important national and societal interests.[92] It can help as we try to develop standards for the permissible limitations on fundamental rights and freedoms.[93] Recognizing the universal and reciprocal character of human dignity encourages responsible human rights advocacy, and is a corrective to positions claiming rights for some but not for others.[94]

Human dignity for everyone everywhere reminds us to focus on the most egregious abuses of human rights, including genocide, crimes against humanity, war crimes, and other atrocities.[95] It also reminds us to focus our attention on individuals and groups who are particularly vulnerable to human rights violations. At the same time, it encourages efforts to respond to problems that may be amenable to practical and feasible solutions.[96]

The "Human Dignity for Everyone Everywhere" project

The Punta del Este Declaration commemorates the 70th anniversary of the adoption of the UDHR, celebrating its recognition of human dignity at the core of the panoply of human rights and recommitting to protecting it for everyone everywhere.

The Punta del Este Declaration's focus on dignity derives from the language of the Preamble of the UDHR itself, which states, "Whereas recognition of the inherent dignity and of the equal and inalienable rights of all members of the human family is the foundation of freedom, justice, and peace in the world …", and from Article 1 of the UDHR, which proclaims, "All human beings are born free and equal in dignity and rights. They are endowed with reason and conscience and should act towards one another in a spirit of brotherhood." This simple idea – human dignity for everyone everywhere – is the central idea of human rights

The Punta del Este Declaration was adopted at a **conference convened in Punta del Este**, Uruguay from December 2–4, 2018, shortly before the formal 70th anniversary of the UDHR (December 10, 2018).

The conference was the culmination of a series of conferences held during 2018 that explored the notion of human dignity, its relation to freedom of religion or belief, and the important role it has played in forming, guiding, and sustaining consensus on core human rights values despite tensions in a highly pluralized world. The hope is that the Punta del Este Declaration will serve as a spur to further discussion and debate and that it can be supplemented and elaborated by individual comments, responses from other conferences or group efforts, and other initiatives that seek to build on the Declaration. An example of such an effect is the collective voice document, African Perspectives on Human Dignity for

92 See Punta del Este Declaration, Article 8.
93 See Punta del Este Declaration, Article 8.
94 See Punta del Este Declaration, Article 9.
95 See Punta del Este Declaration, Article 10.
96 See Punta del Este Declaration, Article 10.

Everyone Everywhere, which was drafted by a large and diverse group of scholars at a meeting of the African Consortium of Law and Religious Studies at a conference in Gaborone, Botswana in May 2019 and which is reproduced in Appendix B.

The "Human Dignity for Everyone Everywhere" project has endeavored to identify and organize a distinguished group of human rights experts, from a variety of viewpoints and professional backgrounds to draft, discuss, and refine a set of principles based on the idea of human dignity for all people in all places. In 2018, a series of consultations, workshops, and conferences were held to explore and develop a deeper understanding of the ways the idea of human dignity for everyone everywhere can help illuminate and further the implementation of human rights.

Conferences dedicated to different dimensions on human dignity for everyone everywhere included:

- On June 1–2, 2018, the conference "Human Dignity for Everyone Everywhere: From Tensions and Conflict to Reconciliation" was convened in cooperation with the Central European University (CEU) in Budapest.
- On August 3–4, a conference on "Human Dignity for Everyone Everywhere: Founding Figures, Foundations, and the Uses of Human Dignity" was held at Christ Church College, Oxford University.
- On October 7–10, the 25th Annual Law and Religion Symposium at BYU Law School was devoted to "Human Dignity and Freedom of Religion or Belief: The Universal Declaration of Human Rights at 70."
- On October 10–12, 2018, the Washington DC Symposium 2018, "Human Dignity and Religious Freedom in Washington, D.C.," was held.

The **CEU conference** brought together a small group of experts from a variety of backgrounds to launch the project, in presentations and discussions elucidating linkages between the idea of dignity and particular human rights claims, exploring in particular whether a more nuanced understanding of dignity can provide a basis for principled reconciliation or at least mutual protection of otherwise conflicting rights claims.

The **Oxford Conference** was co-sponsored with the *Oxford Journal of Law and Religion*; the Programme for the Foundations of Law and Constitutional Government, University of Oxford Faculty of Law; and the Religion, Law and International Relations Programme at the Centre for Christianity and Culture, Regent's Park College, Oxford. Approximately 40 conference participants were invited to consider the ideas that motivated and illuminated the human rights project 70 years ago:

- Can the idea of human dignity for everyone everywhere help with the implementation of human rights, through progressive measures?
- Can it enable the vision of human rights to become a common standard of achievement for all people and nations?

- Can the idea of human dignity help reconcile competing human rights claims, and resolve tensions with other important national and social interests?
- Can the idea of human dignity provide insight into the nature of dignitary harms and identity politics in the conscience wars?

The hope is that answers to such questions hold the key to finding solutions for building stable and just communities in an inevitably highly pluralistic world. To this end, participants in the 2018 Oxford Conference (1) reviewed specific thinking about human dignity by some of the founding figures of the UDHR; (2) considered conceptual and ideological foundations of human dignity, including a variety of religious and philosophical approaches to human dignity (including Jewish, Christian, Muslim, and concepts based upon Confucianism); and (3) explored specific ways that the fecundity of the concept of human dignity can be tapped in fruitful and practical ways.

The informative presentations and intense conversations at the Oxford Human Dignity Conference revealed perspectives and raised issues, including candid recognition of the risk that the notion of human dignity can be weaponized in certain contexts. Recognition of this risk moved the discussion forward in useful ways, leading to a more comprehensive framing of principles built upon shared notions of human needs in plural societies, with human dignity as common ground.

The **BYU Conference**, "Human Dignity and Freedom of Religion or Belief: The Universal Declaration of Human Rights at 70," brought together more than 100 delegates – religious and civic leaders, legal scholars, members of the judiciary, and representatives of governments, NGOs, and the media from roughly 50 countries to gather global perspectives on the theme. This provided an opportunity to help distill insights about the role dignity principles can play in fostering respect for the dignity of everyone everywhere. The symposium then moved to Washington DC where a smaller group continued with discussions on the issue of human dignity.

The long-term aim of this project, extending beyond the 2018 Budapest, Oxford, BYU, and DC conferences, is to identify and provide in-depth explanations for a set of dignity-based principles that can help anchor the protection of dignity for everyone everywhere. Such principles can be found at the level of foundations, objectives, and criteria for evaluating human rights. But they can also address building common understanding, finding better ways to implement or realize human rights, including finding principles for reconciling or adjudicating human rights claims in plural societies.

These conferences and additional meetings and consultations laid the groundwork for the preparation of the culminating event of 2018, the Punta del Este Declaration.

The Punta del Este Conference was convened under the auspices of the European Academy of Religion, with the leadership of **Ján Figel'**, Special Envoy for Freedom of Religion or Belief outside the European Union, and with the support of the International Center for Law and Religion Studies at Brigham Young

University. The Punta del Este Conference and the preparatory conferences held earlier in 2018 benefited from the thought, recommendations, and assistance of an informal organizing committee including **Carmen Asiaín Pereira** (Uruguay), Alternate Senator in the Parliament of Uruguay, former President of the Latin American Consortium for Freedom of Religion and Belief, and Professor of Law and the University of Montevideo (Uruguay); **Heiner Bielefeldt** (Germany), former UN Special Rapporteur for Freedom of Religion or Belief; **Tahir Mahmood** (India), Chairman, Amity University Institute of Advanced Legal Studies and Former Chair, Minorities Commission of India; **Christopher McCrudden** (Northern Ireland), Queens University, Belfast; **Alberto Melloni** (Italy), UNESCO Chair on Religious Pluralism and Peace; **Dicky Sofjan** (Indonesia), Professor of the Core Doctoral Faculty of the Indonesian Consortium for Religious Studies, University of Gadjah Mada University (Yogyakarta); **Renata Uitz** (Hungary), Chair, Constitutional Law Program, Central European University; and **Robin Fretwell Wilson** (USA), Roger and Stephany Joslin Professor of Law, University of Illinois College of Law.

What the Punta del Este Declaration is not

In understanding the purposes and background of the Punta del Este Declaration, it is helpful to clarify what the document is not.

The Punta del Este Declaration is not a restatement or recapitulation of the specifically enumerated rights in the UDHR. Rather, the focus is on one primary concept, human dignity, and the role it played in the remarkable achievement of global consensus about human rights that resulted in the adoption of the UDHR in 1948, and the many ways that human dignity remains a useful concept in understanding, respecting, protecting, and promoting human rights today.

The purpose of the Punta del Este Declaration is not to replace human rights with a more general or theoretical concept of human dignity. Rather the purpose is to recognize the importance of human dignity as a foundational concept that underlies human rights. The drafters of the Punta del Este Declaration believe that human dignity was central to the success of generating worldwide support for and agreement regarding the UDHR.[97]

97 Human dignity and rights are integrally connected, but they are distinct concepts; dignity is foundational to but only part of human rights, which "affirms both moral (equal human dignity) and prudential (universal human interests) elements of human rights." John Tasioulas, "Human Dignity and the Foundations of Human Rights" in Christopher McCrudden (ed.), *Understanding Human Dignity* (Oxford University Press: Oxford, 2013) 291, 304–305. The UDHR drafters emphasized human dignity to reflect post-World War II "prolific constitution and treaty-making activity," and, with dignity at the helm of the document, the drafters highlighted interdependence to accomplish the aims of the UDHR. Glendon (2001) 174. Dignity was emphasized in the UDHR in order to foster global support by illustrating "a non-negotiable marker against the denial of human dignity. From the Declaration onwards, governments should not be permitted to say to any human being, 'you do not count, you have no value as an individual.' This did not require a deep philosophical justification; and it

The Punta del Este Declaration is not an attempt to reformulate, renegotiate, or retreat from the progress that has been made since 1948 in specifying, articulating, and creating legally binding obligations regarding human rights.[98] As the Punta del Este Declaration is made in commemoration of the 70th anniversary of the adoption of the UDHR, it focuses on the UDHR rather than subsequent human rights instruments, and in particular, focuses on the centrality of the concept of human dignity to the UDHR and the broader human rights project. Participants in the drafting of the Punta del Este Declaration have a wide variety of views about human rights. The goal was to create a document that reflects a broad consensus about human dignity and the important role it plays in connection to human rights.

The Punta del Este Declaration does not take a position on the important question of whether human dignity is itself a human right, or whether it is better understood as being a background or foundational concept that lies behind and beneath human rights. The drafters and signatories recognized that in practice,

was a cosmopolitan principle that applied to all humans in their dealings with governments." Roger Brownsword, "Human Dignity from a Legal Perspective" in Marcus Düwell et al. (eds.), *The Cambridge Handbook of Human Dignity: Interdisciplinary Perspectives* (Cambridge University Press, 2014) 1, 3. "Human dignity and human rights can be distinguished, and they must be distinguished, but they must not be separated. The basic rights are guaranteed for the sake of human dignity." Christoph Goos, "Restoring Human Dignity in Post-Nazi Germany" in Christopher McCrudden (ed.), *Understanding Human Dignity* (Oxford University Press: Oxford, 2013) 79, 89. Human dignity is not only applicable to every person in and of itself, but it also foundational to the overall idea of human rights and "[g]iven this relationship between human dignity and human rights, the primary *practical* and *political* discourse becomes that of human rights; and, while those who seek a deeper justification for human rights might need to revisit the idea of human dignity, the practical business of pressing one's interests against others (particularly against powerful states) will be conducted in terms of claimed human rights." Roger Brownsword, "Human Dignity from a Legal Perspective" in Marcus Düwell et al. (eds.), *The Cambridge Handbook of Human Dignity: Interdisciplinary Perspectives* (Cambridge University Press, 2014) 1, 3. Because of the connection between dignity and human rights, most issues that arise will be decided under analysis of human rights, while human dignity will be preserved as an inherent quality for all people. *Id.*

98 Glendon emphasized that "[t]he most impressive advances in human rights – the fall of apartheid in South Africa and the collapse of the Eastern European totalitarian regimes – owe more to the moral beacon of the [UDHR] than to the many covenants and treaties that are now in force." Glendon (2001) 236. Morsink reinforced that point when he said, "[t]he [UDHR] performs [a] canonical function for the enormous human rights movement that has sprung up since the end of World War II and that has covered the globe, so that now there is not a single nation on earth that is not caught up in the moral web woven by the articles." Johannes Morsink, *Inherent Human Rights: Philosophical Roots of the Universal Declaration* (University of Pennsylvania Press: Philadelphia, 2009) 2 (Later cited as Morsink (2009)). See also W. Cole Durham and Brett G. Scharffs, *Law and Religion: National, International, and Comparative Perspectives* (Wolters Kluwer: New York, 2019) 84, 86. (Later cited as Durham and Scharffs (2019)).

human dignity has been utilized both ways.[99] The Punta del Este Declaration and this book enumerate places where the issue of whether human dignity is itself a human right might arise.

The Punta del Este Declaration is not an attempt to shift the focus of human rights from individual rights to group rights. It is clear that the UDHR was focused on individual human rights and this project is in no way an attempt to backtrack from or renegotiate that focus.[100] It is also clear that there was a

99 An "interesting duality of uses [of dignity] has to do with the distinction between dignity as the ground of rights and dignity as the content of rights. On the one hand, we are told that human rights 'derive from the inherent dignity of the human person.' On the other hand, it is said that people have a right to be protected against 'degrading treatment' and 'outrages on personal dignity.'" Jeremy Waldron (Meir Dan-Cohen ed.), *Dignity, Rank and Rights: The Tanner Lectures on Human Values* (Oxford University Press: New York, 2012) 13, 17. In the first usage, "human dignity serves as part of the foundation of human rights law, at least in the sense that recognition of this value gives us reason to construct a system of legal rights, calculated to protect individual against treatment inconsistent with human dignity." Gerald L. Neuman, "Discourses of Dignity" in Christopher McCrudden (ed.), *Understanding Human Dignity* (Oxford University Press: Oxford, 2013) 631, 638. Using human dignity in this way, it is "a grounding value of human rights, perhaps even as their exclusive normative basis. Hence, the 1966 Covenants on Civil and Political Rights and on Economic, Social, and Cultural Right both assert that the right they enumerate 'derive from the inherent dignity of the human person.'" John Tasioulas, "Human Dignity and the Foundations of Human Rights" in Christopher McCrudden (ed.), *Understanding Human Dignity* (Oxford University Press: Oxford, 2013) 291, 292. This sentiment was reiterated by numerous international, regional, and domestic instruments. *Id.* In the second usage described above, human dignity is treated as its own individual right.

100 In John Humphrey's initial draft of the UDHR, "his text stated that everyone owes a duty to his *state*. Humphrey could or should have known that this reference to the state would probably create problems, for the First Session of the Commission the delegates had engaged in a 'debate' on the relationship between the individual and the state or society." Johannes Morsink, *The Universal Declaration of Human Rights: Origins, Drafting, and Intent* (University of Pennsylvania Press, 1999) 242 (Later cited as Morsink (1999)). However, the drafters ultimately created the UDHR with a focus on individuals. In the first session of the Human Rights Commission, Eleanor Roosevelt stated the importance of protecting individual's freedoms, saying, "It seems to me that in much that is before us, the rights of the individual are extremely important. It is not exactly that you set the individual apart from his society, but you recognize that within any society the individual must have rights that are guarded." Glendon (2001) 40. In that same session, the Soviet Union's delegate, Valentin Tepliakov, acknowledged the relation the significance of the individual's freedoms and their connection to collective rights, stating that individual rights "must be seen in relation to the individual's obligations to the community, which is 'the main body which provides for his existence, and the enjoyment of the human rights which belong to him.'" *Id.* René Cassin similarly noted the priority of an individual's freedom of conscience and because this "gives man his value and dignity." *Id.*, 41. A focus on the individual was vital to the UDHR because a person's personal identity cannot be completely encompassed by his or her group identities; "[b]etween a person and his or her sometimes numerous affiliations stand the rights that come with being born into the family of humankind." Morsnik (1999) 212. In the long run, this debate between

conscious effort by the drafters of the UDHR to include the concerns of groups by emphasizing that human rights are often realized in community with others. In the 70 years since the adoption of the UDHR, there has been an increased appreciation and recognition of the importance of human rights to groups collectively as well as to individuals.[101] Denials of human rights have often focused on groups as well as individuals, so it is natural to speak of human rights as a matter of concern to groups as well as individuals.[102] But the Punta del Este Declaration is not an effort to reorient human rights away from individual rights to focus more explicitly on group rights. Human dignity is a characteristic of human beings, not groups, but groups can be treated in ways that violate the dignity of their members.[103]

The Punta del Este Declaration does not propose a definitive definition of human dignity. There is a common understanding of the general meaning of dignity, that it relates to an individual's worth and that we "should value the human person, simply because he or she is human."[104] However, the drafters of

a collective or an individualist focus is somewhat artificial because if individuals' rights are mutually respected, "the society becomes a community." *Id.* at 248. What is for the good of the community is also for the good of the person. Paul Groarke and J. L. A. West, "Individual Rights and the Common Good" in William Sweet (ed.), *Philosophical Theory and the Universal Declaration of Human Rights* (University of Ottawa Press, 2003) 155, 161.

101 Glendon (2001) 236. Morsink reinforced that point when he said that, "[t]he [UDHR] performs [a] canonical function for the enormous human rights movement that has sprung up since the end of World War II and that has covered the globe, so that now there is not a single nation on earth that is not caught up in the moral web woven by the articles." Morsnik (2009) 2.

102 The UN Convention on the Prevention and Punishment of the Crime of Genocide (the Genocide Convention) was drafted at the same time as the UDHR and was adopted by the UN's General Assembly only one day prior to the UDHR. Johannes Morsink, *The Universal Declaration of Human Rights and the Challenge of Religion* (University of Missouri Press: Columbia, MO, 2017) 57–58 (later cited as Morsink (2017)). Ultimately, the Genocide Convention established a duty upon all state parties to criminalize the crime of genocide, crime with the specific intent to destroy a protected group in whole or in part.

103 For example, Christian Neuhäuser strives to explain collective dignity, especially in connection with individualism; the relationship is close because individual dignity becomes shared as soon as more than a single individual possesses it "(for example, individual dignity is usually thought to be 'shared' by all human beings)." Micha Werner, "Individual and Collective Dignity" in Marcus Düwell et al. (eds.), *The Cambridge Handbook of Human Dignity: Interdisciplinary Perspectives* (Cambridge University Press, 2014) 343, 346. Neuhäuser describes three possible dignity violations that could be shared by a group: direct, symbolic, or representative group humiliation. *Id.* "In the case of *direct* group humiliation, 'all members of a group are directly humiliated precisely because they are members of this group'. *Symbolic* group humiliations are acts that are directed against symbols of a group that express or are intentionally linked to a real threat against the group. *Representative* group humiliations means that 'a whole group is humiliated through the humiliation of one or more of its members.'" *Id.*

104 Christopher McCrudden, "In Pursuit of Human Dignity: An Introduction to Current Debates" in Christopher McCrudden (ed.), *Understanding Human Dignity* (Oxford University Press: Oxford, 2013) 1.

the UDHR did not specifically define "dignity" and the term remains somewhat flexible for interpretation and application. However, there have been efforts made by different individuals to articulate a more concrete definition for "dignity."[105]

Indeed, the working group that drafted the Punta del Este Declaration does not all agree upon a definition. There is much about human dignity that can be gleaned from the Punta del Este Declaration, but it does not seek to provide a simple uncontroverted definition. This omission was intentional. A definition by its nature would invite disagreement rather than agreement. Our hope is rather to

105 The following are examples of such efforts: Judge Christian Byk describes dignity as "what ma[kes] [each human being] unique, sacred. Therefore, dignity is the founding value of the respect due to each human person, whatever his or her biological or social condition might be." Christian Byk, "Is Human Dignity a Useless Concept? Legal Perspectives" in Marcus Düwell *et al.* (eds.), *The Cambridge Handbook of Human Dignity: Interdisciplinary Perspectives* (Cambridge University Press, 2014) 363. Margaret Farley defined the requirements to protect human dignity are "obligating features of personhood" and such features include "autonomy (the capacity to be self-determining and not have one's life simply shaped by other persons or external powers), and relationality (the fact that persons cannot survive, thrive, or even exist as persons without some fundamental relatedness to other persons)." David Hollenbach, "Experience and History, Practical Reason and Faith" in Christopher McCrudden (ed.), *Understanding Human Dignity* (Oxford University Press: Oxford, 2013) 123, 129. David A. Jones, "Dignity Language in Bioethical Discussions" in Christopher McCrudden (ed.), *Understanding Human Dignity* (Oxford University Press: Oxford, 2013) 525, 526.

Roger Brownsword, "Human Dignity from a Legal Perspective" in Marcus Düwell et al. (eds.), *The Cambridge Handbook of Human Dignity: Interdisciplinary Perspectives* (Cambridge University Press, 2014) 1, 3–4. David Hollenbach emphasizes that "[r] especting human dignity means avoiding those violations of the human person that are so grave that all (or nearly all) persons see them as outrageous and shocking." David Hollenbach, "Experience and History, Practical Reason and Faith" in Christopher McCrudden (ed.), *Understanding Human Dignity* (Oxford University Press: Oxford, 2013) 123, 126–27. Meanwhile, Catherine Dupré posits that dignity's definition alters depending on when it's presumed that the legal concept of dignity began. Assuming that the legal concept of dignity began in 1789 with the French Declaration of the Rights of Man, dignity is defined "as a foundational principle of liberal democracy, strongly connected to claims of liberty and equality"; assuming it began in 1848 with France outlawing slavery, dignity "sheds light on the fundamental connection between dignity, humanity, work, and working conditions"; assuming it began in 1949, post-World War II, dignity has a negative connotation, that it "is a 'never again' response to the systematic denial and destruction of humanity, which leaves out its arguably much needed positive and complementary dimensions"; and assuming 2009 as the beginning with the Lisbon Treaty, dignity's novelty is emphasized, but appears an "EU-made concept, whereas the story is much more complex." Catherine Dupré, "Constructing the Meaning of Human Dignity" in Christopher McCrudden (ed.), *Understanding Human Dignity* (Oxford University Press: Oxford, 2013) 113, 117–18. Ultimately, dignity's definition is not concrete and it has been used in various senses. Nevertheless, these variations in meaning do not necessarily imply equivocation. There are, rather, 'a family of concepts clustered around the practice of moral evaluation'. Indeed, that the search for the essential characteristics of a concept should lead to a family of meanings is not a special feature of the word 'dignity'. It is, rather, a common property of meaning in ordinary language."

create an invitation for individuals or groups to suggest definitions that capture the meaning of human dignity from a variety of theoretical, conceptual, ideological, or religious perspectives. The Punta del Este Declaration is based on the idea that human dignity is a complex concept that is susceptible to many conceptions, formulations, and definitions. In this sense, the Punta del Este Declaration is what philosophers have referred to as an "incompletely theorized agreement."[106] The goal is to invite the creation of what John Rawls described as an "overlapping consensus,"[107] or what Norwegian philosopher Tore Lindholm has called an "overlapping justification" for human rights. In Tore Lindholm's alternative theory of "overlapping justification," human rights derive

106 The use of incompletely theorized agreements by legal systems, as described by Cass Sunstein, are when individuals involved in legal controversies "agree on the result and on relatively narrow or low-level explanations for it. They need not agree on a fundamental principle. They do not offer larger or more abstract explanations than are necessary to decide the case. When they disagree on an abstraction, they move to a level of greater particularity." Cass R. Sunstein, "Commentary: Incompletely Theorized Agreements" (1995) 108 *Harvard Law Review* 1733, 1735–36. Incompletely theorized agreements are beneficial when the ultimate desired result is mutually understood, but the underlying reasoning or methods are not. With this concept, "religious believers can continue to affirm their beliefs as the most important part of their lives while living and participating in society, tolerating others, and obeying the laws of the land." Durham and Scharffs (2019) 77. *See* Cass R. Sunstein, "Commentary: Incompletely Theorized Agreements" (1995) 108 *Harvard Law Review* 1733, 1737, 1742–1743 (1995) (using *Roe v. Wade* as an example of an incompletely theorized agreement explaining that many individuals support the ultimate decision in *Roe*, but some support it for women's equality, other for privacy protection, others for separation of church and state, and still others support because fetuses would not be protected anyway).

107 John Rawls conveyed his hope that political institutions could carry out international affairs through overlapping consensus, rather than comprehensive views. Robert P. George, "Response to Tollefsen and Cameron" in Christopher McCrudden (ed.), *Understanding Human Dignity* (Oxford University Press: Oxford, 2013) 501, 501. Overlapping consensus is a helpful theory because though there can be significant differences in individual ideas about justice, these different ideas can still lead to the same conclusion; the theory requires reciprocity in that each side believes that all other views also support the shared conclusion. John Rawls, *A Theory of Justice* 387–388 (Harvard University Press, 1971). In overlapping consensus, "the reasonable doctrines endorse the political conception, each from its own point of view." The political conception is a framework encouraging "deliberation and reflection which helps [to] reach political agreement on at least the constitutional essentials and the basic questions of justice." John Rawls, *Political Liberalism* (Columbia University Press: New York, 1993) 134, 156. Marcus Düwell noted how overlapping consensus could be an effective theory, particularly with the UDHR as it was intended to be accepted globally with differing views on dignity. Using overlapping consensus "would have the advantage that it would give room for a diversity of ways to access the concept, and … it would account for the genuinely political nature of struggles about human dignity." Marcus Düwell, "Concepts, Discussions, Philosophical Perspectives" in Marcus Düwell et al. (eds.), *The Cambridge Handbook of Human Dignity: Interdisciplinary Perspectives* (Cambridge University Press, 2014) 23, 46.

> from the public global commitment to heed the inherent dignity of every human being but only by way of complex processes of deliberation and negotiation with moral, religious, cultural, political, economic, diplomatic, and other inputs … Justification of a problematic moral norm, at the level of the individual, does not require that the norm be deduced from unproblematic (or "certain" or "self-evident") higher principles … Reasonable justification has to be holistic and fallibilist: we have good reason to accept only what "best" fits into the totality of our knowledge, values, commitments, and beliefs (remembering that among our cherished commitments we may include open-mindedness, taking arguments seriously, and respect for fellow human beings and their plights).[108]

The Punta del Este Declaration does not offer a metaphysics or ontology of human dignity.[109] In this respect, it is an invitation to depth and discussion rather

108 Tore Lindholm, "Philosophical and Religious Justification of Freedom of Religion or Belief" in Tore Lindholm, W. Cole Durham and Bahia Tahzib-Lie (eds.), *Facilitating Freedom of Religion or Belief: A Deskbook* (Martinus Nijhoff, 2004) 49–50.

109 There have been various descriptions of moral, metaphysical, or ontological bases for human rights. P. C. Chang at the 95th United Nations' meeting discussed the purpose of the United Nations in relation to morality, stating, "[E]thical considerations should play a greater part in the discussion … The aim of the United Nations was not to ensure the selfish gains of the individual but to try and increase man's moral stature. It was necessary to proclaim the duties of the individual for it was a consciousness of his duties which enabled man to reach a high moral standard." Pinghua Sun, *Historic Achievement of a Common Standard: Pengchun Chang and the Universal Declaration of Human Rights* (Springer: Singapore, 2018) 236. Immanuel Kant also used morality as a gauge for human dignity and rights. He believed that the only thing to have dignity is morality (and humanity so long as it is capable of morality) and to preserve morality, each individual must be given respect and treated as an end, rather than a means for another end. "The value of a human being – the person's dignity – is beyond price." Michael Rosen, "Dignity: The Case Against" in Christopher McCrudden (ed.), *Understanding Human Dignity* (Oxford University Press: Oxford, 2013) 143, 146. "Things with price can be exchanged for each other in the marketplace, but humans, having dignity, are valuable in themselves and thus cannot be simply traded one for another." David Hollenbach, "Experience and History, Practical Reason and Faith" in Christopher McCrudden (ed.), *Understanding Human Dignity* (Oxford University Press: Oxford, 2013) 123, 126. David Walsh acknowledges that human dignity is an eschatological concept that cannot be completely understood and articulated but describes one avenue to approach the topic of human dignity. David Walsh, "Dignity as an Eschatological Concept" in Christopher McCrudden (ed.), *Understanding Human Dignity* (Oxford University Press: Oxford, 2013) 245, 245. Walsh states that as a person "who holds his or her existence in his or her own hands, we must not take that away by treating them as objects of control. Autonomy is too thin a word for what autonomy identifies. It is the whole metaphysical significance of the person that is at issue when we confront the question of human dignity. Our difficulty is that we live in a world without metaphysics, and therefore have to say what cannot be said." *Id.* John Tasioulas explained his philosophy about human nature and dignity by admitting it as "an inexhaustible topic," but generally described it as belonging to a group that has "a characteristic form of embodiment; a finite lifespan of a certain rough magnitude; capacities for physical growth and reproduction;

itself a deep and definitive statement about the nature of human dignity.[110] The goal is to identify a large number of ways that human dignity can be a useful concept, even if we don't have complete agreement on all of the specific grounds of dignity or its meaning and implications. The hope of the drafters and adopters of this Declaration is that it will have the practical effect of refocusing on human dignity as a way of generating broader support for human rights around the world, including in places where human rights are met with suspicion or resistance.

Conclusions

The human rights project, initiated by the UDHR, is not yet finished. While the UDHR was a truly historic achievement, it is crucial to emphasize that the road towards universalism is long. Over the years, the recognition, realizations, and protection of the human rights identified in the UDHR have been slow, but we believe that it is crucial to explore ways to refocus and reinvigorate the human rights project so it will continue to grow and not stagnate. The Punta del Este Declaration aims to be a part of that effort.

psychological capacities, … and, specifically rational capacities." John Tasioulas, "Human Dignity and the Foundations of Human Rights" in Christopher McCrudden (ed.), *Understanding Human Dignity* (Oxford University Press: Oxford, 2013) 291, 305. However, there is not universal agreement that such philosophies based on morality or metaphysics are necessary. In fact, Michael Ignatieff "believes we should forgo efforts to ground [human rights] on claims about a dignity or nature allegedly shared by all human beings. Support for human rights will be more secure if we avoid metaphysical or religious claims about their foundations and rely simply on historical, prudential, or pragmatic evidence that support for rights is desirable." David Hollenbach, "Experience and History, Practical Reason and Faith" in Christopher McCrudden (ed.), *Understanding Human Dignity* (Oxford University Press: Oxford, 2013) 123, 125.

110 The abstract quality of human dignity does not weaken its value to furthering human rights. Dignity's lack of clarity is similar to that of "the rights to equality or liberty. Constitutional democracy has apparently already become accustomed to the idea that the rights to liberty and equality, for all of their vagueness, are essential features of every constitutional bill of rights." Aharon Barak, "The Constitutional Value and the Constitutional Right" in Christopher McCrudden (ed.), *Understanding Human Dignity* (Oxford University Press: Oxford, 2013) 361, 379–80. Bills of rights, which have broad applications within a nation, rarely strictly define the rights they outline, leaving the interpretation to the applicant. Dieter Grimm, "Dignity in a Legal Context and as an Absolute Right" in Christopher McCrudden (ed.), *Understanding Human Dignity* (Oxford University Press: Oxford, 2013) 381, 382. "Vagueness does not deprive a norm of its legal nature. Vagueness has to be reduced by way of interpretation." *Id.*, 383.

2 An introduction to the Punta del Este Declaration and its Preamble

Introduction

This chapter focuses on the Preamble to the Punta del Este Declaration and provides an expanded explanation of the preambular paragraphs focusing on the meaning and scope of the concept of human dignity.

Expanded explanation of the Declaration's title

Preliminary consideration: human dignity "of" and "for" everyone everywhere

The working group on the Punta del Este Declaration carefully scrutinized whether the Declaration should be titled "human dignity *for* everyone everywhere," "human dignity *of* everyone everywhere" or a hybrid of the two options, "human dignity *of and for* everyone everywhere." The wording divided the working group over issues of meaning, usage, and emphasis. The primary argument for using the phrase "human dignity *of* everyone" was that human dignity is inherent in all human beings and the preposition "of" most clearly expresses the inherent and inalienable character of human dignity and human rights.[1] Human dignity is not something that depends upon action by states for it to exist; rather it describes a state of affairs that simply is. Human rights are not created by states enacting

1 See Article 1 of the UDHR. Kateb emphasized that "[T]he human species is indeed something special [in] that it possesses valuable, commendable uniqueness or distinctiveness that is unlike the uniqueness of any other species. It has high[er] dignity than all other species, or a qualitatively different dignity from all of them … Humanity is not only natural, whereas all other species are only natural." George Kateb, *Human Dignity* (Harvard University Press, 2011) 5. (Later cited as Kateb (2011)). Morsink claims that "The [UDHR] consists of two complementary theses about the universality of human rights … The first universality thesis is a metaphysical one about the way the world is. It states that people everywhere and at all times have right that are not man-made, but inherent in the human person from the moment of birth." Morsink (2009) 17. See also: Erin Daly, *Dignity Rights: Courts, Constitutions, and the Worth of the Human Person* (University of Pennsylvania Press, 2013) 13.

DOI: 10.4324/9781003207030-3

positive law; states enact positive law to fulfill their obligations to recognize and protect human rights.[2]

The Preamble of the UDHR begins with a "recognition *of* the inherent dignity and of the equal and inalienable rights of all members of the human family …"[3] Indeed, the UDHR itself emphasizes the inherent and inalienable character of human rights with its title, "The Universal Declaration *of* Human Rights" (emphasis added).

The primary argument for using the phrase "human dignity *for* everyone" was that the preposition "for" is a more active word that emphasizes the need for action in light of the inherent nature of human dignity. The word "for" does not suggest that human dignity is not inherent or inalienable but emphasizes that action is needed – by us as human beings –for human dignity to be realized in the world. The primary argument for using the phrase "human dignity *of and for* everyone" was that this included both ideas, although at the expense of brevity. There was also a concern by some that this made the document seem overly legalistic, which is contrary to the intent of the project.

While there was disagreement among the Punta del Este Declaration working group about how to best express the inherent and inalienable nature of human rights as well as the need for specific action in recognition of human dignity, there was no disagreement about the inherent nature of human dignity as a feature of human existence and that it is not something that awaits being granted or recognized by the state before it becomes operative. There was also no disagreement about the need for action by all sectors of society to implement and realize human dignity for all people.

While the working group on the Punta del Este Declaration ultimately settled upon the word "for" in the title of the Punta del Este Declaration, the inherent character of human dignity is emphasized in the first sentence of Article 1 of the Punta del Este Declaration, which states,

> The inherent human dignity *of* all people and the importance of respecting, promoting, and protecting human dignity *for* everyone everywhere is the foundational principle and the key objective or goal of human rights, as well as an invaluable criterion for evaluating laws, policies, and government actions for how well they accord with human rights standards.[4]

2 Kateb emphasized that "When the state respects human rights, supposedly the only thing that matters is that the state is, by and large, acting by positive policies or by avoidance and restraint to reduce human suffering, whatever else the state may imaginatively do for the good." Kateb (2011) 28–33.

3 Preamble of the UDHR [emphasis added]. See also Martti Koskenniemi, "Preamble of the Universal Declaration of Human Rights" in Gudmundur S. Alfdredsson and Asbjørn Eide (eds.), *The Universal Declaration of Human Rights* (Martinus Nijhoff Publishers, 1999) 27–39. The drafters used the passive voice in phrases such as this to indicate the irrevocability of dignity and human rights; this phrase with the passive voice "affirms an eternal truth, independent from anyone's recognition." *Id.*, 32.

4 Emphasis added. See: full text of Punta del Este Declaration on Human Dignity for Everyone Everywhere, in Appendix A.

The use of the word "for" in the title should in no way call into question the inherent and inalienable nature of human dignity.

Expanded explanation of the Declaration's Preamble

The Preamble to the Punta del Este Declaration states background reasons and considerations that were viewed by the working group as explanations for the motivations behind the document and the reasons for promulgating it.

The "whereas" clauses

The first five preambular clauses begin with the word *whereas*. These clauses state the general background reasons for issuing the Punta del Este Declaration. These clauses recall the significant event of the adoption of the UDHR and the important role that the concept of human dignity played as the foundational principle of human rights. The Punta del Este Declaration is made in recognition of the importance of remembering, reaffirming, and recommitting ourselves to the basic principle of human dignity for everyone everywhere.

The following is a more detailed explanation of each of the *whereas* clauses.

> ***Whereas* seventy years ago in the aftermath of World War II, the nations and peoples of the world came together in solidarity and solemnity and without dissent adopted the Universal Declaration of Human Rights (UDHR) as a common standard of achievement for all peoples and all nations**

The UDHR was drafted and adopted in the shadow of the mass atrocities and severe human rights violations perpetrated by Nazi fascism and Japanese imperialism during WWII.[5] The specter of World War I was also a powerful reminder

5 The delegates were "part of an alliance against a common enemy, nazism/fascism, whose violations of human rights had been widely condemned." Asbild Samnoy, "The Origins of the Universal Declaration of Human Rights" in Gudmundur Alfredsson and Asbjørn Eide (eds.), *The Universal Declaration of Human Rights* (Martinus Nijhoff Publishers, 1999) 11. According to Morsink, "During the final General Assembly debate in December 1948 the drafters made it abundantly clear that the Declaration on which they were about to vote had been born out of the experience of the war that had just ended." and "The Cold War, the women's lobby, and the tradition of Latin American socialism were also major forces that shaped the writing of this pivotal document. But none of them match the Holocaust in importance." Morsink (1999) 36, 37. Johnson and Symonides stressed that "The bestial behavior of fascist regimes on the eve of and during the Second World War, however, so offended the global conscience that statesmen and citizens alike began to search for international protection for some basic standard of human dignity and worth." M. Glen Johnson and Janusz Symonides, *The Universal Declaration of Human Rights: A History of Its Creation and Implementation 1948–1998* (UNESCO, 1998) 26. Quataert credited the success of the project to "Nazi and Axis policies [that] included the mass deportations of people; abuses of prisoners of war; extensive reliance on slave labor;

that the horrors of the war just completed was not an anomaly.[6] The founding figures[7] of the human rights project were motivated by a powerful desire that "never again" would the world see the horrors of World War II, a conflict in which some 60 million people lost their lives.[8]

Before World War II, even though the international community had recognized some common values, there were no univocally defined and codified human rights triggering international protection.[9] This was one of the challenges that arose in

and, for the Japanese, the widespread use of women as sex slaves for their imperial army." Jean H. Quataert, *Advocating Dignity: Human Rights Mobilizations in Global Politics* (University of Pennsylvania Press, 2009) 1. Similarly, Morsink stressed that "Charles Malik, the representative from Lebanon, said that the document 'was inspired by opposition to the barbarous doctrines of Nazism and fascism.' Lakshimi Menon, his colleague from India, told the Assembly that the Declaration was 'born from the need to reaffirm those rights after their violation during the war.' Like Bodil Begtrup, the Danish delegate, all the drafters wanted 'to avoid the horrors of a new war.' 'From the ruins of destruction wrought by the Second World War,' said Jorge Carrera Andrade, the delegate from Ecuador, 'man had once again fanned the immortal flame of civilization, freedom and law.' Now that Nazism, fascism, and their 'brutal totalitarian States' had been destroyed, the United Nations, he said, should 'strive for a new democratic internationalism.' The Belgian delegate, Count Henry Carton de Wiart, thought that 'the essential merit of the Declaration was to emphasize the high dignity of the human person after the outrages to which men and women had been exposed during the recent war.' René Cassin, the French delegate, pointed out that indeed the Declaration 'was the most vigorous and the most urgently needed of humanity's protest against opposition.'" [internal citations omitted]. Morsink (1999) 36–37. See also: Roger Normand and Sarah Zaidi, *Human Rights at the U.N.: The Political History of Universal Justice* (Indiana University Press, 2008) 143–144.

6 In justifying the need for a Declaration, Ernest Davies of the United Kingdom noted that "'previous declarations had lived in history long after the wars and disputes which had given rise to them' had been forgotten." World War II was the impetus for this Declaration, but it was not first war to prompt such a response. Morsink (1999) 37.

7 Key members of the Human Rights Commission who were tasked with drafting the UDHR included Eleanor Roosevelt, P.C. Chang, René Cassin, Charles Malik, and John Humphrey. The "triumvirate" of Eleanor Roosevelt, the unanimously elected chair, P. C. Chang, vice chairman and head of the Chinese UN Delegation, and Charles Malik of Lebanon, "symbolically representing West, East, and in the case of Malek, a crossroads of many cultures, constituted the leadership of the Human Rights Commission throughout the entire period of the preparation of the document that became the Universal Declaration of Human Rights." Glendon (2001) 33.

8 While the exact number is unclear, according to Olmstead, "The general consensus is that 50 million to 80 million people died." Dan Olmstead, "Did More Russians or Americans Die during WWII?" (Sept. 17, 2018) *The National WWII Museum*. For an interactive video that crunches the data of WWII casualties, see *The Fallen of World War II*, an interactive documentary film by Neil Halloran at http://www.fallen.io/ww2/

9 As the drafters were grappling with what the role the Nuremberg Trials should play in the UDHR, they included the term "international law" to recognize the need for some checks after national law failed to protect human rights. "The [principles of the Hague Convention of 1907] protected the law of humanity against violation by national law (as had happened in the case of Nazi Germany)." The Nuremberg Trials served to prosecute violations of customs of warfare, but the Hague Convention did

the trials of Nazi military leaders at Nuremberg. During the International Military Tribunals at Nuremberg (the Nuremberg Trials), prosecutors resorted to a creative argument that although human rights were not codified (at the time when the Nazis perpetrated the mass atrocities), there existed commonly recognized higher values under international law that required protection.[10] The Nuremberg Trials established the supremacy of international law over domestic law. As a result, the perpetrators could be prosecuted for acts that were authorized by the state and in accord with domestic law at the time.[11]

The UDHR began the process of codifying human rights into terms that would eventually have the status of enforceable international law. The UDHR was a remarkable achievement, and the window of opportunity for accomplishing it was narrow.[12] The United Nations was in its infancy, and the deep freeze of the Cold War was fast approaching. In retrospect, it is a wonder that agreement was achieved on such a sweeping and comprehensive statement of shared principles of human rights.[13] Indeed, as Glendon describes it, "Shortly after the

not spark protectionist intervention on behalf of any individual. Morsink (2017) 52–58. As Bennett emphasizes, "In retrospect, it might seem that given the horrors of World War II the turn to human dignity as a foundation for political thinking – the proposal that universal human dignity can provide the warrant for new regimes of governance and care – was an obvious one." This "post-war formulation of human dignity as self-evident" created "new political and ethical practices." Gaymon Bennett, *Technicians of Human Dignity: Bodies, Souls, and the Making of Intrinsic Worth* (Fordham University Press, 2016) 3.

10 H. Lauterpacht, "The Law of Nations and the Punishment of War Crimes" in Guenael Mettraux (ed.), *Perspectives on the Nuremberg Trial* (Oxford University Press: New York, 2010) 28.

11 *Trial of Major War Criminals Before the International Military Tribunals*, published in 1947, Nuremberg, Volume 1, *Judgment*, 295. See also: Andrew Clapham, "Issues of Complexity, Complicity and Complementarity: From the Nuremberg Trials to the Dawn of the New International Criminal Court" in Philippe Sands, *From Nuremberg to the Hague. The Future of International Criminal Justice* (Cambridge University Press: Cambridge, 2003).

12 According to Quataert, "John P. Humphrey, the Canadian jurist and prominent architect of the U.N. human rights project, described so vividly the atmosphere of 'optimistic excitement' in these early years of human rights history. In his own words, the undertaking to remake the law was 'nothing short of revolutionary.'" Quataert continues, "Competing in the arena of global politics, human rights consciousness defied the odds." Later, Quataert declares that "Probably no other document of any kind, certainly no other statement of human rights, has ever been debated so extensively and intensively by such a diverse group of people representing such varied cultures and backgrounds. It was a remarkable achievement merely to have reached such wide agreement on such a text." Jean H. Quataert, *Advocating Dignity: Human Rights Mobilizations in Global Politics* (University of Pennsylvania Press, 2009) 2–3, 61–62

13 The Declaration was adopted during the "brief interlude between the end of World War II and the definitive collapse of the Soviet-American alliance." Glendon (2001) xix. "As the UDHR was being drafted, vital factors in its favor were changing and gradually, but inexorably, lessening the chances for adoption: the memory of the horrors of World War II was becoming less vivid; the Cold War

[UDHR]'s adoption, the window of opportunity closed, to remain shut for forty years."[14]

The UN General Assembly proclaimed the UDHR as,

> a common standard of achievement for all peoples and all nations, to the end that every individual and every organ of society, keeping this Declaration constantly in mind, shall strive by teaching and education to promote respect for these rights and freedoms and by progressive measures, national and international, to secure their universal and effective recognition and observance, both among the peoples of Member States themselves and among the peoples of territories under their jurisdiction.[15]

This common achievement, arguably, made the UDHR the most important international document over the subsequent decades and will continue to be such for many generations to come, having been widely ratified and used as a basis for other international treaties, constitutions and domestic laws. No other international document has come close to such a status.

> ***Whereas* the Preamble of the UDHR declares that "recognition of the inherent dignity and of the equal and inalienable rights of all members of the human family is the foundation of freedom, justice, and peace in the world"**

It was the recognition of the inherent dignity and the equal inalienable rights of all people that was the starting point for the recognition and enumeration of human rights. Here the Punta del Este Declaration quotes the preambular paragraph 1 of the UDHR to reconfirm the inherent and inalienable nature of human dignity. The inherent and inalienable nature of human dignity is essential to the idea of the universality of human dignity and human rights.

The concept of human dignity came to have "pride of place" in the Preamble of the UDHR. As Glendon emphasized:

> The Preamble begins by linking freedom, justice, and peace and by asserting that these goals *depend* upon the recognition of human dignity and rights. The proposition that human rights are *universal*, belonging to "all members of the human family," challenged the traditional view that the relation between a sovereign state and its own citizens was that nation's own exclusive business.[16]

was intensifying; the question of self-determination was becoming increasingly sensitive." Asbild Samnoy, "The Origins of the Universal Declaration of Human Rights" in Gudmundur Alfredsson and Asbjørn Eide (eds.), *The Universal Declaration of Human Rights: A Common Standard of Achievement* (Martinus Nijhoff Publishers: The Hague, 1999) 20.

14 Glendon (2001) xix.

15 See Preamble, UDHR.

16 Glendon (2001) 175–176. The document is "a declaration of interdependence – interdependence of people, nations, and rights." *Id.*, 174.

Similarly, P. C. Chang stressed that the Preamble of the UDHR was to incorporate foundational premises of the document and a "standard should be established with a view to elevating the concept of man's dignity."[17] Similarly, Charles Malik believed that the Preamble, and the inclusion of human dignity in the Preamble, would set the tone for interpreting the UDHR.[18]

The concept of human dignity was the key to generating agreement and energizing and propelling the UDHR project. Indeed, after the atrocities of World War II, there was a general understanding and agreement among the drafters that human dignity must be protected from anything that helped create such horrors.[19]

> ***Whereas* Article 1 of the UDHR proclaims that "All human beings are born free and equal in dignity and rights. They are endowed with reason and conscience and should act towards one another in a spirit of brotherhood"**

This clause recites Article 1 of the UDHR to confirm that all human beings are born free and equal in dignity and rights. Article 1 is meant to assert the universality of human dignity and the rights enshrined in the UDHR. As Norwegian philosopher Tore Lindholm has observed, this declaration is "now widely accepted, taken seriously, and rarely contested throughout the world, may count as a major political achievement to be associated with the UDHR."[20]

The drafters of the UDHR focused on the unifying broad concepts of "reason," "conscience," and the need to treat each other with a "spirit of brotherhood."[21] For example, the idea of being endowed with conscience is founded in Confucian ethics, from the word *ren* which in English terms means, "humaneness towards others" or "consciousness of his fellow men."[22] René Cassin when commenting on the phrase "spirit of brotherhood" emphasized that the "expression was all-inclusive and had the further advantage of stressing the inherent equality of human beings, a concept which had recently been attacked by Hitler and his ideological disciples. The idea of the solidarity of men should be made explicit in the Article to convince the peoples of the world that the United Nations firmly believed in their essential brotherhood."[23]

Despite this recognition constituting a part of international law (international customary law), since the adoption of the UDHR the empirical reality is still far from the aspirations of the drafters of the UDHR. Many individuals and groups continue to be denied their rights or have their rights limited to the point that the

17 Glendon (2001) 38.
18 Glendon (2001) 117–118. Lindholm (1999) 44.
19 Morsink (1999) 37.
20 Lindholm (1999) 66.
21 See the second section of this chapter.
22 Lindholm (1999) 43. See also: Glendon (2001) 67.
23 William Schabas, *The Universal Declaration of Human Rights: The "Travaux Préparatoires."* (Cambridge University Press: Cambridge, 2013) 1670. (Later cited as Schabas (2013)).

rights are not meaningful, or have their dignity nullified altogether. Some of the most affected groups continue to be, for example, women and girls, children, refugees, internally displaced persons, stateless persons, minorities, indigenous persons, persons with disabilities, older persons, HIV-positive persons, and members of LGBTQ communities.

Over the years, the UN has launched campaigns focused on ensuring that all human beings are recognized as free and equal. For example, under Human Rights Council resolution 6/15 of September 28, 2007, the UN established the forum on minority issues to provide a platform for national, ethnic, religious, and linguistic minorities, and to promote their rights and implement the Declaration on the Rights of Persons Belonging to National or Ethnic, Religious and Linguistic Minorities. In July 2013, the Office of the United Nations High Commissioner for Human Rights (OHCHR) launched the "Free & Equal" campaign to promote equal rights and fair treatment of LGBTQ people. Despite such proactive steps, more needs to be done to achieve the aim expressed in Article 1 of the UDHR.

> ***Whereas* the equal human dignity of everyone everywhere is the foundational principle of human rights and reminds us that every person is of value and is worthy of respect**

Human dignity is the foundational principle of human rights. At times human dignity is regarded as a human right itself, whereas at other times it is considered to be the value that underlies all human rights. In either event, human dignity is a marker of the fact that every person has inherent value and is worthy of respect.

When human rights questions arise, human dignity is always implicated. When trying to guarantee and protect human rights, it is crucial to consider the implication of any such attempts upon the human dignity of everyone everywhere. The idea that human dignity is the foundational principle of human rights is developed further in Article 1 of the Punta del Este Declaration.

While the Punta del Este Declaration does not attempt an extensive definition of "human dignity," this sentence identifies an important component of such a definition, the idea that "every person is of value and is worthy of respect." Again, this recognition was fundamental to the drafters of the UDHR who continued to face up to the horrors of Nazi atrocities and the denial of human dignity to groups of people they considered unworthy of protection.[24]

> ***Whereas* it is important to remember, reaffirm, and recommit ourselves to these basic principles**

Despite the passage of 70 years since the adoption of the UDHR, human rights and its underlying principles are not yet univocally and universally recognized and implemented around the world. It is crucial to remember, reaffirm, and recommit

24 Glendon (2001) 176; Morsnik (1999) 87.

to the basic principle of human dignity to ensure that the aim behind the UDHR, namely, to become a truly universal mechanism for the recognition, respect, and realization of human rights, is fulfilled.

The Punta del Este Declaration is not designed to be an expansion, restatement, or reformulation of the UDHR; rather it is adopted in the spirit of commemorating the achievement of the UDHR and is consciously striving to facilitate a global "remembering," "reaffirmation," and "recommitment" to the basic principles underlying human rights.[25]

The "recalling" clauses

The five "recalling" clauses of the Punta del Este Declaration focus on perspectives from the time of the drafting and adoption of the UDHR in the aftermath of World War II. These include the grave violations of human rights that occurred during World War II and in other wars of the first half of the 20th Century, as well as the realization that domestic laws alone had not been sufficient to safeguard against grave violations of human rights. These clauses also focus on the role that human dignity played in bringing the peoples and nations of the world together to adopt the UDHR. Despite many political, economic, and ideological differences, human dignity was a concept that became a rallying point for the UDHR. It became the wellspring for and an underpinning of the rights enumerated in the UDHR. The UDHR in turn became the inspiration for numerous international and regional conventions, as well as a wide array of national constitutions, bills and charters of rights, and legislation concerning human rights.

> ***Recalling*** **that it was grave violations of human dignity during the wars of the 20th Century that preceded and precipitated the UDHR**

The UDHR was not an afterthought or a special interest project. This sentence is a recognition of the grave violations of human rights, including the atrocities perpetrated by the Nazi regime, that focused the world's attention on the need for the UDHR.[26] The UDHR was adopted in large measure to help ensure that the grave violations of human dignity that took place during the first and second world wars would not be repeated and was designed to motivate the nations and peoples of the earth to unite in the common effort to protect human rights of everyone everywhere. Before the brutality of World War II, it was commonly

25 See Chapter 1, "What the Punta del Este Declaration Is Not" for discussion on this point.

26 The atrocities of World War II caused people around the world "to realize the urgency and importance of human rights protection. The establishment of the United Nations and the publication of the UN Charter provided a historical background" for the UDHR. Pinghua Sun, *Historic Achievement of a Common Standard: Pengchun Chang and the Universal Declaration of Human Rights* (Springer: Singapore, 2018) 137. (Later cited as Pinghua Sun (2018)).

believed that concerns of human rights were issues confined to domestic governments; however, after the deep violations of human dignity in the war, it was understood that human rights were instead

> a common concern for all mankind and the whole world should unite to defeat fascism and protect human rights of every individual and in every place. Thus, "[t]he atrocities of World War II, with its intensive and unbelievable repression and brutality, provide the immediate background for the drafting and adoption of the UDHR."[27]

The UDHR was not motivated by simple idealism or as a theoretical exercise. Rather it was a solemn and serious response to egregious human rights violations that had occurred during the first half of the 20th Century.[28]

Indeed, among the drafters of the UDHR, there was a shared agreement that "[a]fter the repeated condemnations by the Allies of the Nazi violations of human rights and fundamental freedoms, many countries had come to look upon the United Nations as the new world organization that was to have some teeth in

27 Pinghua Sun (2018) 139–140. Dignity was at the forefront of the political agenda and became a legal concept used to change laws because "human dignity can be understood as a solemn constitutional commitment 'never again' to deny people their humanity and to destroy it in a systematic manner." Catherine Dupré, "Constructing the Meaning of Human Dignity" in Christopher McCrudden (ed.), *Understanding Human Dignity* (Oxford University Press: Oxford, 2013) 113, 119. Glendon, quoting Charles Malik, Lebanon's representative during the UDHR's drafting, about World War II's influence on the UDHR, stressed that: "Certainly the sense of urgency and drive that characterized the preparation of the Declaration back in 1947 and 1948 are absent … The Declaration in 1948 was really something of a miracle, so that if it were not proclaimed then, possibly we would still be working on it now." Glendon (2001) 208. See also: Asbjørn Eide and Gudmundur Alfredsson, "Introduction" in Gudmundur Alfredsson and Asbjørn Eide (eds.), *The Universal Declaration of Human Rights* (Martinus Nijhoff Publishers, 1999) xxv, xxvi.

28 The statesmen and women who drafted and adopted the UDHR were not starry-eyed idealists. Rather, they were experienced and seasoned military, political and religious leaders who had received a hard lesson in the brutality that humankind was capable of unleashing on itself. Morsink stresses the experience and qualifications of the key drafters of the Declaration. John Humphrey had taught law at McGill University before serving as the UN Secretariat's Human Rights Director in 1946. René Cassin was a respected international jurist and France's delegate to the League of Nations Assemblies and the Geneva Disarmament Conferences. Hernan Santa Cruz, the Chilean delegate, "had been a professor of criminal procedure and military procedure at various military academies" and served as a judge of Chile's Superior Military Court. Eleanor Roosevelt, the widow of President Franklin Roosevelt and a significant political figure in her own right, served on various UN committees before being elected chair of the Commission on Human Rights and of its Drafting Committee. Morsink states "In the years 1946–1948 there was no other public figure dedicated to the cause of human rights who was respected and trusted by both of the great powers. Very few other American diplomats could have worked with the Soviet Union the way Roosevelt did without having undercut domestic support for the project." See Morsink (1999) 28–31.

it."[29] At the outset of the UDHR, the drafters wrote that the UDHR was created because of the "barbarous acts which ha[d] outraged the conscience of mankind," particularly those during and leading up to World War II.[30] Morsink emphasizes that in the aftermath of World War II, there was a "shared, humanity-wide revulsion help[ing] explain why the criticisms leveled at the Declaration as a Western ethnocentric document are shortsighted and often plain wrong, for that revulsion affected all the delegations and not just those from around the North Atlantic ... This explains how a human rights consensus could and did develop among delegations from a great variety of cultural, economic, and religious traditions."[31]

> ***Recalling* the international consensus that domestic law alone had not been sufficient to safeguard against and avoid the human rights violations of the World Wars**

One of the lessons of the World Wars was that domestic law alone had not been sufficient to safeguard against severe human rights violations.[32] This is true now as it was decades ago.

Domestic law provisions should be deeply grounded in respect for human dignity and international standards of human rights. Though the UDHR outlines essential and universal standards of human rights, these standards must be implemented on a more intimate level than only a broad international level. Fortunately, the UDHR's standards have gained more presence and force in national legal systems.[33] This will help prevent situations where domestic laws that are contrary to international human rights standards permit human rights violations.

29 Morsink (1999) 12.

30 Morsink (1999) 91.

31 Morsink stressed that "Taking a position diametrically opposed to Hitler's, they believed that any morally healthy human being would have been similarly outraged when placed in similar circumstances. This shared outrage explains why the Declaration has found such widespread support." Morsink (2009) 64.

32 Pinghua Sun (2018) 168. The UDHR is a call for global efforts and this unified call is clear from the beginning of the document. Making an international declaration not only helped unify nations around the world, but in some respects, an international document was necessary, especially because "[n]ational constitutions are not addressed to worldwide audiences and hence do not usually speak of rights which require more than one nation to implement, such as the right to move between countries ([UDHR] Article 13), the right to asylum ([UDHR] Article 14), and the right to a nationality ([UDHR] Article 15). Morsink (1999) 72–73. For people to enjoy these rights various countries have to cooperate and hence give up a piece of their sovereignty .... [T] he question of the problem of sovereignty can no longer be hidden behind the veil of positive national law." *Id.*

33 Glendon (2001) 237. "It would be hard to overestimate the importance of that development. Though the Declaration is rightly hailed for establishing that nations are accountable to others for the way they treat their own people, the fact is that international institutions can never provide first-line protection for victims of rights violations. When protection at the national level is absent or breaks down, there are severe limitations to what international enforcement mechanisms can accomplish." Glendon (2001) 237. On the importance of domestic laws reflecting human rights in the

At a fundamental level, the "rule of law" should triumph over "ruled by law."[34] It is noteworthy that the crimes perpetrated by the Nazis were authorized by law, including killing disabled children and those with mental handicaps.[35]

UDHR, R. J. Vincent stressed that "human rights arrangements at the regional level are made to carry global standards into all the provinces of international politics … While the standards are universal, their implementation will be the more successful the closer the attention to local circumstances. States … are more likely to accept machinery for implementation if it is established among a group of neighboring and like-minded countries than if it allows the snooping of strangers." Morsink (1999) 20.

Barak presents a thorough analytical study of human dignity as a value and right in international documents and constitutions. Aharon Barak, "The Constitutional Value and the Constitutional Right" in Christopher McCrudden (ed.), *Understanding Human Dignity* (Oxford University Press: Oxford, 2013) 34–64. De Gaay Fortman explains how several different countries' legal systems have implemented human dignity and struggles and successes of such implementation. Bas de Gaay Fortman, "Equal Dignity in International Human Rights" in Marcus Düwell et al. (eds.), *The Cambridge Handbook of Human Dignity: Interdisciplinary Perspectives* (Cambridge University Press, 2014) 355, 355–436.

34 "[T]he rule of law presupposes an underlying uniformity and stability of official behavior" and "creates the baseline of regularity that allows us to see outrages for what they are." David Luban, *Legal Ethics and Human Dignity* (Cambridge University Press, 2007) 3–4. (Later cited as Luban (2007)). In the rule of law, laws are applicable to both lawmakers as well as citizens. "Governance through rules implies that the governed and the governors belong to the same interpretive community and have roughly equivalent powers of intellect and will …. To be a lawgiver rather than a command-giver is to treat the citizen as a self-determining agent." *Id.*, 111. "[O] pression is far more easily accomplished outside the rule of law than within … [and] human dignity has been better served in nations with mature legal systems and independent legal professions." *Id.*, 5–6. In the third clause of its Preamble, the UDHR notes the importance of the rule of law to protect fundamental human rights. This clause "gives prominence to a key concept: the importance and the fragility of the rule of law … remind[ing] the nations that they ignore human rights at their peril …. If people are not to resort to violence against oppression, 'human rights should be protected by the rule of law.'" Glendon (2001) 175–177.

35 Mary Ann Glendon explained, "[p]rior to World War II, legal positivism (the view that there are no rights other than those granted by the laws of the state) flourished in the United States and Europe and was dogma in the Soviet Union. But legally sanctioned atrocities committed in Nazi Germany had caused many people to reevaluate the proposition that there is no higher law by which the laws of nation-states can be judged." Glendon (2001) 176. Morsink illustrates the danger in laws that are based on the whims of leaders rather than inherent rights: "We can see this if we think of how a dictator like Hitler calculated the general welfare of the German people. He figured that the greatest happiness of the greatest number of Germans would be best served by the extermination of Jews, gypsies, and homosexuals. For that reason, *merely* calculating cannot be the key move in the justification of our belief in human rights. Too much depends on who does the calculating and on what the scope of the general welfare is taken to be. This pragmatic approach overlooks the main thesis of this book, which is that human rights are *inherent* in all human beings, who have or possess them from birth. The dignity of the persons who have these rights should be respected because these are their moral birth right and not merely (though that may be the case as well) because of certain rough calculations concerning general welfare. While such calculations are very important, human rights are not derived from them or based on

Recalling **that despite all of their differences, nations of the world concurred that the dignity of all people is the basic foundation of human rights and freedom, justice, and peace in the world**

Here is a recognition of the wide diversity of views that existed at the time of the adoption of the UDHR.[36] The Human Rights Committee tasked with drafting what would become the UDHR was comprised of representatives of states that represented a wide diversity of economic, political, developmental, geographical, and religious viewpoints.[37] Thus, it is noteworthy that despite these differences, or

them." Morsink (2009) 14. Morsink continued, "[t]o have our possession of human rights based on calculations of the general welfare leaves open the possibility that should – God forbid – the calculations turn out some other way, then some unfortunate individual or group may no longer be protected and instead be killed, tortured, or oppressed. That method of justifying human rights flies in the face of the idea of inherent possession." *Id.*

36 "The UN documents show that 58 states participated in the drafting process of the Declaration, including the developed and developing, the Eastern and Western countries. Because they came from states of different cultures, philosophies, religions, and political traditions, representatives hoped to exert influence on the epoch-making instrument. As Western scholars pointed out: 'The Chinese wanted to base the Declaration on the philosophy of Confucius, the Catholics on the teachings of St. Thomas Aquinas, the liberals on those of Locke and Jefferson, and the Communists on the doctrines of Karl Marx.'" Pinghua Sun (2018) 168. While the drafters were working on the UDHR, the UNESCO philosophers' committee sent questionnaires for outside opinions on human rights. The committee got responses from "Chinese, Islamic, Hindu, and customary law perspectives, as well as from American, European, and socialist points of view." But despite all the differences between cultures and countries involved, they were all invested in human rights and drafting a supported Declaration. Thus, the UDHR was written with an intentionally open structure to allow for broad application. "They had established a 'common standard of achievement' that could be interpreted and implemented in a legitimate variety of ways. They were comfortable with the idea that there would always be different visions of freedom within one human family." Glendon (2001) 191. Glendon stressed that there was tension among the drafters of the UDHR from the different ideologies and conflicts on their home fronts, such as the Cold War conflicts between the Soviet bloc and the United States, Russia's support of communism in China, among others. Glendon (2001) 53. Similarly, Morsink emphasized that "The delegations came from nations with very different political, cultural, religious, ethnic, economic, and legal traditions. What this shows is that when atrocities or gross violations are clear enough, moral outrage against them will also be clearly shared." Morsink (2009) 63.

37 The first Commission of Human Rights included 18 representatives from Australia, Belgium, Byelorussia, Chile, China, Egypt, France, India, Iran, Lebanon, Panama, Philippines, Ukraine, USSR, United Kingdom, United States, Uruguay, and Yugoslavia. Glendon (2001) 32. From these countries, the Commission elected Eleanor Roosevelt from the United States as chairman, Peng-chun Chan from China as vice chairman, and Charles Malik from Lebanon as secretary; these elected delegates "symbolically represent[ed] West, East, and in the case of Malik, a crossroads of many cultures, constituted the leadership of the Human Rights Commission throughout the entire period of the preparation of the document that became the Universal Declaration of Human Rights." Glendon (2001) 33. The differences between the countries' priorities and ideologies were prevalent in during the drafting, but as the USSR's

perhaps in part because of these differences, the principle that was capable of generating agreement of everyone was the idea of human dignity.

The drafters of the UDHR, coming from different backgrounds and having different interests and positions on issues, agreed that the human dignity of all people was the basic foundation of human rights and freedom, justice, and peace in the world.[38] Human dignity is the cornerstone of human rights and other values that require international protection.

delegate Alexei Pavlov noted, the "Commission's discussions had clearly shown the divergences which existed between the members in the fields of philosophy and ideology; that difference of ideas had not prevented fruitful co-operation," allowing the Commission to achieve agreement on the application of human rights. Morsink (1999) 316–317. Glendon emphasized that "Before the whole two-year process from drafting and deliberation to adoption reached its end, literally hundreds of individuals from diverse backgrounds had participated. Thus, Malik could fairly say, 'The genesis of each article, and each part of each article, was a dynamic process in which many minds, interests, backgrounds, legal systems and ideological persuasions played their respective determining roles.'" Glendon (2001) 225. Johnson and Symonides credited the success to the fact that "The range of backgrounds and interests among the Commission members, the staff and NGOs working with them undoubtedly deepened and broadened the perspective which informed the deliberations leading to the Declaration." M. Glen Johnson and Janusz Symonides, *The Universal Declaration of Human Rights: A History of Its Creation and Implementation 1948–1998* (UNESCO, 1998) 26. See Pinghua Sun (2018) 168.

38 Each of the UDHR's major drafters (Eleanor Roosevelt, Pen Chung Chang, Charles Malik, René Cassin, and John Humphrey) had unique backgrounds leading up to their work on the UDHR as well as individual opinions on aspects of human rights. Roosevelt grew up neglected because her mother saw her as an ugly duckling, which motivated Roosevelt to help others in society who similarly felt neglect. Glendon (2001) 22. She was especially passionate about women's rights, racial discrimination, and living and working conditions; she even criticized her husband's administration at times, such as when one program's implementation would lay off married women. *Id.*, 24. After her husband's death, Roosevelt was asked by President Truman to be the United States representative at the United Nations, to which she responded, "How could I be a delegate to help organize the United Nations when I have no background or experience in international meetings?" *Id.*, 21. However, a little lost after her husband's passing, she accepted Truman's call as she thought the UN could "be a place where her talents and energies would be useful and where she could pursue her lifelong interest in humanitarian causes." *Id.*, 24. Compared to Roosevelt's relatively little experience as a delegate, Chang had spent a significant amount of time as a delegate for China. Chang first studied in China before coming to American universities for further degrees with a Master of Arts, a Master of Science in Education, and a doctor's degree in philosophy, which influenced Chang's philosophical thinking. Pinghua Sun (2018) 21–22, 28. Then when his Chinese university, Nankai University, was bombed by Japanese troops, Chang served as a diplomat for anti-Japanese propaganda and was a representative at the National Political Council; Chang was the Minister Plenipotentiary to Turkey and the Chinese Ambassador to Chile; additionally, he was the permanent representative to the Economic and Social Council during the UN's first General Assembly conference. Pinghua Sun (2018) 24–26. Chang was elected as vice chairman in preparation for drafting the UDHR, recognized for his diverse abilities as "a playwright, musician, educator, and seasoned diplomat, devoted to traditional Chinese music and literature but conversant with Islamic and Western

At the time of the adoption of the UDHR, the UN had only 58 members.[39] The UDHR represented the aspirations to independence and freedom of many areas of the world that were under colonial rule.

culture as well." Glendon (2001) 33. Malik's parents were Greek Orthodox Arabs, but he attended a Protestant school, leading to a degree in philosophy and ultimately his attendance and work at Harvard concerning Arab youth. Glendon (2001) 124–126. During a fellowship in Germany for Harvard, Malik was beaten up for his Semitic looks and was bothered by the uniformity and hatred engrained in Nazi Germany. *Id.*, 125–126. Malik reluctantly left his academic work for politics but felt a sense of isolation for himself and for his newly independent country of Lebanon; however, Malik "gradually turned his loneliness into a source of strength." *Id.*, 128. "He gained a reputation for independence, for which he was respected even by those who opposed his positions." *Id.* Lebanon is a multireligious country and Malik represented this quality by urging the UDHR drafter to "recognize the fundamental right of differing fundamental human convictions, as in religion, to exist in the same national entity. The fact that a single nation is obligated by international law, to recognize the diversity of fundamental points of view on ultimate matters should, he believed, be considered an essential and fundamental right." Morsink (2017) 62. Like Malik, Cassin had a diverse religious background with an Orthodox Jewish education because of his mother, an anti-religious father, and Catholic friends in his youth. Glendon (2001) 61. Cassin later fought for France in World War I and afterwards because a professor of civil law and a founder of an international veterans' organization. *Id.*, 61. Cassin's experience led him to becoming General Charles de Gaulle's legal advisor during World War II, reestablishing administrative and judicial systems as well as the nation's credibility. *Id.*, 62–63. Cassin had a deep belief in "the universality of human rights" which was "rooted in his Jewish heritage." Morsink (2017) 27. During the drafting of the UDHR, Cassin was asked to outline a list of the Declaration's rights, to which he wrote: "All men are brothers. Being endowed with reason, members of one family, they are free and possess equal dignity and rights." This text referenced ideas of liberty, equality, and fraternity embedded in the French Revolution. Among his many contributions, Cassin's prominent role in drafting the UDHR "is an outstanding example of Jewish participants who welcomed the secularism of the Declaration." *Id.*, 27–28. Finally, Humphrey was a Canadian international lawyer who wrote a draft of the UDHR and was closely involved throughout the drafting process, but he admitted that he "had practically no experience drafting documents." Glendon (2001) 43, 63. Humphrey's childhood "had given him a lively sense of empathy for the disadvantaged: as a boy of six he had lost his left arm in an accident; then, orphaned at eleven, he was placed in a boys' boarding school, where he learned to detest the abuse of authority. From an early age he had dreamed of helping to 'make the world a better place.'" *Id.*, 48. Humphrey wrote articles on international law and had experience with civil and common law, multinational staff, and "linguistic ability that led to his appointment at the UN." *Id.*

39 Morsink emphasized that "Cassin had expressed the hope that '[t]he declaration of human rights was to be the expression of the rights of all the peoples of the world and not only the fifty-eight nations then constituting the United Nations.'" and "The drafting structure was such that the entire United Nations membership was given a chance to participate and actually did so." Morsink (1999) 11, 28. More than 50 member states participated in the drafting. Eight states abstained from ratification for various reasons, but significantly, none dissented. See Morsink's discussion of the abstentions at 21–28.

Recalling **that human dignity is the wellspring of and underpins all the rights and freedoms recognized in the UDHR as fundamental**

The Declaration does not take a position on whether human dignity is itself a human right, or whether it is the foundational source of all human rights.[40] Some legal instruments recognize human dignity as a right, but there are other approaches to human rights that view dignity as foundational rather than as a right itself.[41]

Here the Declaration introduces two additional metaphors that are often used when describing the role of dignity to human rights – the idea of being a wellspring[42]

40 Bennett, summarizing the work of legal scholar Klaus Dicke, wrote that "In the declaration, human dignity is declaimed as the ground for human rights. What proves to be the case, however, is that human rights, which are subsequently elaborated, effectively define the substance of human dignity ... Dignity and rights share a mutually formative and constraining relation, and that relation defines what it means to be human, politically speaking." Gaymon Bennett, *Technicians of Human Dignity: Bodies, Souls, and the Making of Intrinsic Worth* (Fordham University Press, 2016) 142.

41 For example, Goos considers the various definitions of human dignity in the German context. These ideas included Theodor Heuss' contention human dignity is foundational: "Human dignity must rest in itself. It must not be derived from any governmental position." Goos does not define the exact relationship between human dignity and human rights, but he asserts that "[h]uman dignity and human rights can be distinguished and they must be distinguished, but they must not be separated." Christoph Goos, "Restoring Human Dignity in Post-Nazi Germany" in Christopher McCrudden (ed.), *Understanding Human Dignity* (Oxford University Press: Oxford, 2013) 89.

42 The second definition of "wellspring" in the *Oxford English Dictionary* uses this figurative sense: a wellspring is "a source or origin providing a constant or abundant supply of something." See: *Oxford English Dictionary*. Much like the idea of a wellspring, in the Confucianist philosophy, "[h]uman rights originate from human dignity, which generates from man's reason and conscience. Man [sic] finds himself fundamentally different from the animal because of the reason and conscience endowed." Pinghua Sun (2018) 280. Some countries adopt the idea of dignity as a wellspring of human rights by making dignity its own right within the legal system. For example, in the German Constitution, Article 1 paragraph 1 states: "'Human dignity shall be inviolable. To respect and protect it shall be the duty of all state authority.' This norm has become absolutely outstanding and increasingly dominating in the legal order of the German Federal Republic ... Any ... possibility of balancing or compromising between competing constitutional rights or values is impossible .... Every intrusion upon human dignity is inevitably a violation of the Constitution." Horst Dreier, "Human Dignity in German Law" in Marcus Düwell et al. (eds.), *The Cambridge Handbook of Human Dignity: Interdisciplinary Perspectives* (Cambridge University Press, 2014) 375, 375–376. South Africa also implemented dignity as an actual right in their Constitution, which provides that everyone's dignity need be both respected and protected. Anton Fagan, "Human Dignity in South African Law" in Marcus Düwell et al. (eds.), *The Cambridge Handbook of Human Dignity: Interdisciplinary Perspectives* (Cambridge University Press, 2014) 401, 401. South Africa "also recognizes human dignity as one of three values (the others are equality and freedom) upon which the Republic of South Africa was founded and which the South African Bill of Rights affirms. *Id.* Bennet, for example, considers human dignity as an archaic concept that acts as a moral mandate. As he continues: "Human dignity, as a given, is also a

and the idea of being an underpinning.[43] The image of a wellspring is evocative since it suggests the image of pure water as a life source that is flowing and ongoing. The idea here is that human dignity is akin to a spring of water that provides an important source for the sustenance of human rights.

The image of an underpinning is a metaphor that is related to a foundation.[44] The idea is that human dignity can help support and undergird human rights.[45]

moral mandate and places an absolute obligation on conscience and thereby political action. However, in the course of the declaration, human dignity does not remain a matter of pure form. Where explicit substantive definition might be lacking, tacit and operational definition quickly fills in." Bennett explores the idea of human dignity using concepts from anthropology and Foucault. The Declaration framers did not actually define human dignity, but they did set it up as something that all individuals have and that states have an obligation to protect. Dignity then has not a substantive definition, but a functional one – that which must be protected. As dignity is protected, so too are more concretely defined human rights. Gaymon Bennett, *Technicians of Human Dignity: Bodies, Souls, and the Making of Intrinsic Worth* (Fordham University Press, 2016) 142.

43 Schlink stressed that "Human dignity is also used as a foundational concept for human rights, as a concept that at least justifies and at best requires the existence of human rights." Bernhard Schlink, "The Concept of Human Dignity: Current Usages, Future Discourses" in Christopher McCrudden (ed.), *Understanding Human Dignity* (Oxford University Press: Oxford, 2013) 631, 631. He continued that the "concept of human dignity can keep the idea of human rights rich and complex; once it is understood that human dignity can serve as the foundational concept for human rights, it follows that every aspect of a good life that is associated with human dignity must find its place in the system of human rights." 631, 634. According to Jones, dignity can be utilized to provide "a basis for human rights in respect for other persons as person … Used in this way it does not serve to identify a particular aspect of the human good that is to be protected. It rather serves as a placeholder for the recognition of other persons as worthy of moral consideration, as making moral claims on us." David A. Jones, "Dignity Language in Bioethical Discussions" in Christopher McCrudden (ed.), *Understanding Human Dignity* (Oxford University Press: Oxford, 2013) 525, 526.

44 Yehoshua Arieli stressed that "[i]f one looks for a philosophical underpinning for the principles contained in the Universal Declaration of Human Rights, Kant may serve as a guide, as his philosophy presents a feasible link between a possible metaphysic and secularism which is the existential dimensions of modernity and of modern history. This was basically the core contention of Immanuel Kant. Whether dealing with the nature and limits of pure reason or the nature of ethics, morality, human freedom and history, or the true aims of a cosmopolitan order, his basic assumption is man's capacity to shape his individual and collective existence according to the highest ideals implied in the concept of the dignity of man and his existential autonomy and freedom." Yehoshua Arieli "On the Necessary and Sufficient Conditions for the Emergence of the Doctrine of the Dignity of Man and His Rights" in David Kretzmer and Eckart Klein, *The Concept of Human Dignity in Human Rights Discourse* (Brill, 2002) 7.

45 The *Oxford English Dictionary* gives the second, figurative definition of the verb "underpin" as "to support, corroborate," which accords with common descriptions of the relationship between human dignity and human rights. As a noun, the OED first defines "underpinning" as "the action of supporting or strengthening a building, etc., from beneath."

The key idea here is that human dignity is a basic and foundational principle that underlies and gives life to the human rights project. Any interpretation of human rights that neglects or ignores human dignity is unlikely to be successful. Human rights cannot be adequately protected or guaranteed without due consideration to human dignity.

> ***Recalling* that the UDHR has served as the inspiration for an array of international and regional covenants and other instruments, as well as numerous national constitutions, bills and charters of rights, and legislation protecting human rights**

The UDHR was not intended to be a legally binding instrument.[46] Indeed, at the time of drafting, there were significant discussions about whether the commission should create a binding document or agree to a declaration that lacked enforcement power.[47] The UDHR is not legally binding. Nonetheless, the UDHR is generally considered to constitute a part of international customary law, and hence is binding upon all states.[48] Furthermore, parts of the UDHR have been "re-introduced" in several subsequent international (legally binding) treaties, including the International Covenant on Civil and Political Rights (ICCPR). The UDHR served as the inspiration for and to a remarkable extent the blueprint for a wide variety of legally binding instruments of international and national law. The rights enumerated in the UDHR have also been incorporated, sometimes with modification, into many national constitutions, national bills, and charters of rights.[49]

46 The representatives at the drafting of the UDHR argued whether the Declaration should be legally binding or not. However, the "role of human rights as a political weapon was one of the motivations for not giving the human rights text binding status … The further the text was considered to be legally binding, the greater the effort to restrict its content." Ultimately, it was decided the delegates would first create a non-legally binding declaration and then there would be a convention later with legal force. Åshild Samnøy, "The Origins of the Universal Declaration of Human Rights" in Gudmundur Alfredsson and Asbjørn Eide (eds.), *The Universal Declaration of Human Rights* (Martinus Nijhoff Publishers, 1999) 3, 10. "As the irony of history had it, what worried many of the delegations – that their declaration was not attached to or accompanied by a covenant – has proved to be a very beneficial feature of the document, one that has helped rather than hindered the process of implementation." Morsink (1999) 19. The UDHR led to two legally binding covenants (the International Covenant on Civil and Political Rights and the International Covenant on Economic, Social, and Cultural Rights) as well as various other regional binding instruments, but the "fact that the Declaration itself is not intertwined with any piece of this machinery of implementation gave it from the start an independent moral status in world affairs and law." *Id.*, 20.

47 See Morsink (1999).

48 See, for example: Hurst Hannum, "The Status of the Universal Declaration of Human Rights in National and International Law" (1998) 3 *Health and Human Rights* 145; Louis Henkin, *The Age of Rights* (Columbia University Press: New York, 1990) 9.

49 These are discussed in Chapter 3 ff.

The "recognizing" clauses

The six "recognizing" clauses contain a series of observations about human dignity as a human rights concept. These recognitions conclude that human dignity is not a static concept that is easily defined or captured; that while dignity has been criticized by some as being too abstract to be useful, it has been quite useful in the effort to define and specify human rights; and that human dignity reinforces the uniqueness and worth of every human being and the importance of each person being able to seek to find or create meaning in his or her own life.

The three remaining "recognizing" clauses identify ways that human dignity can be abused, fragmented, eroded, and neglected, and the problems that arise when the dignity of some people is placed ahead of the dignity of others.

> ***Recognizing*** **that human dignity is not a static concept but accommodates respect for diversity and calls for a dynamic approach to its application in the diverse and ever-changing contexts of our pluralistic world**

This sentence reflects a recognition that capturing human dignity in a single definition is difficult if not impossible. One of the strengths of human dignity as a concept is that it affords numerous conceptions. While specific definitions may be helpful or even necessary in certain contexts, human dignity should be understood to be a living and dynamic concept that can be adaptable to new contexts and issues that arise in our pluralistic world.

Attempts to define human dignity as a static concept could be used to exclude some people or groups from its protection as contexts change. Such an approach would undermine the universality of the concept and result in human dignity benefiting only some people.

The ambition of the Punta del Este Declaration is not to provide a definitive definition of human dignity, but rather it is to provide an invitation for discussions and analyses of human dignity from a variety of perspectives – including political, philosophical, and religious perspectives. Human dignity can serve as a source for finding areas of agreement about human rights, but it also can help us describe and define our conceptions of human rights. The expectation is not that we will arrive at a complete agreement about the meaning and implications of human dignity, but we can achieve more agreement than might have seemed possible, and we can also achieve a better understanding of our own and others' views.

> ***Recognizing*** **that although the notion of dignity has been criticized by some as being too abstract, it has been and remains a powerful organizing force that points humanity towards its highest ideals and has proven itself as an influential heuristic in constitutional and human rights discourse**

Some critics of human dignity have argued it is a concept that is too abstract or too vague to be practically useful. While this criticism has some merit in that it is a concept with many conceptions, this "weakness" of human dignity is also to some extent its strength as it ensures that the concept is flexible and progresses with changing contexts rather than becomes an empty and outdated value.[50]

Furthermore, the concept of human dignity is not as abstract and empty as some of its critics have suggested. Human dignity has been a fundamental concept in various foundational legal documents including the German Basic Law, the Basic Law of Israel, and the Constitution of South Africa.[51]

It is true that human dignity can be misused as a concept and that it is easy to try to overspecify the demands of human dignity. Human dignity is not particularly useful as a major premise in simple syllogisms designed to mandate certain political outcomes.[52] It is a concept that is more helpful for starting conversations than it is for winning arguments.

> ***Recognizing*** **that the concept of human dignity emphasizes the uniqueness and irreplaceability of every human being; that it implies a right of each individual to find and define the meanings of his or her own life; that it presupposes respect for pluralism and difference; and that it carries with it the responsibility to honor the dignity of everyone**

Human dignity for everyone everywhere recognizes and emphasizes the uniqueness and irreplaceability of every life. Human dignity in this sense is not an abstract concept but is a descriptive declaration about the nature of every human being. Every human being has a status and value. Human dignity is not just a feature of the human race, but rather a descriptor of every human life.

Human dignity for everyone everywhere will recognize and respect the right of each human being to seek, find, and define the meanings of his or her own life. It recognizes that human beings are seekers and strivers towards values, including truth, beauty, love, and meaning, among many others. Human dignity recognizes that different people will identify different answers, paths, and recipes concerning those important values. Recognizing and respecting the value and uniqueness of every human being allows pluralism to flourish.

50 Most important political and moral concepts, including justice, equality, freedom and fairness, are susceptible to similar criticism.

51 See discussions of Articles 7 and 8 of the Punta del Este Declaration in Chapters 9 and 10.

52 For example, human dignity has been used by proponents of abortion rights to justify abortion on demand, and by defenders of the right to life to argue against abortion under most if not all circumstances. Arguments like these may be appealing to those who already agree, but are unlikely to persuade others. Human dignity may be helpful in seeking to reach accommodations for life in a pro-abortion legal regime, or in seeking to reach accommodations for choice in a pro-life regime. It is most likely to be helpful in trying to reach compromise measures on issues of stark moral valence such as abortion if the emphasis on "everyone" and "everywhere" is remembered. Human dignity will not necessarily be a vehicle for wholesale victory of one of these values over the other, but it may be helpful in finding our way to a destination that strives to be respectful to the values on both sides.

Recognizing the irreplaceability of every human being underscores the importance of protecting the right to life of every human being and ensures that when other values are at stake, human life is afforded maximum consideration.[53]

> ***Recognizing*** **that severe violations and abuses of human dignity continue to this day, including through wars, armed conflicts, genocides, crimes against humanity, war crimes, and the global crises concerning refugees, migrants, asylum seekers, and human trafficking victims, and that such depredations continue to threaten peace, justice, and the rights of all**

Seventy years after the UDHR, we do not speak from a posture of satisfaction or complacency. We are all too aware that violations of human dignity and fundamental human rights are all too common in the world in which we live today.

We are mindful that while the post-World War II period has not seen mass atrocities of the type and scale of the Holocaust, there have been many severe human rights abuses in the past 70 years, some of which have risen to the scale and scope of genocides, crimes against humanity, and other atrocities.[54] Even in

53 The issue of irreplaceability was one of the conclusions of the decision of the German Federal Constitutional Court when considering the constitutionality of the legal provision allowing the shooting down of a hijacked plane with innocent people if there was a suspicion that the plane would be used as a weapon. It concluded that causing the deliberate deaths of innocent people as the result of shooting down the plane violates the right to life of Article 2(2) sentence 1 and Article 1(1) of the German Basic Law. See: Aviation Security Act, BVerfG,1 BvR 357/05.

54 By some manners of reckoning, the post World War II era has been extremely brutal with respect to human dignity. The Soviets committed many atrocities in the decades leading up to and throughout World War II. And those atrocities did not end with the war. As R. J. Rummel put it in his book *Lethal Politics*, "in Soviet history [the end of World War II] only shut down one death machine, the most visible one of clashing armies that historians and journalists write about. To the other death machine – terror against 'enemies of the people,' social prophylaxis, purges, deportations, labor camps, and utopian campaigns – this historical boundary was nonexistent." Rudolph J. Rummel, *Lethal Politics: Soviet Genocide and Mass Murder Since 1917* (Routledge, 1990) 192. Rummel estimates that Stalin's regime murdered 15,613,000 individuals between the end of World War II in 1945 and Stalin's death in 1953. *Id.*, 191.

Mao's "Great Leap Forward" is estimated to have killed 20–30 million between 1958 and 1962. Jonathan Glover, *Humanity: A Moral History of the Twentieth Century* (Yale University Press, 1999) 284. Glover explained that "[t]he Great Leap Forward was an ambitious plan to involve everyone in producing vast quantities of steel and food. It caused mass starvation. Famine was familiar in China. Civil war and rivalries between warlords had resulted in millions of armed men criss-crossing the country and taking the food from peasants. But the famine caused by the Great Leap Forward was on a new scale." *Id.* It is estimated that Pol Pot and the Khmer Rouge killed around 2 million individuals in Cambodia with their "Four Year Plan to build Socialism in All Fields" which began in 1976. *Id.*, 303, 309. And while 2 million is relatively fewer than other mass atrocities, 2 million was roughly a quarter of the Cambodian population, which numbered less than 8 million at the time. *Id.*, 309. One of the more recent mass atrocities took place in Rwanda in 1994 when Hutus killed as many as a million Tutsis. *Id.*, 120. Glover explained that "[i]n pre-colonial times, the Tutsis were

our day, we are mindful of mass atrocities that amount to genocide, most notably, in Syria, Iraq, and Myanmar. Thus, in our day as well as in the aftermath of World War II, it is crucial to strengthen the global commitment to protect human rights and human dignity for everyone everywhere.

The 20th Century has been marked with wars, mass atrocities, and severe human rights violations. States, international actors, and all people need to work together to ensure that such atrocities are not repeated. However, despite being far from the dark history of the 20th Century, the beginning of the 21st Century has been marked with mass atrocities amounting to genocide and crimes against humanity. The case of the atrocities perpetrated by the Burmese military against the Rohingya Muslims and other religious minorities shows that states not only continue to have little if any respect for human dignity or human rights of individuals belonging to groups they deem as unworthy of protection, but also that the international community is slow and reluctant to act to protect such endangered groups.

The cases of the Daesh genocide against religious minorities in Syria and Iraq, and the mass atrocities perpetrated by Boko Haram in Nigeria and surrounding states show that a new danger has emerged – that of mass atrocities being perpetrated by powerful non-state actors who managed to gain the support of thousands of fighters from all over the world (or in the case of Boko Haram – from African states). Such new danger poses challenges that require new solutions.

Despite the recognition of the universal status of human dignity in the UDHR, human dignity continues to be violated in many places in our world. Some violations are severe and may amount to mass atrocities like genocide, crimes against humanity, and war crimes. War, armed conflicts, and global crises create conditions where severe violations of human dignity are likely.

Thus, it is with a renewed sense of urgency that this Declaration seeks to remember, revisit, and recommit all people to the importance of the fundamental value of human dignity and of the urgent and ongoing need to find ways to vindicate this value for all people in all places.

the ruling tribe and sometimes exploited the Hutus ruthlessly. The dominant status of the Tutsis had been supported by German and Belgian colonial rule. At the end of the colonial period, the Hutus rose up and seized power, killing many Tutsis. A legacy of Hutu resentment continued after the Tutsis' dominance ended. In the 1960s, after independence, there were outbreaks of mass killing of Tutsis by Hutus. In 1990, the Rwandan Patriotic Front, mainly made up of Tutsi exiles, invaded Rwanda from Uganda. Genocidal killing of Tutsis started in 1994 after Juvenal Habyarimana, the (Hutu) president of Rwanda was killed in a plane crash. The Tutsis, probably unfairly, were blamed." Glover continued, "road blocks were set up and the country was scoured for Tutsis, each ten houses having one man appointed to conduct a systematic search. Tutsis were denounced by their neighbors and then killed. Thousands of their corpses floated down river to Tanzania and Uganda." *Id.*

***Recognizing* that human rights can easily be fragmented, eroded, or neglected and that constant vigilance is necessary for human rights to be implemented, realized, and carried forward in the world**

Human rights can easily be fragmented when attention is paid to one important aspect of human rights without recognizing other related and connected rights. Such a pick-and-choose approach cannot sustain the project of human rights. As the International Law Commission, a UN body tasked with helping to develop and codify international law, when commenting on the fragmentation of international law more broadly, observed that:

> Fragmentation puts to question the coherence of international law. Coherence is valued positively owing to the connection it has with predictability and legal security. Moreover, only a coherent legal system treats legal subjects equally.[55]

Focusing on human dignity, interpreting human rights via the spectrum of human dignity, and understanding that human dignity is the end goal of human rights helps to counter such fragmentation and ensure coherence.

Human rights can be eroded when other important values such as security or stability are invoked as reasons for placing unnecessary limits on them. Indeed, national security has been used and abused to limit (in various degrees) the human rights of people in different parts of the world. One of the main issues is that what constitutes a threat (predominately within the traditional geopolitical meaning) that falls within the ambit of national security continues to expand,[56] and hence posing a risk of related human rights restrictions.[57] However, it is crucial to emphasize: first, not all rights can be

55 Martti Koskenniemi, *Fragmentation of International Law: Difficulties Arising from the Diversification and Expansion of International Law* (International Law Commission, Study Group on Fragmentation, 2006). The report further notes that: "Coherence is, however, a formal and abstract virtue. For a legal system that is regarded in some respects as unjust or unworkable, no added value is brought by the fact of its being coherently so. Therefore, alongside coherence, pluralism should be understood as a constitutive value of the system. Indeed, in a world of plural sovereignties, this has always been so." *Id.*, 248. See also: Lucas Lixinski, "Choice of Forum in International Human Rights Adjudication and the Unity/Fragmentation Debate: Is Plurality the Way Forward?" (2008) XVIII *Italian Yearbook of International Law* 183–200.

56 See: Office of the Director of National Intelligence, "Scenarios: Alternative Futures the IC Could Face" (2004) 4 *Quadrennial Intelligence Community Review* 1.

57 Lord Falconer emphasized that when considering the national security argument, "courts are not conducting the fight against terrorism. Nor are they deciding the measures to be used. The level of threat, and the extent to which exceptional measures are required, are for the executive, or the legislature. The questions the courts in the UK ask are: first, do these measures infringe any individual's fundamental human rights; second if they do, is there a justification for the infringement; and third, is the infringement the minimum necessary to protect our democracy." Rt. Hon. Lord

restricted, and second, even where the rights can be limited,[58] such limitations are subject to limits.[59]

And human rights can be neglected due to other pressing concerns and the overwhelming magnitude of unfinished work. The human rights project is significant, and one that will sometimes be placed second to other considerations. However, where human dignity is at risk, human rights aiming for the protection of human dignity should be prioritized.

Thus, on occasions such as the 70th anniversary of the UDHR, it is important to recall and recommit ourselves to the implementation and realization of human rights through progressive measures throughout the world.

Ongoing and sustained vigilance is crucial to ensure that human dignity and human rights for everyone everywhere are guaranteed. Small steps in this direction, while they should be recognized, should not overshadow the great amount of work that remains to be done to achieve the ultimate aim of human dignity for everyone everywhere.

> ***Recognizing* that human dignity for everyone everywhere and at every level is threatened when the needs, interests, and rights of one group or individual are placed ahead of those of other groups and individuals**

Human rights apply to individual human beings, but those rights are often exercised in community with others, and sometimes the needs or interests of

Falconer, "The Role of Judges in a Modern Democracy" (Sep. 13, 2006) The Magna Carta Lecture, Sydney.

58 For example, see Article 4 of the ICCPR stating:

"1. In time of public emergency which threatens the life of the nation and the existence of which is officially proclaimed, the States Parties to the present Covenant may take measures derogating from their obligations under the present Covenant to the extent strictly required by the exigencies of the situation, provided that such measures are not inconsistent with their other obligations under international law and do not involve discrimination solely on the ground of race, colour, sex, language, religion or social origin.

2. No derogation from articles 6, 7, 8 (paragraphs 1 and 2), 11, 15, 16 and 18 may be made under this provision.

3. Any State Party to the present Covenant availing itself of the right of derogation shall immediately inform the other States Parties to the present Covenant, through the intermediary of the Secretary-General of the United Nations, of the provisions from which it has derogated and of the reasons by which it was actuated. A further communication shall be made, through the same intermediary, on the date on which it terminates such derogation."

59 See for example, Article 19(3) of the ICCPR stating that:

"3. The exercise of the rights provided for in paragraph 2 of this article carries with it special duties and responsibilities. It may therefore be subject to certain restrictions, but these shall only be such as are provided by law and are necessary:

(a) For respect of the rights or reputations of others;

(b) For the protection of national security or of public order (*ordre public*), or of public health or morals."

members of one group, or the group as a collectivity, are given priority over the rights and interests of other individuals and the groups to which they belong.

Human dignity should not be invoked as a reason to protect the rights or interests of one individual or a group at the expense of denying the rights and interests of others. Human dignity is a meaningful concept only if it is afforded to everyone everywhere.

Human dignity for everyone everywhere is a powerful antidote to the perils of identity politics that are prevalent in many parts of the world today. Identity politics focuses on particular features or interests of groups of people and places those features and interests ahead and above those of "others." Identity politics depends for its force on identifying an "other" that is the problem or the enemy and then seeking power or privilege over that other. What identity politics always fails or refuses to do is to take seriously the interests and needs, indeed often the human dignity, of others, and in particular, the "other" that is identified as the nemesis of the group.

The "emphasizing" clauses

The three "emphasizing" clauses identify several features of human dignity that deserve special emphasis. Human dignity is a statement of fact, but its realization in the world requires it to be learned, nurtured, and lived. Violations of dignity require appropriate redress. And human dignity is now a time-tested principle that can help resolve conflicts involving human rights.

> ***Emphasizing* that equal human dignity is a status with which all human beings are endowed, but also a value that must be learned, nurtured, and lived**

Contemporary academic discussions of human dignity often revolve around whether human dignity is best understood as a concept involving status or value.[60] It seems clear that human dignity invites and incorporates both ideas.

The fact that human dignity is an inherent and inalienable feature of human beings does not guarantee that this value or status will be recognized or understood by us or others. Human dignity is a truth to be understood and recognized, but it is in the understanding and the recognition that it is most likely to be protected. Human beings must learn to recognize and respect the human dignity with

60 Waldron, in particular, argues for a conception of human dignity that fits with "the old hierarchical system of dignity" connected to "noble rank or high office." He sees human dignity as equalizing a high status on all human beings, which is then vindicated by the law through constitutional and human rights law employing "human dignity" to recognize every person's high legal rank or status. This understanding of dignity moves away from the Kantian concept of *Würde*, which is more based on value than based on status. Jeremy Waldron (Meir Dan-Cohen, ed.), *Dignity, Rank and Rights. The Tanner Lectures on Human Values* (Oxford University Press: New York, 2012) 47.

which they are endowed which is an inherent feature of their life and the lives of others. Respecting and valuing human dignity, our own, and that of others, is something that must be nurtured and lived.

The importance of education in this regard is evident, but so is the importance of developing habits of regard for self and others that will vindicate human dignity.

> ***Emphasizing* that violations of human dignity require appropriate redress**

When we have a deep appreciation of the human dignity of all people, then we will understand that violations of human dignity require appropriate redress.

Violations of human rights, regardless of their severity, need to be adequately redressed. Indeed, as the Hon. John von Doussa QC stresses,

> When an individual's rights are violated as a result of the misuse or abuse of national security or counter-terrorism powers, the individual should have access to an effective remedy, which may, depending on the damage suffered, include compensation. This approach is consistent with article 2(3) of the ICCPR, which provides that a person has a right to an effective remedy if his or her human rights are violated.[61]

The more severe the violation, the more complex and multilayered the redress that is needed. What will count as "appropriate" redress will often be an issue of disagreement, but the idea of human dignity can help guide the pursuit of the answer to such questions.

> ***Emphasizing* that human dignity is now a time-tested principle that can help find common ground, reconcile competing conceptions of what justice demands, facilitate the implementation of human rights, and guide adjudication in case of conflicts, and that can also help us respond to distortions, abuse, and hostility towards human rights**

Human dignity is neither a new nor an untested idea. One of the lessons of the struggle to draft and complete the UDHR is that human dignity was a concept that helped people with very different backgrounds and values find common ground and reach an agreement about the content of the UDHR. It was a concept that helped reconcile competing conceptions of justice, and it has helped in facilitating the implementation of human rights.

61 The Hon. John Von Doussa QC, "Incorporating Human Rights Principles into National Security Measures" (Oct. 16–17, 2007) International Conference on Terrorism, Human Security and Development: Human Rights Perspectives, City University of Hong Kong.

Human dignity has been widely recognized in positive law, including in international and regional human rights treaties, in constitutions and bills and charters of rights, and legislation. Human dignity has also been a useful guide in the adjudication of human rights claims. It also helps in responding to distortions of human rights into something that looks like the protection of state interests or the interests of those with political power. Human dignity is also a powerful rejoinder to abuses of human rights, which will invariably include negative repercussions for human dignity. And human dignity for all is a powerful response to those who are hostile to human rights since those people will inevitably be concerned with their rights and interests, as well as their human dignity. Human dignity is an enemy of tyrants and despots, those with all-embracing utopian visions of how society should be structured and organized.

Human dignity, apart from being a wellspring and underpinning of all rights and freedoms, is also the ultimate common ground that can help to reconcile differences in the pursuance of a solution that will respect and accommodate the rights of all.

The "believing" clauses

These three clauses express beliefs about human dignity, including that it can help make human rights discourse less divisive, that it reminds us that human rights must be read and realized together, and that human dignity can be helpful in our ongoing efforts to understand, protect, and implement human rights around the world.

> ***Believing*** **that human rights discourse might be less divisive than it often is and greater efforts might be made to find common ground**

From the very beginning, human rights discourse has often been divisive. On the most obvious macro level, there was a strong disagreement between liberal democracies in the West that wanted to emphasize important civil and political rights, and the communist countries of the East that wanted to emphasize social and economic rights. Eventually, this led to two different international covenants, one focusing on political and civil rights and the other on economic and social rights. But at the end of the day, both covenants received widespread global support, suggesting that the divisions were not as broad or insurmountable as they appeared to be. Today as well, human rights discourse is often quite contentious, with nations accusing each other of human rights violations, which usually results in counter-recriminations.

By focusing on the idea of human dignity for everyone everywhere, this pattern of accusation and counter-accusation can be mitigated. Efforts to navigate our way through disagreements about human rights will be facilitated if the "north star" of human dignity for everyone is kept in view as we steer our way through the inevitable controversies and stormy seas that will arise. Over the years, human rights conflicts have often divided individuals, groups, communities, and whole nations. Focusing on the human dignity of everyone everywhere helps to neutralize such divisions and nurture the understanding of differences that should be respected.

> ***Believing* that human rights must be read and realized together**

Human rights are often thought of as individual rights held by individual people. This is a useful perspective, but experience has shown that human rights are most likely to be realized when they are realized together with other rights, and those rights are realized for other people as well. Human rights will not be realized if only some rights for some people are protected. The goal, the standard of achievement, is for the realization of all human rights for all people in all places. This suggests that strategies for defining and protecting human rights should take into account complementary rights and the rights of everyone affected by that strategy.

> ***Believing* that the concept of human dignity can help us understand, protect, and implement human rights globally**

The concept of human dignity of all people, in all places, at all times is an idea that can help reinvigorate a human rights project that at times seems to be weary. The Punta del Este Declaration is made with the belief that human dignity is the lens through which human rights should be understood, protected, and implemented. A human dignity-oriented understanding of human rights will facilitate the protection and implementation of human rights and is the means for achieving an increase in the effective recognition and protection of human rights for everyone everywhere. When human rights remain unimplemented, they will remain only a dream. And left unfulfilled, that dream can generate disappointment or despair, skepticism or cynicism, and even anger or rage.

The "hoping" clause

The preliminary clauses conclude with a single statement of hope – that the 21st Century will be more humane, just, and peaceful than the 20th Century was. This hope is the underlying motivation for the time and effort that was put into preparing, discussing, negotiating, drafting, and adopting the Punta del Este Declaration on Human Dignity for Everyone Everywhere.

> ***Hoping* that the present century will be more humane, just, and peaceful than the 20th Century**

This Declaration was drafted and adopted with the hope that by focusing on the fundamental concept of human dignity for everyone everywhere, human rights can be reinvigorated and reinforced. The Punta del Este Declaration is made with the hope that the 21st Century can be more humane, just, and peaceful than the

20th Century. The Punta del Este Declaration is made with hope, but with a clear realization that the promise of human rights is far from complete. The hope behind the Punta del Este Declaration is that it will be used as a guide throughout the process of improving the legacy of human rights for future generations.

Expanded explanation of the reaffirmation of the initial declaration of the UDHR

The operative part of the Punta del Este Declaration begins by quoting at length the preliminary declaration from the UDHR. This statement is important because it sets forth in spare, elegant prose the understanding of the adopters of the UDHR of what it was and what it hoped to achieve. Quoting the UDHR, the Punta del Este Declaration states:

> **We, the undersigned, do solemnly reaffirm:**
> **The Universal Declaration of Human Rights continues to be "a common standard of achievement for all peoples and all nations, to the end that every individual and every organ of society, keeping the Declaration constantly in mind, shall strive by teaching and education to promote respect for these rights and freedoms and by progressive measures, local, national and international, to secure their universal and effective recognition and observance."**

A common standard of achievement

The UDHR is described as "a common standard of achievement," suggesting both its universality, its aspirational quality, and that it can be used as a measure for assessing progress. As Eleonor Roosevelt noted at the time of adoption of the UDHR:

> In giving our approval to the declaration today, it is of primary importance that we keep clearly in mind the basic character of the document. It is not a treaty; it is not an international agreement. It is not and does not purport to be a statement of law or legal obligation. It is a declaration of basic principles of human rights and freedoms, to be stamped with the approval of the General Assembly by a formal vote of its members, and to serve as a common standard of achievement for all peoples of all nations.[62]

62 Statement by Eleonor Roosevelt to the UN on December 10, 1948. quoted in Mary Ann Glendon, "The Rule of Law in the Universal Declaration of Human Rights" (2004) 2 *Northwestern University Journal of International Human Rights* 1, 5. See also: Eleanor Roosevelt, "On the Adoption of the Universal Declaration of Human Rights" in James Daley (ed.), *Great Speeches by American Women* (Dover: Mineola, NY, 2008) 128–129.

The aspirational quality of the "common standard of achievement" language can be seen in Abraham Lincoln's explanation of the statement "all men are created equal" in the Declaration of Independence:

> They [the drafters] did not mean to assert the obvious untruth, that all were then actually enjoying that equality, nor yet, that they were about to confer it immediately upon them. In fact, they had no power to confer such a boon. They meant simply to declare the right so that the enforcement of it might follow as fast as circumstances should permit. They meant to set up a standard maxim for free society which should be familiar to all: constantly looked to, constantly labored for, and … thereby constantly spreading and deepening its influence and augmenting the happiness and value of life to all people, of all colors, everywhere.[63]

For all peoples and all nations

It is for "all peoples and all nations," with the modifier "all" repeated, again emphasizing the universal scope and reach of its aspirations. It is for nation-states, enumerating specific obligations of government, but it is also for all people and all peoples.

In June 1947, the American Anthropological Commission wrote a letter to the Human Rights Commission to provide advice and perspective as the UDHR's drafting was underway; the letter noted that the task would be "to formulate a statement of human rights that will do more than just phrase respect for the individual as an individual. It must also take into full account the individual as member of the social group of which he is part, whose sanctioned modes of life shape his behavior, and with whose fate his own is thus inextricably bound."[64] The drafters' primary intended audience was the members of the human race; the phrase preceding Article 1, "every individual and every organ of society," which according to Morsink, "refers to the secondary addressees of the document and [the phrase 'all peoples and all nations'] refers to the third level of addressees. Both of these other levels are crucial in educating people about their own and other people's human rights and in the fight for the recognition and observance of these rights on a national and international scale."[65]

For every individual and every organ of society

It creates obligations for "every individual and every organ of society" to promote respect for the rights and freedoms enumerated in the UDHR and to work

63 Mary Ann Glendon, "The Rule of Law in the Universal Declaration of Human Rights" (2004) 2 *Northwestern University Journal of International Human Rights* 1, 11–12, quoting Abraham Lincoln (Roy P. Basler (ed.)), *The Collected Works of Abraham Lincoln* (Abraham Lincoln Association, 1953) 301.

64 Glendon (2001) 222.

65 Morsink (1999) 34–35. See Glendon (2001) 177 (quoting Eleanor Roosevelt's explanation that the UDHR was a standard of achievement applicable to all peoples, nations, individuals, and organs of society).

towards the effective recognition and observance of those rights and freedoms.[66] The repetition of the word "every" again emphasizes the universal character of the duties associated with the UDHR.[67] Mary Ann Glendon writes,

> The Declaration's "Everyone" is an individual who is constituted, in important ways, by and through relationships with others. "Everyone" is envisioned as uniquely valuable in himself ... but "Everyone" is expected to act toward others "in a spirit of brotherhood." "Everyone" is depicted as situated in a variety of specifically named, real-life relationships of mutual dependency: families, communities, religious groups, workplaces, associations, societies, cultures, nations, and an emerging international order.[68]

Human rights are not viewed as just being the province of states or governments. Here the Punta del Este Declaration reaffirms that no longer are states the sole subjects of international law; human beings are as well. Since the UDHR's adoption, the document has been the foundation for several monitoring mechanisms for the United Nations, bringing human rights under international inspection, rather than leaving human rights issues under purely domestic examination.[69]

66 As Glendon stresses, "The Preamble [of the UDHR] begins by linking freedom, justice, and peace and by asserting that these goals *depend* upon the recognition of human dignity and rights." Glendon (2001)175-176. Koskenniemi, clarified that the UDHR "is an essentially individualistic document that sees States, nations and international politics as a means for guaranteeing rights, thereby endowing these institutions with a powerful cloak of cosmopolitan legitimacy." Martti Koskenniemi, *Fragmentation of International Law: Difficulties Arising from the Diversification and Expansion of International Law* (International Law Commission, Study Group on Fragmentation, 2006) 27, 38. Morsink quoted the Brazilian delegate Belarmino Austregesilio de Athayde to say that "It was impossible to draw up a declaration of rights without proclaiming the duties implicit in the concept of freedom which made it possible to set up a peaceful and democratic society." Morsink (1999) 249.

67 William Hodgson of Australia said, "Every one of these rights [in the UDHR] has a corresponding duty." See UN Doc. AC.1/3Add.1/p.5. Johannes Morsink explains that eventually only Article 29 of the UDHR, which comes towards the end of the document, specifically refers to duties of individuals. Morsink (2009) 40. This means the emphasis on duties gets overlooked by legal theorists, yet "[e]ven after being moved to the end, Article 29 is still a formidable article." *Id.* According to Glendon, in general the UDHR emphasizes the duty that "everyone" has to each other and to society. Glendon (2001) 227.

68 Glendon (2001) 227.

69 Asbjørn Eide and Gudmundur Alfredsson, "Introduction" in Gudmundur Alfredsson and Asbjørn Eide (eds.), *The Universal Declaration of Human Rights* (Martinus Nijhoff Publishers, 1999) xxv, xxxi. "Largely thanks to the UDHR, States can no longer use domestic jurisdiction arguments to defend themselves against international scrutiny. The United Nations has repeatedly undertaken investigations and commented on the human rights performance of States notwithstanding such internal affairs arguments, as confirmed in the 1993 Vienna Declaration which states the 'the promotion and protection of all human rights is a legitimate concern of the international community.' *Id.* That the UDHR stated that human rights are

Referring to the UN Charter and the changes it made to international law, Morsink stressed the limitations it placed on "what until then had been almost limitless sovereignty of the nation-states that make up the international system." He said, "[one] limitation was on the internal sovereignty of states, telling states that they could no longer do to the people within their borders as they wished."[70] According to Hans Ingvar Roth, "[w]hat made the UDHR such a landmark was that the individual, the single human being, for the first time in history was accorded a status within international law."[71]

Keeping the Declaration constantly in mind

The UDHR, and in turn the Punta del Este Declaration, becomes operative and becomes powerful by being kept "constantly in mind" by all people and all organs of society. This phrase in the UDHR's Preamble highlights the individual's and society's responsibility to actively remember the UDHR's material.[72]

> From the point of view of each individual, it is necessary to bear in mind the individual rights and to respect others' enjoyment of the same rights. Both familiarizing with the content of the UDHR and understanding its rights system are essential to enhance the awareness of human rights, to improve the level of human rights protection, and to fully realize the common standard of the international human rights.[73]

universal, "belonging to 'all members of the human family,' challenged the traditional view that the relation between a sovereign state and its own citizens was that nation's own exclusive business." Glendon (2001) 175–176. Glendon further emphasized that, "[b]y the close of the Geneva meeting it was clearer than ever that the chief obstacle to unanimous approval of the Declaration was not going to be its content, but its potential for legitimating outside interference in a country's internal affairs. The behavior of the Communist delegates at Geneva suggested that the Soviet bloc might oppose the Declaration when the actual day of decision came. Despite its defects, Cassin argued, the Declaration 'contributes something new: the individual becomes a subject of international law in respect of his life and liberty; principles are affirmed, side by side with those already laid down by the majority of national laws, which no national or international authority had hitherto been able to proclaim, let alone enforce.' He was referring specifically to three 'international' rights – the rights to freedom of movement, to seek asylum, and to a nationality – that the closed societies of Eastern Europe both protested and feared." *Id.*, 96. Morsink made this point when he said, "[t]he Nuremberg legal reflections on the Holocaust ... raised the individual human person to the status of being a subject of international law." Morsink (2009) 79.

70 Morsink (2009) 124.

71 Hans Ingvar Roth, *P. C. Chang and the Universal Declaration of Human Rights* (University of Pennsylvania Press, 2018) 135.

72 See Pinghua Sun (2018) 332.

73 *Id.*

The guarantees found in the UDHR are not self-executing or automatic in their implementation.[74] Memory, vigilance, and mindfulness will all be necessary for the promise of human rights to be fulfilled. The idea of constancy suggests that the realization of human rights will require ongoing attention and effort.

Striving through teaching and education

The Punta del Este Declaration emphasizes the importance of all people and every organ of society, through constant mindfulness, to "strive by teaching and education to promote respect for these rights and freedoms."[75] The inclusion of this phrase in the Preamble of the UDHR shows the drafters' "optimistic view of the human ability to know the 'good' and to realize it spontaneously, without there being any incompatibility between the different 'goods' and, most importantly, any public process of negotiation and adjustment."[76] It is noteworthy that the implementation and realization of human rights are contemplated to take place primarily through teaching and education, rather than through law.[77] Human

74 In the Human Rights Commission's third session for drafting the UDHR, the delegates spent a large portion of time debating how rights should be implemented, especially the newer social and economic rights. Glendon (2001) 117. The representatives recognized that implementation would vary between political structures and thus Eleanor Roosevelt reminded the delegates that the UDHR was not self-executing and should not rigidly outline how countries should realize human rights. *Id.* Indeed, she stated that the variations in human rights implementation "should be considered not only inevitable but salutary." *Id.* Because of this flexibility of implementation, the UDHR "has been and continues to be a source of inspiration and direction for the standard-setting and monitoring activities of the United Nations in the field of human rights. This is also true for the work of other intergovernmental and non-governmental organizations, at both international and regional levels." Asbjørn Eide and Gudmundur Alfredsson, "Introduction" in Gudmundur Alfredsson and Asbjørn Eide (eds.), *The Universal Declaration of Human Rights* (Martinus Nijhoff Publishers, 1999) xxv, xxx.

75 Martti Koskenniemi, "Preamble of the Universal Declaration of Human Rights" in Gudmundur Alfredsson and Asbjørn Eide (eds.), *The Universal Declaration of Human Rights* (Martinus Nijhoff Publishers, 1999) 27, 33. Human rights education is both an effective measure and a vital component of protecting and increasing awareness of human rights. Pinghua Sun (2018) 332–33.

76 Martti Koskenniemi, "Preamble of the Universal Declaration of Human Rights" in Gudmundur Alfredsson and Asbjørn Eide (eds.), *The Universal Declaration of Human Rights* (Martinus Nijhoff Publishers, 1999) 27, 33.

77 Article 26 of the UDHR concerns education and places obligations for access to and attendance for education because education "is an important, maybe the most important, condition for the development of society." Pentti Arajärvi, "Article 26" in Gudmundur Alfredsson and Asbjørn Eide (eds.), *The Universal Declaration of Human Rights* (Martinus Nijhoff Publishers, 1999) 551, 554. According to Morsink, the Brazilian delegate, Belarmino Austregesilio de Athayde, made this point stating that, "Without education the individual could not develop his personality, which was the aim of human life and the most solid foundation of society." Morsink (1999) 212. There was a shared understanding on the importance of the rights to education; thus "[t]here was consensus on the Commission that education was crucial to the aim of

rights will be realized when respect for these rights is promoted by all of us and by all organs of society.[78]

By progressive measures

The preliminary declaration also notes that the rights and freedoms enumerated in the UDHR will be implemented and realized "by progressive measures." For example, P. C. Chang emphasized that,

> In the eighteenth century, when progressive ideas with respect to human rights had been first put forward in Europe, translations of Chinese philosophers had been known to and had inspired such thinkers as Voltaire, Quesnay, and Diderot in their humanistic revolt against feudalistic conceptions. Chinese ideas had been intermingled with European thought and sentiment on human rights at the time when that subject had been first speculated upon in modern Europe. Stress should be laid upon the human aspect of human rights. A human being had to be constantly conscious of other men, in whose society he lived. A lengthy process of education was required before men and women realized the full value and obligations of the rights granted to them in the declaration; it was only when that stage had been achieved that those rights could be realized in practice. It was therefore necessary that the declaration should be approved as soon as possible, to serve as a basis and a programme for the humanization of man. A declaration of human rights should be brief and readily understandable by all. It should be a document for all men

establishing 'freedom, justice, and peace in the world,' and the first paragraph of Article 26 was drafted to reflect that belief." Glendon (2001) 189.

78 The founders of human rights intended human rights education to reach beyond formal educational institutions such as schools and universities. The right to education encompasses traditional education in schools, such as the expressly noted elementary education and higher education, but during the drafting of the UDHR, it was discussed that this should also include vocational and technical training. Pentti Arajärvi, "Article 26" in Gudmundur Alfredsson and Asbjørn Eide (eds.), *The Universal Declaration of Human Rights* (Martinus Nijhoff Publishers, 1999) 551, 552. But even beyond job skills, the right to education can be understood to encompass civic education and public virtues. Morsink (2017) 214. Many South American constitutions had citizenship goals integrated into their education systems; while the drafters could not require any one "particular brand [...] of civic education being practiced," they were able to "prescribe a set of guidelines that are valid in different cultural settings and not dependent on any specific level of development" in Article 26. *Id.*, 215. Other organs of society and, indeed, all human beings have obligations to promote respect for human rights. "The expression [in Article 26] 'education shall be directed to the full development of the human personality' indicates the general ethical aim of education, as it should influence the individual. The development of the entire personality includes all the dimensions of the human being: physical, intellectual, psychological, and social. The aim is that each individual develop, according to his or her abilities and talents, into a well-balanced person." Pentti Arajärvi, "Article 26" in Gudmundur Alfredsson and Asbjørn Eide (eds.), *The Universal Declaration of Human Rights* (Martinus Nijhoff Publishers, 1999) 551, 555.

> everywhere, not merely for lawyers and scholars. It was with that object in mind that the Chinese delegation had introduced, at the third session of the Commission on Human Rights, a brief declaration containing ten articles and it was gratified by the fact that the document had aided in making the present draft declaration clear and relatively brief.[79]

The standard of achievement is a tool for measuring our progress towards the implementation and realization of the right enunciated in the UDHR. The UDHR was created to explicitly tell nations and individuals what inherent rights each human being possesses and then the very same document can be used as a measurement tool to know if human rights are sufficiently protected.[80]

Local, national, and international

The measures to promote and implement human rights will be "local, national and international."[81] It seems significant that the starting point is local implementation.

As Eleonor Roosevelt reminds us,

> Where, after all, do universal human rights begin? In small places, close to home – so close and so small that they cannot be seen on any maps of the world. Yet they are the world of the individual person; the neighborhood he lives in; the school or college he attends; the factory, farm, or office where he works. Such are the places where every man, woman, and child seeks equal

79 Schabas (2013) 2056. Cassin added that "The Committee should try to draft a declaration which would be both effective and restrained, a declaration whose influence on men's lives would increase progressively with the signature of the conventions to which it would give rise. Moreover, the USSR amendment was incomplete in that it did not mention liberty and security of person, which were essential to complete the idea of the right to life." *Id.*, 2244.

80 Morsink (1999) 325. "People can measure their enjoyment of human rights against this standard and see where they are being repressed or in what manner their dignity is being violated … Whenever and wherever the full enjoyment of any of these inherent rights is lacking the standard set by the Declaration has not been fully achieved." *Id.*, 325.

81 "The Declaration's architects expected that its fertile principles could be brought to life in a legitimate variety of ways. Their idea was that each local tradition would be enriched as it put the Declaration's principles into practice and that all countries would benefit from the resulting accumulation of experiences." Glendon (2001) 230. The drafters were aware that each country would implement the rights in the UDHR differently from one another; to explicitly allow such variations Egypt's delegate, Omar Loutfi, (alongside Malik, Cassin, and Roosevelt) included in the UDHR that "the rights in question would be implemented 'in accordance with the organization and resources of each State.'" *Id.*, 115–117. Article 29 is an example of the drafters acknowledging different levels of implementation when they intentionally left out any mention of the "state" and instead outlined the responsibilities of the "community" and the "democratic society." Morsink (2017) 239. This word choice "kept the state out and pulled the community into the range of an individual's duties." *Id.*

> justice, equal opportunity, equal dignity without discrimination. Unless these rights have meaning there, they have little meaning anywhere.[82]

Hence, human rights will be best realized on the ground in particular places and locales. Morsink stressed that "While the [UDHR's] standards are universal, their implementation will be the more successful the closer the attention to local circumstances."[83] It will then be through national and international measures that human rights will be secured and recognized.

Securing their universal and effective recognition and observance

The goal is that the rights of everyone everywhere will be secured in "universal and effective recognition and observance."[84] It is not enough that human rights be recognized, they must be secured, observed and implemented, and as such, effectively recognized. To sufficiently protect human rights, every individual must actively "respect the rights of all the others while having his rights respected by all others so that there must be a mutual sharing of the benefits of rights and the burdens of duties."[85] It is through this mutual recognition that a mere society is elevated to a community. The UDHR itself necessitates "continuous efforts at all levels to realize the universal enjoyment of human rights. The UDHR does not stop at proclaiming rights but also calls for a transformation of the social and international order in such a way that the rights established will be enjoyed in practice."[86] The drafters showed that the pathway to social progress is established on respect for human dignity, "which requires the final elimination of all forms of inequality, exploitation of people

82 Eleanor Roosevelt, "The Great Question" (March 27, 1958) United Nations, New York.

83 Morsink (1999) 20. De Gaay Fortman explained that difficulties with implementation of human rights derive from reliance on international enforcement, when its force is "rather weak. Indeed, the responsibility for implementing all those internationally *declared* rights still rests basically at the national and local level." Bas de Gaay Fortman, "Equal Dignity in International Human Rights" in Marcus Düwell et al. (eds.), *The Cambridge Handbook of Human Dignity: Interdisciplinary Perspectives* (Cambridge University Press, 2014) 355, 359.

84 When analyzing the Preamble to the UDHR, Mary Ann Glendon states that the word "universal" in this phrase contradicted the traditional notion that the relationship between a state and its citizens was purely a domestic issue. Glendon (2001) 176. Additionally, the word "recognition" in the phrase is significant because "[p]rior to World War II, legal positivism (the view that there are no rights other than those granted by the laws of the state) flourished in the United States and Europe and was dogma in the Soviet Union ... The Declaration implicitly rejected the positivist position by stating that fundamental rights are recognized, rather than conferred." *Id.*

85 Morsink (1999) 246 (quoting Alan Gewirth).

86 Asbjørn Eide and Gudmundur Alfredsson, "Introduction" in Gudmundur Alfredsson and Asbjørn Eide (eds.), *The Universal Declaration of Human Rights* (Martinus Nijhoff Publishers, 1999) xxv, xxx.

and individuals, and the recognition and effective implementation of civil and political rights as well as economic, social and cultural rights."[87]

Conclusion

This chapter with its focus on the preambular paragraphs of the Punta del Este Declaration has explored several dimensions of human dignity, setting the tone for further discussion in subsequent chapters. The Preamble is a remarkable summary of the understanding that existed at the time the UDHR was adopted about how its ideals would be achieved.[88] As the working group gathered in Punta del Este, they wanted to begin by "solemnly reaffirm[ing] these basic principles" and emphasizing their continuing relevance.

87 Asbjørn Eide, "Article 28" in Gudmundur Alfredsson and Asbjørn Eide (eds.), *The Universal Declaration of Human Rights* (Martinus Nijhoff Publishers, 1999) 597, 617.

88 The UDHR masterfully declares compelling ideas concisely. "[T]he UDHR has a special place because of its approach to and balancing of civil cultural, economic, political, and social rights, together with its express reference to duties and an international order for the realization of the rights." Asbjørn Eide and Gudmundur Alfredsson, "Introduction" in Gudmundur Alfredsson and Asbjørn Eide (eds.), *The Universal Declaration of Human Rights* (Martinus Nijhoff Publishers, 1999). With its concise and powerful ideas, the Declaration has influenced the monitoring standards of the United Nations and other international and regional organizations, as well as maintained its status "a possible bridge … between different points of view." *Id.*, xxix–xxx. With its structure of human rights, the UDHR "marked the beginning of the global transformation of human rights from moral or philosophical imperatives in the international community into a framework of rights that are legally [recognized] between nations." Joy Liddicoat, "Dignity Online and Offline" in Edward Sieh and Judy McGregor (eds.), *Human Dignity: Establishing Worth and Seeking Solutions* (Palgrave Macmillan, 2017) 3–5.

3 Article 1

Foundation, objective, and criterion

Article 1 of the Punta del Este Declaration reads as follows:

> The inherent human dignity of all people and the importance of respecting, promoting, and protecting human dignity for everyone everywhere is the foundational principle and the key objective or goal of human rights, as well as an invaluable criterion for evaluating laws, policies, and government actions for how well they accord with human rights standards. Protecting, promoting, and guaranteeing respect for the human dignity of everyone is a fundamental obligation of states, governments, and other public bodies, whether local, regional, national, or international. Promoting human dignity is also a responsibility of all sectors of society, and of each of us as human beings. Doing so is the key to protecting the equal and inalienable rights of all members of the human family, and remains the foundation of freedom, justice, and peace in the world.

The following is an expanded explanation of each part of Article 1.

a. The inherent human dignity of all people and the importance of respecting, promoting, and protecting human dignity for everyone everywhere is the foundational principle and the key objective or goal of human rights

The project of developing the UDHR was fraught with difficulty. Indeed, the entire project could have collapsed because of the ideological conflicts of those drafting[1] and political divides between East (influenced by Marxist theory)[2] and West (reinforcing liberal theory), North (more developed) and South (less developed), and nations that were independent and free and those that were still under colonial rule or still emerging from colonial rule. The dialogue during the drafting

1 Rebecca Adami, "Intersectional Dialogue: Analyzing Power in Reaching a Universal Declaration of Human Rights in 1948 on Conflicting Grounds" (2018) 17 *Journal of Human Rights* 357–366.

2 Morsink (1999).

DOI: 10.4324/9781003207030-4

of the UDHR would not have been possible but for the unwritten rule in the Commission on Human Rights that delegates were not to refer to specific violations in other countries.[3]

Foundational principle

There was a need for a set of basic, foundational principles that could be widely embraced by peoples and countries with very different political and legal systems.[4]

The drafters started by adopting a process of surveying existing legal documents, and engaging experts and non-governmental organizations. Indeed, John Humphrey,[5] who was tasked with developing the first draft, grounded his work in existing documents (especially constitutions) and instructions received from the First Session of the Commission and the Economic and Social Council.[6] He incorporated proposals from several drafts (including the drafts submitted by the American Law Institute and the Inter-American Juridical Committee) to ensure that the document was inclusive. Several experts submitted drafts for consideration, including H. G. Wells,[7] Wilfred Parsons,[8] Rollin McNitt,[9] Irving Jacobs, Gustavo Gutierrez,[10] Hersch Lauterpacht,[11] and several non-governmental organizations, for example, the American Bar Association, Free World, American Jewish Conference, and the Commission to Study the Organization of Peace.[12] Furthermore, after the Second Session of the Committee, the draft was sent to governments for feedback.[13]

The idea of human dignity emerged as an idea that could be embraced by a wide variety of viewpoints.[14] According to Tore Lindholm, "By making a public

3 Morsink (1999) 23.

4 The principal framers of the UDHR intended for the document to be widely applicable, capable of enriching "each local tradition … as it put the Declaration's principles into practice" and they "never envisioned that the document's 'common standard of achievement' would or should produce completely uniform practices." Glendon (2001) 230. Tore Lindholm, "Article 1" in Gudmundur Alfredsson and Asbjørn Eide (eds.), *The Universal Declaration of Human Rights: A Common Standard of Achievement* (Martinus Nijhoff Publishers, 1999) 42, 68.

5 An international lawyer and the Director of the UN Secretariat's Division for Human Rights.

6 Morsink (1999) 5.

7 English novelist, journalist, sociologist, and historian.

8 Jesuit priest and author.

9 Honorary Dean of the Law School of Southwestern University (Los Angeles).

10 Peruvian philosopher, theologian, and Dominican priest.

11 British international lawyer and judge at the International Court of Justice. (From his book *An International Bill of the Rights of Man*.)

12 William A. Schabas, *The Abolition of the Death Penalty in International Law* (Cambridge University Press, 2009) 27. See also: UN Doc. E/CN.4/W.16.

13 Morsink (1999) 18.

14 Tore Lindholm, "Article 1" in Gudmundur Alfredsson and Asbjørn Eide (eds.), *The Universal Declaration of Human Rights: A Common Standard of Achievement* (Martinus Nijhoff Publishers, 1999) 55–63.

commitment to the inherent freedom and equal dignity of every human being the thin, but mandatory normative underpinning of universal rights," the drafters designed the UDHR inclusively from the very beginning, such that the UDHR does not "exclude people who subscribe to any religion or major normative tradition from building support for human rights on their own grounds."[15] With human dignity at the foundation of human rights, the UDHR "is flexible enough to allow for differences in emphasis and means of implementation, but not so malleable as to permit any basic human right to be completely eclipsed or unnecessarily subordinated for the sake of other rights."[16]

The aim or end of human rights

In addition to being a foundational concept, human dignity is also the aim or end point of human rights. When human dignity is recognized, respected, and realized everywhere, the goal or objective of human rights will be realized.

Identifying human dignity as the aim or end of human rights has received wide support in the scholarly literature.[17] Donnelly claims that "human rights present only one path to the realization of human dignity"[18] and "human rights appear as the natural response to changing conditions, a logical and necessary evolution of the means for realizing human dignity."[19] However, he considers that there are other ways to achieve human dignity that are not grounded in human rights. According to Mary Ann Glendon, Eleanor Roosevelt defended the inclusion of human dignity in the UDHR "to emphasize that every human being is worthy of respect … it was meant to explain why human beings have rights, to begin with."[20] Furthermore, the understanding of human dignity as the aim of human rights is clear from the wording of Article 1 of the German Basic Law affirming that human dignity shall be inviolable and "the German people, therefore, acknowledge inviolable and inalienable human rights as the

15 Tore Lindholm, "Article 1" in Gudmundur Alfredsson and Asbjørn Eide (eds.), *The Universal Declaration of Human Rights: A Common Standard of Achievement* (Martinus Nijhoff Publishers, 1999) 42, 68.

16 Glendon (2001) 232.

17 Jack Donnelly, "Human Rights and Human Dignity: An Analytic Critique of Non-western Conceptions of Human Rights" (1982) 76 *American Political Science Review* 303; Christopher McCrudden, "Human Dignity and Judicial Interpretation of Human Rights" (2008) 19 *European Journal of International law* 655; Oscar Schachter, "Human Dignity as a Normative Concept" (1983) 77 *American Journal of International Law* 848; David Kretzmer and Eckart Klein, *The Concept of Human Dignity in Human Rights Discourse* (Brill, 2002).

18 Jack Donnelly, "Human Rights and Human Dignity: An Analytic Critique of Non-western Conceptions of Human Rights" (1982) 76 *American Political Science Review* 303.

19 *Id.*, 312.

20 Glendon (2001) 146.

basis of every community, of peace and of justice in the world."[21] The primary reason it is important to protect human rights is to vindicate and realize human dignity. Human dignity for everyone everywhere is the primary goal of human rights.[22]

It is interesting and significant that human dignity for everyone everywhere is not only the foundational principle of human rights but also the objective, goal, *telos,* or end of human rights.[23]

Human rights are not a goal in themselves but a way to protect and strengthen the human dignity of everyone everywhere. The goal of human rights is to protect human dignity for everyone everywhere.[24]

b. Human dignity for everyone everywhere is an invaluable criterion for evaluating laws, policies, and government actions for how well they accord with human rights standards

Assessing human rights performance is a difficult task. There are many important data-driven efforts to measure and evaluate how well countries perform in the protection and realization of human rights. Comprehensive human rights

21 Article 1(2) of the Basic Law.

22 For example, Kateb claims that "Human dignity is … perceived to be the basis for human rights." Kateb (2011) 1.

23 Schlink suggests two ways that dignity may be used. In the first depiction, "[h]uman dignity is used as a flag under which people unite and fight for freedom, equality, and decent living conditions that enable them to take care of their needs." In the second depiction, human dignity is used "as a foundational concept for human rights, as a concept that at least justifies and at best requires the existence of human rights." Bernhard Schlink, "The Concept of Human Dignity: Current Usages, Future Discourses" in Christopher McCrudden (ed.), *Understanding Human Dignity* (Oxford University Press: Oxford, 2013) 631, 631. Tasioulas identified three functions of human dignity: first, that human dignity and human rights are essentially identical; second, dignity distinguishes human rights from other moral or legal rights and is "a threshold at which the operative grounding values … give rise to the rights that individuals can claim"; and third, dignity is "a grounding value of human rights." John Tasioulas, "Human Dignity and the Foundations of Human Rights" in Christopher McCrudden (ed.), *Understanding Human Dignity* (Oxford University Press: Oxford, 2013) 291–292.

24 According to Neuman, "The principle of human dignity serves as part of the foundation of human rights law, at least in the sense that recognition of this value gives us reason to construct a system of legal rights, calculated to protect individuals against treatment inconsistent with human dignity … The international human rights system also rests on the conviction that empowering individuals, by configuring many of the rules that protect them as legal rights that they can assert, best serves their human dignity." Gerald L. Neuman, "Discourses of Dignity" in Christopher McCrudden (ed.), *Understanding Human Dignity* (Oxford University Press: Oxford, 2013) 631, 635–639. Roth claims that "Protection of the individual human being's dignity always lies at the heart of any human rights ethics." Hans Ingvar Roth, *P. C. Chang and the Universal Declaration of Human Rights* (University of Pennsylvania Press, 2018) 136. (Later cited as Roth (2018)).

performance indices include those produced by the Pew Research Center,[25] Human Rights Watch,[26] Amnesty International,[27] and Freedom House.[28]

From 2007 to 2017, the Pew Research Center analyzed "the extent to which governments and societies around the world impinge on religious beliefs and practices."[29] Pew took data and information from "more than a dozen publicly available, widely cited sources of information, including annual reports on international religious freedom by the U.S. State Department[30] and the U.S. Commission on International Religious Freedom,[31] as well as publications by a variety of European and UN bodies and several independent, nongovernmental organizations."[32] The data is categorized into two main indexes, the Government Restrictions Index (GRI) and the Social Hostilities Index (SHI), with four categories within each index. The conclusion in its most recent version of the report (Pew Research Center 2019) was that "in 2017, about a quarter of the 198 countries studied (26%) experienced 'high' or 'very high' levels of government restrictions" on religious freedom and belief, and "[t]he share of countries with 'high' or 'very high' levels of social hostilities involving religion" was 28% in 2017.[33] The study found that in general "in 2017, 83 countries (42%) experienced high or very high levels of overall restrictions on religion."[34]

Another important source of data on human rights is Human Rights Watch, a non-profit advocacy organization founded in 1978 and based in New York, USA.[35] Human Rights Watch has a team of "roughly 450 people of 70-plus nationalities who are country experts, lawyers, journalists, and others" who use a more hands-on approach to identifying human rights data.[36] Their researchers

25 Pew Research Center, "How Religious Restrictions Around the World Have Changed over a Decade" (July 16, 2019). Available at: https://www.pewresearch.org/fact-tank/2019/07/16/how-religious-restrictions-around-the-world-have-changed-over-a-decade/

26 Human Rights Watch, *World Report 2020*. Available at: https://www.hrw.org/world-report/2020

27 Amnesty International, *Report 2017/2018*. Available at: https://www.amnesty.org/en/documents/pol10/6700/2018/en/#:~:text=The%20Amnesty%20International%20Report%202017%2F18%20documents%20the%20state,in%20their%20own%20countries%20or%20across%20international%20borders

28 Freedom House, *Freedom in the World*. Available at: https://freedomhouse.org/reports

29 Pew Research Centre, "A Closer Look at How Religious Restriction Have Risen Around the World" (July 15, 2019) Pew Forum: Religion. Available at: https://www.pewforum.org/2019/07/15/a-closer-look-at-how-religious-restrictions-have-risen-around-the-world/

30 US State Department, *Report on International Religious Freedom*. Available at: https://www.state.gov/reports/2019-report-on-international-religious-freedom/

31 USCIRF, *Annual Report*. Available at: https://www.uscirf.gov/reports-briefs/annual-report/2020-annual-report

32 *Id.*

33 *Id.*

34 *Id.*

35 Human Rights Watch, "About Us" https://www.hrw.org/about-us

36 *Id.*

conduct personal interviews with those who claim to be victims of human rights violations in several locations throughout the world, review "media reports, domestic legislation, international law, policy papers, academic reports, and civil society reports," and lately even satellite technology.[37] Their 2019 *World Report* focused on "key human rights issues in more than 90 countries and territories worldwide, drawing on events from late 2017 through November 2018."[38] The report incorporates country-focused chapters detailing "human rights abuses, examines the freedom of local human rights defenders to conduct their work, and surveys the response of key international actors, such as the United Nations, European Union, African Union, United States, China, and various regional and international organizations and institutions."[39]

Amnesty International, a charity organization based in London, England, uses research, advocacy, and campaigning to address human rights issues.[40] Its mission statement specifically says: "Amnesty International's vision is of a world in which every person enjoys all of the human rights enshrined in the Universal Declaration of Human Rights and other international human rights instruments."[41] Its 2017/18 *Annual Report* surveyed 159 countries and territories, with regional overviews, specific country focus, and calls for action directed at "anyone with an interest in human rights."[42] The report on the Amnesty International website does not provide information about the methodology of their research, but it does provide case studies that highlight the effectiveness of their work.[43]

In addition to these data-driven matrices, when assessing how governments are doing in protecting human rights perhaps the single most important qualitative criterion will be the extent to which human dignity is protected, promoted, and realized for all people living within the government's jurisdiction. Currently, no human rights index focuses on human dignity specifically.

For example, when we consider the extent to which human rights are protected in important institutional settings, such as prisons, hospitals, refugee and internally displaced persons (IDP) camps, one key – perhaps *the* key question – is whether the institutions' policies and practices accord human dignity to the people in their charge.[44]

37 Human Rights Watch, "About Our Research." https://www.hrw.org/about-our-research.

38 Human Rights Watch, *World Report 2019*, VIII. https://www.hrw.org/sites/default/files/world_report_download/hrw_world_report_2019.pdf

39 *Id.*

40 Amnesty International, "What We Do." https://www.amnesty.org/en/what-we-do/

41 Amnesty International, "Amnesty International's Statute." https://www.amnesty.org/en/about-us/how-were-run/amnesty-internationals-statute/

42 Amnesty International, *Amnesty International Report 2017/18: The State of the World's Human Rights* (2018) 409. Available at: https://www.amnesty.org/download/Documents/pol1067002018english.pdf

43 Amnesty International, "Assessing Impact." https://www.amnesty.org/en/what-we-do/

44 See for example, the UN General Assembly's "Basic Principles for the Treatment of Prisoners: Resolution Adopted by the General Assembly," stating that "All prisoners

The impact of human rights protections on human dignity provides a useful tool for evaluating the strength of such protections and the implications of practices and procedures, enabling us to consider and find better approaches that would maximize the human rights of everyone everywhere. Nonetheless, we believe the concept of human dignity will be more directly relevant in qualitative evaluations of human rights rather than quantitative evaluations and matrices.

Many states have introduced mechanisms to monitor and assess human rights protections domestically and/or internationally. Several states have human rights commissions that consider their domestic implementation of human rights. For example, the Equality and Human Rights Commission in the UK, a statutory non-departmental public body established by the Equality Act 2006 and a national human rights institution, "seeks to maintain and strengthen this heritage, while identifying and tackling areas where there is still unfair discrimination or where human rights are not being respected."[45] Other governments have established domestic mechanisms to focus on the situation of particularly vulnerable groups. For example, the Norwegian government established an action plan against antisemitism, for the years 2016–2020, with a special monitoring mechanism on human rights violations.

Among the monitoring mechanisms with a truly global focus, the Office of International Religious Freedom within the U.S. State Department monitors the protection of the right to freedom of religion or belief globally and "recommends and implements policies in respective regions or countries, and develops programs to promote religious freedom."[46] In 2016 the government of Hungary established the State Secretariat for the Aid of Persecuted Christians to monitor the situation of human rights violations against Christians "providing direct support for persecuted Christian communities and raising domestic and international political and public awareness of the phenomenon and increasing scale of Christian persecution in the 21st century."[47] The mechanism continues to expand to focus on other religious minorities such as the Yazidis in Iraq and other countries.

The UN has comprehensive monitoring mechanisms in place. For example, the Universal Periodic Review (the UPR), a periodically conducted state-driven mechanism, reviews all the human rights compliance of all UN member states.[48]

shall be treated with the respect due to their inherent dignity and value as human beings." UN General Assembly, "Basic Principles for the Treatment of Prisoners": Resolution Adopted by the General Assembly, 28 March 1991, A/RES/45/111.

45 Equality and Human Rights Commission, "About Us." Available at: https://www.equalityhumanrights.com/en/about-us/who-we-are

46 US State Department, "About Us – Office of International Religious Freedom." Available at: https://www.state.gov/about-us-office-of-international-religious-freedom/

47 Hungarian Government, "State Secretariat for the Aid of Persecuted Christians and for the Hungary Helps Program." Available at: https://www.kormany.hu/en/prime-minister-s-office/state-secretariat-for-the-aid-of-persecuted-christians-and-for-the-hungary-helps-program

48 UN Secretary-General, "In Larger Freedom: Towards Development, Security and Human Rights for All", 21 March 2005, A/59/2005. World Summit Outcome, General Assembly Resolution 60/1, 24 October 2005.

Additionally, the UN has several other mechanisms that can be used to monitor the state of human rights compliance, whether focused on special treaty obligations, particular rights, or particular localities. Several UN treaty bodies[49] can receive complaints brought before them and adjudicate them in terms of a state's compliance with human rights. Lastly, the UN established mandates for special rapporteurs who monitor human rights within their mandates. For example, the UN Special Rapporteur on Freedom of Religion or Belief has a mandate to:

a to promote the adoption of measures at the national, regional, and international levels to ensure the promotion and protection of the right to freedom of religion or belief;

b identify existing and emerging obstacles to the enjoyment of the right to freedom of religion or belief and present recommendations on ways and means to overcome such obstacles;

c continue her/his efforts to examine incidents and governmental actions that are incompatible with the provisions of the Declaration on the Elimination of All Forms of Intolerance and Discrimination Based on Religion or Belief and to recommend remedial measures as appropriate;

d continue to apply a gender perspective, inter alia, through the identification of gender-specific abuses in the reporting process, including in information collection and recommendations.[50]

c. Protecting, promoting, and guaranteeing respect for the human dignity of everyone is a fundamental obligation of states, governments, and other public bodies, whether local, regional, national, or international

The primary human rights obligation of states, governments, and other public bodies is to promote, protect, and guarantee respect for the human dignity of everyone within their jurisdictions. Human dignity must be protected, promoted, and guaranteed by all states, governments, and other public bodies, whether local, regional, national, or international.[51]

The UDHR and the key human rights covenants, for example, the ICCPR and the ICESR, focus predominately on the duties of states and state actors to protect human rights. Indeed, international human rights law, whether the UDHR (as part of the customary law) or the covenants (as international treaties), imposes

49 E.g., CCPR, CERD, CAT, CEDAW, CRPD, CED, CMW, CESCR and CRC.

50 UN Human Rights Council Resolution 6/37, Elimination of All Forms of Intolerance and of Discrimination Based on Religion or Belief, 14 December 2007, UN Doc A/HRC/RES/6/37. 18.

51 "The world is divided into individual nation-states, and human rights protection is premised on each state being (primarily) responsible for protecting the human rights of all those within its territorial borders." Sabine C. Carey, Mark Gibney, and Steven C. Poe, *The Politics of Human Dignity: The Quest for Human Dignity* (Cambridge University Press, 2010) 50.

duties that states are bound to respect. States assume human rights duties under international law when they voluntarily become parties to international treaties. On the other hand, customary international law imposes duties as arising from established international practices rather than voluntary acceptance of treaty obligations.

Apart from states having obligations to fulfill their human rights obligations, they may also have duties regarding human rights conditions in other states. The UN Charter calls upon member states to take "joint or separate action"[52] to promote the UN's purposes, including:

a higher standards of living, full employment, and conditions of economic and social progress and development;
b solutions of international economic, social, health, and related problems; and international cultural and educational cooperation; and
c universal respect for, and observance of, human rights and fundamental freedoms for all without distinction as to race, sex, language, or religion.[53]

Additionally, Article 22 of the UDHR prescribes that "everyone, as a member of society … is entitled to realization, through national effort and international co-operation and in accordance with the organization and resources of each State, of the economic, social and cultural rights indispensable for his dignity and the free development of his personality."[54]

d. Promoting human dignity is also a responsibility of all sectors of society, and each of us as human beings

For human dignity to be guaranteed and adequately protected for everyone everywhere, all sectors of society should be engaged in its promotion. As stated in the preliminary declaration of the UDHR, the implementation of human rights depends upon "every individual and every organ of society."[55] It is not enough to recognize the duty of states if other sectors of society fail to collaborate in this goal. Only by involving all sectors of society will the aim of ensuring the human dignity of everyone everywhere be achieved.

While the primary duty to protect human rights rests with the state, all sectors of society have duties and responsibilities relating to human rights. Indeed, the issue was discussed during the drafting of the UDHR. For example, the first draft of the UDHR prepared by John Humphrey stated: "that man does not have rights only; he owes duties to the society of which he forms part."[56] The draft further stated that "Everyone owes a duty to his State and to the United Nations.

52 See Article 56 of the United Nations, *Charter of the United Nations*, 24 October 1945, 1 *UNTS* XVI.
53 *Id.*, Article 55(A)–(C).
54 Article 22 of the UDHR.
55 Preamble to the UDHR.
56 See: Glendon (2001) 271.

He must accept his just share of responsibility for the performance of such social duties and his share of such common sacrifices as may contribute to the common good."[57] However, the proposal received some criticism and René Cassin and Eleanor Roosevelt suggested alternative wording to Humphrey's draft.[58]

The adopted version of the UDHR only briefly refers to duties in Article 29(1). Article 29(1) of the UDHR prescribes that "Everyone has duties to the community in which alone the free and full development of his personality is possible." Similarly, Article 30 of the UDHR recognizes the duties of actors other than states where it confirms that "nothing in this Declaration may be interpreted as implying for any State, group or person any right to engage in any activity or to perform any act aimed at the destruction of any of the rights and freedoms set forth herein." Lastly, the Preamble of the UDHR also refers to duties of every organ of society "to promote respect for these rights and freedoms and by progressive measures, national and international, to secure their universal and effective recognition and observance, both among the peoples of Member States themselves and among the peoples of territories under their jurisdiction."[59]

Subsequent international documents covered the issue more comprehensively. For example, the ICCPR and the ICESCR, in their preambles, indicate that "the individual, having duties to other individuals and to the community to which he belongs, is under a responsibility to strive for the promotion and observance of the rights recognized in the present Covenant." Among others, Jordan J. Paust claims that the Preamble means that "at a minimum, individuals have duties to not violate human rights."[60]

Similarly, corporations and other business organizations have duties to respect human rights.[61] As Paust has explained, "a corporation can recognizably become involved in violations of human rights law either directly as a private actor; as an actor colored by a connection with a state, state entity, or other public actors; or as a participant in a joint venture or complicitous relation with another human rights violator."[62] In recognizing the role they may play in human rights abuses, it is evident that corporations have duties to comply with human rights standards.

To reinforce this argument, Professor John Ruggie, the UN Special Representative on business and human rights, developed the UN Guiding Principles on Business and Human Rights (the Guiding Principles) that were subsequently endorsed by the UN Human Rights Council.[63] The Guiding Principles impose

57 Morsink (1999) 241.

58 *Id.*, 245.

59 See: Preamble, UDHR.

60 Jordan J. Paust, "Human Rights Responsibilities of Private Corporations" (2002) 35 *Vanderbilt Journal of Transnational Law* 813; Jordan J. Paust, "The Other Side of Right: Private Duties under Human Rights Law" (1992) 5 *Harvard Human Rights Journal* 51.

61 Jordan J. Paust, "Human Rights Responsibilities of Private Corporations" (2002) 35 *Vanderbilt Journal of Transnational Law* 801.

62 *Id.*, 825.

63 UN Human Rights Council, *Human Rights and Transnational Corporations and Other Business Enterprises*, 16 June 2011, A/HRC/17/4.

obligations on companies to respect human rights, independently from the state's ability or willingness to protect human rights.[64] As Surya Deva notes, "due diligence is the cornerstone of executing the corporate responsibility to respect human rights."[65] Indeed, Principle 17 of the Guiding Principles prescribes that:

> In order to identify, prevent, mitigate, and account for how they address their adverse human rights impacts, business enterprises should carry out human rights due diligence. The process should include assessing actual and potential human rights impacts, integrating and acting upon the findings, tracking responses, and communicating how impacts are addressed.[66]

While the Guiding Principles are not legally binding per se, they reflect the international and domestic norms applicable to corporations and other businesses. As articulated in the UDHR, the primary point is not narrowly legal. Rather, the point is that from the beginning the drafters and adopters of the UDHR recognized it would take a "whole of society" approach to implementing human rights.

e. Promoting human dignity is the key to protecting the equal and inalienable rights of all members of the human family, and remains the foundation of freedom, justice, and peace in the world

Human dignity for everyone everywhere is the foundation of freedom, justice, and peace in the world. The Preamble of the UDHR declares that "recognition of the inherent dignity and of the equal and inalienable rights of all members of the human family is the foundation of freedom, justice, and peace in the world."[67] The central goal of the UDHR of promoting "freedom, justice, and peace in the world" is based upon a global recognition of the "inherent dignity and equal and inalienable rights" of all human beings. Indeed, the importance of this foundational principle was an important topic for discussions during the drafting process.

For example, René Cassin when discussing the right to freedom of conscience, emphasized that the right was "absolutely unconditional … it was this right to the freedom of conscience which gave the human person his worth and dignity."[68] When considering the importance of freedom and human dignity, Charles Malik suggested,

64 See Principle 11 of the UN Guiding Principles on Business and Human Rights. United Nations, "Guiding Principles on Business and Human Rights: Implementing the United Nations' 'Protect, Respect and Remedy' Framework." 2011.

65 Surya Deva, "Guiding Principles on Business and Human Rights: Implications for Companies" (2012) 9 *European Company Law* 106. See also: Tineke Lambooy, "Corporate Due Diligence as a Tool to Respect Human Rights" (2010) 28 *Netherlands Quarterly of Human Rights* 404.

66 Principle 17 of the UN Guiding Principles on Business and Human Rights. United Nations. "Guiding Principles on Business and Human Rights: Implementing the United Nations 'Protect, Respect and Remedy' Framework." 2011.

67 See Preamble of the UDHR.

68 Schabas (2013) 201.

> Man might live in a perfect state, have all material security, be free from all social maladjustments, and yet not be the man which the Charter of the United Nations had in mind, a man with a worth and a dignity of his own. This exact worth and dignity must be determined. Man must be able to think and choose freely and even to reject freely and to rebel freely.[69]

Mr. George Marshall, Representative of the US, stated,

> Freedom of thought, conscience and religion, freedom of opinion and expression, freedom from arbitrary arrest and detention, the right of a people to choose their own government, to take part in its work, and, if they become dissatisfied with it, to change it, the obligation of government to act through law – these are some of the elements that combine to give dignity and worth to the individual.[70]

Mr. Charles Theodore Te Water, Representative of South Africa,

> had questioned the advisability of the reference to dignity in article 1 since the various articles should be devoted to statements of fundamental rights whereas the dignity of the individual was a deeper and broader concept than a right. If the fundamental human rights were respected, the dignity of the individual would be automatically recognized.[71]

Mrs. Bodil Begtrup, Representative of Denmark, emphasized the importance of dignity,

> in order to lay stress on the dignity of the wife and mother, to indicate that husband and wife were on a footing of absolute equality, both legally and morally. It was also important to emphasize in article 14 the fact that the dignity of the human person could only be safeguarded if every possibility of discrimination was eliminated.[72]

René Cassin, when referring to the issue of justice, emphasized that

> there could be no question of issuing directives to sovereign States; but there were degrees between absolute equality and the denial of all rights, and it was the United Nations' duty to ensure not only that all human beings had juridical personality, but also that they should be guaranteed certain elementary rights indispensable to their wellbeing and to their dignity. The recognition of everyone as a person before the law was the first and most important step.[73]

69 *Id.*, 1490.
70 *Id.*, 2025.
71 *Id.*, 2149.
72 *Id.*, 2463.
73 *Id.*, 1742.

Mr. Carrera Andrade, Representative of Ecuador, indicated that "the historic moment had come to proclaim the dignity of man and his faith in the progress of society, as well as in legal standards which would lead him towards a new era of justice and culture."[74]

John Humphrey, in the Preamble of his first draft of the UDHR, identified the importance of peace for human dignity by stating that "there can be no human dignity unless war and the threat of war is abolished."[75] Mr. Katz-Suchy, Representative of Poland, emphasized that

> It was not sufficient merely to say that human rights had been violated during the war. It should be emphasized that violation of human rights and contempt of human dignity lay at the very roots of fascist ideology. The Declaration must condemn fascism first of all, and then make it impossible for fascism to rise again.[76]

Eleanor Roosevelt stressed that

> it was clear that the declaration was inspired by a sincere desire for peace. The declaration was based on the conviction that man must have the freedom to develop his personality to the full, and have his dignity respected. The fact that the declaration had the moral support of 58 nations would help in the adoption of the measures necessary for its implementation.[77]

Count Carton de Wiart, Representative of Belgium, emphasized that

> the essential merit of that declaration was to emphasize the high dignity of the human person after the outrages to which men and women had been exposed during the recent war. It was essential that the dignity of the human person should be safeguarded against the recurrence of such acts and also against the excessive risks of individualism and of State control.[78]

The Punta del Este Declaration reflects and reiterates the central role that protecting and promoting human dignity will have in the protection and promotion of human rights. If human dignity is not protected, human rights will not be protected either. If human dignity is protected, human rights will be protected.

74 *Id.*, 3079.
75 *Id.*, lxxxviii. See also: Robert Kolb, "The Relationship between International Humanitarian Law and Human Rights Law: A Brief History of the 1948 Universal Declaration of Human Rights and the 1949 Geneva Conventions" (1998) 324 *International Review of the Red Cross* 409.
76 *Id.*, 1996.
77 *Id.*, 3030.
78 *Id.*, 3044.

4 Article 2

Generating agreement and building common understanding

Article 2 reads as follows:

> The inherent dignity of every human being was the key idea that helped generate agreement and a common understanding at the time of the adoption of the UDHR about human rights of all people, in spite of diversity and deep differences, notwithstanding divergent political and legal systems.
>
> Human dignity for everyone everywhere is valuable as a point of departure for exploring and understanding the meaning of human rights, as a basis for finding common ground regarding human rights and consensus about their content and meaning. It provides an approach to building bridges between various normative justifications of human rights, including those with religious and secular theoretical groundings. Respecting human dignity for everyone everywhere facilitates discussions on different conceptions of shared values. Human dignity is a broad concept that nevertheless invites in-depth reflection within differing traditions and perspectives.
>
> Human dignity for all reminds us that human rights are universal, inalienable, indivisible, interdependent, and interrelated.

The following is an expanded explanation of each part of Article 2.

a. The inherent dignity of every human being was the key idea that helped generate agreement and a common understanding at the time of the adoption of the UDHR about human rights of all people, in spite of diversity and deep differences, notwithstanding divergent political and legal systems

At the time of drafting the UDHR in 1947 and 1948, the drafters spent considerable time and placed specific focus on agreeing upon a vocabulary and approach to the specification of human rights that could be widely embraced as being universal. This is because of the strong differences between delegates and the countries they represented that had to be overcome to create a document that

DOI: 10.4324/9781003207030-5

could be accepted by all.[1] Mary Ann Glendon summarizes the differences as a great "divide between the Soviet-bloc representatives and others at the first meeting. Other divisions were ominous, too – such as those between the philosophically inclined and the more practical-minded members; between representatives of small or weak nations and the major powers; and between proponents of enforceable instruments and supporters of a declaration of principles."[2]

Human dignity emerged as one of the key ideas that helped to generate agreement. Indeed, the Preamble of the UN Charter that explains the rationale for the creation of the United Nations includes an important reference to human dignity in the recitation of the purpose of the United Nations:

> We the peoples of the United Nations Determined to save succeeding generations from the scourge of war, which twice in our lifetime has brought untold sorrow to mankind, and to reaffirm faith in fundamental human rights, *in the dignity and worth of the human person*, in the equal rights of men and women and of nations large and small ...[3]

This rationale for the establishment of the United Nations, as well as the memory of the atrocities of World War II, became the guiding principle for the drafting of the UDHR.[4] At this time in 1945, the delegates felt an urgency to,

> Include an international bill of rights in the Charter of the United Nations. The national and international pressure for such a bill had been steadily building throughout World War II ... All this international and national pressure paid off when ... Secretary Stettinius accepted the idea that the United Nations Charter should include, if not an outright bill of rights, then certainly explicit references to the need for international recognition and protection of human rights.[5]

From this, the members of this United Nations formation decided to meet again to form the UN Human Rights Commission and further discuss actions for human rights.[6]

Dignity became the central concept of the UDHR. For example, P. C. Chang emphasized that "after the myopia of the last hundred and fifty years, nations were

1 Morsink (2009) 68–69.
2 Glendon (2001) 43.
3 UN Charter, Preamble (emphasis added).
4 In 1945, shortly before the UDHR drafting process began, representatives of 50 states met in San Francisco at the United Nations Conference on International Organization to compose the United Nations Charter from the proposals drafted by China, the Soviet Union, the UK and the US in late 1944. Roth (2018) 118.
5 Morsink (1999) 1–2.
6 Roth (2018) 118.

at last on the threshold of a new humanistic period. The bill envisaged should be based on the aspiration for a new humanism."[7] P. C. Chang stressed the need to:

> affirm and enlarge the difference existing between man and animal. A standard should be established with a view to elevating the concept of man's dignity and emphasizing the respect of man: that principle should be embodied in a preamble to the International Bill of Rights.[8]

He further emphasized that "the principle of human rights should be given universal application regardless of human level … a minimum standard as a means of increasing the stature of man as opposed to animal."[9]

Similarly, Charles Malik considered that in the UDHR, the United Nations was allowed to answer "What is man?" The declaration would provide meaning to the phrase "dignity and worth of the human person" in the Preamble of the Charter of the United Nations.[10] Charles Malik stated that he wanted to ensure that the phrase "human dignity" was given greater meaning,

> It would indeed be a dead letter if they refused to admit that the human person had the right to choose in full liberty, that is, without being exposed to reprisals or persecutions … [T]he human person had not been created for the sake of the State, but that the State existed rather for the sake of the human person. The Bill of Rights ought, therefore, to subordinate everything to the interest of the human person, even the State.[11]

Similarly, political and military leaders of the Allies during World War II had emphasized the importance of human dignity. For example, General Douglas MacArthur, aboard the USS *Missouri* in Tokyo Bay on September 2, 1945, at the time of Japan's surrender at the end of World War II, expressed his sentiments as follows:

> It is my earnest hope and indeed the hope of all mankind that from this solemn occasion a better world shall emerge out of the blood and carnage of the past – a world founded upon faith and understanding – *a world dedicated to the dignity of man* and the fulfillment of his most cherished wish – for freedom, tolerance and justice.[12]

Nevertheless, it was not primarily the Great Powers (the US, the UK, and the Soviet Union) that emerged from World War II that was the moving force behind

7 Schabas (2013) lxxxvii.
8 Schabas (2013) 170.
9 Schabas (2013) 170.
10 Schabas (2013) lxxxvii.
11 Schabas (2013) 201.
12 Douglas MacArthur (Vorin E. Whan, Jr., ed.), *A Soldier Speaks: Public Papers and Speeches of General of the Army Douglas MacArthur* (Praeger, 1965) 148–149 (emphasis added).

the UDHR. Rather, to a remarkable extent, it was small countries, many still yearning for freedom from colonial subjugation, adamant that human rights receive priority, along with non-governmental organizations, civil society groups, and religious groups. Today, some observers mistakenly characterize human rights as a Western imposition upon developing countries, but as will be explained in more detail below, that is not congruent with the history of why the human rights instruments came to be drafted. If anything, the exact opposite is closer to the truth.[13]

It is also important to recognize that the UDHR was not the work of starry-eyed idealists. It was the work of statesmen and stateswomen who had come through the fiery crucibles of not only World War II but World War I.[14] They had seen the horrors of the atrocities perpetrated by Nazi Germany and their effort to annihilate the Jewish race.[15] They knew the consequences of Japanese

13 When the UDHR was adopted, the United Nations membership was made up of 36% of representatives from North and South America, 27% from Europe, 24% from Asia, 6% from Africa, and 5% from the South Sea Islands. Morsink (1999) 96. However, "[a]s far as participation by developing countries in the framing of the Declaration is concerned, we have seen that it was by no means negligible. It is true that much of the world's population was not represented in the UN in 1948" – countries under colonial rule in Asia and Africa, as well as World War II's Axis powers were absent. Glendon (2001) 225. "But Chang [from China], Malik [from Lebanon], Romulo [from the Philippines], Mehta [from India], and Santa Cruz [from Chile] were among the most influential, active, and independent members of the Human Rights Commission. And members of the third committee … represented a wide variety of cultures." *Id.*

14 In direct response to the atrocities of World War I, the League of Nations was created, which eventually evolved into the United Nations. Glendon (2001) 3–4. In 1944, representatives from China, the UK, the US, and the Soviet Union met in Washington, D.C. to discuss the need to form an organization for peace and security. They invited countries that had similarly fought the Axis powers to send representatives to San Francisco in 1945, where they drew up the UN Chapter and chose to also create the UN Human Rights Commission to pave the way for the UDHR. Roth (2018) 118. The delegates remembered their motivation from the world wars throughout the drafting process. Among others, Geoffrey Wilson, a delegate from the UK, reminded the delegates "of the historical situation in which the Committee met. It was one, he said, where Germany and other enemy countries during the war had completely ignored what mankind had regarded as fundamental rights and freedoms. The [UN Human Rights] Committee met as a first step toward providing the maximum possible safeguard against that sort of thing in the future." Morsink (2009) 63. Similarly, Lakshimi Menon, representative of India, emphasized that the UDHR was "born from the need to reaffirm those rights after their violation during the war." Morsink (1999) 36.

15 The "legally sanctioned atrocities committed in Nazi Germany had caused many people to reevaluate the proposition that there is no higher law by which the laws of nation-states can be judged." Glendon (2001) 176. Indeed, throughout the whole process of drafting the UDHR, several representatives commented on their abhorrence of the human rights violations of World War II and their desire to address those issues with the UDHR. Pierre Ordonneau, Representative of France, felt it "was essential that the Declaration should at least recall the dangers of Nazism" and advocated for ensuring that the document stressed the duties of not only states or individuals but also the duties of groups to protect human rights, in Article 30 of the

imperialism.[16] This was a group of people who had been through an ordeal unlike anything most of us have experienced today. Thus, to suggest that the UDHR was the work of unrealistic romantics does a tremendous disservice to this group of people. However, while these individuals were not naïve idealists, there was indeed a profound idealism involved: an earned idealism that arose from the ashes of World War I and World War II.[17]

The drafting and debate were diverse and inclusive. It is important to recognize that this was not just a group of elite drafters, it was a process that was very

UDHR. Morsink (1999) 87. Similarly, Fernand Dehousse, Representative of Belgium, "was firmly convinced of the necessity to stop the activities of subversive groups and thus to prevent a repetition of the experience … immediately preceding the war." *Id.*, 88. Lastly, Charles Malik stressed the need to ensure that for wording the UDHR would refer to the need to "check … and prevent … the growth of nascent Nazi, fascist or other totalitarian ideologies." *Id.*, 87.

16 The Japanese were known to carry out mass extermination orders in cities they occupied. Most notable was the Nanking massacre of 1937, dubbed "one of the worst instances of mass extermination" and the "Symbol of Japanese Evil." Though the numbers are disputed, the Nanking War Crimes Tribunal puts those killed by Japanese troops at 190,000, over 28 mass slaughters and 150,000 in 858 sporadic killings where some were buried and burned alive. This was over a period of six weeks from December 1937 to January 1938. See Frank Jacob, "Banzai! and the Others Die – Collective Violence in the Rape of Nanking" in Michael J. Pfeiffer (ed.), *Global Lynching and Collective Violence, Vol 1: Asia, Africa and the Middle East* (University of Illinois Press, 2017); Iris Chang, *The Rape of Nanking. The Forgotten Holocaust of World War II* (Basic Books: New York, 2011) 5; Ian Buruma, "The Nanking Massacre as a Historical Symbol" in Fei Fei Li, Robert Sabella, and David Liu (eds.), *Nanking 1937: Memory and Healing* (M. E. Sharpe: Armonk, NY, 2002). See also the Sook Ching Massacre in Singapore. Kevin Blackburn, "The Collective Memory of the Sook Ching Massacre and the Creation of the Civilian War Memorial of Singapore" (2000) 73(2) *Journal of the Malaysian Branch of the Royal Asiatic Society* 73–75. http s://www.jstor.org/stable/41493428?seq=1> accessed 6 July 2020. Amongst other atrocities, the Japanese also forced women into sexual slavery. These "comfortwomen" were taken from Korea, China, Taiwan, Indonesia, Malaysia and the Philippines and had to sexually please up to 40 Japanese soldiers a day. Kazuko Watanabe, "Trafficking in Women's Bodies, Then and Now: The Issue of Military "Comfort Women" (1999) 27(1/2) *Women's Studies Quarterly* 20; Frank Jacob, "Banzai! And the Others Die: Collective Violence in the Rape of Nanking" in Michael J. Pfeiffer (ed.), *Global Lynching and Collective Violence, Vol 1: Asia, Africa and the Middle East* (University of Illinois Press, 2017). In addition, the Japanese sought to impose an Asian nationalism that was based on the "Japanese spirit." This meant condemning any forms of western influence, including the use of the English language and English-medium schools and instituting Japanese as lingua franca as well as the use of propaganda to cultivate Japanese ideals. See Victor Gosiengfiao, "The Japanese Occupation: 'The Cultural Campaign'" (1966) 14 (2) *Philippine Studies* 228–242; Paul H. Kratoska, *The Japanese Occupation of Malaya and Singapore, 1941–45: A Social and Economic History* (NUS Press, 2018).

17 Morsink claimed that "What the drafters discussed most is what rights they needed to list in order to protect individual human beings from abuses of state power such as Hitler had perpetrated." Morsink (2009) 130. In fact, "clauses and even whole articles of the Declaration were adopted simply because the drafters agreed that this would prevent another Holocaust." *Id.*, 58.

inclusive and wide-ranging. It began with an extensive survey of existing national and international rights instruments, including treaties, national constitutions, bills and charters of rights, and other relevant legislation.[18] The drafting process also included an extensive survey of experts and the general public about the scope of the document.[19]

The UDHR was aimed to become, as Mary Ann Glendon has explained, "an instrument, as well as the most prominent symbol, of changes that would amplify the voices of the weak in the corridors of power."[20] After all, the UDHR empowers individuals by emphasizing the rights that individuals can claim against their states.[21]

18 Morsink explained that: "Humphrey grounded his first draft in existing material and in the instructions he received from the First Session of the Commission and from the Economic and Social Council. He had before him a collection of drafts, from which he borrowed freely. This scavenging for the best articles from the various drafts made for an inclusive first draft and explains, among other things, why there are social, economic, and cultural rights in the Universal Declaration." Morsink (1999) 6. The collection included drafts from Cuba, the American Law Institute, the American Association for the United Nations, the American Jewish congress, the World Government Association, the Institut de Droit International, and the editors of *Free World*. See: Schabas (2013) 147; E/CN.4/W.16/p. 9–11. Glendon comments that "Roosevelt, Malik, and Chang were taken aback by the sheer volume of this material when they first met with him. Malik later confessed that the commissioners initially felt 'completely lost; we had no conception of how to proceed with the task entrusted to us.'" Glendon (2001) 50. See further: Schabas (2013) 111, 153, 333, 336.

19 Glendon states that this process included UNESCO recruiting "some of the leading thinkers of the day for a Committee on the Theoretical Bases of Human Rights." Glendon (2001) 51. This committee, which was formed in January 1947, wanted to be useful to the UN Human Rights Commission. *Id.* In March 1947, the group of philosophers sent "a questionnaire to statesmen and scholars around the world – including such notables as Mohandas Gandhi, Pierre Teilhard de Chardin, Benedetto Croce, Aldous Huxley, and Salvador de Madariaga – soliciting their views on the idea of a universal declaration of human rights." *Id.* Glendon adds that in June of 1947, "the UNESCO philosophers' committee was coming to some very practical conclusions. They had received about seventy responses to their questionnaire asking for reflections on human rights from Chinese, Islamic, Hindu, and customary law perspectives, as well as from American, European, and socialist points of view. The replies included letters from Mohandas Gandhi, French Jesuit paleontologist Pierre Teilhard de Chardin, Italian philosopher Benedetto Croce, and *Brave New World* author Aldous Huxley." *Id.*, 73. Glendon claims that "the results of the UNESCO survey were encouraging: they indicated that the principles underlying the draft Declaration were present in many cultural and religious traditions, though not always expressed in terms of rights. Somewhat to the UNESCO group's surprise, the lists of basic rights and values submitted by their far-flung correspondents were broadly similar." *Id.*, 76.

20 Glendon (2001) xvi. See Louis Henkin, "Human Rights: Ideology and Aspiration, Reality, and Prospect" in Samantha Power and Graham Allison (eds.), *Realizing Human Rights: Moving from Inspiration to Impact* (St. Martin's Press: New York, 2000) 3, 12.

21 While the UDHR is "aimed at *prevention* rather than punishment," Glendon claims that, "[t]ogether with the Nuremberg Principles of international criminal law developed by the Allies in 1946 for the trials of German and Japanese war criminals and the 1948 Genocide Convention, the Universal Declaration of Human Rights became a pillar of a new international system under which a nation's treatment of its own

It primarily places duties upon states to protect and limitations on the way states and state actors can treat those subject to their jurisdiction.[22]

Importantly, the UDHR introduces the idea that human beings, and not just states, are the subjects of international law.[23] The drafters intended to forestall the repeat of Holocaust-type abominations through formulating an international (later changed to universal) bill of rights, according to a view that all human beings are "members of one and the same family of mankind, each one of them born with inherent human rights."[24] This bill of rights would elevate the individual above domestic law and as a subject of international law.[25] As René Cassin states, the UDHR

> [C]ontribute[d] something new: the individual [became] a subject of international law in respect of his life and liberty; principles are affirmed, side by side with those already laid down by the majority of national laws, which no national or international authority had hitherto been able to proclaim, let alone enforce.[26]

Since the treaty of Westphalia in 1648, which largely ended the European wars of religion, international law had been viewed as a matter of the relations between states as a secularization of relations between states began to emerge.[27] However,

citizens was no longer immune from outside scrutiny." Glendon (2001) xvi. See para. 6 of the Preamble, UDHR.

22 Pinghua Sun states that the UDHR "makes a clear and detailed list of human's freedoms and basic rights; on the other hand, it set responsibilities and obligations for the states, which become the moral regulations for member states in political government." Pinghua Sun (2018) 354. Glendon cautions that although "[t]he Declaration is rightly hailed for establishing that nations are accountable to others for the way they treat their own people, the fact is that international institutions can never provide first-line protection for victims of rights violations." Glendon (2001) 237.

23 Morsink (2009) 149.

24 Morsink (2009) 149.

25 *Id.*, 78–79.

26 Economic and Social Council, Commission on Human Rights Report to the Economic and Social Council on the Second Session, at 20, UN Doc. E/600 (1948).

27 The Treaty of Westphalia helped to officially end the Thirty Years' War that affected Northern and Central Europe. Karel Blei, *Freedom of Religion and Belief: Europe's Story* (Van Gorcum Ltd., 2002) 79. (Later cited as Blei (2002)). The Thirty Years' War was part of ongoing conflicts over the spread of Protestantism in countries where Roman Catholicism had been the dominant religion. *Id.*, 84. Cole Durham, founding director of the International Center for Law and Religion Studies at the J. Reuben Clark Law School and Brett Scharffs, the current director, said that international religious freedom's "earliest incarnations were far different from and much more restrictive than current protections." Durham and Scharffs (2019) 80. For example, "[t]he Peace of Augsburg is the source of the famous principle of *cuius regio, eius religio* (whose realm, his religion), which shaped the religious landscape of Europe for centuries." *Id.* The Religious Peace of Augsburg (1555) created a system where "the religion of the prince … will also be the religion of all the inhabitants of his territory." Blei (2002) 83. The only permitted religions were Roman Catholicism and one form

the Declaration not only identified human beings as subjects of international law, but also challenged that long-held assumption that international law is primarily a matter of state-to-state relations, and explicitly rejected the claim that human rights are only a matter of domestic concern.[28]

of Protestantism: Lutheranism (Calvinism was excluded). *Id.* However, conflict over which religion dominated the state was especially great in Germany, where princes of both the Roman Catholic and Protestant churches (mainly Lutheranism and Calvinism) formed rival leagues in attempts to protect themselves from one another. *Id.*, 84. Because Roman Catholicism was still the dominant religion, Protestants did not feel protected in Germany. *Id.* This tension is what triggered the Thirty Years' War, after Calvinist Bohemians in Prague rose up in rebellion against Roman Catholic rule. *Id.* Mary Ellen O'Connell, Research Professor of International Dispute Resolution for the Kroc Institute for International Peace Studies at the University of Notre Dame, explained that: "By 1648, European rulers were ready to end their long war and to agree to limits on resort to force. The peace treaties, known as the 'Peace of Westphalia', were negotiated over a period of three years in the 'first European Congress'. The treaties committed the various kings, princes, and noblemen to refrain from resort to war in religious causes and to collectively enforce the treaties' provisions." Mary E. O'Connell, "Peace and War" in Bardo Fassbender and Anne Peters (eds.), *The Oxford Handbook of the History of International Law* (Oxford University Press: Oxford, 2012) 276–277. According to Durham and Scharffs, the basic principle of "whose realm, his religion" – the fact that the prince determined the religion of the state – "was reinforced and clarified by the Peace of Westphalia, concluded in the treaties of Osnabrück and Münster in 1648. The Westphalia accords accepted the Reformed (Calvinist) tradition as well as the Lutheran and Catholic religions … In general, the focus of the first phase was on freedom of religion for rulers and states, and the provision for individuals remained quite restrictive. This stage was marked by the emergence of a secular international order that served for years to come as a technique for achieving religious peace." Durham and Scharffs (2019) 80. O'Connell stressed that, "Arthur Nussbaum called [the Peace of Westphalia] the 'first attempt at international organization for peace.'" Mary E. O'Connell, "Peace and War" in Bardo Fassbender and Anne Peters (eds.), *The Oxford Handbook of The History of International Law* (Oxford University Press: Oxford, 2012) 277. O'Connell adds that "the new peace order contained elements for a new challenge to legal restraints on war. The secularization of the legal regime and the establishment of equal, sovereign States undermined conceptions of community and community law. '[T]he Peace of Westphalia, while paying lip service to the idea of a Christian commonwealth, merely ushers in the era of sovereign absolutist states which recognized no superior authority.'" *Id.*, 277.

28 Nikolas Politis, Greek jurist and diplomat, long before the UDHR, has emphasized the changes to the way international law was being understood. According to Winter and Prost, Politis believed that "international law had come to a turning point. It used to be the case that international law was essentially and exclusively the law of the states; individual people were ignored. It used to be the case as well that states acted as if they were 'sovereign moral persons, who were not subject to the authority of the rule of law, save when through their free and independent assent, they accepted its compulsory force.'" Jay Winter and Antoine Prost, *René Cassin and Human Rights: From the Great War to the Universal Declaration* (Cambridge University Press: Cambridge, 2013) 223. They cited Politis stating that "The dominant feature of our times is the intertwining of human relations both within and across borders." *Id.*, 223. Winter and Prost claimed that "Individuals now mattered in international law, and no state stood outside of its reach. 'What will assure the final triumph of this new conception of international law', [Politis] wrote, 'is the ruin into which the alternative

When the UN Charter was drafted in 1945, the great Powers – the United States, Great Britain, and the Soviet Union – showed little interest in the human rights project.[29] While the UN Charter briefly mentions human dignity and human rights, it does not give content to the idea of human rights.[30] However, the Allied Powers had described the war as a fight for freedom and democracy,

principle of classical theory – that of sovereignty – will fall irreversibly.' Only if a new idea penetrated the fog of legal and political inertia could an international organization like the League of Nations survive and another war be averted." *Id.*, 223–224 (internal citations omitted). Similarly, the drafters of the UDHR grappled with the question of state sovereignty as they discussed the approach to be adopted in the UDHR. Morsink describes the drafters of the UDHR as globalists or cosmopolitans, and not internationalists. Morsink (2009) 149. To Morsink, this meant several of the drafters' minds were set on "individual human beings," and nation-states were "no more (and no less) than the most important vehicles for the delivery of the enjoyment of people's ... inherent birthrights." *Id.* René Cassin said that the Third Committee's "duty was to proclaim to the whole world that there was not a single human being who could not possess both rights and obligations." Morsink (1999) 44–45. However, the Soviet representatives consistently cautioned against taking sovereignty away from the state and giving power to an international organization. See Glendon (2001) 71, 85, 110. The British delegate Sir Alexander Cadogan also pushed back on the idea of infringing on state sovereignty, because "international concerns for human rights might lead the future organization to criticize internal matters of the Member States." Åshild Samnøy, "The Origins of the Universal Declaration of Human Rights" in Gudmundur Alfredsson and Asbjørn Eide (eds.), *The Universal Declaration of Human Rights* (Martinus Nijhoff Publishers, 1999) 4. Yet even with differing opinions on state sovereignty, Morsink writes that "[m]ost of the delegations had little difficulty voting for many of the rights in the Declaration, for more often than not their own national constitutions also contained the particular right to be voted upon." Morsink (1999) 72.

29 Representatives from the Great Powers were united in their desire to win the war, yet their goals and concerns for peace differed. At the suggestion of the United States, human rights were mentioned once in the draft proposal for the UN Charter. Glendon (2001) 6. The original Great Powers (the US, the UK, and the Soviet Union) decided, however, before China arrived, "to bury any references to human rights deep within the text [of the UN Charter] and confine it to social and economic cooperation." Schabas (2013) ixxv. The Soviets' chief concern was to "protect the frontiers of the motherland" and perhaps establish a "'US-UK-Soviet hegemony in international affairs.'" Glendon (2001) 5 (internal citations omitted). While Churchill was more concerned with "post-war cooperation among the Western European nations than in a world-wide organization." *Id.*

30 The drafters of the UN Charter left out the language regarding human rights that were present in the Atlantic Charter and the Declaration of the United Nations, as well as an American proposal to list human rights as one of the main purposes of the UN Charter. Schabas (2013) ixxv. The final draft of the UN Charter contained only one reference to human rights. *Id.* However, documents from the Dumbarton Oaks Proposals do contain several proposed amendments from Mexico, Panama, and a handful of other countries clearly emphasizing human rights. All were rejected. UN Conference on International Organization, San Francisco, 1945, Dumbarton Oaks Proposals for a General International Organization, UN Doc. 1 G/1 (Apr. 25, 1945) 176, 266, 271.

and those who longed most for such freedom were slow to forget the world they envisioned.[31]

Today, it comes as a surprise to some people to learn that it was not the Western powers (primarily the US, the USSR, the UK, and France) who were most insistent on the United Nations creating a detailed instrument regarding human rights. This is in part because the Great Powers were primarily concerned with matters involving peace and security.[32] It is also because each of these countries had reasons for wanting to not place human rights issues front and center on the international agenda. In the post-World War II period, the United States was not especially interested in human rights because of its domestic issues surrounding race. At the time, the United States was facing the issue of widespread segregation and racial discrimination. The promulgation of human rights at the time would serve as a basis for uncomfortable claims of racial equality.[33] The Soviet Union was

31 Indeed, Stalin's main concern at a meeting in Yalta – following the meeting at Dumbarton Oaks – between the Big Three leaders was to "reach a firm agreement with the United States and Britain to protect his country from any resurgence of German military ambitions." Glendon (2001) 7. He held disdain for the vision of an "inclusive 'universal organization'" as part of the discussion at Yalta. *Id.*, 9. Churchill in turn hoped to "dilute the Soviet Union's power in the European continent" by proposing that France should have an active role in the UN Security Council to help police postwar Europe. *Id.*, 7. France was added to the UN Security Council as the fifth permanent member (China was the fourth). *Id.* During this debate concerning the shape and purpose of the United Nations, the "promotion of fundamental rights and freedoms was far from central" until the "details of the Nazi reign of terror" came to light. *Id.*, 9.

32 According to Glendon, "the Great Powers had gone along with the human rights language in the UN Charter, but they made sure that the Charter also protected their national sovereignty." Glendon (2001) 19. Indeed, Article 2 of the UN Charter states that "nothing contained in the present Charter shall authorize the United Nations to intervene in matters which are essentially within the domestic jurisdiction of any State, or shall require the Members to submit such matters to settlement under the present Charter; but this principle shall not prejudice the application of enforcement measures under Chapter VII." The only exception to this being limited situations where the UN Security Council determines that international peace and security are threatened. Glendon (2001) 19. Samnø stressed that "The extent of genuine concern for human rights is difficult to judge, but an important motive – in particular for the most powerful States – was the need to avoid criticism and, at the same time, to have an opportunity to criticize others." Åshild Samnøy, "The Origins of the Universal Declaration of Human Rights" in Gudmundur Alfredsson and Asbjørn Eide (eds.), *The Universal Declaration of Human Rights* (Martinus Nijhoff Publishers, 1999) 9. "Thus, a particular policy on human rights might have been adopted mainly as a strategic means to obtain a superior goal." *Id.*, 8–9.

33 Carlos Romulo and other delegates "pressed in San Francisco for a position on racial discrimination – much to the discomfort of the United States and some colonial powers. Their combined effort, supported by China, France, and the Soviet Union, produced the Charter's radical challenge to the social status quo throughout the world: an emphatic statement that human rights b`elong to everyone 'without distinction as to race, sex, language, or religion.'" Glendon (2001) 13. The issue was further raised during the drafting process of the UDHR by the Soviet Union. Schabas (2013) 1520.

uninterested in human rights because the collectivist ideology of communism prescribed that the individual's interest must be subordinate to the community's interest.[34] Additionally, Great Britain did not prioritize the human rights project because it was hopeful of preserving what it could of its global empire.[35]

The most vocal proponents of the human rights project were delegates from countries that were subject to imperial powers. For example, Carlos Romulo of the Philippines, a statesman, diplomat, and journalist said that he would not be deterred from pressing issues of human dignity. He wrote that he became "a nuisance, a gadfly, a pest. I prowled corridors, buttonholed delegates, cornered unwilling victims in hotel lobbies, and men's rooms."[36] This quotation illustrates the sentiment that there was an adamancy, an advocacy, an insistence on holding the Great Powers accountable to the promise of what they said the war had been about. Additionally, as appalling photographs from the Nazi concentration camps were becoming widely circulated, the US agreed, somewhat reluctantly, to the creation of a special committee on human rights.[37]

34 During the early stages of the drafting process, the Soviet Union sent a representative that did not have the power to vote. During the Geneva draft review by the Human Rights Commission, the Soviet Union sent a new representative, Alexei P. Pavlov who, according to Glendon "proved more difficult to deal with than any of his predecessors." Glendon (2001) 110. He said his government could not accept any part of the Geneva draft "because it was riddled with serious defects, including some provisions 'which would violate the principle of sovereignty of states.'" *Id.* See also Schabas (2013) 1486–1487. Pavlov complained that the draft overlooked the "individual's obligations to the state." *Id.* At the adoption of the UDHR, the Soviet bloc made its last effort to "have the matter put over to the next session of the General Assembly." Glendon (2001) 167. While acknowledging the "many good features" of the UDHR, the Soviet bloc believed it was "still seriously defective". *Id.* Though the basis of their objections were inconsistent, they did believe the "project was mostly empty words, but it was also a threat to national sovereignty." *Id.* With four minutes until midnight the president of the UN "called the roll and drew by lot the name of the country to vote first, Burma. After Burma voted yes, Byelorussia, next in order, abstained, as did the other members of the Soviet bloc when their turns came up – Czechoslovakia, Poland, the Ukraine, the USSR, and Yugoslavia." *Id.*, 169.

35 During negotiations in 1943 and 1944 between the Great Powers, "the British delegate, Sir Alexander Cadogan, was the most profound critic of any inclusion of the human rights issue. His main objection was simple: international concerns for human rights might lead the future organization to criticize internal matters of the Member States. The reality behind this argument was British colonial policy." Åshild Samnøy, "The Origins of the Universal Declaration of Human Rights" in Gudmundur Alfredsson and Asbjørn Eide (eds.), *The Universal Declaration of Human Rights* (Martinus Nijhoff Publishers, 1999) 4. In 1945, in San Francisco, Churchill sided with Stalin's disdain for a universal organization. "As prime minister of a country with a vast if crumbling colonial empire … Churchill became agitated" when Stettinius, the recently appointed secretary of state for the US, "broached the subject of establishing UN trusteeships in non-self-governing territories (a euphemism for colonies)." Churchill swore that "'not one scrap of British territory' would ever be included in such arrangements if he could prevent it." Glendon (2001) 9.

36 Glendon (2001) 12.

37 *Id.*, 18.

President Harry Truman insisted that Eleanor Roosevelt, the still-mourning widow of President Franklin Delano Roosevelt, join the US delegation to the United Nations.[38] Many politicians in the US opposed Eleanor Roosevelt's appointment because of her inexperience in international relations.[39] Others opposed her appointment because of her liberal and outspoken nature.[40] Indeed, she herself doubted her capacity to tackle such a project as human rights.[41]

Nevertheless, when she agreed to spearhead the human rights project, she threw herself into the task with tremendous energy and hard work.[42] She used

38 Glendon attributes President Truman's reasoning to his concern with "keeping the prestige of the Roosevelt name associated with his administration", saying he was less concerned with the possible risks of the appointment. Glendon (2001) 22. "Truman was the last person in the world to be dissuaded by Mrs. Roosevelt's inexperience in foreign affairs. When he was thrust into the highest office in the land preceding April, he had to work hard to bring himself up to speed on foreign policy." *Id.* Joseph P. Lash, a friend to Eleanor Roosevelt, said Roosevelt thought "the president was wise ... in thinking that someone connected with F.D.R ... would remind the delegates" just by her being in London, of F. D.R.'s "hopes and aims for the new international organization." Joseph P. Lash, *Eleanor Roosevelt: A Friend's Memoir* (Doubleday, 1964) 297.

39 Glendon remarks that the "opposition to [Eleanor Roosevelt's] nomination included not only prominent Republicans such as John Foster Dulles, who would later be Dwight Eisenhower's Secretary of State, but distinguished Democrats, including Senator William Fulbright." Glendon (2001) 22. John Foster Dulles viewed Roosevelt as too inexperienced, while Fulbright "was concerned that [Roosevelt's] presence on the delegation would signal a lack of seriousness about the UN." *Id.* Foreign policy professionals also feared that "the outspoken former First Lady would be a loose cannon in her new environment. As a political activist and popular journalist, she had developed a formidable reputation for her independence of mind and determination to champion progressive causes." *Id.*

40 After her approval by the United States Senate, Eleanor Roosevelt remarked, "[a]s it turned out, some senators did protest to the President against my nomination but only one, Senator Theodore G. Bilbo of Mississippi, actually voted against me. He had been critical of statements I made previously in regard to discrimination against Negroes, but when some newspapermen in Washington asked him why he opposed my nomination he replied only that he had so many reasons he would have to write a book in order to cover them all. Anyway, my nomination was confirmed by the Senate, and I still marvel at it." Eleanor Roosevelt, *The Autobiography of Eleanor Roosevelt* (Da Capo Press, 1958) 299–300.

41 When President Harry Truman sent a message to Eleanor Roosevelt in December 1945 asking her to serve as a member of the United Nations delegation, Roosevelt's first reaction was this: "Oh no! It would be impossible! ... How could I be a delegate to help organize the United Nations when I have no background in international meetings?" Eleanor Roosevelt, *The Autobiography of Eleanor Roosevelt* (Da Capo Press, 1958) 299. Despite this reaction, she said later, "At last I accepted in fear and trembling. But I might not have done so if I had known at that time that President Truman could only nominate me as a delegate and that the nomination would have to be approved by the United States Senate, where certain senators would disapprove of me." *Id.* In a letter to her daughter, Anna, Roosevelt said, "Say prayers that I'm really useful on this job for I feel very inadequate." Glendon (2001) 25.

42 Glendon commented that Roosevelt had a great willingness to work coupled with a "quickness in grasping the gist of the technical material [that] did not go unappreciated" by her fellow members of the US delegation. Glendon (2001) 27.

preparation and organizational skills to compensate for what she lacked in ready knowledge and experience.[43] She proved to be a powerful and valuable asset to the US delegation as well as to the UN's efforts to create the UDHR.[44]

Her most effective diplomatic strategy involved inviting key participants to her home. She had a town house on Washington Square Park in Greenwich Village where she would invite Commission members to enjoy tea, discuss the relevant issues, and eventually engage in preliminary negotiations. By the time the formal negotiations commenced, a variety of views had already been exchanged during the social aspects of the delegates' visits, and thus they were better positioned to make progress.[45]

43 Eleanor Roosevelt, *The Autobiography of Eleanor Roosevelt* (Da Capo Press, 1958) 303. See Åshild Samnøy, "The Origins of the Universal Declaration of Human Rights" in Gudmundur Alfredsson and Asbjørn Eide (eds.), *The Universal Declaration of Human Rights* (Martinus Nijhoff Publishers, 1999) 6–7.

44 Eleanor Roosevelt chaired the UN Commission on Human Rights during the whole drafting process of the UDHR. Åshild Samnøy, "The Origins of the Universal Declaration of Human Rights" in Gudmundur Alfredsson and Asbjørn Eide (eds.), *The Universal Declaration of Human Rights* (Martinus Nijhoff Publishers, 1999) 6. According to Åshild Samnøy, who has widely written on the origins of the UDHR, "Roosevelt's leadership was unchallenged. Her international prestige ... attracted a great deal of attention to the work of the Human Rights Commission." *Id.*, 6. "[Roosevelt] organized her time well and she ruled over the Commission with impatience and energy. Thanks to her energy, the Declaration was drafted quickly. Eleanor Roosevelt's greatest contribution to the drafting of the Universal Declaration of Human Rights lay in her effectiveness and speed in directing its affairs." *Id.*, 6–7. In contrast, Roth says, "It is true that Roosevelt played a very important role by virtue of her personality and her diplomatic abilities, but she was not involved in writing the actual text to the same degree as other members of the core drafting team." Roth (2018) 129. One of her colleagues said that Roosevelt was "the hardest-working delegate of all and the one who made the least demands on her colleagues." Joseph P. Lash, *Eleanor Roosevelt: A Friend's Memoir* (Doubleday, 1964) 303. John Humphrey, the delegate from Canada, believed that such "prestige was one of the chief assets of the Human Rights Commission in the early years." *Id.*, 4. Senator Vandenberg proclaimed all over Washington that, "She was a stateswoman," partly because she had supported "his pleas for a stronger line with the Russians than Byrnes had been willing to take." *Id.*, 302. Lash writes that "to the world, and especially the younger nations, [Roosevelt] had become the symbol of this 'common standard of achievement for all peoples and all nations' as the General Assembly proclaimed the Declaration." *Id.*, 303.

45 Eleanor Roosevelt's unique contribution to the Human Rights Commission "consisted of fostering and providing a setting for cross-cultural understanding" through dinners and tea parties "[enabling] delegates to get to know one another as human beings and to exchange views off the record." Glendon (2001) 114. When Roosevelt, Chang, Malik, and Humphrey were commissioned to write the preliminary draft of the UDHR – which at that time was supposed to be an international bill of rights – Roosevelt invited the group "for tea at her Washington Square apartment." *Id.*, 45, 47. Roosevelt recalls the experience: "[T]hinking that our work might be helped by an informal atmosphere, I asked this small group to meet at my apartment for tea ... As we settled down over the teacups, one of them made a remark with philosophic implications, and a heated discussion ensued." Eleanor Roosevelt, *The Autobiography*

The UN Commission on Human Rights appointed representatives of 18 nations tasked with drafting the UDHR.[46] These countries were Australia, Belgium, Byelorussia, Chile, China, Egypt, France, India, Iran, Lebanon, Panama, Philippines, Ukraine, the Soviet Union, the United Kingdom, the United States, Uruguay, and Yugoslavia.[47] The careful composition of this list is rather remarkable, especially considering that at the time of the adoption of the UDHR at the end of 1948 there were only 58 countries in the United Nations.[48] The UN Human Rights Commission included nations aligned with the western democracies as well as with the Soviet Union; countries from the north and the south; developed as well as developing countries; and both Christian, Hindu, and Islamic majority countries as well as countries with explicitly secular ideologies. Indeed, it would have been difficult to come up with a more careful, nuanced, and balanced group of countries than those that the UN Human Rights Commission identified and appointed.

Eleanor Roosevelt was elected chair of the UN Human Rights Commission and the 18-member delegation almost immediately found that drafting an international bill of human rights as a whole was challenging.[49] Consequently, a drafting committee was organized. The Commission voted unanimously to have the first

of Eleanor Roosevelt (Da Capo Press, 1958) 316–317. Several comments were exchanged regarding Western ideas, Thomas Aquinas, and Confucianism. *Id.* Glendon claims that Roosevelt "saw from the beginning that there were two individuals on the Commission who were going to be the dominant intellectual figures." Pinghua Sun (2018) 66. Those dominant figures were Charles Malik and P. C. Chang. *Id.* Glendon believes that because Roosevelt saw that Malik and Chang's "personalities were going to be in tension with one another … she very wisely said, 'It's better to get these two in a small group where they can get to know each other better because they are going to have to work and cooperate if everything is going to succeed.'" *Id.*

46 See Åshild Samnøy, "The Origins of the Universal Declaration of Human Rights" in Gudmundur Alfredsson and Asbjørn Eide (eds.), *The Universal Declaration of Human Rights* (Martinus Nijhoff Publishers, 1999) 6.

47 *Id.*

48 See United Nations, "Growth in United Nations Membership, 1945–Present" https://www.un.org/en/sections/member-states/growth-united-nations-membership-1945-present/index.html

49 The first meeting of the Commission proved to be somewhat contentious and confusing as delegates debated the duties of the UN Human Rights Commission and how to start on an international bill of human rights. See Glendon (2001) 35–41. Cold War politics often resulted in finger-pointing by the Soviets and the United States on each other's weaknesses, petitions poured in from all over the world from people who claimed they were victims of human rights violations and the UN had no mechanism for dealing with such petitions, and philosophical debates concerning the whether the individual was recognizable under the law or only as part of society all slowed the progress of a written bill of rights. *Id.* A cartoon of the day shows members of the Human Rights Commission caricatured "as a class of schoolboys, with Mrs. Roosevelt as the teacher, saying, 'Now, children, all together: "The rights of the individual are above the rights of the state."'" Glendon remarks that "the cartoon captures the disarray that often afflicted the UN committees." *Id.*, 42 (internal citations omitted).

draft of the UDHR written by Eleanor Roosevelt, Charles Malik,[50] Lebanese philosopher, diplomat, and secretary of the commission, and P. C. Chang,[51] Chinese philosopher, diplomat, and playwright who served as vice-chairman of the commission.[52] John Humphrey, a Canadian international law expert assigned to

50 Charles Malik was the representative from Lebanon, with a Ph.D. in philosophy from Harvard University. Pinghua Sun (2018) 84. "He served almost at all important positions in UN affairs: Rapporteur of the Commission on Human Rights (1947–1948), President of the Economic and Social Council (1948), Chairman of the Commission on Human Rights (1951), and the thirteenth President of the General Assembly (1958–1959). *Id.*, 85. Charles Malik "became rapporteur, or secretary, responsible ... for summarizing and preparing official reports on the committee's work." Glendon (2001) 33. In 1948, Malik became the "president of the Economic and Social Council, to which the Commission had to submit its draft Declaration. That fall he was elected chairman of the UN's Third Committee (the Social, Humanitarian, and Cultural Affairs Committee), which had to present the Declaration for approval by the UN General Assembly at its December meeting in Paris." *Id.*, 124. He found himself in an interesting position, "wearing three big hats as the Declaration moved through its crucial final stages in the fall of 1948." *Id.* Malik says he "found himself 'as Rapporteur submitting to myself, as President of the Economic and Social Council at its summer session in Geneva, the draft of the declaration prepared by the Commission, and then submitting, as President of ECOSOC, again to myself as Chairman of the Third Committee, the draft text as passed on by ECOSOC.'" *Id.* According to Morsink, "Charles Malik and General Carlos Romulo from the Philippines were ... among the most influential of drafters." Morsink (2017) 31. Glenn Mitoma, Assistant Professor of Human Rights and Education and Director of the Thomas J. Dodd Research Center at University of Connecticut, said of Malik that "[w]ith the possible exception of John Humphrey, no individual contributed more" as Malik played a crucial role in making sure the covenants on human rights did not stall out when he replaced Eleanor Roosevelt as chair of the Commission on Human Rights. Glenn Mitoma, ***Human Rights and the Negotiation of American Power*** (University of Pennsylvania Press, 2013) 104. See generally Glendon (2001) 124–130.

51 Chang has been described as a "globetrotter" throughout the world due to his assignments as a diplomat and then as a representative from China for the United Nations. Roth (2018) 100. Roth quotes Chang's son's journal entry describing what he saw as he accompanied his father to the Declaration drafting meetings at Lake Success, "As soon as any questions came up relating to formulation or logical organization, the other members of the working group expected my father to be able to give an answer." *Id.*, 115. "Although Mrs. Roosevelt was the chair, in reality it was my father who managed the greater part of the negotiations." *Id.* According to Glendon, "Chang played a mediating role time and again throughout the third committee debates in the fall of 1948. The Chinese ambassador to the UN was uniquely suited for his role as explainer of the Declaration to the committee's diverse membership." Glendon (2001) 33. Of Chang, Professor Pinghua Sun said, "It was P. C. Chang who proposed the master plan for drafting the Declaration, which was readily approved by the committee. He was in fact a mastermind or principal architect of the Declaration, contributing to every item in drafting the Declaration using his wisdom and knowledge." Pinghua Sun (2018) 31. He also comments on Chang's mediating role during the Third Committee debates in the fall of 1948: "The Chinese ambassador to the UN was uniquely suited for his role as explainer of the Declaration to the committee's diverse membership." *Id.*, 147. See generally *Id.*, 22–24, 27.

52 Other members of the Commission could submit "orally or in writing, any observations and suggestions" or be enlisted to help with the draft by the chairman. *Id.*

act as the director of the Human Rights Division of the UN Secretariat, assisted the three drafters and was tasked with providing the first draft of the UDHR.[53] In time, the drafting committee was expanded to include René Cassin, the legal genius of Free France; Colonel William Hodgson of Australia; Hernan Santa Cruz of Chile; Geoffrey Wilson representing the United Kingdom; and Vladimir Koretsky (followed by other Soviet officials) as the representative of the Soviet Union.[54]

For nearly two years, the drafting committee and the UN Human Rights Commission as a group repeatedly revised and debated the document that became the Universal Declaration of Human Rights. The document passed through multiple committees and votes, eventually earning the unanimous approval of the UN General Assembly.[55]

Setting aside the difficulties of those who were trying to undermine the attempt to reach an agreement, including the Soviet representatives, it was difficult to find common ground between philosophical, ideological, political, and religious perspectives.[56]

53 John Humphrey played an interesting role "as a member of the UN bureaucracy rather than of the Commission itself." Glendon (2001) 43. Humphrey was at nearly all of the Commission meetings, and his role was "as important as that of most commissioners in the shaping of the Universal Declaration." *Id.* He was also appointed to be the "first director of the Secretariat's Division on Human Rights." Morsink (2009) 70. While director, he was asked to write the first draft of the Declaration. *Id.* According to Mary Ann Glendon, "the decision to entrust the first draft [of the UDHR] to Humphrey made good sense. He and his multinational staff had been collecting and studying pertinent material from all over the world. Humphrey himself was well grounded in both civil and common law and fluent in French and English. [H]e had already built a solid academic reputation as the author of several learned articles on international law and a monograph dealing with the relations among nations in the Americas." *Id.*, 48.

54 See Glendon (2001) 49. The Soviet Representative changed multiple times throughout the drafting process and included: Valentin Tepliakov, Vladimir Koretsky, Alexander Bogomolov, and Alexei Pavlov. See *Id.*, 54, 83, 110.

55 Jakob Th. Möller, "The Universal Declaration of Human Rights: How the Process Started" in Gudmundur Alfredsson and Asbjørn Eide (eds.), *The Universal Declaration of Human Rights* (Martinus Nijhoff Publishers, 1999) 23. See *Id.*, 25, documenting the timeline of the drafts of the UDHR as it passed through each committee.

56 By replacing the original delegate Valentin Tepliakov with Vladimir Koretsky, the Soviets seemed to be taking the human rights initiative more seriously. Glendon (2001) 54. "Koretsky was the USSR's most distinguished international lawyer." *Id.* Neither Tepliakov or Koretsky received specific instructions from the government in Moscow. *Id.*, 59. However, Koretsky made his opinion clear concerning "threat[s] to the principle of national sovereignty." *Id.* To internationalize rights already found in national constitutions, like the right to freedom of movement and the right to a nationality, Koretsky warned, was "pushing the Commission 'beyond the limit of international law.'" *Id.* (internal citations omitted). He told the Russian Foreign Ministry in a report that he was worried the Declaration might "'make it easier to intervene in the internal affairs of sovereign states.'" *Id.*, 71 (internal citations omitted). His suggestion was that the Soviet Union submit its own draft before the next

For example, some delegates wanted to include references to God or a creator as the basis of human rights.[57] Other delegates insisted that references to a deity

meeting of the Human Rights Commission and "that the USSR should support an international bill of rights in the form of a multilateral convention to which the signers could append any reservations they deemed necessary." *Id.* At the Geneva meeting of the Human Rights Commission in 1947, the Soviets sent another new representative, Alexander Bogomolov, who proved "easier to work with than his predecessors," and perhaps the "most cooperative of all the men the Soviet Union ever sent," according to John Humphrey. *Id.*, 83. Bogomolov kept the Soviet Foreign Minister V. M. Molotov informed throughout the Geneva meeting, making sure that the Soviet Union was protected "from outside meddling in its internal affairs." *Id.*, 85. When it came time for the UN Human Rights Commission to vote on the Geneva draft, the USSR abstained because the draft was too vague and did not include "references to enforcement by the state." *Id.*, 93–94. Bogomolov also urged the Soviet Foreign Minister that a draft should be submitted by the USSR. *Id.*, 97. When Alexei Pavlov, yet another Soviet representative, was sent by the Soviet Union, his insistence on scrapping the Geneva draft of the Declaration completely led to the committee going through each article again one by one to make the document clearer. *Id.*, 110–11. Eleanor Roosevelt described her experience with the Russian delegate Alexei Pavlov: "[W]hile it would be possible to reach some kind of agreement on the Declaration, we were going to be in for a great deal of controversy with the Russian representatives, particularly Dr. Pavlov, who attempted at every opportunity to write a bit of Communist philosophy into the document. For example, at the end of practically every article the Russian proposed to amend the Declaration to read: 'This shall be enforced by the State.'" Eleanor Roosevelt, *The Autobiography of Eleanor Roosevelt* (Da Capo Press, 1958) 317. Western delegates, including Roosevelt, argued against the amendment "on the ground that this was an international declaration … and that we did not believe it should be imposed by the power of the individual governments." *Id.* Such amendments were voted against and defeated, "[b]ut as soon as the next article was completed the Soviet delegate would again propose the same amendment" and the United Nations had to go through the same process over and over again to defeat the Soviet proposal." *Id.* Roosevelt remarks, "This naturally became monotonous, but the Russians never gave up trying." *Id.* Another of Pavlov's techniques was his long-winded speeches during UN meetings, causing the drafting process to slow down significantly. *Id.*, 320. According to Roosevelt, Pavlov "delivered many long propaganda harangues that appeared to be more for the purpose of publicizing the Communist point of view than in the hope of making changes in the Declaration. *Id.* To stop this tactic, Charles Malik brought a stopwatch to the meetings, "'mercilessly[] warning each speaker by a stroke of the gavel 30 second before the end of the time allotted to him.'" Glendon (2001) 152–153. Ultimately, when it came time for each country to vote on the final draft of the UDHR, even after all of the obstruction techniques, all six countries from the Soviet bloc ended up abstaining from voting. *Id.*, 169.

57 Article 1 of the Declaration did not include references to specific human rights "because it was meant to explain why human beings have rights to begin with." Glendon (2001) 146. The wording saying, "human beings were endowed 'by nature' with reason and conscience" – which was included in one of the drafts of Article 1 – sparked controversy because some representatives believed this reference seemed to be excluding the existence of God. Summary Record of the Ninety-Sixth Meeting for the Third Comm., UN Doc. A/C.3/SR.96 at 97 (Oct. 7, 1948). Because of the controversy, Glendon explains that members of the Belgium delegation sought to remove the words "by nature", while the Brazilian delegation proposed an amendment that

should be avoided so those who do not believe in God would not find it impossible to sign up to the concept of human rights.[58] The formulation found in the Preamble of the US Declaration of Independence, that it is self-evidently true "that all men are created equal, that they are endowed by the Creator with certain unalienable Rights, that among these are Life, Liberty and the pursuit of Happiness,"[59] was rejected in favor of the simple declaration that all human beings are

would say, "all human beings are created in the image and likeness of God." See Glendon (2001) 146. "The most persistent attempt to include the source of human rights in the UDHR came from those who supported a reference to God as the Creator." Åshild Samnøy, "The Origins of the Universal Declaration of Human Rights" in Gudmundur Alfredsson and Asbjørn Eide (eds.), *The Universal Declaration of Human Rights* (Martinus Nijhoff Publishers, 1999) 17. According to Malik, who was the chairman of the United Nations committee that heard the draft proposals, the intent behind drafting article 1 "had not been to imply that man had been endowed with reason and conscience by some entity beyond himself." Summary Record of the Ninety-Sixth Meeting for the Third Comm., UN Doc. A/C.3/SR.96 at 97, (Oct. 7, 1948). Malik told the committee that "[t]he English text would be clearer if the order of the words were changed so that they read: 'They are by nature endowed …'" *Id.* Glendon writes that "[i]t was Chang, again, who carried the majority by reminding everyone that the Declaration was designed to be universally applicable. His own country, he pointed out, comprised a large proportion of humanity, and its people had ideals and traditions different from those of the Christian West … Yet he, as the Chinese representative on the Human Rights Commission, had refrained from proposing those ideals for inclusion in the Declaration. He hoped his colleagues would show similar consideration." Glendon (2001) 146.

58 "In the process of debate in the Third Committee of the United Nations General Assembly, some representatives attempted to contain [sic] 'God', 'human nature', or 'God' phrase in the first article, which sparked fierce debate about the origin of human rights. It was just because P. C. Chang insisted on deleting these containing philosophical views of 'natural law' that the contradictions were finally resolved, differences were cut off and agreement was finally reached." Pinghua Sun (2018) 54. Chang reminded the assembly "that the Declaration was designed to be universally applicable." Glendon (2001) 146. In Chang's opinion, the first line of Article 1 "should refer neither to nature nor to God. Those who believed in God, he suggested, could still find the idea of God in the strong assertions that all human beings are born free and equal and endowed with reason and conscience." *Id.* See Summary Record of the Ninety-Sixth Meeting for the Third Comm., UN Doc. A/C.3/SR.96 at 98–99 (Oct. 7, 1948) and Summary Record of the Ninety-Eighth Meeting for the Third Comm., UN Doc. A/C.3/SR.98 at 113–14 (Oct. 9, 1948). According to Pavlov, the USSR representative, to put language in the UDHR referring to a creator as the source of human rights – like the Brazilian amendment proposed – should not be included in order to separate Church and State. Summary Record of the Ninety-Eighth Meeting for the Third Comm., UN Doc. A/C.3/SR.98 at 111 (Oct. 9, 1948). He also said that "the declaration should be a document to which all the nations, or at least the majority, could subscribe", and referencing a creator would conflict with the constitutions of other countries. *Id.*

59 The United States Declaration of Independence states in the second paragraph: "We hold these truths to be self-evident: that all men are created equal; that they are endowed, by their Creator, with certain unalienable rights; that among these are life, liberty, and the pursuit of happiness." Para. 2 of the Declaration of Independence (US, 1776).

"endowed with reason and conscience."[60] This was a conscious effort to avoid religious language that could limit the scope of agreement about the universality of the rights being identified.

Human dignity proved to be a concept that was widely acceptable to representatives of a broad range of philosophical and ideological backgrounds.[61] For example, Paweł Łuków, professor of philosophy and ethics at the University of Warsaw, attributed it to two main factors:

> The first was establishment of renewed legal orders after World War II, which saw human dignity as the value to be protected by them. In such remakings of legal arrangements, the idea of dignity, which was known to many influential politicians and social activists, could be readily identified with the dignity from the founding human rights documents. Thus, legal rights could be seen as instruments of protection of human dignity. The second factor that made dignity as a founding value a more and more attractive idea were changes in societies and, later, progress in science and technology.[62]

Tore Lindholm suggests that the doctrine in Article 1 of the UDHR that "'all human beings are born free and equal in dignity, and hence, in rights …' is now widely accepted, taken seriously, and rarely contested throughout the world, [and may be counted] as a major political achievement to be associated with the UDHR."[63]

Significantly, human dignity was cited both in the Preamble of the UDHR and in Article 1 of the UDHR. This was important because of the different roles the preambular paragraphs and the operative paragraphs play. P. C. Chang emphasized that the Preamble of the UDHR should incorporate clear reference to foundational premises of the document and a "standard should be established with a view to elevating the concept of man's dignity."[64] Charles Malik, who drafted

60 In René Cassin's original draft of Article 1, the language read: "All men are brothers. Being endowed with reason, members of one family, they are free and possess equal dignity and rights." Schabas (2013) 789; Draft International Declaration of Rights Submitted by Working Group of Drafting Committee (Preamble and Articles 1–6), Commission on Human Rights, 2, UN Doc. E/CN.4/AC.1/W.1 (Jun. 16, 1947). The phrase "endowed with reason", which was kept in later drafts, was attributable to Charles Malik, while the addition, "and conscience" is the result of a proposal by P. C. Chang. Lindholm (1999) 43. The idea of being endowed with conscience is somewhat founded in Confucian ethics, from the word *ren* which in English terms means, "humaneness towards others" or "consciousness of his fellow men." *Id.* The final draft of Article 1 reads: "All human beings are born free and equal in dignity and rights. They are endowed with reason and conscience and should act towards one another in a spirit of brotherhood."

61 See Article 3 of the Punta del Este Declaration below.

62 Paweł Łuków, "A Difficult Legacy: Human Dignity as the Founding Value of Human Rights" (2018) 19 *Human Rights Review* 313.

63 Lindholm (1999) 66.

64 Glendon (2001) 38.

the final version of the Preamble, considered human dignity was key in setting the tone for interpreting the UDHR.[65]

Dr. Guy Pérez Cisneros, representing Cuba, suggested that since the content of Article 1 was a statement of fact rather than a right itself, it should be moved to the Preamble.[66] This was supported by representatives of Guatemala, the Netherlands, and South Africa.[67] Carton de Wiart representing Belgium objected to such a transfer, emphasizing that, "Article 1 was important as the first article of a solemn document since it affirmed a principle which in some measure summed up the articles that followed."[68] According to Mary Ann Glendon, Eleanor Roosevelt stressed that "in the scheme of the Declaration, Article 1 did not refer to specific rights because it was meant to explain why human beings have rights, to begin with."[69] Eleanor Roosevelt "said that the word *dignity* had been considered carefully by the Human Rights Commission, which included it to emphasize that every human being is worthy of respect."[70] This was supported, among others, by P. C. Chang and René Cassin. Ultimately, once the issue of removing the reference to human dignity from Article 1 was put to a vote, Panama, South Africa, Venezuela, Guatemala, the Netherlands, and New Zealand voted in favor, while 26 voted against the proposal (and 10 abstained).[71]

b. Human dignity for everyone everywhere is valuable as a point of departure for exploring and understanding the meaning of human rights

As it was in 1947–48, focusing on human dignity for everyone everywhere is a good place to start conversations about human rights, including places where human rights are suspect or unpopular.

For example, when this project was in its early stages of formation, Ján Figel', the European Union Special Envoy for Freedom of Religion or Belief Outside the EU, shared an experience he had in trying to set up a visit to Pakistan to talk with government officials about his area of concern. Religious freedom is a very controversial and sensitive subject in Pakistan. Thus, it wasn't surprising that his suggestion of visiting Pakistan was met with considerable hesitancy by Pakistani officials. When the government asked him what he wanted to talk about, he said he wanted to talk about the concept of human dignity, and how it is important for all people, and at all times, and in all places. This broke the ice. He was told that human dignity is an important concept in Islam, *Karama* (in the Koran), and that it could be valuable to have some meetings and discussions about human dignity. With this opening, he went to Pakistan on multiple occasions, engaged in

65 Glendon (2001) 117–118; Lindholm (1999) 44.
66 Lindholm (1999) 53.
67 *Id.*, 53.
68 *Id.*, 53.
69 Glendon (2001) 144.
70 *Id.*
71 Lindholm (1999) 53.

meaningful discussions with government and academic leaders about human dignity, and participated in public meetings about religious freedom, using human dignity as a point of departure. He even established sufficient trust that he was able to help with the release of Asia Bibi, a Christian woman who had been in prison for many years on charges of blasphemy.[72]

Nearly every human right, including those that are quite sensitive, has important implications for human dignity. For example, human dignity can help start conversations about women's and children's rights, about non-discrimination, and about the right way to treat prisoners or other people in state-supervised institutional settings such as hospitals or facilities that care for the elderly or disabled. It is important for discussions on police misconduct and other possible abuses of authority by state officials. It is a concept that has clear implications for freedom of thought, conscience, and belief.

Human dignity is a concept that encourages other concerns. It is more difficult for discussions of human rights to descend into special pleading for the rights of oneself or one's group when the focus is on human dignity, because dignity as a concept applies to everyone. Human dignity points us towards the universality of human rights. Despite the many ways that individuals, or groups are different from each other, they are all the same in their basic human dignity.

A historical example helps illustrate how dignity can play a role in resolving divisive political issues. In the United States, towards the end of the Civil War in early 1865, President Abraham Lincoln wanted to press for the passage of the Thirteenth Amendment to constitutionalize the freeing of slaves before the war ended. Proponents of freedom were accused of failing to see the differences between the races. These proponents responded by saying that despite their differences, there was a deep way in which all are the same, including having equality under the law and equality in our status as human beings.

For example, when discussing the issue of equality, Senator Henry Wilson, Republican of Massachusetts, emphasized that:

> We must see to it that the man made free by the Constitution … is a freeman indeed; that he can go where he pleases; work when and for whom he pleases; that he can sue and be sued; that he can lease and buy and sell and own property, real and personal; that he can go into the schools and educate himself and his children; that the rights and guarantees of the good old common law are his, and that he walks the earth, proud and erect *in the conscious*

72 Asia Bibi, a Christian Pakistani woman, was convicted and sentenced to death by a Pakistani court in November 2010. The court found her guilty of making derogatory remarks about the Prophet Mohammed during an argument with another woman. In 2014, the Lahore High Court upheld her death sentence. The execution was stayed in July 2015, when the Pakistani Supreme Court agreed to hear her appeal. It was listed to take place during October 2016 when the appeal had to be adjourned after one of the three judges, Justice Iqbal Hameed-ur-Rehman, recused himself quoting a conflict of interests. On October 31, 2018, the Supreme Court of Pakistan acquitted.

> *dignity of a free man* who knows that his cabin, however humble, is protected by the just and equal laws of his country.[73]

He explained further:

> By the equality of man, we mean that the poorest man, be he black or white ... is as much entitled to the protection of the law as the richest and proudest man ... We mean that the poor man, whose wife may be dressed in a cheap calico, is as much entitled to have her protected by equal law as is the rich man to have his jeweled bride protected by the law of the land ... That the poor man's cabin though it may be the cabin of a poor freedman in the depths of the Carolinas is entitled to the protection of the same law that protects the palace of a Stewart or an Astor.[74]

When conflicts exist between individuals or groups, it is important to remember that the interests and rights of everyone are important. While everyone wants to have rights adequately protected and implemented, it is crucial to recognize that the rights of others are equally important.

Human rights as defined, protected, and implemented should enrich and strengthen human dignity for everyone everywhere. If human rights fail to do so, it is crucial to consider the shortfalls and how they could be addressed to promote human dignity for everyone everywhere.

Indeed, when commenting in 1864 upon the issue of equality and slavery, Timothy H. Howe, Senator from Wisconsin, stressed that,

> It belonged to republican institutions to carry out, to execute the doctrines of the Declaration of Independence, to make men equal. That they are not equal in social estimation, that they are not equal in mental culture, that they are not equal in physical stature, I know very well; but I have thought the weaker they were the more the government was bound to foster and protect them. If government be designed for the protection of the weak, certainly the weaker men are the more they need its protection.[75]

c. Human dignity for everyone everywhere is a basis for finding common ground regarding human rights and consensus about their content and meaning

Human dignity is helpful not only for starting conversations about human rights but also for finding common ground regarding human rights and consensus about their content and meaning.

73 *The Congressional Globe*, 39th Cong., 1st Sess. 111 (1865) (emphasis added).
74 *The Congressional Globe*, 39th Cong., 1st Sess. 343 (1864).
75 *The Congressional Globe*, 39th Cong., 1st Sess. 438 (1864).

The development of the UDHR was not built upon a deep philosophical agreement about the ontological or metaphysical bases of human rights. Rather, the specific rights were recognized as being important and generated widespread agreement.[76] The rights were universal because they were universally recognized and embraced as being universal. Part of the genius of the human rights project was that it generated agreement on specific rights without requiring agreement – religious, philosophical, moral, legal, or political – about the underlying systematic justifications for human rights.

Because of deep differences between these various types, there was a need to find common ground or a common vocabulary that could express the universal truths that the drafters sought to express. Human dignity was a key component of that common vocabulary. As was the case at the time of the drafting of the UDHR, human dignity for everyone everywhere remains the most promising basis for ***finding common ground*** regarding human rights and achieving an overlapping consensus[77] or finding

76 Indeed, according to the French Catholic philosopher Jacques Maritain, "people can come to agree on a list of human rights regardless of different ideological backgrounds." Bradley R. Munro, "The Universal Declaration of Human Rights, Maritain, and the Universality of Human Rights" in William Sweet (ed.), *Philosophical Theory and the Universal Declaration of Human Rights* (University of Ottawa Press, 2003) 109, 110. In his speech to the Opening Plenary of UNESCO in 1947, Maritain says, "How… is an agreement conceivable among men assembled for the purpose of jointly accomplishing a task dealing with the future of the mind, who come from the four corners of the earth and who belong not only to different cultures and civilizations, but to different spiritual families and antagonistic schools of thought? Since the aim of UNESCO is a practical aim, agreement among its members can be spontaneously achieved, not on common speculative notions, but on common practical notions, not only on the affirmative of the same conception of the world, man, and knowledge, but on the affirmation of the same set of convictions concerning action … It is, however, enough to undertake a great work; and it would mean a great deal to become aware of this body of common practical convictions." Jacques Maritain, *Man and the State* (Catholic University of America Press, 1998) 77–78. Åshild Samnøy commented on the issue that the "drafters of the UDHR agreed to disagree on these philosophical matters in order to attain a practical goal, the adoption of the Universal Declaration." Åshild Samnøy, "The Origins of the Universal Declaration of Human Rights" in Gudmundur Alfredsson and Asbjørn Eide (eds.), *The Universal Declaration of Human Rights* (Martinus Nijhoff Publishers, 1999) 18.

77 "Overlapping consensus" is a term John Rawls, the moral and political philosopher, defined in a lecture he gave at Oxford that was later revised for the *Oxford Journal of Legal Studies.* John Rawls, "The Idea of an Overlapping Consensus" (1987) 7 *Oxford Journal of Legal Studies* 1,1. According to Rawls, a constitutional democratic society has an important goal to present "a political conception of justice that can not only provide a shared public basis for the justification of political and social institutions but also helps ensure stability" – especially of constitutional ideals – "from one generation to the next." *Id.*, 1. Such a political conception of justice, Rawls writes, should "specify the aims the constitution is to achieve and the limits it must respect." *Id.* According to Rawls, "the historical and social conditions of a modern democratic society require us to regard a conception of justice for its political institutions in a certain way," to work within the boundaries of democratic politics. *Id.*, 2. He describes three features of a political conception of justice that illustrate how the conditions of a modern democratic society "affect the features of a practicable

incompletely theorized agreements,[78] about the content and meaning of human rights. This is not to say that the idea of human dignity will resolve all disputes about the boundaries of human rights or all questions about the permissible limitations on human rights. These are matters that will remain controversial and difficult to resolve.

conception." *Id.*, 3. First, even though a political conception of justice "is, of course, a moral conception, it is a moral conception worked out for a specific kind of subject, namely for political, social and economic institutions." *Id.* He clarifies that the morality he speaks of is "certain ideals, principals and standards" that guide what he calls "the 'basic structure' of a modern constitutional democracy." *Id.* A political conception of justice should be focused on "the framework of basic institutions and the principles, standards and precepts that apply to them." *Id.* The second feature of a political conception of justice is that even as a moral conception, it is not a conception that "involves, so far as possible … prior commitment to any wider doctrine" such as utilitarianism or Marxism. *Id.*, 4. In order for a political conception of justice to be effective, is must be "different from many familiar moral doctrines, for these are understood as general and comprehensive views." *Id.*, 3. To create this kind of conception of justice, Rawls says it cannot be based on "self- or group-interests alone," or even religious or philosophical ideas, but must be a "political conception … such that there is some hope of its gaining the support of an *overlapping consensus*, that is, a consensus in which it is affirmed by the opposing religious, philosophical and moral doctrine likely to thrive over generations." *Id.*, 1 (emphasis added). In a democratic society based on a political conception of justice by an overlapping consensus, "[q] uestions of political justice can be discussed on the same basis by all citizens, whatever their social position, or more particular aims and interests, or their religious, philosophical or moral views." *Id.*, 5–6. Such diversity of doctrines and beliefs – pluralism – Rawls believes is "a permanent feature of the public culture of modern democracies" and "not a mere historical condition that will soon pass away." *Id.*, 4. The third feature of a political conception of justice based on an overlapping consensus is that the conception is not "formulated in terms of a general and comprehensive religious, philosophical or moral doctrine but rather in terms of certain fundamental intuitive ideas viewed as latent in the public political culture." *Id.*, 6. These intuitive ideas come from "a tradition of democratic thought, the content of which is at least intuitively familiar to citizens generally." *Id.* An example of a political conception based on an overlapping consensus is "'justice as fairness'… [where] the problem of justice is then understood as that of specifying the fair terms of social cooperation between citizens." *Id.*, 7. Such a conception of justice "will be acceptable to a wide range of comprehensive doctrines and hence supported by an overlapping consensus." *Id.*, 8. Because pluralism is not likely to go away in the future, "the point of the idea of an overlapping consensus on a political conception is to show how, despite a diversity of doctrines, convergence on a political conception of justice may be achieved and social unity sustained in long-run equilibrium, that is, over time from one generation to the next." *Id.*, 5.

78 Cass R. Sunstein, professor at Harvard Law School and former Administrator of the White House Office of Information and Regulatory Affairs, wrote an article for the *Harvard Law Review*, summarizing his "special strategy for producing agreement amidst pluralism" in a democratic society. Cass R. Sunstein, "Commentary: Incompletely Theorized Agreements" (1995) 108 *Harvard Law Review* 1733, 1735. This strategy is called "incompletely theorized agreements." *Id.*, 1736. What Sunstein means by incompletely theorized agreements is that "[p]articipants in legal controversies… agree on the result and on relatively narrow or low-level explanations for it," rather than agreeing on fundamental principle like utilitarianism. *Id.*, 1735–1736.

For example, when judges use incompletely theorized agreements, "[t]hey do not offer larger or more abstract explanations than are necessary to decide [a] case. When they disagree on abstraction, they move to a level of greater particularity. The distinctive feature … is that it emphasizes agreement on (relative) particulars rather than on (relative) abstractions. This is an important source of social stability and an important way for diverse people to demonstrate mutual respect, in law specially but also in liberal democracy as a whole." *Id.*, 1736. Sunstein says, "When the convergence on particular outcomes is incompletely theorized, it is because relevant actors are clear on the *result* without being clear, either in their own minds or on paper, on the most general *theory* that accounts for it." *Id.*, 1737 (emphasis added). "When (and if) people who agree on the same course of action are able to do so from different foundations," Sunstein adds, "they need not choose among foundations. So too, people may favor a rule of strict liability for certain torts from diverse starting points." *Id.*, 1736. In advocating for incompletely theorized agreements and focusing less on theories or abstractions, Sunstein does "not suggest that there is no place in society or law for ambitious theories." *Id.*, 1738. He says, "Certainly such theories are legitimately a part of democratic deliberation. To reveal practices as confused or unjust, or to decide whether practices are confused or unjust, it may be necessary to think at high levels of abstraction. Indeed, judges might well raise the level of theoretical abstraction if that is necessary to decide a case, or if a high-level theory can be shown to be a good one and they can be persuaded to agree to it. But participants in adjudicative institutions are – and should be – very cautious before taking this step." *Id.*, 1738. Sunstein says a reason to be cautious is that "[p]articipants in law may be unwilling to commit themselves to large-scale theories of any kind, and they will likely disagree with one another if they seek to agree on such theories." *Id.*, 1735. However, Sunstein believes that "[i]f a good abstraction is available, and if diverse judges can be persuaded that the abstraction is good, there should be no taboo against its judicial acceptance. The claims on behalf of incompletely theorized agreements are presumptive rather than conclusive." *Id.*, 1764. According to Sunstein, incompletely theorized "agreements are especially well suited to the institutional limits of the judiciary, which is composed in significant part of multimember bodies, consisting in turn of highly diverse people who must render many decisions, live together, avoid error to the extent possible, and show each other mutual respect." *Id.*, 1738. He says, "Legal rules are typically incompletely theorized in the sense that they can be accepted by people who disagree on many general issues. People may agree that a sixty-five mile-per-hour speed limit makes sense, and that it applies to defendant Jones, without having much of a theory about criminal punishment, and without making judgments about the domain of utilitarianism and the scope of paternalism. A key social function of rules is to allow people to agree on the meaning, authority, and even the soundness of a governing legal provision in the face of disagreements about much else." *Id.*, 1741. Yet Sunstein does not shy away from the value of disagreement: "Of course, it is not always disrespectful to disagree with someone in a fundamental way; on the contrary, such disagreements may reflect profound respect. For example, objections to judgments based on prejudice may reflect respect for the person at the same time that they attempt to overcome the judgments at issue. When defining commitments are based on demonstrable errors of fact or logic, it is appropriate to contest them. The same is true when those commitments are rooted in a rejection of the basic dignity of all human beings, or when it is necessary to undertake the contest to resolve a genuine problem." *Id.*, 1747. Perhaps Sunstein and Rawls would agree that an overlapping consensus or raising the level of abstraction would be appropriate here, because an overlapping consensus is not so high-level that intense disagreement over fundamental principles creates a logjam on a desired result. *Id.*, 1735, 1740, 1764.

But human dignity can still serve as a common vocabulary for finding common ground and building consensus.

When groups with different interests and rights with each other engage in bargaining to find mutually acceptable solutions to contentious conflicting rights claims, beginning the conversation with a basic agreement about the human dignity of those on the other side of the controversy can facilitate finding compromises or even principled approaches that vindicate the dignitary interests of both sides. When the interests of both sides are evaluated by both sides in terms of human dignity, there can be the possibility that deeper conversations seeking mutual vindication of rights may occur rather than a winner-take-all approach where rights claims are viewed as being a zero-sum game.[79]

Human dignity is a concept that can be useful in unique ways because it is so widely embraced by a variety of religious and philosophical systems of thought.

Sunstein also breaks down three different types of incompletely theorized agreements. *Id.*, 1739, 1740. One type of incompletely theorized agreement is agreeing on a general principle. *Id.*, 1739. Sunstein says, "Such agreements are incompletely theorized in the sense that people who accept the principle need not agree on what it entails in particular cases. People know that murder is wrong, but they disagree about abortion." *Id.* A second kind of incompletely theorized agreement is that "[p]eople may agree on a mid-level principle but disagree both about the more general theory that accounts for it and about outcomes of particular cases. They may believe that government cannot discriminate on the basis of race, without settling on a large-scale theory of equality, and without agreeing on whether government may enact affirmative action programs or segregate prisons when racial tensions are severe." *Id.* In this way, Sunstein and Rawls might also agree that an overlapping consensus could be similar to a principle or "mid-level principle" that is not based in any "wider doctrine" or on the same outcome when applying such principles. *Id.* A third kind of incompletely theorized agreement is on a particular outcome, "accompanied by agreements on the low-level principles that account for them." *Id.*, 1740. Sunstein says that "we might think of low-level principles as including most of the ordinary material of legal doctrine – the general class of principles and justifications that are not said to derive from any particular large theories of the right or the good." *Id.* In general, Sunstein offers two main reasons for using incompletely theorized agreements. *Id.*, 1746. "The first and most obvious," he writes, "is that incompletely theorized agreements are well suited to a world – especially a legal world – containing social disagreement on large-scale issues. By definition, such agreements have the large advantage of allowing a convergence on particular outcomes by people unable to reach anything like an accord on general principles." *Id.* The second reason is that "incompletely theorized agreements can promote two goals of a liberal democracy and a liberal legal system: to enable people to live together, and to permit them to show each other a measure of reciprocity and mutual respect." *Id.*

79 See Chapter 10 on Article 8. See also: Robin Fretwell Wilson, "The Politics of Accommodation. The American Experience with Same-Sex Marriage and Religious Freedom" in Timothy Shah, Thomas Farr, and Jack Friedman (eds.), *Religious Freedom and Gay Rights: Emerging Conflicts in the United States and Europe* (Oxford University Press: New York, 2016) 144; J. Stuart Adams, "Cultivating Common Ground" in William N. Eskridge, Jr. and Robin Fretwell Wilson (eds.), *Religious Freedom, LGBT Rights, and the Prospects for Common Ground* (Cambridge University Press, 2019) 449; Michael O. Leavitt, "Shared Spaces and Brave Gambles" in William

Human dignity is an important concept in many religious traditions, as well as many non-religious moral and ethical systems.[80]

The fact that human rights depend upon overlapping consensus and incompletely theorized agreements reminds us that we should not preemptively try to exclude peoples' reasons from our efforts to discuss and define human rights. While human rights embraces the philosopher John Rawls's idea of "overlapping consensus" it should be wary of another of his major ideas, namely "public reason."

"Public reason" refers to the kinds of reasons that individuals or groups can use in political advocacy and public dialogue. For Rawls, only certain kinds of beliefs should be invoked in the public square, ones that any "reasonable person" could be expected to endorse. Rawls argues that this limitation ensures proper respect for fellow citizens who may not share other's moral or religious beliefs. This is the heart of public reason – the concern for legitimacy in the face of pluralism.[81] Many nations are extremely diverse, with citizens holding widely divergent beliefs about God, religion, morality, and the good life. Yet they must live together and create laws for everyone. This is even more difficult on the international stage, where pluralism reaches new levels. Rawls argues that, in light of this pluralism, individuals should not draw on the entirety of their religious or moral beliefs in the political realm. To do so would disrespect fellow citizens who hold different beliefs and worldviews. Fundamentally, for Rawls, an act of coercive power – like a coercive law – is illegitimate if it does not respect fellow citizens as free and equal.[82] But to respect fellow citizens as free and equal requires that they not be coerced (by the law) without reasons that they could accept. In other words, to respect fellow citizens, I must not support a law that coerces them unless there are reasons for that law that they should accept. To do otherwise treats them as unequal and as a mere means to enforcing my view of what is right and true. Rawls's view of public reason, then, restricts public dialogue to ensure that coercive laws can be legitimate. As such, individuals must only appeal to "presently

N. Eskridge, Jr. and Robin Fretwell Wilson (eds.), *Religious Freedom, LGBT Rights, and the Prospects for Common Ground* (Cambridge University Press, 2019) 462–463.

80 See section (d) below.

81 In *Political Liberalism*, Rawls refers to this as the "fact of reasonable pluralism," namely, that under free institutions, reasonable persons will hold widely different beliefs about philosophical and religious topics. And this is not a result of their failure to think carefully or altruistically, but rather a fact about our epistemic and political environments. *Political Liberalism*, 36. While the fact of reasonable pluralism refers to liberal democracies, the same basic idea influences (to an even stronger degree) his conception of the law of peoples in the international sphere, where pluralism becomes even deeper.

82 Rawls's view on public reason stems from his commitment to what he calls the "liberal principle of legitimacy," which requires that "our exercise of political power is fully proper only when it is exercised in accordance with a constitution the essentials of which all citizens as free and equal may reasonably be expected to endorse in the light of principles and ideals acceptable to their common human reason." Rawls, *Political Liberalism*, 137.

accepted general beliefs and forms of reasoning found in common sense, and the methods of and conclusions of science when these are not controversial."[83] This is "the most appropriate, if not the only, way to specify the guidelines of public inquiry."[84]

To make Rawls's position clearer, consider this example: During the debate surrounding "enhanced interrogation" techniques in the United States during the "War on Terror," a group of evangelicals issued the "Evangelical Declaration against Torture" which argued that "enhanced interrogation" is immoral and should be outlawed.[85] And the reasons for this position were explicitly religious – all humans are created in the image of God, Jesus atoned for the sins of all people, thus every human life has intrinsic value, etc.[86] On Rawls's view of public reason, this declaration would not be an acceptable form of political advocacy, *unless* the evangelical signatories also had – and presented – non-religious and suitably public reasons for their view. Since not all people are Christian or even theistic, to only invoke beliefs about God or Christ is inappropriate and disrespectful.

The scope of public reason varies by the thinker, though Rawls's conception is relatively narrow. For Rawls, "the limits imposed by public reason do not apply to all political questions but only to those involving what we may call 'constitutional essentials' and questions of basic justice."[87] Rawls also allowed that religious citizens could discuss their faith in public dialogue, so long as public reason has priority: "[R]easonable comprehensive doctrines, religious or non-religious, may be introduced in public political discussion at any time, provided that in due course proper political reasons – and, not reasons given solely by comprehensive doctrines – are presented that are sufficient to support whatever the comprehensive doctrines introduced are said to support."[88] Robert Audi took this argument even further to suggest that "if religious considerations are not appropriately balanced with secular ones in matters of coercion, there is a special problem: a clash of Gods vying for social control. Such uncompromising absolutes easily lead to destruction and death."[89] Audi also holds that there is *always* a prima facie duty not to bring religious beliefs into public dialogue concerning restrictive laws, not simply on constitutional essentials (as with Rawls).[90]

For religious believers, public reason requires that they not utilize their faith when advocating for political measures or bring their religion to bear on basic matters of justice. Instead, they should bring forth "public reasons," ones that any

83 *Id.*, 224.
84 *Id.*
85 "An Evangelical Declaration Against Torture," adopted by the National Association of Evangelicals Board of Directors in 2007. https://www.nae.net/an-evangelical-declaration-against-torture/
86 *Id.*, 2.4–2.10.
87 John Rawls, *Political Liberalism* (Columbia University Press: New York, 1993) 214.
88 John Rawls, "The Idea of Public Reason Revisited" (1997) 64 *University of Chicago Law Review* 784.
89 Robert Audi, *Religious Commitment and Secular Reason* (Cambridge University Press: Cambridge, 2000) 103.
90 Robert Audi, *Democratic Authority and the Separation of Church and State* (New York: Oxford University Press, 2011), 65–66.

reasonable person could endorse, regardless of their belief. Rawls argues that this restriction is not one of anti-religious bias, however.

According to Rawls, "central to the idea of public reason is that it neither criticizes nor attacks any comprehensive doctrine, religious or non-religious, except insofar as that doctrine is incompatible with the essentials of public reason and a democratic polity."[91] The duty to only utilize public reasons applies to all individuals, and it does not require a person to abandon their faith or their comprehensive view of the world. But public reason does discount and exclude "religious reasons" and other "comprehensive views" from public advocacy. Rawls emphasized that "there is no reason ... why any citizen, or association of citizens, should have the right to use the state's police power to decide constitutional essentials or basic questions of justice as that person's, or that association's, comprehensive doctrine directs."[92]

While the basic aims of public reason are laudable, its categorical duty to restrain individuals from bringing forth their best reasons – public or not – in political dialogue presents serious problems for the human rights project.[93] First, it has the effect of privileging non-religious liberal views, since those are more easily translated into public reason. As Kent Greenawalt has observed:

> Rawls's approach requires that one decide what counts as public reasons as compared with reliance on comprehensive reasons. The problem about religious comprehensive views is relatively minor. Rawls assumes that in genuine liberal democracies, citizens are not going to accept with near universality any particular Christian view, or Christianity in general, or Islam, Judaism, Hinduism, etc. Nor will they accept theism as opposed to nontheism. Thus, the exclusion of comprehensive views bars direct reference to Christian, Jewish, Islamic, theist, or atheist premises. Subtle questions arise about the status of religious stories and references to religious traditions as sources of general human or particular cultural understanding, but when they are carefully presented in the right way, such stories and references can fall within the domain of public reasons. A more serious concern arises over nonreligious comprehensive views, particularly liberal non-religious comprehensive views. When someone urges that the value of autonomy be respected, it may be virtually impossible for him and others to tell whether he is relying on a particular comprehensive perspective or the widely-shared value of autonomy in our culture. Liberal nonreligious comprehensive perspectives are bound to "suffer less" from a principle of self-restraint than both religious views and nonreligious, nonliberal views. This difference may reasonably be thought to involve a kind of inequity.[94]

91 John Rawls, "The Idea of Public Reason Revisited" (1997) 64 *University of Chicago Law Review* 766.
92 John Rawls, *Political Liberalism* (Columbia University Press: New York, 1993) 62.
93 We speak here of public reason generally, recognizing that Rawls's use of that concept slightly differs with liberal societies versus the international law of peoples.
94 Kent Greenwalt, "On Public Reason" (1994) 69 *Chicago Kent Law Review* 687–688.

This possible inequity and privileging of non-religious views threatens the consensus around human rights. This is especially true for highly religious nations outside the "West," whose religious character is central to their political outlook. An insistence upon public reason in the human rights realm – even a less restrictive, international version of public reason – will alienate those who feel it privileges non-religious, secular worldviews. An insistence on public reason may bar those who might otherwise agree with the human rights project (albeit for non-public reasons) since they would be expected to suspend their own deeply held beliefs in the international realm. Human rights may then appear as nothing more than a secular imposition upon religious or non-Western nations, rather than a universal aspiration for all.

The insistence on public reason can also create mistrust and prompt suspicions of bad faith. When human rights must be discussed from within a public reason framework, participants in that discussion may worry that some use the language of public reason as a cloak for imposing their comprehensive worldview. And this concern cuts both ways: secular groups may question whether religious groups are seeking to impose their faith using the language of public reason, and religious groups may also fear that "public reason" is a pretext for militant secularism. From a historical point of view, the UDHR and other international agreements on human rights push against the public reason project. These agreements were not based on any shared theory or justification of human rights. Quite the opposite. The writers of the UDHR, for example, intentionally avoided such issues to reach a consensus.[95] Each nation may have its conception of human rights, but the project of human rights is based on a shared *consensus*, not shared *reasons*. Rawls's public reason cuts against this history – the purpose of public reason is to restrict public dialogue to shared reasons, rather than pursuing a common acceptance of human rights for quite different (and even incompatible) reasons. To insist categorically on public reason may reignite the contentious issues that were carefully avoided by the authors of the UDHR.

Being honest and forthright about one's reasons for supporting human rights can also create understanding and mutual respect. Indeed, respecting individuals or peoples may have much more to do with seeking to understand their reasons – all of their reasons – rather than insisting on limiting what considerations can come to bear on the question of human rights. Generating commitment to human rights seems far more likely when each party can be authentic to their full range of beliefs, rather than when they must base that commitment on the narrow category of "public reasons."

Of course, there is great value in finding common ground and avoiding the assumption that one's worldview is (or should be) universally accepted. But the lesson of pluralism is not to exclude any viewpoint, but to foster a dialogue that both respects the uniqueness of each tradition while also seeking consensus and common ground.

The opinions or public policy proposals of individuals or organizations should not be discounted or disqualified from consideration in the public sphere just

95 *Supra* n. 376.

because they are motivated by religious beliefs. Throughout history, many important advances in the protection of human rights were motivated by religious belief. The fact that a political proposal may be motivated or instructed by some religious belief does not mean that it does not have a place in public debate. At the same time, even if believers are deeply persuaded of the correctness or Divine approval of their opinions or policy proposals, it is not reasonable to expect those who do not share the same belief systems to accept their proposals without critical discussion and review. Proposals and opinions regarding sensitive social issues should be aired and evaluated on their merits in the public square, and religiously motivated ideas should not be either disqualified or automatically accepted because of their religious origin, but neither should believers expect others to accept such opinions or proposals with the same authority that they do.

Human dignity does not aspire to serve as a kind of "public reason," but rather as a shared value that helps generate consensus about human rights. As with human rights, there are varying conceptions and theories of human dignity. We do not hold that human dignity simply erases any controversies about human rights. What it does do, however, is shine a light on a fundamental value that many (if not all) can accept in the human rights project. Moreover, whatever theory or reason one has for embracing human dignity, this value helps us understand why we care about human rights in the first place and how we might seek to avoid the zero-sum-game of my rights versus your rights. As a basic value, human dignity for everyone everywhere helps establish common ground and provides a framework for promoting human rights.

d. Dignity provides an approach to building bridges between various normative justifications of human rights, including those with religious and secular theoretical groundings

Human dignity is a concept that resonates in various religious and secular traditions and doctrines as a justification for human rights. When these different conceptions of human dignity are drawn into conversation with each other, the goal is not to overcome the view of others, but to better understand ourselves and others, and to find ways to expand areas of agreement.[96]

96 "[J]ust as there are differences among the precise religious visions adhered to by different sects within Christianity, there are differences among the precise visions adhered to by different world religions. Again, the analogical imagination does not yield precisely the same vision in every time or place. But such differences ought not obscure the fact that the experience of all human beings as sacred is widely shared among different sects and religions, albeit expressed or mediated differently in different traditions; and that common, ecumenical ground helps to explain the emergence of the idea of human rights as a point of convergence among peoples from different religious traditions." Michael J. Perry, "Is the Idea of Human Rights Ineliminably Religious?" (1993) 27 *University of Richmond Law Review* 1048. See also: Michael J. Perry, *The Idea of Human Rights: Four Inquiries* (Oxford University Press: Oxford, 1998) 22.

"Ecumenical politics aspires to discern or achieve, in a religiously and morally pluralistic context, a common political ground." Michael J. Perry, *Love and Power* (Oxford

Sometimes religious and other ideological divides that separate us seem unbridgeable. While we should not overestimate the ability of one idea to help us bridge these divides, human dignity for everyone everywhere can help us find ways of bridging differences.

For example, while the UDHR does not provide religious or philosophical justifications for human rights, various thinkers and authors have provided such justifications. For example, normative defenses of human rights have been proposed from a variety of philosophical,[97] religious,[98] and moral perspectives. For Catholics, human dignity is

University Press, 1991) 44. "Notwithstanding its substantial religious/moral pluralism, American society is a genuine political community. There are underlying grounds of political judgment – grounds concerning how the life in common is to be lived – which we Americans, qua members of a judging community, share, and which can and do serve to unite us in dialogue, notwithstanding our (sometimes radical) disagreements. The most apparent such shared standards of political judgment derive from our constitutional tradition, especially from that part of the tradition concerned with the rights of citizens and others against the state – standards concerning, for example, religious liberty; political freedom, including the freedoms of speech and of the press; racial and others sorts of discrimination, 'due process' and other procedural rights ... Such constitutional standards are, for most of us Americans, fundamental standards of political morality ... But it would be a mistake to conclude that constitutional norms are morally authoritative for us because they are legally authoritative for us. Rather they are legally authoritative for us ... because they are morally authoritative for us. The fundamental standards of American political morality with which I am principally concerned in this book ... derive from the religious traditions of American society, in particular the biblical heritage." *Id.*, 88. "[P]erhaps meaningful participation in ecumenical political dialogue is possible even for those who are not fallibilists or pluralists. Perhaps fallibilism and pluralism are better understood, not as prerequisites to ecumenical political dialogue, but as attitudes or positions for which it is sometimes fitting to contend, depending on the particular question at issue, in ecumenical political dialogue. (It does seem to me, however, that the kind, or quality, [of]participation in ecumenical political dialogue available to one who is neither fallibilist nor pluralist is inferior to that available to one who is both fallibilist and pluralist.)" *Id.*, 140.

97 John Tasioulas, "Human Dignity and the Foundations of Human Rights" in Christopher McCrudden (ed.), *Understanding Human Dignity* (Oxford University Press: Oxford, 2013) 291. On Kant see: Immanuel Kant (Thomas E. Hill, Jr. and Arnulf Zweig, eds.), *Groundwork for the Metaphysics of Morals* (Oxford University Press, 2002); Jeremy Waldron, "Citizenship and Dignity" in Christopher McCrudden (ed.), *Understanding Human Dignity* (Oxford University Press: Oxford, 2013); Thomas E. Hill, Jr., "In Defence of Human Dignity: Comments on Kant and Rosen" in Christopher McCrudden (ed.), *Understanding Human Dignity* (Oxford University Press: Oxford, 2013); Michael Rosen, *Dignity: Its History and Meaning* (Harvard University Press, 2012). On Aristotle see: Michael Pakaluk, "Aristotle on Human Rights" (2012) 10 *Ave Maria Law Review* 379; Fred D. Miller, Jr., "Aristotle and the Origins of Natural Rights" (1996) 49 *The Review of Metaphysics* 873; Fred D. Miller, Jr., *Nature, Justice and Rights in Aristotle's "Politics"* (Oxford University Press, 1997); *Marquette Law Review*, "Legal Philosophers: Aristotle, Aquinas and Kant on Human Rights" (1972) 55 *Marquette Law Review* 64.

98 Musa Hitam, former chairman of the UN Commission on Human Rights, and current leader of the Malaysian Delegation to that Commission, said, "The Declaration should be universally accepted as a code of conduct for the use of states and individuals. Indeed, the Declaration contains the teachings of all the major religions of the world and merits adherence as close as possible by all." *The Star*, "Weighing Our Rights and

grounded on the fact that human beings are created in the image of God. *Dignitatis Humanae*, the Second Vatican Council's (Vatican II) Declaration on Religious Freedom, recognizes this relationship between dignity and freedom.[99] It is human dignity, the dignity of the person, that leads to the right of religious freedom. Indeed, Vatican II explains that

> the right to religious freedom has its foundation in the very dignity of the human person as this dignity is known through the revealed word of God and by reason itself. (2) This right of the human person to religious freedom is to be recognized in the constitutional law whereby society is governed and thus it is to become a civil right.[100]

Freedoms," December 10, 1998, Section 2, 3. For an introduction to human rights and its interaction with various religions including Christianity, Islam, Hinduism, Confucianism, Buddhism, and Indigenous Religion, see John Witte, Jr. and M. Christian Green (eds.), *Religion and Human Rights: An Introduction* (Oxford University Press, 2011).

On Catholicism see: James Hanvey, "Dignity, Person, and Imago Trinitatis" in Christopher McCrudden (ed.), *Understanding Human Dignity* (Oxford University Press: Oxford, 2013); Walter Kasper, "The Theological Foundations of Human Rights" (1990) 50 *The Jurist* 148.

On Orthodox Christianity see: David P. Gushee, "A Christian Theological Account of Human Worth" in Christopher McCrudden (ed.), *Understanding Human Dignity* (Oxford University Press: Oxford, 2013); Richard Amesbury and George M. Newlands, *Faith and Human Rights: Christianity and the Global Struggle for Human Dignity* (Fortress Press, 2008).

See also: Janet Soskice, "Human Dignity and the Image of God" in Christopher McCrudden (ed.), *Understanding Human Dignity* (Oxford University Press: Oxford, 2013); David Walsh, "Dignity as an Eschatological Concept" in Christopher McCrudden (ed.), *Understanding Human Dignity* (Oxford University Press: Oxford, 2013); Tina Beattie, "The Vanishing Absolute and the Deconsecrated God: A Theological Reflection on Revelation, Law, and Human Dignity" in Christopher McCrudden (ed.), *Understanding Human Dignity* (Oxford University Press: Oxford, 2013);

On Buddhism see: Perry Schmidt-Leukel, "Buddhism and the Idea of Human Rights: Resonances and Dissonances" (2006) 26 *Buddhist-Christian Studies* 33; Sallie B. King, "Buddhism and Human Rights" in John Witte, Jr. & M. Christian Green (eds.), *Religion and Human Rights: An Introduction* (Oxford University Press, 2011).

On Hinduism see: Arvind Sharma, *Hinduism and Human Rights: A Conceptual Approach* (Oxford University Press, 2004); Martha Tarasco, "Hinduism and Human Rights" in Joseph Tham et al. (eds.), *Religious Perspectives on Bioethics and Human Rights* (Springer, 2017).

See also Chandra Muzaffar, *Rights, Religion and Reform: Enhancing Human Dignity through Spiritual and Moral Transformation* (Routledge, 2002).

99 Declaration on Religious Freedom, *Dignitatis Humanae*, on the Right of the Person and of Communities to Social and Civil Freedom in Matters Religious Promulgated by His Holiness Pope Paul VI on December 7, 1965. Available at: www.vatican.va/archive/hist_councils/ii_vatican_council/documents/vat-ii_decl_19651207_dignitatis-humanae_en.html

100 Vatican II, Section 2. See also Section 9:

"The declaration of this Vatican Council on the right of man to religious freedom has its foundation in the dignity of the person, whose exigencies have come to be are

It isn't freedom that enables dignity; it is dignity that enables freedom.

Dignitatis Humanae explains that the responsible exercise of that freedom includes a search for truth and for God.[101] The Catholic fathers were confident that the responsible exercise of freedom will lead human beings to embrace the truths of the Catholic Church. Human dignity gives us the capacity to seek and choose truth; as the New Testament teaches, it is the truth that makes us free.[102]

Friedrich Schweitzer, a prominent Protestant thinker, emphasized that "human dignity is itself seen as founded in the human's likeness of God, in the sense of Genesis 1:26f. In other words, this dignity is a special gift from God who created humans as special beings in God's likeness. Then God said, 'Let us make man in our image, after our likeness' (KJV). Human rights are considered the outgrowth of this biblical understanding."[103] He further added that "the Council of the Evangelical Church in Germany emphasized the central position of human dignity in the Protestant understanding, calling it the 'foundation' of 'European basic values'… 'To shape European politics according to these values means to make the criteria of human dignity and of a corresponding understanding of the human being its guideline.'"[104]

The idea of human dignity exists in Judaism as *kavod*. Doron Shulzinger has stressed that while the concept of human dignity (*Kvod Ha'adam*), in such wording, is not found in the Bible, "the word Kavod is widespread throughout the

fully known to human reason through centuries of experience. What is more, this doctrine of freedom has roots in divine revelation, and for this reason Christians are bound to respect it all the more conscientiously. Revelation does not indeed affirm in so many words the right of man to immunity from external coercion in matters religious."

101 Vatican II, Section 1: "… On their part, all men are bound to seek the truth, especially in what concerns God and His Church, and to embrace the truth they come to know, and to hold fast to it."

Section 2: "It is in accordance with their dignity as persons – that is, beings endowed with reason and free will and therefore privileged to bear personal responsibility – that all men should be at once impelled by nature and also bound by a moral obligation to seek the truth, especially religious truth. They are also bound to adhere to the truth, once it is known, and to order their whole lives in accord with the demands of truth … Therefore, the right to religious freedom has its foundation not in the subjective disposition of the person, but in his very nature. In consequence, the right to this immunity continues to exist even in those who do not live up to their obligation of seeking the truth and adhering to it and the exercise of this right is not to be impeded, provided that just public order be observed."

Section 3: "… Truth, however, is to be sought after in a manner proper to the dignity of the human person and his social nature. The inquiry is to be free, carried on with the aid of teaching or instruction, communication and dialogue, in the course of which men explain to one another the truth they have discovered, or think they have discovered, in order thus to assist one another in the quest for truth. Moreover, as the truth is discovered, it is by a personal assent that men are to adhere to it."

102 John 8:32: "and you will know the truth, and the truth will set you free."

103 Friedrich Schweitzer, "Human dignity and education – A Protestant view". Available at: https://hts.org.za/index.php/hts/article/view/3436/7806

104 *Id.*

Bible."[105] *Kavod* may mean "dignity, honor and glory, and respect." Another usage of the word refers to the God of Israel or divine source. Shulzinger identified that "three characteristics of human dignity in Jewish thought can be identified as 1) the extrinsic divine source of human dignity; 2) the precedence of 'dignity of the people' over personal autonomy and liberty; 3) the diminution of personal autonomy and liberty with regard to God's dignity."[106] Shulzinger further explained that "The Jewish conception of human dignity is multifaceted. The first and central aspect is the source of human dignity. Human beings have dignity because they were endowed with dignity by an external divine entity and not because of their autonomous rational capabilities or any other capacity ... Human dignity in Jewish thought is intertwined with the sanctity of life. Dignity is defined by life, regardless of physical characteristics, mental capabilities, or racial belonging."[107]

In Islam, the concept of human dignity is closely associated with the idea, *al-karama*. According to Malaysian professor Mohammad Hashim Kamali, who has written about human dignity in Islamic thought, "the Shari'ah would normally not sacrifice the basic rights and liberties of the individual and his human dignity and honour in the name of the common good, or of communal interest and maslahah. The individual is thus seen, not just as a member of the community and subservient to its will, but as a morally autonomous agent who plays a distinctive role in shaping the community's sense of direction and purpose."[108] He further adds that "the commitment of the Shari'ah to the dignity of man is so strong and pervasive as to warrant the identification of human dignity as one of the higher goals and objectives (maqasid) of the Shari'ah. This means that the dignity of man is identified as a strategic value of overall significance, and therefore all measures that are devised to protect and promote human dignity are a priori upheld and sanctified by the Shari'ah. An explicit commitment of this kind in the applied constitutions of present-day Muslim

105 Doron Shultziner, "A Jewish Conception of Human Dignity. Philosophy and Its Ethical Implications for Israeli Supreme Court Decisions" (2006) 34 *Journal of Religious Ethics* 666.

106 *Id.*, 672.

107 *Id.*, 680. Shultzinger further added that "The recognition that different conceptions of human dignity exist can, however, also lead to the understanding that some conflicts are not a matter of misconceptions or misunderstandings. Some moral disputes would not be solved by resolving conceptual differences or by employing the same terms such as human dignity. Rather, there are different notions of human dignity that stem from different worldviews. Ethical and political disputes are not necessarily a matter of misunderstandings regarding the true definition of human dignity. Rather, sometimes the source of these disputes is in irreconcilable ideological disagreements about how human dignity requires us to behave, and in irreconcilable interests and relations between individuals or groups of different political power. Finally, it has been observed that there is a prominent communitarian character to human dignity in Jewish religious thought."

108 Mohammad Hashim Kamali, *The Dignity of Man: An Islamic Perspective* (The Islamic Texts Society: Cambridge, 2002).

countries is highly recommended, if only to show a visible commitment to the clear mandates of the Qur'an."[109]

Some Muslim scholars have pointed out that the Arabic word *karama* does not translate explicitly into the word dignity as it is understood in English. The Koran explains that when Allah created Adam, he did so out of an attitude of generosity, or *karama*. The idea is that *karama* is an expression of the generosity that God shows to humankind. The righteous, in turn, exhibit the same generosity to other human beings that Allah exhibits to them when they treat each other with the same love and respect with which Allah treated Adam. The concepts of generosity and reciprocity contribute an important dimension to our understanding of dignity. On this understanding, human beings receive dignity from God due to God's generosity; and human beings reciprocate this generosity by giving dignity to others by treating them as God does us. Recognizing that God's generosity extends to other human beings (and not just to me) is a powerful route to recognizing that human dignity is important for everyone everywhere.

Human dignity is one of the central ideas developed by Immanuel Kant's systematic philosophy. Throughout his works, he refers to human dignity as not only as *Menschenwürde*, but uses also *Würde des Gebots* ("dignity of law"), *Würde der Pflicht* ("dignity of duty"), and *Würde der Sittlichkeit* ("dignity of morality"), particularly *Würde eines vernünftigen Wesens* ("dignity of a rational being") and *Würde der Menschheit* ("dignity of humanity").[110]

Dieter Schönecker and Elke Elisabath Schmidt suggest that

> A two-level-model of being is an end in itself. According to this model, every human being is an end in itself and has intrinsic value because every human being has a noumenally-good will and therefore the capacity to be moral. And since every human being (even a scoundrel) has this noumenally-good will, every human being is an end in itself and has to be respected. On a second level (in another respect), however, one has to take into consideration whether someone actually intends and acts morally, i.e., whether she also has a practically-good will. And if she does, she is an end in itself in an elevated sense and therefore has value in an elevated sense.[111]

Indeed, according to Kant, "for as such (*homo noumenon*) he is not to be valued merely as a means to the ends of other people, or even to his own ends, but as an end in himself. This is to say, he possesses a dignity (an absolute inner worth) by

109 Mohammad Hashim Kamali, *The Dignity of Man: An Islamic Perspective* (The Islamic Texts Society: Cambridge, 2002) 2.

110 Dietmar von de Pfordten, "On the Dignity of Man in Kant" (2009) 84 *Philosophy* 372.

111 Dieter Schönecker and Elke E. Schmidt, "Kant's Ground-Thesis. On Dignity and Value in the Groundwork" (2018) 52 *The Journal of Value Inquiry* 81.

which he exacts respect for himself from all other rational beings ..."[112] He further adds that one should "act in such a way that you always treat humanity, whether in your own person or in the person of any other, never simply as a means, but always at the same time as an end."[113] For Kant, human dignity is the absolute and inner value or unconditioned, incomparable value. Again, as Kant has been using various phrases associated with dignity, he has also spoken of dignity as a "way of thinking" (*Denkungsart*, 435,25), i.e., of the "morally good disposition or virtue" (435,29), or of the "*dignity* in a person who fulfills all his duties" (440,1). Thus, every rational being in its capacity to give the moral law and to obey it has dignity; and every finite rational being has its own level of dignity, depending on how virtuous it is.[114]

We can learn about dignity from each other's unique personalities and as such we can build bridges of understanding and appreciation. Indeed, human dignity can be a powerful force for finding a common ground among persons with different religious and secular theoretical groundings.

e. Respecting human dignity for everyone everywhere facilitates discussions on different conceptions of shared values

The same concept can often have various conceptions.[115] For example, complex concepts such as justice, fairness, equality, and non-discrimination are often understood in very different ways.

Human dignity is a unifying value that can help bridge divides between different conceptions. For example, when we are discussing two very different conceptions of an idea such as justice, it can be helpful to ask the question, what are the implications of those conceptions for human dignity? By doing this, we may find that although these conceptions of justice are very different, there are still significant areas of agreement. It may also help us determine that a particular conception of justice is deficient if it does not address important concerns about human dignity.

112 Immanuel Kant (Mary Gregor, trans. and ed.), *The Metaphysics of Morals. Metaphysical First Principles of the Doctrine of Virtue* (Cambridge University Press, 1996) 434f. 1. 33.

113 See: Immanuel Kant (Thomas E. Hill, Jr. and Arnulf Zweig, eds.), *Groundwork for the Metaphysics of Morals* (Oxford University Press, 2002).

114 Dieter Schönecker and Elke E. Schmidt, "Kant's Ground-Thesis. On Dignity and Value in the Groundwork" (2018) 52 *The Journal of Value Inquiry* 81.

115 The *Oxford English Dictionary* defines "concept" as a "general idea or notion, a universal; a mental representation of the essential or typical properties of something, considered without regard to the peculiar properties of any specific instance or example." "concept, n." *OED Online*, Oxford University Press, June 2019, www.oed.com/view/Entry/38130. Accessed 12 July 2019. See W. B. Gallie, "Essentially Contested Concepts" (1956) *Proceedings of the Aristotelian Society* 167. For more examples of concept v. conception with words like "justice" or "equality," see generally John Rawls, *A Theory of Justice* (2001) and Ronald Dworkin, *Law's Empire* (HarperCollins, 1988).

To portray the difference in approaching such concepts like justice or equality, here is an example. There are several conceptions of equality, namely, equality of resources, equality of opportunity, equality in the treatment by law, or equality of outcome. Equality of resources refers to the equal distribution of resources in that "the resources devoted to each person's life should be equal."[116] Ronald Dworkin says that "[u]nder equality of resources, however, people decide what sorts of lives to pursue against a background of information about the actual cost their choices impose on other people."[117]

Rawls, on the other hand, proposes fair equality of opportunity, which means that

> assuming there is a distribution of natural assets, those who are at the same level of talent and ability and have the same willingness to use them should have the same prospects of success regardless of their initial place in the social system.[118]

More than one may be important in assessing the strengths of various conceptions and their implications for other values.

f. Human dignity is a broad concept that nevertheless invites in-depth reflection within different traditions and perspectives

Human dignity is a dynamic concept not only for facilitating discussion and understanding between different religious or ideological points of view, but it is also a powerful mechanism for centering reflection within particular intellectual traditions.

Human dignity is a concept that not only invites breadth but depth as well. Thus, human dignity is useful not only for starting conversations, finding common ground, or building bridges, it is also a concept that invites searching and specific explorations within particular intellectual and faith traditions.

A good example of this is the serious and sustained examination of the meaning of human dignity within the 1960s Roman Catholic religious tradition, an examination that culminated in the issuance of Vatican II. In January 1959, Pope John XXIII announced the creation of the Second Vatican Council (Vatican II), the first such ecumenical council in close to a century. An ecumenical council is an assembly comprised of Roman Catholic religious leaders tasked to settle doctrinal issues. The rationale for it was the aftermath of World War II and the cultural changes that followed. Vatican II is considered to have shaped the modern Catholic church.

116 Ronald Dworkin, "What Is Equality? Part 2: Equality of Resources" (1981) 10 *Philosophy and Public Affairs* 289.

117 *Id.*, 288.

118 John Rawls, *A Theory of Justice* (Harvard University Press: Cambridge MA, 1999) 63.

Part of the shift came in refocusing discussion from the "dignity of truth" to the "dignity of human beings" as moral agents who are obliged to seek and adhere to the truth.

A similar in-depth examination of human dignity could be the subject of inquiry in other intellectual traditions and communities, both religious and non-religious. One of the aims of the Punta del Este Declaration is to encourage communities and individuals to reflect deeply on the meanings and implications of human dignity from within their own religious, moral, and intellectual traditions. This will facilitate not only a better understanding by those belonging to specific communities of the meaning and commitments of their principles, traditions, and doctrines, it will also help others understand those communities and to know how to engage with them in discourse and dialogue. For example, if Christians and Muslims each understand better their way of thinking about human dignity, as well as the other's way of thinking about human dignity, this will help build bridges between these normative worlds.

g. Human dignity for all reminds us that human rights are universal, inalienable, indivisible, interdependent, and interrelated

Human dignity is inherent and inalienable. Because the goal of human rights is to protect and strengthen human dignity for all people, human rights must be universal. In important ways, human rights are also indivisible, interdependent, and interrelated.

This formulation emerged from the 1993 Vienna World Conference on Human Rights, an international conference that has gained unprecedented participation of governments and a broad variety of civil society representatives, resulting in the adoption of the Vienna Declaration and Program of Action (Vienna Declaration). Among its successes, the Vienna Declaration has resulted in strengthening the UN mechanisms for protecting human rights, including the UN General Assembly resolution 48/121 establishing the UN High Commissioner for Human Rights.

Article 5 of the Vienna Declaration states:

> All human rights are universal, indivisible and interdependent and interrelated. The international community must treat human rights globally in a fair and equal manner, on the same footing, and with the same emphasis. While the significance of national and regional particularities and various historical, cultural and religious backgrounds must be borne in mind, it is the duty of States, regardless of their political, economic and cultural systems, to promote and protect all human rights and fundamental freedoms.

The Vienna Declaration affirms the universality of human rights, but also affirms a flexible pluralism, noting that "the significance of national and regional particularities and various historical, cultural and religious backgrounds must be borne in mind."[119]

119 See Article 5 of the UN General Assembly, Vienna Declaration and Programme of Action, 12 July 1993, A/CONF.157/23.

Universal

As Mary Ann Glendon and Seth D. Kaplan explain, "The framers [of the UDHR] wisely confined themselves to a small set of principles so basic that no country or group would openly reject them."[120] This was not only a practical necessity to gain broad political support for the UDHR, but it also helped ensure that this support would last.[121] Universality means that rights should be enjoyed by everyone, everywhere.

However, universality does not mean that human rights are absolute. Glendon and Kaplan explain, "One of the surest ways to misconstrue – or misuse – human rights is to think that any particular right is absolute, or that all the diverse rights can be wholly in harmony with one another. On the contrary, every right has certain boundaries and exists within a constellation of other rights."[122]

Universality also does not demand homogeneity in the implementation of rights.[123] As Jacques Maritain explained, human rights allow "different kinds of music" to be "played on the same keyboard."[124] However, a minimum standard of human rights should be ensured. Universality is compatible with modesty. It is noteworthy, that the UDHR is satisfied with 30 succinct statements of rights. One of the challenges facing human rights today is that so many claims are made in the name of human rights that the concept has become overburdened. As emphasized in the Vienna World Conference, "It is the duty of States to promote and protect all human rights and fundamental freedoms, regardless of their political, economic and cultural systems."[125]

Inalienable

Inalienable means that a human right cannot be sold or separated from the human being to which it belongs or adheres. This does not mean that rights cannot be subject to limitations, but those limitations are subject to limits. "They should not be taken away, except in specific situations and according to due process. For example, the right to liberty may be restricted if a person is found guilty of a crime by a court of law."[126]

120 Mary Ann Glendon and Seth D. Kaplan, "Renewing Human Rights" (February 2019) *First Things* 36.

121 Glendon and Kaplan continue, "This was essential not only in order to gain broad political support within the U.S., but also to ensure that the Declaration would have deep and long-lasting support across vastly different cultures, belief systems, and political ideologies." *Id.*, 36.

122 *Id.*, 37.

123 As Glendon and Kaplan explain, the principal drafters of the UDHR "were universalists but not homogenizers. They crafted a document that was flexible enough to respond to different needs in terms of emphasis and implementation, but not so malleable that any basic right could be ignored." *Id.*, 36.

124 Quoted in *Id.*, 37.

125 UN OHCHR, "What are human rights?" https://www.ohchr.org/EN/Issues/Pages/WhatareHumanRights.aspx

126 *Id.*

Indivisible

Indivisible means that human rights should be pursued in ways that are complementary and inclusive of other rights. It suggests the dangers of special pleading on behalf of a single right for some people to be pursued at the expense of other rights for other people.

Interdependent

As Glendon and Kaplan explain, "The framers of the Universal Declaration took care to ensure that it would be read as a holistic document containing a small number of interdependent, mutually reinforcing rights."[127] They note,

> Today, we are so accustomed to viewing the UDHR as a list of separate guarantees that hardly anyone realizes the document has a structure, includes duties as well as rights, and must be read as a whole. By isolating each part from its place in the overall design, misreadings of the Declaration facilitate misuse. Clashes of rights are treated as winner-takes-all contests. Forgotten are the sections of the Declaration making it clear that everyone's rights depend on respect for the rights of others, on the rule of law, and on a healthy civil society.[128]

That rights are interdependent does not mean that some rights are not prioritized. As Glendon and Kaplan explain, "A handful of rights … were prioritized, tightly drafted so as to allow little scope for variation. They include protections for freedom of religion and conscience, as well as prohibitions of torture, enslavement, degrading punishment, of retroactive penal measures, and of other grave violations of human dignity made non-derogable under the International Covenant on Civil and Political Rights."[129] The non-derogable status means that the rights cannot be suspended even in a state of emergency.[130]

Interrelated

The important insight of recognizing human rights as interdependent and interrelated is that they are meant to work together, "rather than to be pitted against each other – and to resist the notion that any basic right can be ignored."[131]

127 Mary Ann Glendon and Seth D. Kaplan, "Renewing Human Rights" (February 2019) *First Things* 37. They cite a statement published by the Ramsey Collequium in *First Things* on the fiftieth anniversary of the UDHR, which pointed out, "Far from asserting a random collection of unconnected rights, the Declaration is an integrated document that turns on a concept of the human person in community, and of the free and just society required for human flourishing." *Id.*

128 Mary Ann Glendon and Seth D. Kaplan, "Renewing Human Rights" (February 2019) *First Things* 37.

129 *Id.*

130 See: Articles 6, 7, 8, 11, 15, 16, and 18 of the ICCPR.

131 Mary Ann Glendon and Seth D. Kaplan, "Renewing Human Rights" (February 2019) *First Things* 37.

5 Article 3

Defining and specifying human rights

Article 3 reads as follows:

> Dignity is an essential part of what it means to be human. Respect for human dignity for everyone everywhere helps us define and understand the meaning and scope of all human rights. Focusing concretely and in actual situations on human dignity and its implications for particular human rights claims can help identify the specific content of these rights as well as how we understand human dignity itself.

The following is an expanded explanation of each part of Article 3.

a. Dignity is an essential part of what it means to be human

Dignity is an essential part of what it means to be a human. Denying or violating the dignity of a person entails denying or violating the very cornerstone of what it means to be a human.

Definitions of human dignity

As we have seen, as the drafters of the UDHR looked for principles upon which they could build the edifice of human rights, human dignity emerged as one of the key concepts sufficiently broad enough to be accepted (by the drafters with diverse backgrounds and representing different *Weltanschauung*) and morally appealing enough to further the work, along with related concepts such as "reason," "conscience," and the need to treat each other with a "spirit of brotherhood."

As we've also seen, dignity is an important concept in a large number of religious and non-religious normative systems. We can learn a lot about the shape and meaning of dignity by looking closely at how the term is defined by various thinkers and authorities within a variety of (religious and non-religious) traditions and (philosophical and non-philosophical) systems of thought. We can also learn from thoughtful ordinary people who reflect upon what dignity means in their eyes.

DOI: 10.4324/9781003207030-6

There are a variety of typologies for defining dignity.[1] One of the most important differences is between definitions that focus on "status" versus those that focus on "Würde" ("worth").[2] For example, Jeremy Waldron explains,

> A person may have dignity (in the sense that interests us) because he or she has worth (or "Würde" in Kant's sense): but this is a genuine derivation, not synonymy. We can distinguish the ideas also in terms of appropriate responses to value and status, respectively. The thing to do with something of value is to promote it or protect it, perhaps maximize things of that kind, at any rate to treasure it. The thing to do with a ranking status is to respect and defer to the person who bears it. It is important not to elide this difference.

Waldron claims that "dignity is a normative status and that many human rights may be understood as incidents of that status. The relation between a status and its incidents is not the same as the relation between a goal and the various subordinate principles that promote the goal."[3] He adds that

> in general, a status is not a goal or a telos: a status comprises a given set of rights rather than defining them as instrumentalities … A status account will present dignity (however defined) as foundation-*ish* (or, as we might say, foundational), but it may not be a foundation in the simple way that (for example) the major value premises of a consequential argument are a foundation of everything else in the consequentialist's moral theory.[4]

Waldron contrasts the definition of human dignity as status with the understanding of human dignity as "Würde" (worth), and citing Kant, he explains that "'Würde,' in sense of the passage in Kant's Groundwork, expresses a type of value

1 Dr. Mette Lebech, assistant professor of philosophy, explains the concept of human dignity on a taxonomy using time-typical frameworks of human dignity: cosmo-centric, Christo-centric, Logo-centric, and Polis-centric. Leech claims that: "In the cosmo-centric framework human beings are thought to have fundamental value because they have dominion (over their passions, their household or group, or over the brute beasts)"; "In the Christo-centric framework human beings are thought to have fundamental value because they are made in the image and likeness of God, and therefore reflect the creator-God in whom and from whom all things have their being and value"; "In the logo-centric framework human beings have dignity because of Reason, or, in the Kantian expression, because they are capable of understanding the implications of the 'universalisability' of any of the maxims of their actions"; "The polis-centric framework was the result of the political experience of 'reason' being used ideologically by those in power, to make assumptions as to who was to be accounted reasonable." See: Mette Lebech, "What Is Human Dignity?" (2006) *Maynooth Philosophical Papers* 59.

2 Jeremy Waldron (Meir Dan-Cohen, ed.), *Dignity, Rank and Rights. The Tanner Lectures on Human Values* (Oxford University Press: New York, 2012).

3 *Id.*, 212.

4 *Id.*, 215.

or a fact about value. 'Dignity,' by contrast, conveys the idea of a type of status that a person may have."[5]

Dignity as status

These definitions focus on ideas such as the "dignity of one's position" or the "dignity of one's office."[6] These definitions tend to be hierarchical, and so they can seem antiquated in our egalitarian age where equality is such a powerful normative concept.[7] But to the extent that these definitions emphasize the duties of behavior that attend those who are in positions of influence or power they are helpful reminders that we have often expected (and still expect) that those who have unusual power should behave in dignified ways.[8] Even today, when holders of high office behave in undignified ways, our negative judgment of them is of a greater magnitude than our judgment might be of others behaving the same way who do not hold offices of power or influence.[9] George Washington, the first US

5 *Id.*, 218.

6 See Christopher McCrudden, "Human Dignity and Judicial Interpretation of Human Rights" (2008) *European Journal of International Law* 655–724; Hubert Cancik, "'Dignity of Man' and 'Persona' in Stoic Anthropology: Some Remarks on Cicero, *De Officiis I*" in David Kretzmer and Eckart Klein, *The Concept of Human Dignity in Human Rights Discourse* (Kluwer Law International: The Hague, 2002) 19–40.

7 Ben A. McJunkin, "Rank Among Equals" (2015) *Michigan Law Review* 856; Michael Rosen, "Replies to Jeremy Waldron: Dignity, Rank and Rights" (April 21–23, 2009) Tanner Lectures, Berkeley; Remy Debes, "Review of Dignity, Rank, and Rights" (2013) *Notre Dame Philosophical Reviews*, http://ndpr.nd.edu/news/24692; Pablo Gilabert, *Human Dignity and Human Rights* (Oxford University Press: Oxford, 2018); David Estlund, "Jeremy Waldron on Law and Disagreement" (2000) 99 *Philosophical Studies* 117; Robert Mark Simpson, "Dignity, Harm, and Hate Speech, Law and Philosophy" (2013) 32 *Law and Philosophy* 701.

8 Generally, there is an expectation that those in power/with higher power will conduct themselves with dignity and decorum. This understanding has infiltrated all aspects of our lives. Even comic book heroes understand this principle; as Spider-Man put it, "with great power comes great responsibility." Though commonly attributed to Uncle Ben in *Spider-Man* (Columbia Pictures, 2002), variations of the phrase "With great power comes great responsibility" have been appearing since the Enlightenment. Indeed, similar statements are attributed to Winston Churchill ("Where there is great power there is great responsibility, where there is less power there is less responsibility, and where there is no power there can, I think, be no responsibility" February 28, 1906, *The Parliamentary Debates*), Franklin D. Roosevelt ("Today we have learned in the agony of war that great power involves great responsibility." April 14, 1945, *Daily Illinois State Journal*), and Theodore Roosevelt ("I believe in a strong executive; I believe in power; but I believe that responsibility should go with power, and that it is not well that the strong executive should be a perpetual executive." Letter of June 19, 1908 from Theodore Roosevelt to Sir George Otto Trevelyan) among others.

9 The *Merriam-Webster Dictionary* defines "noblesse oblige" as "the obligation of honorable, generous, and responsible behavior associated with high rank or birth." This concept has promoted and accepted in works from Homer's *Iliad* to present day films like *Thor* (Marvel Studios, 2011), not to mention studied by political scientists,

president, set the tone of expectations for this office by his dignity and decorum. David Brooks wrote about George Washington:

> Washington absorbed, and later came to personify what you might call the dignity code. The code was based on the same premise as the nation's Constitution – that human beings are flawed creatures who live in constant peril of falling into disasters caused by their own passions. Artificial systems have to be created to balance and restrain their desires.[10]

As Brooks writes, "The dignity code commanded its followers to be disinterested – to endeavor to put national interests above personal interests. It commanded its followers to be reticent – to never degrade intimate emotions by parading them in public. It also commanded its followers to be dispassionate – to distrust rashness, zealotry, fury, and political enthusiasm."[11] In commenting upon the state of contemporary politics, Brooks notes that the dignity code has been "completely obliterated."[12] Lest we think that Brooks was taking a swipe at President Donald Trump, we recall that Brooks wrote this in 2009, eight years before Trump was elected President.

The idea that those who hold an office of power and influence should model decorum and dignity remains powerful, even if notable exceptions remind us of the importance of the role. For example, various codes of conduct for judges and other public officials often place expectations of dignified behavior. Codes of conduct for people with authority will vary depending on the profession, state, and other variables. Below are some examples of how the concept of dignity has been incorporated within such codes of conduct.

Among others, judges are to uphold the dignity of the profession. For example, the Code of Conduct for United States Judges, states:

> (3) A judge should be patient, dignified, respectful, and courteous to litigants, jurors, witnesses, lawyers, and others with whom the judge deals in an official capacity. A judge should require similar conduct of those subject to the judge's control, including lawyers to the extent consistent with their role in the adversary process.[13]

Canon 4 further states that,

> A judge may engage in extra activities, including law-related pursuits and civic, charitable, educational, religious, social, financial, fiduciary, and governmental activities, and may speak, write, lecture, and teach on both law-related and

economists, and sociologists. See also David Brooks, "In Search of Dignity" (July 6, 2009) *New York Times*, for a discussion of this idea in politics.

10 David Brooks, "In Search of Dignity" (July 6, 2009) *New York Times.*

11 *Id.*

12 *Id.*

13 Code of Conduct for United States Judges, Canon 3.

> nonlegal subjects. However, a judge should not participate in extrajudicial activities that detract from the dignity of the judge's office, interfere with the performance of the judge's official duties, reflect adversely on the judge's impartiality, lead to frequent disqualification, or violate the limitations set forth below.[14]

Similarly, lawyers are bound by codes of conduct. For example, the New York Lawyer's Code of Professional Responsibility states in its Preamble that,

> The continued existence of a free and democratic society depends upon recognition of the concept that justice is based upon the rule of law grounded in respect for the dignity of the individual and the capacity of the individual through reason for enlightened self-government. Law so grounded makes justice possible, for only through such law does the dignity of the individual attain respect and protection. Without it, individual rights become subject to unrestrained power, respect for law is destroyed, and rational self-government is impossible.[15]

Rule EC 1–7 of the Code further states "A lawyer should avoid bias and condescension toward, and treat with dignity and respect, all parties, witnesses, lawyers, court employees, and other persons involved in the legal process." Rule EC 7–36 indicates that,

> Judicial hearings ought to be conducted through dignified and orderly procedures designed to protect the rights of all parties. Although a lawyer has the duty to represent the client zealously, the lawyer should not engage in any conduct that offends the dignity and decorum of proceedings. While maintaining independence, a lawyer should be respectful, courteous, and above-board in relations with a judge or hearing officer before whom the lawyer appears. The lawyer should avoid undue solicitude for the comfort or convenience of judge or jury and should avoid any other conduct calculated to gain special consideration.[16]

The same is true for professions of trust, including, the medical profession.[17] Section 1 of the American Medical Association (AMA) Principles of Medical Ethics clearly states that "The principal objective of the medical profession is to render service to humanity with full respect for the dignity of man. Physicians should merit the confidence of patients entrusted to their care, rendering to each a full measure of service and devotion."[18] Furthermore, Section 4 prescribes that,

14 *Id.*, Canon 4.
15 New York Lawyer's Code of Professional Responsibility.
16 *Id.*, Rule EC 7–36.
17 *Id.*, Rule EC 1–7.
18 American Medical Association (AMA) *Principles of Medical Ethics* (1957), Section 1.

> The medical professional should safeguard the public and itself against physicians deficient in moral character or professional competence. Physicians should observe all laws, uphold the dignity and honor of the profession and accept its self-imposed disciplines. They should expose, without hesitation, illegal or unethical conduct of fellow members of the profession.[19]

Similarly, Article I of the AMA Code of Medical Ethics states "A physician shall be dedicated to providing competent medical care, with compassion and respect for human dignity and rights."[20]

Lastly, the clergy is expected to act with dignity and decorum. About two-thirds of US adults consider clergy (religious leaders) to have high or very high ethical standards.[21] The clergy is subjected to various codes of conduct that differ depending on the denomination and even region. For example, the Code of Conduct for Clergy (Code) of the Archdiocese of St. Paul and Minneapolis (Archdiocese) prescribes policies and provides guidance for clergy belonging to the Archdiocese that is to ensure that their conduct comports with their professed faith.[22] Furthermore, the code provides practical guidance to enable the clergy to effectively serve their communities and protect people coming into contact with the clergy (and especially those vulnerable).[23]

It is not an accident or coincidence that we have particular expectations of judges, lawyers, doctors, and clergy. These were the three earliest recognized professions, each governed by special rules of conduct and comportment reflecting the unique power these professions held over various aspects of human life – doctors concerning physical health, lawyers concerning material wealth, and clergy concerning spiritual health.

Human dignity as worth

Another family of definitions of dignity focuses on worth. The idea here is that dignity is an expression of the inherent and inalienable value of human

19 *Id.*, Section 4.

20 AMA Code of Medical Ethics, Article I.

21 Pew Research Center, "Americans Have Positive Views about Religion's Role in Society, but Want It Out of Politics" (2019). Available at: https://www.pewforum.org/2019/11/15/most-congregants-trust-clergy-to-give-advice-about-religious-issues-fewer-trust-clergy-on-personal-matters/#fn-32346-6

22 Archdiocese of St. Paul and Minneapolis, *Code of Conduct for Clergy* 104 (2016). Available at: https://safe-environment.archspm.org/100-ministerial-standardssafe-environment/104-code-conduct-clergy/.

23 *Id.*, Section 1. "1.1 Clergy will maintain appropriate boundaries in professional relationships, and not use the power inherent in their position to exercise unreasonable or inappropriate authority over others.

1.2 Clergy will relate to others respectfully and professionally, and will work collaboratively and cooperatively with others serving the Church.

"1.3 Clergy must not engage in physical, psychological, or sexual harassment of any person, and must not tolerate such harassment by others serving the Church. Harassment may be a single incident or a persistent pattern of behavior where the purpose is to create a hostile, offensive, or intimidating work environment."

beings.[24] By being human, people have value and worth that is intrinsic and should be recognized and respected by others and defended and protected by the state.

Both the idea of status and worth inform our understanding of dignity in the human rights context. The idea of status is sometimes inverted to focus not on hierarchies of office, class, or rank, but on the shared status of being human beings.[25] The idea is that we all share a status based on our shared identity as human beings. Worth is also important to our understanding of human dignity in the human rights context, as one of the key ideas informing contemporary understanding of dignity is that every human being has inherent value and worth simply based on the fact that they are human beings.[26] As is often the case with complex concepts with many conceptions, there is something we can learn from all of these definitions, and insights from different definitions will likely prove helpful when addressing specific human rights issues.

We must be careful to not exaggerate the demands that human dignity places upon states, society, or each other. For example, if dignity were to require us to express equal concern for all people, then special treatment of family, neighbors, friends, and fellow citizens could be construed as blameworthy conduct. This is contrary to sound moral thinking since we should have a special regard for those with whom we share close moral (and sometimes legal) proximity.[27] Thus, overly demanding claims about the requirements of respecting or protecting the dignity of others will be self-defeating, since disregarding such exaggerated demands is entirely reasonable and morally desirable. This is generally true of important moral principles that are applied in the realms of politics and law. We are often better off having realistically thin conceptions of ideas such as human dignity when we are defining the duties of states, or the rights of people under the law, whereas other definitions are often helpful when we are speaking in ways that are aspirational or motivational.

24 Immanuel Kant (Paul Guyer and Allen W. Wood, eds.), *Practical Philosophy* (Cambridge University Press: New York, 1999) 84; Aurel Kolnai, "Dignity" in Robin S. Dillon (ed.), *Dignity, Character, and Self-Respect* (Routledge, 1995); Christopher McCrudden, "Human Dignity and Judicial Interpretation of Human rights" (2008) 19 *European Journal of International Law* 679; Stephen J. Heyman, *Free Speech and Human Dignity* (Yale University Press: New Haven, CT, 2008) 39; George. P. Fletcher, "Human Dignity as a Constitutional Value" (1984) 22 *University of Western Ontario Law Review* 171.

25 Jeremy Waldron (Meir Dan-Cohen, ed.), *Dignity, Rank and Rights. The Tanner Lectures on Human Values* (Oxford University Press: New York, 2012); John Austin (Robert Campbell, ed.), *Lectures on Jurisprudence, or The Philosophy of Positive Law* (John Murray: London, 1885) Volume II, Lecture XL, 687–688; Ronald H. Graveson, *Status in the Common Law* (Athlone Press: London, 1953).

26 Herbert Spiegelberg, "Human Dignity: A Challenge to Contemporary Philosophy" (1971) 9 *Journal of New Paradigm Research* 39–64; Aurel Kolnai, "Dignity" (1976) 51 *Philosophy* 251.

27 See Elizabeth S. Scott and Ben Chen, "Fiduciary Principles in Family Law" in Evan Criddle, Paul Miller and Robert Sitkoff (eds.), *Oxford Handbook of Fiduciary Law* (Oxford University Press, 2019).

For example, Kant's categorical imperative that we must never treat others as means to our ends, but as ends in themselves (which is closely related to his account of human dignity), is useful guidance, even if we can imagine exceptions to the rule that renders the imperative something less than absolutely categorical.[28] Even rules that admit exceptions can be useful rules of thumb or even default rules that we should violate only when reasons for doing so are extraordinarily strong. As the philosopher William D. Ross explained, some duties are *prima facie* duties rather than absolute duties, in that they can be overcome by other important countervailing duties, or perhaps even other important reasons.[29]

Dignity in international and domestic law

Dignity or human dignity is a common feature in several legally binding instruments, including international treaties and domestic constitutions and laws. As is common with other important concepts such as freedom, liberty, equality, non-discrimination, and due process of law, these concepts are often left undefined, especially in foundational or framework documents such as constitutions.

28 The classic examples proffered by philosophers often involve the need to torture a terrorist to find a ticking bomb. David Luban, "Liberalism, Torture, and the Ticking Bomb" (2005) 91 *Virginia Law Review* 1425. That we can imagine an extreme situation where we might need to treat others as means rather than as ends in themselves is not a powerful refutation of the usefulness of the basic principle, nor to the advisability of treating the principle as categorical, since we might otherwise find ourselves resorting to torture in too many situations. Jeremy Davies, "The Fire-Raisers: Bentham and Torture" (2012) 19 *Interdisciplinary Studies in the Long Nineteenth Century* 15.

29 William D. Ross (Philip Stratton-Lake, ed.), *The Right and the Good* (Clarendon Press: Oxford, 2007) 21–22. Ross identified seven *prima facie* duties, namely:

"(1) Some duties rest on previous acts of my own. These duties seem to include two kinds,

(a) those resting on a promise or what may fairly be called an implicit promise, such as the implicit undertaking not to tell lies which seems to be implied in the act of entering into conversation (at any rate by civilized men), or of writing books that purport to be history and not fiction. These may be called the duties of fidelity,

(b) those resting on a previous wrongful act. These may be called the duties of reparation.

(2) Some rest on previous acts of other men, i.e., services done by them to me. These may be loosely described as the duties of gratitude.

(3) Some rest on the fact or possibility of a distribution of pleasure or happiness (or of the means thereto) which is not in accordance with the merit of the persons concerned; in such cases there arises a duty to upset or prevent such a distribution. These are the duties of justice.

(4) Some rest on the mere fact that there are other beings in the world whose condition we can make better in respect of virtue, or of intelligence, or of pleasure. These are the duties of beneficence,

(5) Some rest on the fact that we can improve our own condition in respect of virtue or of intelligence. These are the duties of self-improvement.

(6) I think that we should distinguish from (4) the duties that may be summed up under the title of 'not injuring others.'" *Id.*, 21.

Treaties

The International Covenant on Civil and Political Rights

The International Covenant on Civil and Political Rights (the ICCPR) mentions the concept of human dignity on three occasions. The Preamble to the ICCPR states:

> Considering that, in accordance with the principles proclaimed in the Charter of the United Nations, recognition of the inherent dignity and of the equal and inalienable rights of all members of the human family is the foundation of freedom, justice and peace in the world,
> Recognizing that these rights derive from the inherent dignity of the human person.

Also, Article 10(1) of the ICCPR states, "All persons deprived of their liberty shall be treated with humanity and with respect for the inherent dignity of the human person." Here, the importance of human dignity when the state has heightened power or control over a person is emphasized.

The International Covenant on Economic, Social and Cultural Rights

The ICCPR's preambular paragraphs on human dignity are repeated in the International Covenant on Economic, Social, and Cultural Right (the ICESCR). Also, Article 13(1) of the ICESCR states:

> The States Parties to the present Covenant recognize the right of everyone to education. They agree that education shall be directed to the full development of the human personality and the sense of its dignity, and shall strengthen the respect for human rights and fundamental freedoms.

Here again, dignity is emphasized in a context (education of children) where people are especially vulnerable and the state's power is of a high magnitude.

The International Convention on the Elimination of All Forms of Racial Discrimination

The International Convention on the Elimination of All Forms of Racial Discrimination (the ICERD) refers to human dignity several times in its preambular paragraphs:

> Considering that the Charter of the United Nations is *based on the principles of the dignity and equality* inherent in all human beings and that all Member States have pledged themselves to take joint and separate action, in co-operation with the Organization, for the achievement of one of the purposes of the

> United Nations which is to promote and encourage universal respect for and observance of human rights and fundamental freedoms for all, without distinction as to race, sex, language or religion,
>
> Considering that the Universal Declaration of Human Rights proclaims that *all human beings are born free and equal in dignity and rights* and that everyone is entitled to all the rights and freedoms set out therein, without distinction of any kind, in particular as to race, color or national origin ...
>
> Considering that the United Nations Declaration on the Elimination of All Forms of Racial Discrimination of 20 November 1963 (General Assembly resolution 1904 (XVIII)) solemnly affirms the necessity of speedily eliminating racial discrimination throughout the world in all its forms and manifestations and of *securing understanding of and respect for the dignity of the human person.*
>
> (Emphasis added)

The repeated inclusion of dignity in the preambular clauses reminds us that dignity is a touchstone in understanding the purpose of the convention as well as the rights of nondiscrimination that is the primary focus.

The Convention on the Elimination of All Forms of Discrimination Against Women

The Convention on the Elimination of All Forms of Discrimination Against Women (the CEDAW) contains similar references to human dignity in its preambular paragraphs. CEDAW's Preamble states:

> Noting that the Charter of the United Nations reaffirms faith in fundamental human rights, in *the dignity and worth of the human person* and in the equal rights of men and women,
>
> Noting that the Universal Declaration of Human Rights affirms the principle of the inadmissibility of discrimination and proclaims that *all human beings are born free and equal in dignity and rights* and that everyone is entitled to all the rights and freedoms set forth therein, without distinction of any kind, including distinction based on sex ...
>
> Recalling that *discrimination against women violates the principles of equality of rights and respect for human dignity*, is an obstacle to the participation of women, on equal terms with men, in the political, social, economic, and cultural life of their countries, hampers the growth of the prosperity of society and the family and makes more difficult the full development of the potentialities of women in the service of their countries and of humanity.
>
> (Emphasis added)

Here, the repeated use of the concept of dignity aims to stress its importance in reaffirming the rights of women, and combating all forms of discrimination that continue to be present in many aspects of life.

The Convention Against Torture and Other Cruel, Inhuman, or Degrading Treatment or Punishment

The Convention Against Torture and Other Cruel, Inhuman or Degrading Treatment or Punishment (CAT) also refers to human dignity in the Preamble, which states: "Recognizing that those rights derive from the inherent dignity of the human person."

The Convention on the Rights of the Child

Among international human rights treaties, the Convention on the Rights of the Child (CRC) is prominent in making clear references to human dignity in its preambular and operative paragraphs. CRC's Preamble states:

> Considering that, in accordance with the principles proclaimed in the Charter of the United Nations, *recognition of the inherent dignity and of the equal and inalienable rights* of all members of the human family is the foundation of freedom, justice and peace in the world,
>
> Bearing in mind that the peoples of the United Nations have, in the Charter, reaffirmed their faith in fundamental human rights and *in the dignity and worth of the human person*, and have determined to promote social progress and better standards of life in larger freedom ... Considering that the child should be fully prepared to live an individual life in society, and brought up in the spirit of the ideals proclaimed in the Charter of the United Nations, *and in particular in the spirit of peace, dignity, tolerance, freedom, equality and solidarity.*
>
> (Emphasis added)

Article 23(1) of the CRC indicates that: "States Parties recognize that a mentally or physically disabled child should enjoy a full and decent life, *in conditions which ensure dignity*, promote self-reliance and facilitate the child's active participation in the community" (emphasis added). Dignity is important for everyone, including children with disabilities.

Article 28(2) of the CRC prescribes that: "States Parties shall take all appropriate measures to ensure that school discipline is administered in a manner consistent with the *child's human dignity* and conformity with the present Convention" (emphasis added). Dignity is important when children are disciplined in school, a setting where harsh or even violent practices have been known to take place.

Article 37(c) of the CRC indicates that:

> Every child deprived of liberty shall be treated with humanity and *respect for the inherent dignity of the human person*, and in a manner, which takes into account the needs of persons of his or her age. In particular, every child deprived of liberty shall be separated from adults unless it is considered in the child's best interest not to do so and shall have the right to maintain contact

> with his or her family through correspondence and visits, save in exceptional circumstances.
>
> (Emphasis added)

Again, dignity is especially recognized at a time when the state's power is at a high ebb, such as when refugees are in state detention.

Article 39 of the CRC states that

> States Parties shall take all appropriate measures to promote physical and psychological recovery and social reintegration of a child victim of any form of neglect, exploitation, or abuse; torture or any other form of cruel, inhuman or degrading treatment or punishment; or armed conflicts. Such recovery and reintegration shall take place in an environment which fosters the health, self-respect, and *dignity of the child.*
>
> (Emphasis added)

Here, the importance of dignity is emphasized when states are dealing with children who are victims of neglect, exploitations or abuse, or in other conditions of severe human rights violations.

Article 40(1) of the CRC states that

> States Parties recognize the right of every child alleged as, accused of, or recognized as having infringed the penal law to be treated in a manner consistent with the promotion of the *child's sense of dignity and worth*, which reinforces the child's respect for the human rights and fundamental freedoms of others and which takes into account the child's age and the desirability of promoting the child's reintegration and the child's assuming a constructive role in society.
>
> (Emphasis added)

Here, the important idea is that the dignity of the child must be promoted when administering juvenile justice.

It is noteworthy that human dignity plays such a prominent role in a convention focusing on children, suggesting that dignity is an especially important consideration at times when human beings are particularly vulnerable.

The Convention on the Rights of Persons with Disabilities

As the CRC, the Convention on the Rights of Persons with Disabilities (CRPD) exceeds any other international treaties in relying on the concept of human dignity. Again, this makes sense given the particular vulnerability of persons with disabilities. The relevant parts of the CRPD are noted below:

> Preamble
>
> (a) Recalling the principles proclaimed in the Charter of the United Nations which *recognize the inherent dignity and worth* and the equal and

inalienable rights of all members of the human family as the foundation of freedom, justice and peace in the world …

(h) Recognizing also that *discrimination* against any person based on disability *is a violation of the inherent dignity and worth* of the human person …

(y) Convinced that a comprehensive and integral international convention *to promote and protect the rights and dignity of persons with disabilities* will make a significant contribution to redressing the profound social disadvantage of persons with disabilities and promote their participation in the civil, political, economic, social, and cultural spheres with equal opportunities, in both developing and developed countries …

Article 1. The purpose of the present Convention is to promote, protect and ensure the full and equal enjoyment of all human rights and fundamental freedoms by all persons with disabilities, and *to promote respect for their inherent dignity* …

Article 3. The principles of the present Convention shall be:

(a) *Respect for inherent dignity*, individual autonomy including the freedom to make one's own choices, and independence of persons …

Article 8.1. States Parties undertake to adopt immediate, effective, and appropriate measures:

(a) To raise awareness throughout society, including at the family level, regarding persons with disabilities, and to *foster respect for the rights and dignity* of persons with disabilities …

Article 16(4). States Parties shall take all appropriate measures to promote the physical, cognitive and psychological recovery, rehabilitation, and social reintegration of persons with disabilities who become victims of any form of exploitation, violence, or abuse, including through the provision of protection services. Such recovery and reintegration shall take place in an environment that fosters the health, welfare, self-respect, *dignity*, and autonomy of the person and takes into account gender- and age-specific needs.

Article 24(1). 1. States Parties recognize the right of persons with disabilities to education. To realize this right without discrimination and based on an equal opportunity, States Parties shall ensure an inclusive education system at all levels and lifelong learning directed to:

(a) The *full development of human potential and sense of dignity and self-worth*, and the strengthening of respect for human rights, fundamental freedoms, and human diversity…

Article 25(d) Require health professionals to provide care of the same quality to persons with disabilities as to others, including based on free and informed consent by, inter alia, raising awareness of the human rights, *dignity*, autonomy, and needs of persons with disabilities through training and the promulgation of ethical standards for public and private health care.

(Emphases added)

These international treaties each emphasize the centrality of human dignity, reaffirming the importance of human dignity not only as a foundational value in human rights law but also as an important means for achieving the goals of these treaties.

Domestic laws

Several states have constitutions or other foundational laws that include prominent references to human dignity. These are especially prominent features of constitutions and foundational laws enacted since World War II. For example, the German Basic Law introduces the concept of human dignity in Article 1, stating: "(1) Human dignity shall be inviolable. To respect and protect it shall be the duty of all state authority." The courts (and especially the Federal Constitutional Court) have used the concept of human dignity to provide redress where other protection failed. The South African Constitution states in Article 1 that "The Republic of South Africa is one, sovereign, democratic state founded on the following values: a. Human dignity, the achievement of equality, and the advancement of human rights and freedoms." Article 7(1) indicates that "This Bill of Rights is a cornerstone of democracy in South Africa. It enshrines the rights of all people in our country and affirms the democratic values of human dignity, equality and freedom." Article 10 confirms that "Everyone has inherent dignity and the right to have their dignity respected and protected." The South African Constitution contains further references to human dignity throughout the document. Neither of the constitutions defines human dignity.

While the UK does not have a written constitution, the issue of human dignity has been raised in case law. For example, in *Ghaidan v. Godin-Mendoza*, Lady Hale of Richmond indicated that "democracy is founded on the principle that each individual has equal value. Treating some as automatically having less value than others not only causes pain and distress to that person but also violates his or her dignity as a human being."[30]

Agreement about core definition

Despite the differences in definitions, there is widespread agreement about the core or fundamental meaning of human dignity. As Paolo G. Carozza, professor of law at Notre Dame Law School, explains,

> At a very high level of generality, one can find human dignity invoked across legal systems of widely divergent traditions to denote two interrelated ideas: (a) an ontological claim that all human beings have an equal and intrinsic moral worth; and (b) a normative principle that all human beings are entitled to have this status of equal worth respected by others and also have a duty to respect it in all others.[31]

30 *Ghaidan v. Godin-Mendoza* [2004] 2 AC (HL) 557, 605 (UK).

31 Paolo G. Carozza, "Human Rights, Human Dignity, and Human Experience" in Christopher McCrudden (ed.), *Understanding Human Dignity* (Oxford University

Denise Rhéaume, professor of law at the University of Toronto, suggests that human dignity "refers to a kind of worth that is not contingent on being useful, or attractive, or pleasant or otherwise serving the ends of others" and "is ascribed to human beings independently of their particular accomplishments or merits of praiseworthiness."[32]

Justice Iacobucci, judge of the Supreme Court of Canada, analyzed human dignity through the equality guarantees found in Section 15(1) of the Canadian Charter of Rights and Freedoms:

> What is human dignity? There can be different conceptions of what human dignity means .... [T]he equality guarantee in s. 15(1) is concerned with the realization of personal autonomy and self-determination. Human dignity means that an individual or group feels self-respect and self-worth. It is concerned with physical and psychological integrity and empowerment. Human dignity is harmed by unfair treatment premised upon personal traits or circumstances which do not relate to individual needs, capacities, or merits. It is enhanced by laws which are sensitive to the needs, capacities, and merits of different individuals, taking into account the context underlying their differences. Human dignity is harmed when individuals and groups are marginalized, ignored, or devalued, and is enhanced when laws recognize the full place of all individuals and groups within Canadian society. Human dignity within the meaning of the equality guarantee does not relate to the status or position of an individual in society per se, but rather concerns the manner in which a person legitimately feels when confronted with a particular law. Does the law treat him or her unfairly, taking into account all of the circumstances regarding the individuals affected and excluded by the law?[33]

Another important explanation of human dignity by Aurel Kolnai, philosopher and political theorist, states that "Dignity means 'being worthy of ...', the completion that most aptly suggests itself would seem to be worthy of being appreciatively acknowledged as worthy to be thus acknowledged and appreciated, sans plus."[34] If one then considers why human dignity was so central to the UDHR

Press: Oxford, 2013) 616. Carozza adds, "The normative principle includes within it the obligations of the state to respect human dignity in its law and policy as well." This core of understood meaning leads to broad agreement across legal systems that certain types of conduct are prohibited. "Prohibitions on genocide, slavery, torture, forced disappearance, and systematic racial discrimination, for instance, represent some important examples of universal acceptance of the implications of the status and basic principle of human dignity. It is not surprising that in international human rights law many of these clearest instantiations of the requirements of human dignity also coincide with the strongest and exceptionless norms of international law, found for example in the definitions of crimes against humanity or *jus cogens*." *Id.*, 616–617.

32 Denise G. Réaume, "Discrimination and Dignity" (2003) 63 *Louisiana Law Review* 645, 675.

33 *Law v. Canada (Minister of Emp't and Immigration)* [1999] 1 S.C.R. 497 (Canada).

34 Aurel Kolnai, "Dignity" in Robin S. Dillon (ed.), *Dignity, Character, and Self-Respect* (Routledge, 1995) 56.

after the Nazi mass atrocities, Kolnai's definition is the direct response to it. Indeed, the Nazis spoke of life that was unworthy of protection and unworthy of living that justified their annihilation ("*Vernichtung lebensunwerten Lebens*").[35]

This explanation of human dignity as equal worth is also visible in the jurisprudence of the South African courts that state that "[t]he new Constitution rejects this [apartheid] past and affirms the equal worth of all South Africans."[36] Furthermore, Albie Sachs, judge of the Constitutional Court of South Africa, emphasized: "there is a core to the individual conscience so intrinsic to the dignity of the human personality that it is difficult to imagine any factors whatsoever that could justify its being penetrated by the state."[37]

Human dignity is broader than human rights

Although human dignity is an "indispensable basis" for human rights, it is a normative concept that goes beyond human rights. As John Tasioulas, Professor of Politics, Philosophy, and Law at King's College London, explains, "[Human dignity] is a broader notion than human rights, with the result that human dignity may be at stake in contexts and in ways not adequately captured by the idea of human rights, and even when no human rights issue arises."[38] For example, desecrating the graves of the dead is a violation of human dignity, even if we do not think of the dead as having human rights.

Christoph Enders has described human dignity as a right to rights, a primordial right.[39] Without recognizing human dignity, human rights will fail. However, without human rights, human dignity still exists (although it may need to be enforced by human rights provisions). Pleading human dignity allows for more flexibility than pleading human rights. Human dignity can be enforced even if the protections of human rights fail. Indeed, Bernard Schlink, lawyer and novelist, argues that "When the goal is to imbue human dignity as a last resort and an absolute right that courts can enforce and the state will respect, it is an obvious move to turn to Kant, because he understands human dignity as an absolute that prohibits each and every instrumentalization and requires to treat everybody as a subject and nobody as an object."[40]

The fact that human dignity is broader (and more flexible) than human rights has also been accepted in the jurisprudence of the German Federal Constitutional Court. Article 1(1) of the German Basic Law protects human dignity, stating that

35 Robert J. Lifton, *The Nazi Doctors: Medical Killing and the Psychology of Genocide* (Basic Books, 1986) 142.

36 *S. v. Makwanyane* 1995 (3) SA 391 (CC) at para. 329 (S. Afr.).

37 *S. v. Lawrence* 1997 (4) SA 1176 (CC) at 128 (S. Afr.).

38 John Tasioulas, "Human Dignity and the Foundations of Human Rights" in Christopher McCrudden (ed.), *Understanding Human Dignity* (Oxford University Press: Oxford, 2013) 308.

39 Christoph Enders, *Die Menschenwürde in der Verfassungsordnung. Zur Dogmatik des Art. 1 GG* (Mohr Siebeck: Tübingen, 1997) 251.

40 Schlink (2013) 632.

"Human dignity shall be inviolable. To respect and protect it shall be the duty of all state authority." The German Federal Constitutional Court has used Article 1 (1) of the German Basic Law to justify the protection of human rights where it is crucial to uphold and protect human dignity. For example, in the *Aviation Security Act Case*, the German Federal Constitutional Court found that:

> Article 1(1) of the German Basic Law protects the individual human being not only against humiliation, branding, persecution, outlawing and similar actions by third parties or by the state itself … [T]he obligation to respect and protect human dignity generally precludes making a human being a mere object of the state. What is thus absolutely prohibited is any treatment of a human being by a public authority which fundamentally calls into question his or her quality as a subject.[41]

Similarly, in the *Microcensus Case*, the German Federal Constitutional Court recognized that:

> The state cannot through any measure, not even a law, violate human dignity or otherwise interfere with the freedom of the person in its essence, beyond the limits drawn in Art. 2 sec. 1 GG. Thus, the Basic Law confers on each individual citizen an inviolable sphere of private life choices that is beyond the influence of public authority (BVerfGE 6, 32 (41), 389 (433)).
>
> In the light of this concept of the human being, all human beings living in a community enjoy a right to social value and recognition. It would violate human dignity to make a human being a mere object within the state (cf. BVerfGE 5, 85 (204); 7, 198 (205)). It would be incompatible with human dignity if the state were to claim the right to compulsorily register and cata logue a human being in his or her entire personality, even under the anonymity of a statistical survey, and thereby to treat one as a commodity, accessible for inventory in every respect.[42]

Furthermore, in the *Life Imprisonment Case*, the German Federal Constitutional Court found that:

> It is contrary to human dignity to make the individual the mere tool (*blosses Objekt*) of the state. The principle that "each person must always be an end in himself" applies unreservedly to all areas of law; the intrinsic dignity of the person consists in acknowledging him as an independent personality …
>
> The constitutional principles of the Basic Law embrace the respect and protection of human dignity. The free human person and his dignity are the highest values of the constitutional order. The state in all of its forms is obliged to respect and defend it. This is based on the conception of man as a

41 *Aviation Security Act Case*, 1 BvR 357/05 (Germany).
42 *Microcensus Case*, BVerfGE 27, 1 (Germany).

spiritual-moral being endowed with the freedom to determine and develop himself.[43]

These cases illustrate ways in which human dignity is broader than human rights and helps to protect important interests where other protections fail to give adequate consideration to aspects of what it means to be human.

b. Respect for human dignity for everyone everywhere helps us define and understand the meaning and scope of all human rights

The Punta del Este Declaration does not reiterate the specific rights enumerated in the UDHR, nor does it explicitly address the proliferation of rights recognized in international human rights instruments. Focusing on human dignity is an explicit effort to renew and refocus human rights.[44] But focusing on the human dignity of everyone everywhere does help us determine the content of rights, their meanings, and permissible limitations.

Defining and understanding the rights of conscience

For example, human dignity for everyone everywhere helps us understand why it is important for governments to protect people in matters of conscience, including conscientious objection to military service,[45] as well as conscientious objections to

43 *Life Imprisonment Case,* BVerfGE 187, 227–228 (1977) (Germany).

44 To some extent, the success of human rights has led to their being asked to do too much. As human rights have been used to frame international agendas and global standards, "Groups harnessed the moral authority of the human rights idea to champion their causes. Today there are calls to make everything from access to the Internet to development aid to free university education a right. The Universal Declaration's modest thirty articles have burst into potentially more than a thousand rights provisions in agreements that many governments have signed." Mary Ann Glendon and Seth D. Kaplan, "Renewing Human Rights" (February 2019) *First Things* 35. Cramming a thousand rights claims into the backpack is enough to break the back of a concept even as resilient and muscular as human rights.

45 Article 9 of the European Convention on Human Rights (ECHR) does not explicitly incorporate the right to conscientious objection. However, the European Court of Human Rights (ECtHR) found that the right to conscientious objection to the military service is protected under Article 9. In *Bayatyan v. Armenia*, the first case to consider whether conscientious objection falls within the ambits of Article 9, the ECtHR found that where the opposition to military service was motivated by a deeply and genuinely held religious or other beliefs, Article 9 protection was engaged. The ECtHR found that the applicant's Article 9 right was violated taking into account that overwhelming majority of European states accommodated alternative service for conscientious objector. In *Adyan and others v. Armenia*, the ECtHR went even further to find that the conscientious objection extended, in the case, not only to performing in the military service but also in the alternative civilian service and so held that there was a violation of Article 9. The reasons for expanding the scope of conscientious objection to the alternative civilian service was that, in the case, it was not sufficiently

participating in capital punishment,[46] or in performing abortions[47] (independently of what others think of those practices or the law surrounding them).

separated from the military system and the alternative civilian service was significantly longer that the military service (18 months longer).

46 The federal conscience protection in 18 U.S.C. §3597(b) states that:

"No employee of any State department of corrections, the United States Department of Justice, the Federal Bureau of Prisons, or the United States Marshals Service, and no employee providing services to that department, bureau, or service under contract shall be required, as a condition of that employment or contractual obligation, to be in attendance at or to participate in any prosecution or execution under this section if such participation is contrary to the moral or religious convictions of the employee. In this subsection, 'participation in executions' includes personal preparation of the condemned individual and the apparatus used for execution and supervision of the activities of other personnel in carrying out such activities."

The provision is far reaching to include a broad range of individuals covered by the protection, and not only in direct involvement, but also covers several preparatory acts and the supervision of others. Several states have express statute or regulation protections to ensure that one cannot be forced to participate in a death penalty. For example, the California Penal Code at §3605(c) indicates that "[n]o physician or any other person invited pursuant to this section, whether or not employed by the Department of Corrections, shall be compelled to attend the execution, and any physician's attendance shall be voluntary." The Connecticut Department of Correction Directive Number 6:15 states that "[e]xcept as provided by statute, no employee of the Department of Correction shall be required to participate in the execution of an inmate." §15–18–82.1(i) of the Code of Alabama indicates that "Nothing contained in this section is intended to require any physician, nurse, pharmacist, or employee of the Department of Corrections or any other person to assist in any aspect of an execution which is contrary to the person's moral or ethical beliefs." For example, §15–18–82.1(i) of the Code of Alabama extends the objection to capital punishment to where such assistance is contrary to person's moral or ethical belief. Similarly, 42 U.S.C. § 300a-7 ("Church Amendments") cover not only requirements contrary to religious beliefs but also contrary to moral convictions. Similarly, the American Medical Association's Code of Ethics in Rule 2.06 recognizes that: "a physician, as a member of a profession dedicated to preserving life when there is hope of doing so, should not be a participant in a legally authorized execution."

47 The majority of the European countries have some protection of the conscientious objection of the medical professionals to abortion. For example, in the UK, the conscientious objection of medical staff is enshrined in Section 4 of the Abortion Act 1967 that states that "no person shall be under any duty, whether by contract or by any statutory or other legal requirement, to participate in any treatment authorized by this Act to which he has a conscientious objection." However, in the case of *Greater Glasgow Health Board (Appellant) v. Doogan and another (Respondents) (Scotland)*, the UK Supreme Court clarified that the provision is to be granted a narrow interpretation and as a result, participation in abortion was limited to mean "hands-on" capacity. In Italy, conscientious objection is protected in Article 9 of the Legalization of Abortion: Law 194 of the Italian Republic, 1978, that states: "Health personnel and allied health personnel shall not be required to assist in the procedures referred to in Sections 5 and 7 or in pregnancy terminations if they have a conscientious objection, declared in advance." In Luxembourg, conscientious objection is protected in Article 13 of Law of 17 December 2014 that sates: "No doctor will be required to perform an abortion. Similarly, no health professional will be required to contribute to such an intervention." Article 350 of the Belgian Penal Code indicates that: "Neither

In the years since the adoption of the UDHR, there has been a gradual expansion in the recognition of the scope of conscience that should be protected – extending beyond those who belong to particular religious groups,[48] to those who have their own religious or non-religious conscientious bases for objecting to some form of government compulsion.[49] For example, in situations dealing with access to medical care, providers of such services should not be obligated to take any actions to which they have sincere conscience-based objections if the persons who would be affected have reasonably available alternative sources of services.[50]

a physician, nor a nurse, nor a medical assistant is obliged to cooperate with the termination of a pregnancy. The physician is obliged to inform a patient interested in abortion, during the first visit, of his refusal." In the US, the pharmacists' right to conscientious objection was affirmed in the case of *Morr-Fitz, Inc. v. Quinn (Morr-Fitz, Inc. v. Quinn*, 2012 IL App (4th) 110398).

Furthermore, the ECtHR indirectly ruled on conscientious objection for medical professionals in that: "States are obliged to organize the health services system in such a way as to ensure that *an effective exercise of the freedom of conscience of health professionals in the professional context* does not prevent patients from obtaining access to services." (*R.R. v. Poland*, no. 27617/04, ECHR 2011, § 83).

48 The history of conscientious objectors in the US goes as far as the American Revolutionary War. The conscientious objectors would have to pay a fine, and those who refused to pay would have seen their properties confiscated. During the American Civil War, conscientious objectors had the option to pay a substitute for the military service, and during World War I they could undertake a non-combatant role. During World War II, conscientious objectors were given the option of an alternative service. As the history has shown, conscientious objectors have greatly contributed to the military, and for example, Desmond Doss received a Medal of Honor for his heroic efforts during combat.

49 The ECHR has found violations of Article 9 where the applicant did not mention religious belief but relied on their belief that violence or war are unjustifiable under any circumstances (pacifism) (*Savda v. Turkey; Tarhan v. Turkey*). Furthermore, a person does not have to adhere to a religion or belong to a pacifist organization to be recognized as a conscientious objector, by virtue of the negative freedom protection in Article 9 (*Papavasilakis v. Greece*). In *Löffelmann v. Austria, Gütl v. Austria* and *Lang v. Austria*, the ECtHR found a violation of Article 14 (prohibition of discrimination) in conjunction with Article 9 where the three Jehovah's Witnesses ministers were denied the exception from absolute military service and alternative civilian service as such was reserved for ministers of recognized religious associations only (and ministers for Jehovah Witnesses did not meet the requirement).

50 Michael A. Fragoso, "Taking Conscience Seriously or Seriously Taking Conscience: Obstetricians, Specialty Boards, and the Takings Clause" (2011) 86 *Notre Dame Law Review* 1687; J. Paul Kelleher, "Emergency Contraception and Conscientious Objection" (2010) 27 *Journal of Applied Philosophy* 290–304; Nancy Berlinger, "Conscience Clauses, Health Care Providers, and Parents" in Mary Crowley (ed.), *From Birth to Death and Bench to Clinic: The Hastings Center Bioethics Briefing Book for Journalists, Policymakers, and Campaigns* (The Hastings Center: Garrison, NY, 2008), 35–40; See also: Survey of State and Federal Conscience Protection Laws in Brief of Amici Curiae 43 Members of Congress in Support of Petitioners, in *Stormans Inc. v. John Wiesman, Secretary, Washington State, Department of Health, et al.* Available at: https://www.libertyinstitute.org/file/ThriftwayNo.-15-862-Members-of-Congress-Amicus-with-Appendix1.pdf

All reasonable alternatives should be considered and implemented before a state actor undertakes to force persons to violate their conscience or beliefs.[51]

51 Albie Sachs J in *Christian Education in South Africa v. Minister of Education*, Case CCT 4/00 found that:

"35. ... The underlying problem in any open and democratic society based on human dignity, equality and freedom in which conscientious and religious freedom has to be regarded with appropriate seriousness, is how far such democracy can and must go in allowing members of religious communities to define for themselves which laws they will obey and which not. Such a society can cohere only if all its participants accept that certain basic norms and standards are binding. Accordingly, believers cannot claim an automatic right to be exempted by their beliefs from the laws of the land. *At the same time, the state should, wherever reasonably possible, seek to avoid putting believers to extremely painful and intensely burdensome choices of either being true to their faith or else respectful of the law.*" (emphasis added).

In *Minister of Home Affairs and Another v. Fourie*, Case CCT 60/04, Albie Sachs J found that:

"94. In the open and democratic society contemplated by the Constitution there must be mutually respectful co-existence between the secular and the sacred. The function of the Court is to recognize the sphere which each inhabits, not to force the one into the sphere of the other. Provided there is no prejudice to the fundamental rights of any person or group, the law will legitimately acknowledge a diversity of strongly-held opinions on matters of great public controversy. I stress the qualification that there must be no prejudice to basic rights. Majoritarian opinion can often be harsh to minorities that exist outside the mainstream. It is precisely the function of the Constitution and the law to step in and counteract rather than reinforce unfair discrimination against a minority. The test, whether majoritarian or minoritarian positions are involved, must always be whether the measure under scrutiny promotes or retards the achievement of human dignity, equality and freedom."

"95. The hallmark of an open and democratic society is its capacity to accommodate and manage difference of intensely-held world views and lifestyles in a reasonable and fair manner. The objective of the Constitution is to allow different concepts about the nature of human existence to inhabit the same public realm, and to do so in a manner that is not mutually destructive and that at the same time enables government to function in a way that shows equal concern and respect for all."

"97... *The effect of this provision is that no minister of religion could be compelled to solemnize a same-sex marriage if such a marriage would not conform to the doctrines of the religion concerned. There is nothing in the matters before us that either directly or indirectly trenches in any way on this strong protection of the right of religious communities not to be obliged to celebrate marriages not conforming to their tenets.*"

"98. It is clear from the above that acknowledgement by the state of the right of same-sex couples to enjoy the same status, entitlements and responsibilities as marriage law accords to heterosexual couples is in no way inconsistent with the rights of religious organizations to continue to refuse to celebrate same-sex marriages. The constitutional claims of same-sex couples can accordingly not be negated by invoking the rights of believers to have their religious freedom respected. The two sets of interests involved do not collide, they co-exist in a constitutional realm based on accommodation of diversity."

"159. ... Religious institutions would remain undisturbed in their ability to perform marriage ceremonies according to their own tenets, and thus if they wished, to celebrate heterosexual marriages only. *The principle of reasonable accommodation could be applied by the state to ensure that civil marriage officers who had sincere religious objections to officiating at same-sex marriages would not themselves be obliged to do so if this*

The right of conscience, like other rights, will not be absolute and will be subject to the same bases for limitation that apply to limits on religious freedom. The idea of human dignity for everyone also helps explain the limits of doctors' rights to conscientiously object. For example, if there is an emergency where the life of the mother is at stake, or if it would be unreasonably burdensome for a woman to otherwise get access to abortion to which she is legally entitled, accommodation of conscience may be circumscribed. Also, in situations where too many people were to make conscientious objection claims, this might so limit the ability of a woman to exercise her right that the rights of conscience might be limited. Focusing on the dignity of everyone involved, however, encourages us to find solutions that can mutually vindicate both the right of conscience and the right of access.

c. Focusing concretely and in actual situations on human dignity and its implications for particular human rights claims can help identify the specific content of these rights as well as how we understand human dignity itself

Human dignity is sometimes criticized as being an abstract or even empty concept.[52] However, the history of human dignity in the seven decades since the end of World War II belies this claim. As detailed in the discussions of education (Article 5), seeking non-legal ways of vindicating dignity through common ground initiatives (Article 6), implementing human rights in legislation (Article 7), and reconciliation and adjudication (Article 7), human dignity has been a useful concept in defining the content and limits of particular rights. Furthermore, human dignity, as an interpretive tool helps us strengthen protections afforded by

resulted in a violation of their conscience. If Parliament wished to refine or replace the remedy with another legal arrangement that met constitutional standards, it could still have the last word." (emphasis added).

52 It is crucial to acknowledge the concerns raised by critics of human dignity. Among others, they claim that the concept is too "abstract" or "empty." See: Steven Pinker, "The Stupidity of Dignity," *The New Republic*, May 28, 2008, 28–31; Michael Rosen, *Dignity: Its History and Meaning* (Harvard University Press, 2012); Oscar Schacter, "Editorial Comment: Human Dignity as a Normative Concept" (1983) 77 *American Journal of International Law* 848, 849; Ruth Macklin, "Dignity Is a Useless Concept" (2003) 327 *British Medical Journal* 1419–20; H. Kuhse, "Is There a Tension Between Autonomy and Dignity?" in P. Kemp et al. (eds.) *Bioethics and Biolaw* (Rhodos International Science and Art Publishers: Copenhagen, 2000) I. de Melo-Martin, "Human Dignity in International Policy Documents: A Useful Criterion for Public Policy?" (2011) 25 *Bioethics* 37–45; Conor O'Mahony, "There Is No Such Thing as a Right to Dignity" (2012) 10 *International Journal of Constitutional Law* 551–574.

Also, the Canadian Supreme Court considered abandoning the concept for being "an abstract and subjective notion that, even with the guidance of the four contextual factors, cannot only become confusing and difficult to apply; it has also proven to be an *additional* burden on equality claimants, rather than the philosophical enhancement it was intended to be." *R. v. Kapp,* [2008] 2 S.C.R. 483, 2008 SCC 41, para. 22.

maintaining focus – and the focus is on protecting the very cornerstone of what it means to be human.

The point of this part of the Punta del Este Declaration is to emphasize that asking questions about the implications for the human dignity of particular rights claims can help in the assessment of those rights claims. This focused analysis, in turn, helps us further specify the meaning and content of human dignity. It also recognizes that the implementation of human rights will differ from place to place. Despite the differences, the focus on human dignity can serve as a unifying factor that will help to decrease the magnitude of the differences.

Human dignity and the rights of enemy combatants

For example, the Israeli Supreme Court considered "human dignity" in the landmark "enemy combatant" case. The court considered "the government's policy of preventative strikes aimed at killing members of terrorist organizations in the West Bank and Gaza Strip, even when they were not actively or immediately engaged in terrorist activities."[53] Petitioners were human rights organizations arguing that the targets of the preventative strikes were alleged criminals who were entitled to the protections afforded to criminal defendants under Israeli law. In upholding the legality of the airstrikes, in a remarkable opinion by President (Emeritus) Aharon Barak, the Israeli Supreme Court nevertheless recognized that there are limits to the military's right to engage in such actions, and his opinion sends a warning to government and military leaders that the Court is watching them. Justice Barak acknowledges that, "[t]he State's fight against terrorism is the fight of the state against its enemies" and that Israel had suffered the loss of innocent lives of its people due to the terrorist attacks directed against it. He then added the following:

> Needless to say, unlawful combatants are not beyond the law. They are not "outlaws." God created them as well in his image; their human dignity as well is to be honored; they as well enjoy and are entitled to protection … by customary international law.[54]

As Jeremy Waldron points out, the reference to human dignity and the alleged terrorist being created in the image of God is a clear reference to Genesis's account of the creation of the world, and he notes that the inclusion of the overtly religious reference is intended to "pull us up short."

53 Jeremy Waldron, "The War on Terror and the Image of God" in John Witte, Jr. and Frank S. Alexander (eds.), *Christianity and Human Rights: An Introduction* (Cambridge University Press 2010). See *The Public Committee against Torture in Israel and Palestinian Society for the Protection of Human Rights and the Environment v. The Government of Israel and others* [2005] HCJ 769/02 (Isr.).

54 *The Public Committee against Torture in Israel and Palestinian Society for the Protection of Human Rights and the Environment v. The Government of Israel and others* [2005] HCJ 769/02 (Isr.) para. 87.

> It is intended to remind us that although we are dealing with an outsider and an evil person, an enemy of the state of Israel and the Jewish people, a threat to our lives and those of our loved ones, one who will kill and maim scores of innocent people if he gets the opportunity – although we are talking about someone who may be justly liable through his actions and intentions to deadly force – we are nevertheless not just talking about a wild beast, or an outsider to our species, or something that may be manipulated or battered or exploited as a mere tool for our own purposes (the purpose of saving the lives of members of our community). The unlawful combatant may be a threat and an outsider and an evil and dangerous man, but [he] is also *man-created-in-the-image-of-God* and the status associated with that characterization imposes radical limits on what may be done with him and radical constraints on how lightly we may treat the question of what may be done with him.[55]

Waldron finds it significant that Justice Barak speaks not just of "human dignity" but of the idea that man is "created in the image of God," a way of communicating to his audience that includes religious believers that there is a deep grounding for human dignity in their religious commitments.[56] Thus, a "proclamation that the individual we may be targeting is created in the image of God serves as the basis of a compelling constraint, in precisely the circumstances in which we may be tempted to say that constraints no longer apply …"[57]

However, it also needs to be considered that, for example, in the War on Terror, a similar question was raised relative to the rights afforded to those accused of terrorism, the so-called unlawful combatant of war. In the case, John Yoo, General Counsel of the Department of Defense, claimed that detainees, and particularly those held in Guantanamo Bay, were not eligible for the Geneva Conventions' protections.[58] This has paved the way for them being subjected to "Enhanced Interrogation Techniques" that can meet the legal definition of torture. The issue of human dignity has not been taken into consideration.

55 Jeremy Waldron, "The War on Terror and the Image of God" in John Witte, Jr. and Frank S. Alexander (eds.), *Christianity and Human Rights: An Introduction* (Cambridge University Press 2010) 225.

56 Waldron notes that in his concurring judgment, Vice President of the Court Rivlin makes the same argument in purely secular language. *Id.*, 225. Rivlin writes, "The duty to honor the lives of innocent civilians is thus the point of departure … but it is not the endpoint. It cannot negate the human dignity of the unlawful combatants themselves … Human dignity is a principle which applies to every person, even during combat and conflict." *The Public Committee against Torture in Israel and Palestinian Society for the Protection of Human Rights and the Environment v. The Government of Israel and others* [2005] HCJ 769/02 (Isr.), Opinion of Rivlin VP, para. 5.

57 Durham and Scharffs (2019) 632.

58 John C. Yoo, "Memorandum to Jim Haynes, Application of Treaties and Laws to Al Qaeda and Taliban Detainees" (January 9, 2002). Later cited as "Yoo's Memorandum."

Flexible universalism and different social, political, legal, and economic contexts

Another important aspect of defining and specifying the scope and content of human rights is the varying social, political, legal, and economic contexts in which human rights are implemented. As Glendon and Kaplan point out,

> The framers [of the UDHR] understood that there would always be different ways of applying human rights to different social and political contexts, and that each country's circumstances would affect how it would fulfill its requirements. Developing countries would have fewer resources than developed countries. Socialist states emphasize different priorities than capitalist ones. Muslim states' values vary from those of Western states. The framers recognized that each part of the world has its particular concerns.[59]

This is particularly true in the case of social and economic rights. Article 22 of the UDHR states that those rights should be put into practice "in accordance with the organization and resources of each State."[60]

The founding figures of human rights often emphasized a pluralistic view of the many different ways of thinking and living. As P. C. Chang stressed,

> In the present times, and more particularly during the years following the First World War, there had been a tendency to impose a standardized way of thinking and a single way of life. With that approach, equilibrium could be reached only at the cost of moving away from the truth, or employing force. However violent the methods employed, equilibrium achieved in that way could never last.[61]

P. C. Chang's human rights philosophy of pluralism recognized that "there is more than one kind of ultimate reality" and this had to be reflected in the UDHR.[62]

59 Mary Ann Glendon and Seth D. Kaplan, "Renewing Human Rights" (February 2019) *First Things* 36–37.
60 *Id.*, 37, quoting Article 22 of the UDHR.
61 Schabas (2013) 3058; A/PV.182.
62 "Dr. Chang was a pluralist and held forth in charming fashion on the proposition that there is more than one kind of ultimate reality. The Declaration, he said, should reflect more than simply Western ideas and Dr. Humphrey would have to be eclectic in his approach. His remark, though addressed to Dr. Humphrey, was really directed at Dr. Malik, from whom it drew a prompt retort as he expounded at some length the philosophy of Thomas Aquinas. Dr. Humphrey joined enthusiastically in the discussion, and I remember that at one point Dr. Chang suggested that the Secretariat might well spend a few months studying the fundamentals of Confucianism!" Eleanor Roosevelt, *On My Own* (Harper: New York, 1958, 77).

6 Article 4

Duties and responsibilities

Article 4 reads as follows:

> Human dignity for everyone everywhere emphasizes the concept in the UDHR that rights include accompanying obligations and responsibilities, not just of states but also of all human beings with respect to the rights of others. Dignity is a status shared by every human being, and the emphasis on everyone and everywhere makes it clear that rights are characterized by reciprocity and involve corresponding duties. Everyone should be concerned not only with his or her own dignity and rights but with the dignity and rights of every human being. Nonetheless, human dignity is not diminished on the ground that persons are not fulfilling their responsibilities to the state and others.

The following is an expanded explanation of each part of Article 4.

a. Human dignity for everyone everywhere emphasizes the concept in the UDHR that rights include accompanying obligations and responsibilities, not just of states but also of all human beings with respect to the rights of others

The drafters of the UDHR were acutely aware of duties as well as rights. The drafters discussed the issue of corresponding duties throughout their deliberations. The UDHR does not limit itself to an elaboration of rights; it speaks in important ways (which are sometimes overlooked) about duties as well, including important insights about the relationship of rights and duties. The duties do not just attend to states, but all organs of society, and all persons.

Human dignity is a ground for both rights and duties. As Jeremy Waldron explains, "[O]ne of the distinctive things about the introduction of the concept of human dignity into modern legal and political discourse is that it is formally capable of grounding duties and responsibilities as easily as it grounds rights and liberties."[1]

1 Jeremy Waldron, "Citizenship and Dignity" in Christopher McCrudden (ed.), *Understanding Human Dignity* (Oxford University Press: Oxford, 2013) 339. Waldron explains, "I don't just mean that it grounds a duty to respect the dignity of

DOI: 10.4324/9781003207030-7

In a sense, the deepest motivations for the UDHR were based upon a sense of duty – a duty recognized by the survivors of World War II that the horrors and atrocities of war that the world experienced in the two devastating wars of the first half of the 20th Century would not repeat. It was not conceptual agreement about human dignity (or any other single generative value) that was the deepest motivation for the UDHR, it was the shared global trauma of the two World Wars and a desire that "never again" would such devastation be visited upon the world.

In the chapter of his treatise on the UDHR, "World War II as the Catalyst," Morsink writes:

> The motif that runs throughout these adoptions and rejections is that the [UDHR] was adopted to avoid another Holocaust or similar abomination. Hearing about and experiencing the horrors of the war convinced the drafters of the rightness of what they were doing. The moral outrage thus created gave them a common platform from which to operate and do the drafting. While they often differed on the specific wording to be used, once it was shown that a violation of a certain clause or article had in some way helped create the horrors of the war, the adoption of that clause or article was virtually assured.[2]

He adds that,

> When Cassin rewrote this text he added the phrase "before and especially during the last world war." … this phrase … was taken out. But – the Declaration being adopted only three years after World War II ended – even without that extra phrase any reader can guess that the "barbarous acts" that "outraged the conscience of mankind" are the ones discussed in this chapter. By using the phrase "the conscience of mankind" the drafters generalized their own feelings over the rest of humanity. Taking a position diametrically opposed to Hitler's, they believed that any morally healthy human being would have been similarly outraged when placed in similar circumstances. This shared outrage explains why the Declaration has found such widespread support.[3]

The driving force and motivation of the drafters of the UDHR were their shared feelings of duty to future generations to ensure that the project becomes successful and helps to prevent abuses such as those perpetrated during World War II. As Morsink notes, "without the delegates' shared moral revulsion against [the Holocaust], the Declaration would never have been written."[4]

others; though it does; any emancipatory concept like rights will generate correlative duties of that kind. I mean that dignity also generates certain responsibilities upon each person conceived as the bearer of dignity; it is not a wholly emancipatory concept." *Id.*

2 Morsink (1999) 37.

3 *Id.*, 91.

4 *Id.*, xiv.

Distortions of a rights-first (or rights-only) approach to human rights

In the years since, a rights-first (or rights-only) approach has sometimes distorted the human rights project.[5] As University of Chicago law professor Eric Posner describes it:

> The weaknesses that would go on to undermine human rights law were there from the start. The universal declaration was not a treaty in the formal sense: no one at the time believed that it created legally binding obligations. It was not ratified by nations but approved by the general assembly, and the UN charter did not give the general assembly the power to make international law. Moreover, the rights were described in vague, aspirational terms, which could be interpreted in multiple ways, and national governments – even the liberal democracies – were wary of binding legal obligations.[6]

Indeed, a rights-first approach to problem-solving may not always work in complex situations involving intractable problems. As professors, Glendon and Kaplan note, "The minimum standards in the UDHR, which blended community-oriented and individualistic concepts, won acceptance from a wide assortment of European, Middle Eastern, Latin American, Asian, communist, capitalist, developed, and developing countries."[7] This agreement was achieved through what Glendon and Kaplan describe as "flexible universalism," which involved "synthesizing and integrating concepts from many parts of the world. Some elements focus on the individual, others on the community, and society. Some focus on freedom, others on solidarity, and duty. The vision of liberty is inseparable from the call for social responsibility."[8] One of the things that made human rights universally acceptable to the drafters of (but also states adopting) the UDHR was that it recognized the connections between rights and duties.[9]

5 Glendon and Kaplan explain, "The West has often tried to use a rights-first approach to solve problems that require more comprehensive and differentiated treatment. The failure of Western attempts, for example, to help developing countries overcome their biggest challenges – ethnic conflict, weak institutions, and exclusionary growth – has undermined the moral authority of human rights in the countries where it is needed most." Glendon and Kaplan quote Michael Walzer, professor emeritus of the Institute for Advanced Study at Princeton, who has argued, that "Politics must sometimes substitute for justice, providing a neutral frame within which a common life slowly develops," producing "negotiated" rather than "imposed" ways of living. Glendon and Kaplan, *First Things*, February 2019, at 35–36.

6 Eric Posner, "The Case Against Human Rights" (Dec. 4, 2014) *The Guardian*.

7 Mary Ann Glendon and Seth D. Kaplan, "Renewing Human Rights" (February 2019) *First Things* 36.

8 *Id.*, 36.

9 Humphrey's draft Preamble of the UDHR incorporated "four freedoms" including "that man does not have rights only; he owes duties to the society of which he forms part." Cassin emphasized that: "The final texts of the declaration welded those elements together, for they implied ties between the individual and society and affirmed the need of an adequate social and international order capable of ensuring that rights

The UDHR on rights and duties

Duties are integrated into the UDHR in a way that is purposeful and complements the overall structure of the document.[10]

The Proclamation clause of the UDHR calls on "every organ of society" to promote respect for the rights and freedoms enunciated in the Universal Declaration. As Professors Glendon and Kaplan note, "[t]he most important are specifically named: families, communities, religious groups, workplaces, associations, societies, cultures, nations, and an emerging international order."[11] The UDHR does not even purport to create legally cognizable rights, so the implementation of human rights will and must involve more than just states recognizing and protecting the legal rights of people.

Article 1 of the UDHR includes the injunction that all human beings "should act towards one another in a spirit of brotherhood." This is a declaration of duty, and not just of states, but rather of all people.

were respected; they provided safeguards or hope of safe-guards, while at the same time also imposing certain limitations upon mankind." See: Schabas (2013) 3033; A/PV.180, 865. He further added that "We have a right to food, we say, but if everybody has a right to food and no-one wants to be compelled to work, how are we going to feed ourselves? This, therefore, is a point upon which we ought to state the opposite rights. On the one hand we ought to state the right of the individual and on the other hand the right of the community. I, myself, admit in a general way at any rate, that when the State or community creates a member who refuses to work and does not want to collaborate with others, then the rights of that individual must be conditioned by the work he is asked to accomplish." Schabas (2013) 336. Hodgson noted that: "Every one of these rights has a corresponding duty. That brings in the points which were raised yesterday as to the interests of the state against the interests of the individual or the interests of the community. Now, none of these rights we are talking about is absolute. Take the best recognized one of all, the right of expression. Now, that right of expression has a corresponding duty. There is a right, there is a duty to respect the rights of others, not to be libellous. If I have, say, a newspaper to express myself, if I speak treasonably or corruptly, or undermine the very foundations of the state by my right of expression, I am automatically limited. So the question comes to my mind: Are we going in every case to put the corresponding duty or are we just going to lay these down as absolute rights?" Schabas (2013) 335; E/CN.4/AC.1/3/Add.1.

Mr. Dukes (United Kingdom) commented: "... I repeat that in the language as used, it appears as though we are throwing the doors wide open and we unduly, I think, awaiting the right of personal freedom without, at the same time, making provision for the obligations as between the individual or individuals who are supposed to benefit by these freedoms and the obligation to the States into which they would move or where they would hope to find asylum ... It is of no use in my opinion of seeking to define personal freedom entirely detached from the obligation of those individuals either to the State or to voluntary organizations and at the same time claim the advantages and the benefits outlined in this group under number 3." Schabas (2013) 336; E/CN.4/AC.1/3/Add.1.

10 For further information, see Article 1.

11 Mary Ann Glendon and Seth D. Kaplan, "Renewing Human Rights" (February 2019) *First Things* 37.

The initial draft of Article 1 said, "All men are brothers," but this wording raised several concerns. Before the drafters settled upon the phrase, they considered other alternatives, including the initially proposed "brothers." Miss Zung (Representative of China) raised her concern about the use of the word, proposing a more general term, for example, "members of the same family." The phrase "in spirit of brotherhood" was proposed by Begum Hamid Ali (Representative of India), and after deliberation was accepted by others.[12] Cassin commented that "[the] expression was all-inclusive and had the further advantage of stressing the inherent equality of human beings, a concept which had recently been attacked by Hitler and his ideological disciples. The idea of the solidarity of men should be made explicit in the Article to convince the peoples of the world that the United Nations firmly believed in their essential brotherhood."[13]

P.C. Chang, when discussing the importance of corresponding duties, raised the issue that, "The aim of the United Nations was not to ensure the selfish gains of the individual but to try and increase man's moral stature. It was necessary to proclaim the duties of the individual for it was a consciousness of his duties which enabled man to reach a high moral standard."[14]

The penultimate article of the UDHR, Article 29, specifically addresses duties, linking them back to all of the rights enumerated in the UDHR, stating, "Everyone has duties to the community in which alone the free and full development of his personality is possible."

Thus, overtly and purposefully, duties are mentioned at the very beginning and the end of the UDHR, creating conceptual bookends or bracketing, of the rights enumerated in the Declaration.

The conceptual connections between rights and duties

Human rights also necessarily implicate duties, but in ways that are more complex than sometimes understood. Rights and duties are not simply reciprocal (with one right triggering a correlative duty), but rather exist in complex webs or networks of relationships. For example, if I have a right to free speech, this implicates duties on the part of the state to protect that right; it also implicates duties of others to respect my right; but it also implicates my duty to respect the right of free speech of others; also, my right may create duties (both moral and legal) for me concerning how I exercise that right, and the restraint I show in exercising that right.[15] None of this is to suggest that the relationship between rights and duties

12 Schabas (2013) 1357.
13 *Id.*, 1670.
14 *Id.*, 2132.
15 Jeremy Waldron makes a similar point in his discussion of the "dignity of citizenship," noting three ways in which duties and responsibilities may be implicated. "As well as (1) the duty to respect others' dignity (the duty that is correlative to the rights-based aspect of their dignity), there is also a distinction between (2) the duty to submit to law and to political defeat, on the one hand, and (3) the responsibility associated with the active exercise of citizenship rights, on the other." Jeremy Waldron, "Citizenship

is self-evident or uncontroversial.[16] The point is that rights always implicate duties, duties of the state, of others, and myself.

Gandhi, when discussing rights and duties, mentioned the story of what he learned from his mother:

> Fundamental rights can only be those rights the exercise of which is not only in the interest of the citizen but that of the whole world. Today everyone wants to know what his rights are, but if a man learns to discharge his duties right from childhood and studies the sacred books of his faith, he automatically exercises his rights too. I learnt my duties on my mother's lap. She was an unlettered village woman … She knew my dharma. Thus, if from my childhood we learn what our dharma is and try to follow it our rights look after themselves … The beauty of it is that the very performance of a duty secures us our right. Rights cannot be divorced from duties. This is how satyagraha was born, for I was always striving to decide what my duty was.[17]

Legal systems can be structured primarily upon the concept of duty rather than rights, including the Hebrew Bible (Old Testament), which speaks extensively of duties in the language of commandments, while the idea of rights is practically nonexistent.[18]

Charles Malik, in his capacity as the rapporteur for the Commission on Human Rights, commented upon the relationship between rights and duties. When discussing the work of the Commission on Human Rights, he referred to the "loyalties" that individuals have, including:

> We here in this Commission represent and defend the individual man in his conscience and in his individual freedom, and there is no other body in the

and Dignity" in Christopher McCrudden (ed.), *Understanding Human Dignity* (Oxford University Press: Oxford, 2013) 339.

16 Liora Lazarus, Benjamin Goold, Rajendra Desai and Qudsi Rasheed, *The Relationship between Rights and Responsibilities* (Ministry of Justice Research Series, 2009); Erica-Irene Daes, *Freedom of the Individual Under Law: A Study on the Individual's Duties to the Community and the Limitations on Human Rights and Freedoms under Article 29 of the Universal Declaration of Human Rights* (E/CN.4/Sub.2/432/Add.1) (United Nations, 1980); Douglas Hodgson, *Individual Duty within a Human Rights Discourse* (Ashgate Publishing, 2003); John H. Knox, "Horizontal Human Rights Law" (2008) 102 *American Journal of International Law*; David Selbourne, *The Principle of Duty: An Essay on the Foundations of the Civic Order* (Sinclair-Stevenson: London, 1994); Ben Saul, "In the Shadow of Human Rights: Human Duties, Obligations and Responsibilities" (2000) 32 *Columbia Human Rights Law Review* 566; Mary Ann Glendon, *Rights Talk: The Impoverishment of Political Discourse* (Simon & Schuster: New York, 1991); Amitai Etzioni, *The Spirit of Community: Rights, Responsibilities and the Communitarian Agenda* (Touchstone: New York, 1995).

17 Speech at prayer meeting (June 28, 1947) CW, 88: 230.

18 Benjamin Porat, "Rights-Based Law v. Duty-Based Law: Old Dilemma, New Perspective" (2015) Hebrew University of Jerusalem Legal Research Paper no. 16–04.

> United Nations to do that. We must defend him against tyranny, against tyranny of the state and the tyranny of systems, because man has other loyalties than his loyalty to the state. He has loyalty to his family, to his religion, to his profession; he has his loyalty to science and to truth. These loyalties are as exacting on him as his loyalty to the state. And, in my opinion, the fight for freedom today consists primarily in asserting the rights of these intermediate institutions.[19]

Subsequently, he states his position on the issue in even stronger terms:

> [I]t is often mentioned that freedom must be coupled with responsibility or else it will lend itself to a good deal of abuse. I grant that. Freedom must be sobered by responsibility. If, in the name of freedom, conditions such as confusion, irresponsibility, commercialism and catering to the lower instincts of mankind have flourished, so also in the name of responsibility [likely means government control] have conditions such as propaganda, willful bias, and rigid imposition from above equally vitiated the free spread of truth. Everything is capable of abuse, including truth itself ...[20]

Nonetheless, when discussing the wording of the UDHR, focusing on the early drafts of Articles 1 and 2, he said that it was "astounding" to say that: "Everyone owes a duty to his State." He indicated that "it might be questioned whether an individual owed such a duty of loyalty regardless of the characteristics of his State." He added that: "it was odd that men ought to first be told that their freedom is limited. If this were done it would be a Bill not of Human Rights but of what man owes society. It was precisely because the balance had been tipped against the individual and in favor of society that human rights had been violated."[21]

The relationship between rights and duties reappeared throughout the deliberations about the wording of various parts of the UDHR.

René Cassin, when proposing a new text of an early draft of Article 2, suggested that the text needed to cover the relationship between man and society and their mutual duties. He distinguished between three different texts that were paramount to their deliberations and continued to reappear in their discussions:

1 The text describing society's duty towards the individual;
2 The text defining the fundamental duties of man;
3 Finally, the text according to which everyone is limited in the exercise of his rights by the rights of others.[22]

19 Commission on Human Rights, February 1, 1947.
20 Commission on Human Rights, July 25, 1947.
21 Schabas (2013) 733.
22 *Id.*, 1680.

Mr. Pavlov (Representative of the USSR) suggested that the need to balance the interest of the society would be by way of incorporating the duties of individuals. He stated that "if all mention of the rights of States were omitted, it would be impossible to include in the declaration any reference to the duties of individual citizens. The declaration already stated some of those duties, although others should be added, to ensure that selfish interests of individuals did not infringe the interests of society."[23] Mr. Harry (Australia) "felt that attention should be drawn to the general duty of the individual comparing to each general right."[24] Mr. Beaufort (Netherlands) stated that "the rights of the individual were not absolute. It was necessary to define the restrictions demanded by respect for the rights of other individuals and different social groups." Furthermore, he noted the "interdependence of the rights and duties which linked an individual with the community. In choosing the word 'community', it was quite rightly desired to point out that the state was not the only social group concerned."[25] However, contrary to the concerns raised by Charles Malik concerning the character of the state, Mr. Beaufort indicated that "an individual had duties towards the community independent of the character of that or the other community. The fact that a State did not grant political rights to a certain category of citizens, though deplorable, was not a sufficient reason for the citizens in question refusing, for instance, to pay their taxes."[26] Mr. Perez Cisneros (Cuba) while recognizing the need to protect individuals against the state, indicated that "the individual should also be reminded that he was a member of society and that he must affirm his right to be deemed a human being by clearly recognizing the duties which were corollaries of his rights."[27]

Not every interest creates a right

Not every interest creates a right, much less a legally enforceable right. Even if rights are based upon particularly important interests, some interests are not of sufficient magnitude to warrant protection as a right. Sometimes it is not possible to protect a putative right through a putative duty.[28] Sometimes protecting a

23 *Id.*, 2109.
24 *Id.*, 733.
25 *Id.*, 2769.
26 *Id.*, 2770.
27 *Id.*
28 As Tasioulas explains, this impossibility may be logical (there can be no duty to provide everyone with an above average standard of living), sometimes it is a matter of scientific law (there can be no duty to provide men the right to give birth), and sometimes it is a matter of scarcity of resources (there can be no duty to provide everyone with a Rodeo Drive lifestyle), and sometimes an interest cannot be served by recognizing a duty (there can be no right to romantic love with one's preferred partner). But duties may be limited for other reasons, including the "capacity to realize other values, including other rights." John Tasioulas, "Human Dignity and the Foundations of Human Rights" in Christopher McCrudden (ed.), *Understanding Human Dignity* (Oxford University Press: Oxford, 2013) 297.

putative right (such as certain health care claims) would be so costly that it could only be achieved at the expense of other important rights and interests. There is much more that could be said about the transition from interests into rights that is beyond the scope of this commentary. The important point, as John Tasioulas reminds us, is that "we cannot satisfactorily establish the existence and content of any one human right without also considering the implications for the existence and content of other putative human rights."[29] Moral reasoning alone will often not be sufficient to establish specific content to many rights.[30]

Human rights advocates sometimes make the mistake of treating all-important interests as human rights, or of advocating rights without regard to the cost of implementing or protecting those rights, or without regard for other rights and societal values. These rights-first oversimplifications and absolutisms seek to find energy from the moral stature of human rights but ultimately enervate the human rights project.

Not every right will be immediately realized

As understood by the drafters of the UDHR, the fact that something is a basic right does not mean it will be immediately and fully implemented or realized.[31]

29 *Id.*, 298.

30 The drafters of the UDHR were explicitly aware that resource limits, and the different levels of wealth of various countries, would have significant implications for the implementation of human rights. For example, when discussing the right to education, Mr. Harry indicated that "no obligation should be laid down for a State to maintain a particular type or particular degree of education; this must vary according to the resources of the country and the type of community. There must be equal opportunity of access to all institutions of higher learning which are maintained by the State or community." Schabas (2013) 876. Mr. Santa Cruz (Chile) appreciated the "provisions to recognize the right to education and the obligation to provide free primary education and equal access to higher education, which should be limited by the resources of the State and the capacity of the beneficiary." Schabas (2013) 876. In relation to social security, Mr. Pavlov indicated that document should stress "the need to ensure for every individual a real opportunity to enjoy all the rights mentioned in the declaration." Furthermore, he discussed ways in which various rights can be assured "with the qualification that due regard should be paid to the organization and resources of each State." Schabas (2013) 2581.

31 The UDHR speaks of human rights being realized through "progressive measures," and the founding figures of human rights were acutely aware of the limits of poverty and of the capacity of institutions. Among others, Mr. Pavlov (USSR) indicated that "The various questions regarding standard of living, social security, social insurance, protection for mothers and children, were vital, especially for the working classes. It was unfortunately manifest that the years which had followed the last war had been marked by a progressive lowering of the standard of living in many capitalist countries, even in countries which had considerable resources. It was to be noted that the expenditure necessitated by the switch-over from a war to a peacetime economy and by the economic revival of those countries had a direct effect on the workers' standard of living. A few examples would suffice to illustrate that fact. In the United States of America, where production had reached 80 per cent of its pre-war level, the profits of the monopolies and private industries had increased; from 24 thousand million dollars

This was recognized by the drafters of the UDHR, which in its Preamble stresses the need to be "pledged ... to achieve, in co-operation with the United Nations, the promotion of universal respect for and observance of human rights and fundamental freedoms."[32] As the UDHR was being adopted by the UN General Assembly, the signatories recognized the UDHR as a "common standard of achievement for all peoples and all nations, to the end that every individual and every organ of society, keeping [the UDHR] constantly in mind, shall strive by teaching and education to promote respect for these rights and freedoms and by progressive measures, national and international."[33] Full implementation of some rights like equal protection of law and non-discrimination are and (highly likely) will always remain aspirational values requiring ongoing vigilance and renewed efforts to strengthen their realization. Indeed, the UDHR was formulated as an inspirational soft law that was not to be legally binding. Eleanor Roosevelt emphasized that

> In giving our approval to the declaration today, it is of primary importance that we keep clearly in mind the basic character of the document. It is not a treaty; it is not an international agreement. It is not and does not purport to be a statement of law or of legal obligation. It is a declaration of basic principles of human rights and freedoms, to be stamped with the approval of the General Assembly by formal vote of its members, and to serve as a common standard of achievement for all peoples of all nations.[34]

Many experts believe that over time it became a part of customary international law and hence became binding upon all states.[35] Besides, the human rights

in 1939, they had risen to 30 thousand million after the Second World War. Similarly, in France the real wages of the workers were now half what they had been before the war, although the profits of the French capitalists represented 43 per cent of the national income. Those examples would be enough to give a fair idea of the particularly difficult living conditions with which the workers were faced in those countries. In the Soviet Union, on the contrary, the rise in the standard of living and the guarantee of social security for the workers had been the constant care of the Government. Salaries had risen to double what they were in 1940, and a general plan was being carried out for the improvement of the workers' standard of living, involving the [563] building of schools and hospitals, for instance. Moreover, the USSR Government was endeavoring to eliminate the underlying causes of hard living conditions for the workers. It combated unemployment for instance, and was striving to forestall economic crises, and it gave the workers real and effectual aid." Schabas (2013) 2649–2650.

32 Preamble, UDHR.

33 *Id.*

34 Quoted in: Marjorie M. Whiteman, *Digest of International Law Volume 5* (Dept. of State Publication 7873: Washington D.C., 1965) 243.

35 It can be fundamental even if they remain aspirational. The secret is to keep improving, rather than to use the impossibility of perfection as an excuse for inattention or performance that is far below what is possible. Hurst Hannum, "The Status of the Universal Declaration of Human Rights in National and International Law" (1998) 3

enumerated in the UDHR have almost all became legally binding international obligations for states who have adopted international conventions including the ICCPR and the ICESCR.

While some fundamental rights remain aspirational, they should be highly prioritized. Consider a right as basic as the right to clean drinking water and access to basic sanitation.[36] These are important interests that surely rise to the level of being fundamental human rights, but we know that there are parts of the world where poverty and government capacity make it difficult for this right to be fully implemented.[37] This does not mean that clean water is not a human right; nor does it mean that the government does not have a duty to provide clean water. But the practical implementation of that right will vary according to local circumstances.[38] The main point is that this right is so fundamental and important that it should be a matter of high priority for both government and non-government actors. Governments cannot avoid the duty of providing clean water and basic sanitation by claiming there is no such human right, or by using limited capacity or resources as an excuse.

Human dignity for everyone everywhere: implications for rights and duties

The idea of human dignity for everyone everywhere can help us think through the implications of the reciprocal character of rights and duties.

The emphasis on human *dignity* is itself a corrective to an overreliance on human *rights*. The emphasis on *everyone* and *everywhere* reminds us that human rights are not just for "me" but for others as well. If we care about the human

Health and Human Rights 145; Louis Henkin, *The Age of Rights* (Columbia University Press: New York, 1990) 9.

36 As derived from Article 11 of the ICESCR and the UN General Assembly Resolution 64/292, The Human Right to Water and Sanitation.

37 According to the World Health Organization, in 2017, 3 in 10 people worldwide, close to 2.1 billion, lacked access to safe, readily available water at home. "Of the 2.1 billion people who do not have safely managed water, 844 million do not have even a basic drinking water service. This includes 263 million people who have to spend over 30 minutes per trip collecting water from sources outside the home, and 159 million who still drink untreated water from surface water sources, such as streams or lakes." World Health Organization, "2.1 Billion People Lack Safe Drinking Water at Home, More Than Twice as Many Lack Safe Sanitation" (July 12, 2017). Available at: https://www.who.int/news-room/detail/12-07-2017-2-1-billion-people-lack-safe-drinking-water-at-home-more-than-twice-as-many-lack-safe-sanitation

38 Mr. Radovanovic (Yugoslavia) identified that "The economic factor had become decisive in the whole social development of the present time. Consequently, the social status of the individual was not based on juridical instruments but was the result of the social and economic conditions in which that individual lived. That meant that the civil and political status of the individual had become in a very great measure dependent upon his social status … The historical development of the capitalistic society had imposed on the individual unfavorable economic conditions. Therefore, a simple declaration of those rights without providing assurances of adequate material conditions in which they could be enjoyed would be illusory." Schabas (2013) 3074–3075.

dignity of all people in all places, it is conceptually impossible for us to think exclusively in terms of rights, because we will be thinking about *our* obligations to others that are triggered by this very commitment.

If we assert a belief in human dignity for everyone everywhere, we announce our duty to treat everyone everywhere with human dignity. This is not a mere tautology; it is how moral obligation works: we hold ourselves accountable (and allow others to hold us accountable) to our asserted convictions. For example, if I assert that I believe in human dignity because I am a Christian who believes God created all human beings in His image, then it is appropriate for me (and others) to hold me accountable for my asserted beliefs.[39]

The duty of the state: duty to protect

Within the human rights framework, duties are not all created equal. This is no different for the UDHR.[40] A state's duties are different from those of individuals and non-state actors.

39 This is one reason interreligious dialogue is important – not just so we can reach agreement, but so we can make clear to ourselves and others what our commitments and deep beliefs are, which makes it possible for them to hold us to account for living up to our own asserted beliefs. Understanding our own deep commitments can also help us hold ourselves to account for our own asserted beliefs. Fr. Michael Perry, in his letter to the General Minister of the Order of Friars Minor on the 800th anniversary of the Encounter between St. Francis and Sultan al-Malik al-Kāmil, emphasized that: "The anniversary of Francis's encounter with al-Malik al-Kāmil at Damietta in 1219 beckons us to ask again what deeds and words, amid the pluralism and complexity of the world today, would be pleasing to God. Discerning the signs of the times (Mt 16:3), the Church increasingly highlights interreligious dialogue as an essential element of the mission of the Church today. The Second Vatican Council exhorted the Christian faithful to engage in 'dialogue and collaboration with the followers of other religions, carried out with prudence and love and in witness to the Christian faith and life' (*Nostra Aetate*, 2). In particular, the Council taught that the Church regards the Muslims 'with esteem,' and urged Christians to work with their Muslim sisters and brothers to promote social justice and moral welfare, peace and freedom, for the benefit of all (*Nostra Aetate*, 3). St. John Paul II carried this mission of dialogue forward in his ministry as Bishop of Rome, most especially when he called religious leaders of the world to our spiritual home, Assisi, to witness there the transcendent quality of peace … It is thus the universal Church calling the Franciscan family to animate this interreligious fraternity in the peaceful spirit of our Seraphic Father. The Church calls us to raise up this seminal moment in our history, the journey of St. Francis to Egypt, to open ourselves anew to the transformation the Saint of Assisi experienced, and to walk together with Muslims and people of all faiths as fellow travelers, as builders of civility, and most fundamentally, as sisters and brothers, children of Abraham, our father in faith." Fr. Michael Perry, Letter to the General Minister of the Order of Friars Minor on the 800th Anniversary of the Encounter between St. Francis and Sultan al-Malik al-Kāmil. Available at: https://ofm.org/blog/letter-of-the-general-minister-on-the-800th-anniversary-of-the-encounter-between-st-francis-and-sultan-al-malik-al-kamil/

40 As Cassin noted that "the obligations of Governments could not be the same with regard to all rights, for instance with regard to the right to life and the right to a

When a human right is protected by law, the state must protect that right. Among others, states have a duty to protect individuals and groups from human rights abuses. This may require them to undertake positive actions to ensure the protection of human rights. To emphasize and strengthen this understanding, the UN General Assembly adopted the Declaration on the Right and Responsibility of Individuals, Groups, and Organs of Society to Promote and Protect Universally Recognized Human Rights and Fundamental Freedoms, which states:

> Each State has a prime responsibility and duty to protect, promote and implement all human rights and fundamental freedoms, inter alia, by adopting such steps as may be necessary to create all conditions necessary in the social, economic, political and other fields, as well as the legal guarantees required to ensure that all persons under its jurisdiction, individually and in association with others, are able to enjoy all those rights and freedoms in practice.[41]

In evaluating a state's performance of its human rights obligations, the effect of laws, policies, and practices on human dignity will be a key mechanism for assessment. When laws, policies, or practices violate or degrade human dignity, governments should expect this to trigger criticism, condemnation, and scrutiny of the government's performance of its obligations.

As noted earlier, the UDHR not only prescribes duties of states,[42] it also refers to duties of every organ of society "to promote respect for these rights and freedoms and by progressive measures, national and international, to secure their universal and effective recognition and observance, both among the peoples of Member States themselves and among the peoples of territories under their jurisdiction."[43] Indeed, as Jordan J. Paust convincingly argues, the UDHR prescribes the duties of individuals[44] and even corporations and businesses.[45]

The Vienna Declaration and Program of Action adopted by the World Conference on Human Rights in Vienna on June 25, 1993 reaffirms:

nationality, or the right to belong to trades unions and the right to health and hygienic housing conditions. Articles would therefore have to be worded differently. No right, moreover, except the right to freedom of thought, was unconditional. Every right had limitations imposed by the exigencies of law and order. These restrictions should also be defined in a special article rather than in connection with each right. The same applied to the principle of non-discrimination." Schabas (2013) 1162.

41 Article 2(1) of the Declaration on the Right and Responsibility of Individuals, Groups and Organs of Society to Promote and Protect Universally Recognized Human Rights and Fundamental Freedoms.

42 See Article 1 discussion on the topic above.

43 See: Preamble, UDHR.

44 Jordan J. Paust, "Human Rights Responsibilities of Private Corporations" (2002) 35 *Vanderbilt Journal of Transnational Law* 813; Jordan J. Paust, "The Other Side of Right: Private Duties Under Human Rights Law" (1992) 5 *Harvard Human Rights Journal* 51.

45 *Id.*, 825.

> The solemn commitment of all States to fulfill their obligations to promote universal respect for, and observance and protection of, all human rights and fundamental freedoms for all in accordance with the Charter of the United Nations, other instruments relating to human rights, and international law. The universal nature of these rights and freedoms is beyond question … Human rights and fundamental freedoms are the birthrights of all human beings; their protection and promotion is the first responsibility of Governments.

Furthermore, the Maastricht Guidelines on Violations of Economic, Social, and Cultural Rights (Maastricht, January 22–26, 1997) state that:

> Like civil and political rights, economic, social and cultural rights impose three different types of obligations on States: the obligations to respect, protect and fulfil. Failure to perform any one of these three obligations constitutes a violation of such rights. The obligation to respect requires States to refrain from interfering with the enjoyment of economic, social, and cultural rights. Thus, the right to housing is violated if the State engages in arbitrary forced evictions. The obligation to protect requires States to prevent violations of such rights by third parties. Thus, the failure to ensure that private employers comply with basic labor standards may amount to a violation of the right to work or the right to just and favorable conditions of work. The obligation to fulfil requires States to take appropriate legislative, administrative, budgetary, judicial, and other measures towards the full realization of such rights. Thus, the failure of States to provide essential primary health care to those in need may amount to a violation.

This duty is far-reaching and includes "the state's responsibility to ensure that private entities or individuals, including transnational corporations over which they exercise jurisdiction, do not deprive individuals of their economic, social, and cultural rights. States are responsible for violations of economic, social, and cultural rights that result from their failure to exercise due diligence in controlling the behavior of such non-state actors."[46]

By becoming parties to international treaties, states assume obligations flowing from these treaties. When states ratify international treaties, they undertake to introduce domestic equivalents of international protections. Indeed, states have an affirmative duty to facilitate human rights and protect their people from abuses. A failure to adhere to the voluntarily accepted international standards may trigger consequences through the monitoring mechanisms. Within the UN system, several mechanisms are engaged in monitoring treaty obligations (including human rights treaty bodies and special procedures).

Consequences of exaggerating the state's duties regarding human rights

Because states have duties to protect human rights, care should be taken to not exaggerate rights claims, because this might have a predictable (even if unintended)

46 *Id.*, 18.

consequence of undermining human rights.[47] For example, if a state cannot protect a right so costly that it is not realistically feasible, asserting such a right as being categorized and requiring immediate complete realization will likely result in skepticism about rights rather than regard for them.[48]

Human rights proliferation and escalation is a real problem that affects the legitimacy of human rights. Echoing a common concern, University of Chicago law professor Eric Posner claims that "Human rights law is too ambitious – even utopian – and too ambiguous: it overwhelms states with obligations they can't possibly keep and provides no method for evaluating whether governments act reasonably or not."[49] Understandably, the more human rights are multiplied and expanded, the states, which have to implement these rights, will struggle to fulfill their duty.

The duty of others: duty to respect and promote

While individual persons do not have the same obligation as states and other branches of government to protect and guarantee human rights, we all have to respect and promote the rights of others. This duty is discussed in greater detail in part (b) below.

Other rights instruments on the relationship between rights and duties

Some human rights instruments draw a much more direct connection between rights and duties than the UDHR does. For example, the American Declaration on the Rights and Duties of Man (American Declaration), adopted in Bogotá, Colombia, in May 1948, announces with its title the connection of rights and duties. The Preamble of the American Declaration emphasizes that:

> The fulfillment of duty by each individual is a prerequisite to the rights of all. Rights and duties are interrelated in every social and political activity of man. While rights exalt individual liberty, duties express the dignity of that liberty.
>
> Duties of a juridical nature presuppose others of a moral nature which supports them in principle and constitute their basis.

It is worth pausing to recognize that dignity is invoked as an idea that can help mediate individual liberties and duties. Chapter II of the American Declaration

47 Eric Posner, "Human Rights Treaties Are Expensive to Follow" (Dec. 28, 2014) *New York Times*.

48 "We all have limited resources, and if the result of all this effort is that it becomes a few percentage points more likely that a state will improve human rights outcomes, we should ask whether our resources might be better used in some other way – for example, through the provision of foreign aid. And if states do not improve their overall human rights outcomes, but merely switch from more measurable abuses to less measurable abuses, then our resources are being wasted." Eric Posner, "Some Skeptical Comments on Beth Simmons's Mobilizing for Human Rights" (2012) 44 *New York University Journal of International Law and Politics* 819, 831.

49 Eric Posner, "Human Rights Law Is Too Ambitious and Ambiguous" (Dec. 28, 2014) *New York Times*.

focuses on duties, identifying ten duties, including duties to society.[50] Article 29 states that "It is the duty of the individual so to conduct himself in relation to others that each and every one may fully form and develop his personality."

Frequently, national laws address more thoroughly the connection between rights and duties. For example, the German Constitution includes several references to the duties of individuals: Article 25, concerning the primacy of international law, states that international law "shall take precedence over the laws and directly create rights and duties for the inhabitants of the federal territory."[51] The South African Constitution clearly states, in Article 3(2)(b), that "all citizens are equally subject to the duties and responsibilities of citizenship."

b. Dignity is a status shared by every human being, and the emphasis on everyone and everywhere makes it clear that rights are characterized by reciprocity and involve corresponding duties

The formulation, "human dignity for everyone everywhere" reminds us that rights involve reciprocity and corresponding duties. Human dignity is a shared and unifying value. This is partly a result of recognizing that others have the same status

50 "Article XXIX. Duties to society: It is the duty of the individual so to conduct himself in relation to others that each and every one may fully form and develop his personality.

Article XXX. Duties toward children and parents:It is the duty of every person to aid, support, educate and protect his minor children, and it is the duty of children to honor their parents always and to aid, support and protect them when they need it.

Article XXXI. Duty to receive instruction: It is the duty of every person to acquire at least an elementary education.

Article XXXII. Duty to vote: It is the duty of every person to vote in the popular elections of the country of which he is a national, when he is legally capable of doing so.

Article XXXIII. Duty to obey the law: It is the duty of every person to obey the law and other legitimate commands of the authorities of his country and those of the country in which he may be.

Article XXXIV. Duty to serve the community and the nation: It is the duty of every able-bodied person to render whatever civil and military service his country may require for its defense and preservation, and, in case of public disaster, to render such services as may be in his power. It is likewise his duty to hold any public office to which he may be elected by popular vote in the state of which he is a national.

Article XXXV. Duties with respect to social security and welfare: It is the duty of every person to cooperate with the state and the community with respect to social security and welfare, in accordance with his ability and with existing circumstances.

Article XXXVI. Duty to pay taxes: It is the duty of every person to pay the taxes established by law for the support of public services.

Article XXXVII. Duty to work: It is the duty of every person to work, as far as his capacity and possibilities permit, in order to obtain the means of livelihood or to benefit his community.

Article XXXVIII. Duty to refrain from political activities in a foreign country: It is the duty of every person to refrain from taking part in political activities that, according to law, are reserved exclusively to the citizens of the state in which he is an alien."

51 Beyond this, there is no reference to duties in the German Basic Law (*Grundgesetz*).

and worth (as human beings) that we have, and partly by understanding the logical and normative connections between rights and duties.

Focusing on human dignity is an antidote to the erroneous understanding of human rights as a one-way street. The human rights project can only work when the expectation of human rights protections is accompanied by corresponding obligations to uphold them. Reciprocity of human rights is a crucial, yet neglected, element in ensuring that human rights are meaningful.

The duty of others: duty to respect and promote

While the state may have a unique duty to protect and guarantee human rights, other institutions and people have a duty to uphold, respect, and promote the human rights of others. In 1958, a decade after the adoption of the UDHR, Eleanor Roosevelt made a speech at the United Nations concerning human rights, reflecting on what had been accomplished as well as what remained to be accomplished. She emphasized the importance of "small places, close to home" for the implementation and realization of human rights, places where the duties we owe each other are most likely to be felt and manifest. Roosevelt asked,

> Where after all do universal human rights begin? In small places, close to home – so close and so small that they cannot be seen on any map of the world. Yet they *are* the world of the individual person: The neighborhood he lives in; the school or college he attends; the factory, farm or office where he works. Such are the places where every man, woman, and child seeks equal justice, equal opportunity, equal dignity without discrimination. Unless these rights have meaning there, they have little meaning anywhere. Without concerted citizen action to uphold them close to home, we shall look in vain for progress in the larger world.[52]

Eleanor Roosevelt clearly understood that it took "concerted citizen action" to uphold the rights of others "close to home," and that without this effort, the hope for larger progress is vain.

My duty to others

The duty to others is not just a general rule; it has specific implications for each of us individually as persons. Echoing sentiments expressed by others involved in drafting and adopting the UDHR, P. C. Chang stated that "The aim of the United Nations was not to ensure the selfish gains of the individual but to try and increase man's moral stature. It was necessary to proclaim the duties of the

52 Eleanor Roosevelt, "Statements at Presentation of 'In Your Hands: A Guide for Community Action for the Tenth Anniversary of the Universal Declaration of Human Rights'" (1958).

individual for it was a consciousness of his duties which enabled man to reach a high moral standard."[53]

Thomas E. Hill, Jr., professor of philosophy, explains Kant's understanding of the connection between human dignity and the duty to respect others. According to Hill,

> Kant held that we acknowledge the dignity of humanity by *treating every person with respect.* Respect for the moral law demands basic respect for every human person, no matter how disliked, useless, or misbehaving. The respect in question is not the special honour and deference we give to those in high office or those who are especially talented or accomplished. It is rather an expressed recognition, appropriate to the context, that the person has the fundamentally equal status and value of dignity as determined by the moral law.[54]

My duty to myself

Recognizing the human dignity of all people includes recognizing that I, too, am a person with human dignity. This creates obligations relating to how I think about and act concerning myself. Jeremy Waldron explains this connection between human dignity and self-respect:

> Kant associated human dignity with certain duties to oneself – not only the sense of duty which lay at the core of the moral capacity that was the ground of dignity but duties of self-respect and self-maintenance in regard to "the dignity of humanity within us." Similar themes are sounded in modern legal discussions of human dignity. Each person is said to bear a certain responsibility to human dignity in her own person, which might call in question certain claims to freedom – the claim to be able to degrade oneself for money, for example, in prostitution or in various forms of demeaning display.[55]

Thomas E. Hill, Jr., echoes this theme of Kant's idea that dignity generates duties to oneself. Hill asserts,

> Although Kant does not make the point explicitly, the relevant standards for dignified behavior must include the duties to oneself not to debase humanity in one's person – by servility, lying, gluttony, drunkenness, or any sexual practices incompatible with respect for oneself and others.[56]

53 Schabas (2013) 2132.

54 Thomas E. Hill, Jr., "In Defence of Human Dignity: Comments on Kant and Rosen" in Christopher McCrudden (ed.), *Understanding Human Dignity* (Oxford University Press: Oxford, 2013) 317–318.

55 Jeremy Waldron, "Citizenship and Dignity" in Christopher McCrudden (ed.), *Understanding Human Dignity* (Oxford University Press: Oxford, 2013) 339.

56 Thomas E. Hill, Jr., "In Defence of Human Dignity: Comments on Kant and Rosen" in Christopher McCrudden (ed.), *Understanding Human Dignity* (Oxford University Press: Oxford, 2013) 317.

For Kant, Hill explains, self-respect was almost a tautology derived from the duty to respect others. "A kind of respect for oneself as a person with rights and responsibilities is virtually inevitable, Kant thought, but we should also try to conduct ourselves in a manner worthy of this status, that is, in self-respecting ways."[57]

This duty to respect one's dignity may place limits on one's ability to consent to act in ways that may appear to reflect autonomy or at least assertions of informed consent. The classic example is the legal limits that are placed on dwarfs to participate in "dwarf-tossing" contests, notwithstanding their consent.[58]

c. Everyone should be concerned not only with his or her own dignity and rights but with the dignity and rights of every human being

It is a basic feature of moral maturity for us to be concerned not only with our dignity and rights but with the dignity and rights of everyone else as well. Nevertheless, it is a common feature of identity politics, and intersectional amplifications of identity politics, to focus on the rights and interests of particular groups to the exclusion of, or even at the expense of, the rights and interests of others. The problems associated with identity politics are discussed in greater detail below in the elaboration of Article 9 of the Punta del Este Declaration.

Rights as shields or spears

When we think exclusively of our rights, we are more likely to make the mistake of thinking of rights as spears to attack others rather than as shields to protect everyone. Professors Glendon and Kaplan express this point elegantly, noting that, "within Western societies, growing political divisiveness and ideological diversity threaten to turn the idea of rights from a shield that protects everyone into a spear that opposing groups hurl at one another."[59]

57 *Id.*, 318.

58 As Michael Rosen explains, a clear example of dignity being given priority over autonomy "is the well-known case of M. Manuel Wackenheim – the French dwarf who was prohibited on grounds of the violation of dignity from participating in a dwarf-tossing context." Rosen notes two important features of this case. First, "dignity was invoked to override M. Wackenheim's vigorously asserted choice …" And second, "M. Wackenheim's own claim that the ban on dwarf-tossing actually violated his dignity was not given weight." Michael Rosen, "Dignity: The Case Against" in Christopher McCrudden (ed.), *Understanding Human Dignity* (Oxford University Press: Oxford, 2013) 151. See: Conseil d'État [CE Ass.] [Supreme Court of Administrative Justice], Oct. 27, 1995, Rec. Lebon 372.

59 For example, "In European countries such as Norway, Denmark, Switzerland, Germany, and France, there is a growing divide between the secular state (backed by a secularized majority population) that pursues animal rights, children's rights, and nondiscrimination, and minority religious groups defending their right to practice their faith. Jewish and Muslim groups, for example, now must defend circumcision –

Overreliance on courts for defining and vindicating rights

An overreliance on courts for defining and vindicating rights amplifies the tendency to think of rights as zero-sum contests. In countries such as the United States, "reliance on rights and courts to solve disputes encourages a winner-takes-all attitude, at the expense of tolerance and compromise."[60] As Glendon and Kaplan note, "Whereas most democracies introduced policies on controversial matters, such as abortion and sexual freedoms, through legislation and compromise, in the U.S. they have often been dictated by courts, thereby alienating parts of the population and reducing the scope for political settlements."[61]

Respecting ourselves

When we recognize that rights entail duties it encourages us to act in ways that are respectful of ourselves as well as others. We show respect to ourselves (and others) by exercising our rights responsibly.

Respecting others

Dignity and human rights are shared responsibilities. Protecting our dignity and human rights but neglecting the dignity and human rights of others will lead to the collapse of the human rights project. Protecting one's dignity and human rights but neglecting the dignity and human rights of others also prevents human dignity and human rights from becoming universal. The need to protect the human dignity and human rights of others is also crucial as some individuals or groups are not able to protect themselves.

Human dignity and freedom

Dignity and freedom are both fundamental values, and each will place limitations on excessive claims made in the name of the other. For example, the Catholic Church's influential Vatican II Declaration *Dignitatis Humanae* reflects upon the relationship between dignity and freedom. As articulated in *Dignitatis Humanae*, human dignity, the dignity of the person leads to the right of religious freedom. It isn't freedom that enables dignity, it is dignity that enables freedom.[62] *Dignitatis*

an ancient ritual integral to their faiths – against human rights groups declaring it a violation of children's right to bodily integrity. The capacious right to religious freedom in the Universal Declaration's Article 18, which includes the right to 'manifest' one's religion in 'teaching, practice, worship and observance,' is being narrowed to mean only a right to believe and worship – not a right to practice and observe." Mary Ann Glendon and Seth D. Kaplan, "Renewing Human Rights" (February 2019) *First Things* 36.

60 *Id.*, 36.

61 *Id.*, 36.

62 Section 9: "The declaration of this Vatican Council on the right of man to religious freedom has its foundation in the dignity of the person, whose exigencies have come

Humanae explains that the responsible exercise of that freedom includes a search for truth and for God.[63] For example, Vatican II confirms that "the right to religious freedom has its foundation in the very dignity of the human person as this dignity is known through the revealed word of God and by reason itself. This right of the human person to religious freedom is to be recognized in the constitutional law whereby society is governed and thus it is to become a civil right."

The drafters were confident that the responsible exercise of freedom will lead human beings to embrace the truths of the Catholic Church. Human Dignity gives us the capacity to seek and choose truth; as the New Testament teaches, it is the truth that makes us free.[64]

d. Nonetheless, human dignity is not diminished on the ground that persons are not fulfilling their responsibilities to the state and others

Even though human rights create duties for us as people, states may not condition the protection of human rights on persons fulfilling their duties. This may seem counterintuitive and requires some explanation.

Human rights are not conditional upon people fulfilling their responsibilities

One way that states sometimes attempt to sidestep their obligation to protect the fundamental human rights of citizens or others within their jurisdictions is to make

to be are fully known to human reason through centuries of experience. What is more, this doctrine of freedom has roots in divine revelation, and for this reason Christians are bound to respect it all the more conscientiously. Revelation does not indeed affirm in so many words the right of man to immunity from external coercion in matters religious."

63 Vatican II, Section 1: "… On their part, all men are bound to seek the truth, especially in what concerns God and His Church, and to embrace the truth they come to know, and to hold fast to it."

Section 2: "It is in accordance with their dignity as persons – that is, beings endowed with reason and free will and therefore privileged to bear personal responsibility – that all men should be at once impelled by nature and also bound by a moral obligation to seek the truth, especially religious truth. They are also bound to adhere to the truth, once it is known, and to order their whole lives in accord with the demands of truth … Therefore, the right to religious freedom has its foundation not in the subjective disposition of the person, but in his very nature. In consequence, the right to this immunity continues to exist even in those who do not live up to their obligation of seeking the truth and adhering to it and the exercise of this right is not to be impeded, provided that just public order be observed."

Section 3: "… Truth, however, is to be sought after in a manner proper to the dignity of the human person and his social nature. The inquiry is to be free, carried on with the aid of teaching or instruction, communication and dialogue, in the course of which men explain to one another the truth they have discovered, or think they have discovered, in order thus to assist one another in the quest for truth. Moreover, as the truth is discovered, it is by a personal assent that men are to adhere to it."

64 John 8:32: "And you will know the truth, and the truth will set you free."

rights conditional. This is problematic because human rights create duties for states regardless of the behavior of the people who have human rights.

Some rights that are of fundamental importance, and that may in some sense be human rights, carry duties as well. As Jeremy Waldron explains, citizenship is such a type of right and status.[65] Waldron argues, "citizens may also have duties to support the state: they may be liable for example to military conscription in time of war, and in some countries even routinely during peacetime. Everywhere they owe a duty of allegiance to the government of the country of which they are a citizen, and may be punished for treason if they aid the country's enemies."[66]

Basic human rights and human dignity exist without conditions or prerequisites

The fact that human rights trigger duties on the part of rights holders makes it easy for states to make the mistake of conditioning the protection of rights on the fulfillment of duties. The failure by some people to fulfill their obligations or responsibilities does not affect their basic human dignity. Human dignity is inherent and inalienable. This is most clearly illustrated in the case of individuals who have committed serious crimes, such as murder or sexual assault of a minor. They have violated their duties regarding the human rights of others, but this does not mean that they have forfeited their basic human rights, for example, the right to a fair trial, due process of law, and the right of not being subject to punishments that are cruel, inhumane or degrading. Indeed, one of the classes of people most in need of human rights protections are those who have (or are suspected as having) violated the law.

It would be a mistake, and contrary to international law, to only recognize human dignity or fundamental human rights for persons acting in a dignified manner.

The state has obligations to respect and protect the dignity of those who violate their duties

The state is obliged to respect and protect the dignity of even those individuals who violate their duties (for example by breaking the law), or even those who act in clearly undignified ways.

65 Although the right to citizenship derives from the right to nationality in Article 15(1) of the UDHR.

66 Jeremy Waldron, "Citizenship and Dignity" in Christopher McCrudden (ed.), *Understanding Human Dignity* (Oxford University Press: Oxford, 2013) 334. Waldron goes on to explain, "These are the normal or normative incidents of citizenship. Together, as I said, they add up to a status in each polity that is special, equal, and pervasive. Citizenship is a high status: it comprises important rights like the franchise and the right to inhabit a certain country; even those incidents of it that involve duties or liabilities are in some sense valued by those who have them and coveted by those who don't." *Id.*

It is a mistake for states to condition the existence of the most basic human rights of people on those people satisfying prerequisites. Of course, some rights are conditional – for example, the right to have a driver's license.[67] But basic human rights are not conditional in this way. People don't have to behave well or satisfy certain requirements to have human rights. The only qualification for having human rights is being human. This is another reason why human rights should not be exaggerated or proliferated. Some rights are and should have conditions placed upon them, but these by definition are not basic human rights.

As noted above, rights and obligations exist in complex webs; having human rights triggers obligations on the part of the rights-holder, both to others, to the state, and to themselves. But a failure to fulfill those obligations by some people is not a valid reason for the state refusing to recognize or protect the human rights of those people.

Acting in a dignified manner is not a prerequisite to having human dignity or human rights

To conclude, it is not a prerequisite to having human rights that a person acts in a dignified manner. Rather, being a human being is the prerequisite for having human rights. When states place conditions or requirements on having basic human rights, the state violates human rights.

67 This is not to say that human rights will be irrelevant to conditional rights. For example, the human right of non-discrimination will have implications for the administration of the licensing regime.

7 Article 5

Education

Article 5 reads as follows:

> Recognition of human dignity is a vital basis for teaching and education. Human rights education is of importance to promoting respect for the equal dignity of everyone. Such education is essential for sustaining dignity and human rights into the future. Equal access to education is a crucial aspect of respecting human dignity.

The following is an expanded explanation of each part of Article 5.

Article 5 recognizes several important connections between human dignity and education, including: human dignity implies the importance of education; education should be built upon principles of human dignity; human dignity is a helpful cornerstone of human rights education; education is vital to the future of human dignity for all; and human dignity implies there should be equal access to education. These themes are further explained below.

a. Recognition of human dignity is a vital basis for teaching and education

If we care about human dignity, a necessary corollary is that we will care about education, because education is essential for human flourishing. Human dignity implies that education is important and human dignity will shape what education looks like. Recognition of human dignity for everyone everywhere should be taught directly and indirectly in education at all levels.[1] A concern for human

1 The Preamble of the UN Declaration on Human Rights Education and Training states: "Reaffirming further that everyone has the right to education, and that education shall be directed to the full development of the human personality and the sense of its dignity, enable all persons to participate effectively in a free society and promote understanding, tolerance and friendship among all nations and all racial, ethnic or religious groups, and further the activities of the United Nations for the maintenance of peace, security and the promotion of development and human rights." UN General Assembly Res. 66/137, United Nations Declaration on Human Rights Education and Training (Dec. 19, 2011).

DOI: 10.4324/9781003207030-8

dignity will result in a concern for education. Education will naturally emphasize the value of human dignity. Hence dignity and education create a virtuous circle.

As former UN Secretary-General Ban Ki-moon said:

> There is no greater tool than education to enhance human dignity, promote a culture of non-violence, and build lasting peace. Through education, we can craft new ways of living with each other and the planet. Education can also lay the foundation for developing new forms of global citizenship and solidarity that are so essential in today's world.[2]

As affirmed in Article 26(1) of the UDHR, everyone has the right to education. However, as Article 26(2) clearly states, "Education shall be directed to the full development of the human personality." The right to education is more than having access to education, rather it is a right to an education that aims at ensuring the full development of personality, which will have positive consequences for the development of human capacities.

This is a broader claim than that human dignity is relevant to human rights education; it is, but it is also relevant to education more broadly. Article 13 of the ICESCR explicitly links human dignity with the right to education.[3] Article 13 provides that "education shall be directed to the full development of the human personality and the sense of its dignity, and shall strengthen the respect for human rights and fundamental freedoms." The General Comment of the Committee on Economic, Social, and Cultural Rights also invokes the idea of dignity in its explanation of why corporal punishment in schools should be prohibited.[4]

b. Human rights education is of importance to promoting respect for the equal dignity of everyone

Education should include education in human rights that is grounded in the principle of human dignity for all. Education should include human rights education that promotes human dignity. The right to education, in itself, is a human right enshrined in Article 26 of the UDHR. Article 26(2) indicates:

2 UN Secretary-General, "Education Greatest Tool to Enhancing Human Dignity, Building Lasting Peace, Secretary-General Says in Message for International Day of Non-Violence" UN Press Release SG/SM/16224-OBV/1380 (Sept. 29, 2014). Available at: https://www.un.org/press/en/2014/sgsm16224.doc.htm

3 See UN General Assembly Res. 2200A (XXI), International Covenant on Economic, Social and Cultural Rights (Dec. 16, 1966). It is noteworthy that the other provisions in the ICESCR enumerating economic, social and cultural rights do not explicitly refer to human dignity in their definitions, suggesting a recognition by the drafters of the ICESCR that education is intimately and expressly linked with human dignity.

4 UN Compilation of General Comments and General Recommendations Adopted by Human Rights Treaty Bodies, UN Doc. HRI/GEN/1/Rev.9 (Vol. I), at 71, 77 (May 27, 2008).

> Education shall be directed to the full development of the human personality and to the strengthening of respect for human rights and fundamental freedoms. It shall promote understanding, tolerance and friendship among all nations, racial or religious groups, and shall further the activities of the United Nations for the maintenance of peace.

Hence, the right to education is not only an end but also the means to achieve an end. It is a means of creating conditions that will facilitate the realization of other human rights, which is education that fosters human rights. The right to education is not value-neutral.[5]

The point that the right to education in itself is not enough was made by Mr. Lebar representing UNESCO who, contributing to the debates on the scope of the right to education to be included in the UDHR, pointed out that:

> It was absolutely necessary to make it clear that education to which everyone was entitled should strengthen respect for the rights set forth in the Declaration and combat the spirit of intolerance.[6]

Similarly, Mr. Bienenfeld from the World Jewish Congress emphasized that:

> Education in Germany and other fascist countries had been carried out in compliance with the principle of the right of education for everyone; yet the doctrines on which that education had been founded had led to two world wars. If the Declaration failed to define the spirit in which future generations were to be educated, it would lose its value as a guide for humanity. The Declaration was not merely an appeal to the State; it was an appeal also to parents, teachers and educators. It was necessary to stress the importance of the article devoted to the spirit of education, which was possibly greater than that of all the other articles of the Declaration.[7]

Hence, the content of such education is paramount. Education that is committed to human dignity and human rights will contribute to the goal of ensuring the full development of each child's personality. Further, such an approach to education is necessary to prevent education from being captured by those with agendas contrary to the spirit of the UDHR.

The UN Declaration on Human Rights Education and Training

On December 19, 2011, the UN General Assembly adopted the UN Declaration on Human Rights Education and Training (UN General Assembly Resolution

5 See Richard Pierre Claude, "The Right to Education and Human Rights Education" (2005) 2 *Revista Internacional de Direitos Humanos* 36, 63.
6 Schabas (2013) 1841.
7 *Id.*, 1842.

66/137). The Declaration builds upon the right to education in Article 26 of the UDHR and elaborates on how this right can be more fully implemented and realized. The Declaration, while not legally binding, incorporates several important recommendations to ensure that human rights education is equipped to deliver on its promise. Article 1 affirms:

1 Everyone has the right to know, seek, and receive information about all human rights and fundamental freedoms and should have access to human rights education and training.
2 Human rights education and training are essential for the promotion of universal respect for and observance of all human rights and fundamental freedoms for all, in accordance with the principles of the universality, indivisibility, and interdependence of human rights.
3 The effective enjoyment of all human rights, in particular the right to education and access to information, enables access to human rights education and training.

It further recognizes the importance of human rights education is based on principles of equality, human dignity, inclusion, and non-discrimination. Article 5 (1) states:

> Human rights education and training, whether provided by public or private actors, should be based on the principles of equality, particularly between girls and boys and between women and men, human dignity, inclusion, and non-discrimination.

The important point here is that human rights education should be built upon basic foundational principles including human dignity.

Effective human rights education can also help combat radicalization. The summary report of the Office of the United Nations High Commissioner for Human Rights of the high-level panel discussion on the implementation of the Declaration notes that

> The lack of human rights education was a central factor leading to radicalization … [T]he fight against extremism needed to target all forms of extremism and adopt a multidisciplinary approach that addressed the main causes, such as lack of empathy and the inability to think critically.[8]

This concern about radicalization is important, especially in recent years as we have witnessed numerous teenagers and young adults leaving their comfortable lives and joining terror organizations such as Daesh in Syria and Iraq.

During the panel discussion on the implementation of the Declaration, the participants noted that,

8 *Id.*, 21.

> Human rights education and training is an effective strategy for preventing and tackling current global challenges, including violent extremism and conflict, as it proposes solutions in line with human rights standards. The training of media professionals and youth is prioritized in this regard.[9]
>
> Human rights education [is] the antidote to a culture of human rights violations and violence against individuals.[10]
>
> Human rights education is a lifelong process that concerns all ages and all parts of society at all levels. It develops the knowledge and skills of learners to promote, defend. and apply human rights in their daily lives.[11]

The report summarized key messages from a documentary, *A Path to Dignity: The Power of Human Rights Education* that stresses the importance of human rights education:

a human rights education starts with the daily life of the learners, engaging them in a critical reflection on the human rights challenges they face;
b human rights education is an empowering process that provides learners with the tools, knowledge, and skills to address their human rights challenges; and
c human rights education leads to action that is consistent with the basic principles of human rights to further promote and protect human rights.[12]

World Program for Human Rights Education

The World Program for Human Rights Education was established by UN General Assembly Resolution 59/113 to "promote a common understanding of basic principles and methodologies of human rights education, to provide a concrete framework for action and to strengthen partnerships and cooperation from the international level down to the grassroots."[13]

Sustainable Development Goals

Target 4 of the 2030 Sustainable Development Goals (SDG) focuses on education. Target 4.7, for example, states:

> By 2030, ensure that all learners acquire the knowledge and skills needed to promote sustainable development, including, among others, through education for sustainable development and sustainable lifestyles, human rights,

9 *Id.*, 28.
10 *Id.*, 18.
11 *Id.*, 27.
12 *Id.*, 13.
13 UN General Assembly Res. 59/113, World Program for Human Rights Education (Dec. 10, 2004). See OHCHR, *World Program for Human Rights Education (2005–ongoing)*. Available at: https://www.ohchr.org/EN/Issues/Education/Training/Pages/Programme.aspx

gender equality, promotion of a culture of peace and non-violence, global citizenship, and appreciation of cultural diversity and of culture's contribution to sustainable development.

The UN Declaration on Human Rights Education and Training, the World Program for Human Rights Education, and other education-related initiatives (for example, target 4.7 of the SDG) contribute to the growing consensus on the crucial role of human rights education in the realization of all human rights and furthering human dignity.

Apart from the efforts of the UN, other international actors have emphasized the importance of human rights education. For example, in 1985, the Council of Europe's Committee of Ministers issued Recommendation no. R (85)7 about teaching on human rights in schools.[14] It recommends that:

> The study of human rights in schools should lead to an understanding of, and sympathy for, the concepts of justice, equality, freedom, peace, dignity, rights and democracy. Such understanding should be both cognitive and based on experience and feelings. Schools should, thus, provide opportunities for pupils to experience affective involvement in human rights and to express their feelings through drama, art, music, creative writing and audiovisual media.[15]

In 1997, the Council of Europe launched a project on Education for Democratic Citizenship. In 2010, the Committee of Ministers adopted the Council of Europe Charter on Education for Democratic Citizenship and Human Rights Education.[16] Article 5(f) states,

> An essential element of all education for democratic citizenship and human rights education is the promotion of social cohesion and intercultural dialogue and the valuing of diversity and equality, including gender equality; to this end, it is essential to develop knowledge, personal and social skills and understanding that reduce conflict, increase appreciation and understanding of the differences between faith and ethnic groups, build mutual respect for human dignity and shared values, encourage dialogue and promote non-violence in the resolution of problems and disputes.

Human rights education helps students understand that we belong to a global society.[17] Human rights education, "unlike the premise of political education,

14 Council of Europe, Committee of Ministers issued Recommendation No. R(85)7. Available at: https://rm.coe.int/16804c2d48

15 *Id.*, 3.3.

16 Council of Europe Charter on Education for Democratic Citizenship and Human Rights Education. Available at: https://search.coe.int/cm/Pages/result_details.aspx?ObjectID=09000016805cf01f

17 Francisco O. Ramírez, David Suárez and John W. Meyer, "The Worldwide Rise of Human Rights Education" in A. Benavot and C. Braslavsky (eds.), *School Knowledge in Comparative and Historical Perspective* (Springer, 2007) 35.

which is based on the notion of 'the citizen,' … takes as its premise the individual as a member of the human race. Human rights education locates moral authority not in the legitimacy of any particular state, but in the inherent dignity and potential of each person as a physical, sensitive, thoughtful and spiritual being."[18]

Human rights education should promote the understanding of and respect for the equal dignity of everyone.[19] Human rights education should emphasize the reciprocity of human rights and that human rights involve the corresponding duties of everyone everywhere.[20]

Nonetheless, the challenges associated with human rights illiteracy continue, and more needs to be done to ensure that a comprehensive human rights education anchored in adequate understanding of human dignity is accessible by everyone. Such human rights education is needed to combat human rights illiteracy and associated challenges, including radicalization, violent extremism, and human rights violations.

In places where human rights education is controversial or faces resistance, focusing on the foundational concept of human dignity can help make human rights less subject to disagreement and opposition. The concept of human dignity for everyone everywhere is such a powerfully intuitive concept, that by starting with this idea, resistance to human rights education can be mitigated. As Eleanor Roosevelt emphasized:

18 Felisa Tibbets, "On Human Dignity: The Need for Human Rights Education" (1996) 60 *Social Education* 428.

19 Article 2 of the UN Declaration on Human Rights Education and Training:

"1. Human rights education and training comprises all educational, training, information, awareness-raising and learning activities aimed at promoting universal respect for and observance of all human rights and fundamental freedoms and thus contributing, inter alia, to the prevention of human rights violations and abuses by providing persons with knowledge, skills and understanding and developing their attitudes and behaviors, to empower them to contribute to the building and promotion of a universal culture of human rights.

2. Human rights education and training encompasses:

(a) Education about human rights, which includes providing knowledge and understanding of human rights norms and principles, the values that underpin them and the mechanisms for their protection;

(b) Education through human rights, which includes learning and teaching in a way that respects the rights of both educators and learners;

(c) Education for human rights, which includes empowering persons to enjoy and exercise their rights and to respect and uphold the rights of others." UN General Assembly Res. 66/137, United Nations Declaration on Human Rights Education and Training (Dec. 19, 2011).

20 Article 4(b) of the UN Declaration on Human Rights Education and Training: "Developing a universal culture of human rights, in which everyone is aware of their own rights and responsibilities in respect of the rights of others, and promoting the development of the individual as a responsible member of a free, peaceful, pluralist and inclusive society." (UN General Assembly Res. 66/137, United Nations Declaration on Human Rights Education and Training (Dec. 19, 2011)).

> It will be a long time before history will make its judgment on the value of the Universal Declaration of Human Rights, and the judgment will depend, I think, on what the people of different nations do to make this document familiar to everyone. If they know it well enough, they will strive to attain some of the rights and freedoms set forth in it, and that effort on their part is what will make it of value in clarifying what was meant in the Charter in the references to human rights and fundamental freedoms.[21]

c. Human rights education is essential for sustaining dignity and human rights into the future

The drafters of the UDHR recognized that the most important feature of creating a human rights culture and ensuring the implementation and stability of human rights would be through teaching and education.[22] The introductory proclamation of the UDHR calls for "every organ of society" through constant mindfulness and vigilance, to "strive by teaching and education to promote respect" for human rights at all levels, beginning with local efforts and progressing through national and international measures.[23]

Teaching human rights and human dignity, and their importance is the only way to ensure that both are not only adequately implemented but also preserved in the future. As time goes by, the atrocities that led to the drafting and adoption of the UDHR will be forgotten, and so the importance of protecting human rights and human dignity of everyone everywhere could easily diminish. Teaching human rights and human dignity, and teaching about the dark history that led the world to muster the political will to draft and adopt the UDHR, will help ensure that human rights and human dignity are strengthened and preserved to benefit (and protect) generations to come.

d. Equal access to education is a crucial aspect of respecting human dignity

It is crucial to ensure equal access to education for all, by following international standards. While over the years some progress has been made, nonetheless it is crucial to recognize that several groups continue to be neglected regarding their

21 Richard Pierre Claude, "The Right to Education and Human Rights Education" (2005) 2 *Revista Internacional de Direitos Humanos* 36, 63.

22 See above, Section (b).

23 "Therefore THE GENERAL ASSEMBLY proclaims THIS UNIVERSAL DECLARATION OF HUMAN RIGHTS as a common standard of achievement for all peoples and all nations, to the end that every individual and every organ of society, keeping this Declaration constantly in mind, shall strive by teaching and education to promote respect for these rights and freedoms and by progressive measures, national and international, to secure their universal and effective recognition and observance, both among the peoples of Member States themselves and among the peoples of territories under their jurisdiction." UDHR.

access to education. Of particular note is that in many parts of the world, women and girls continue to be disproportionally disadvantaged in their access to education.[24]

There are other groups too whose situation is dire and stands in urgent need of being addressed. For example, the UNHCR reports that only 50% of refugee children are enrolled in primary school, while 22% of refugee youth are enrolled in secondary school and only 1% of refugees attend universities.[25] This is critical, especially as there are approximately 25.4 million refugees in the world, with over half of them being children.[26]

Similar barriers are faced by persons with disabilities. According to a 2018 UNESCO report that considered data from 49 states, children with disabilities are less likely to attend school than those without disabilities.[27] The largest gaps between persons with and without disabilities in education have been reported in Vietnam (44% vs. 97% in 2009), Egypt (43% vs. 89% in 2006), and Indonesia (53% vs. 98% in 2010).[28]

Such barriers are also faced by numerous children who belong to ethnic, religious, or linguistic minorities.

A failure to address the issue of equal access to education will result in a commitment failure of human rights education. If one cannot access education (including human rights education), one will be deprived of the very opportunity to learn about their human rights or the human rights of others. The human rights project will only be successful when education (broadly) and human rights education (specifically) are afforded to everyone.

24 UNESCO, Fact sheet no. 48 UIS/FS/2018/ED/48 (Feb. 2018), http://uis.unesco.org/sites/default/files/documents/fs48-one-five-children-adolescents-youth-out-school-2018-en.pdf

25 UNCHR: The UN Refugee Agency, "Missing Out: Refugee Education in Crisis" (Sept. 2006), https://www.unhcr.org/57d9d01d0

26 *Id.*

27 UNESCO, "Education and Disability: Analysis of Data from 49 Countries," Information paper no. 49 (March 2018), http://uis.unesco.org/sites/default/files/documents/ip49-education-disability-2018-en.pdf

28 *Id.*, 4.

8 Article 6

Seeking common ground

Article 6 reads as follows:

> Focusing on human dignity for everyone everywhere encourages people to search for ways to find common ground regarding competing claims and to move beyond exclusively legal mechanisms for harmonizing, implementing, and mutually vindicating human rights and finding solutions to conflicts.

The following is an expanded explanation of each part of Article 6.

a. Focusing on human dignity for everyone everywhere encourages people to search for ways to find common ground regarding competing claims

Human dignity is a unifying value, and hence, an approach to human rights that is oriented around human dignity will help find common ground in solving conflicts between competing rights claims and finding solutions that are beneficial for everyone involved (rather than pronouncing winning and losing parties). Human dignity for all is unlikely to generate winner-takes-all solutions to human rights conflicts. Hence, it is unlikely to be an idea that is appealing to those who view human rights conflicts as contests to be won at any cost, or for a preferred right to be so important that it should be pursued without regard for other rights or interests. Human dignity for everyone everywhere at its very core is an outlook that will seek common ground.

Religious freedom and non-discrimination

Sometimes human rights claims come into conflict, such as when a religious-freedom claim to abstain from some activity clashes with a non-discrimination right (or equality laws). Familiar examples include wedding service providers such as cake makers, florists, and photographers, who as a matter of conscience do not wish to participate in a same-sex wedding. If there is a legal provision prohibiting discrimination based on sexual orientation, the right to conscientious objection may be viewed as conflicting with the prohibition on discrimination. Sometimes,

DOI: 10.4324/9781003207030-9

the clash is less than it appears to be – the objection may not be to serving someone based on their sexual orientation; rather it may be based on communicating a message that a person does not want to be associated with. For example, in the Northern Irish case of *Ashers' Bakery*, the bakers were asked to bake a cake and ice it with a picture of Bert and Ernie and a message stating "support gay marriage." Having learned about the message to be iced on the cake, the bakers declined the order, citing that delivering such a message on the cake would be contrary to their beliefs. This resulted in a long and expensive legal battle.

Once the case arrived at the UK Supreme Court, the Court concluded that:

> The bakery could not refuse to provide a cake – or any other of their products – to Mr. Lee because he was a gay man or because he supported gay marriage. But that important fact does not amount to a justification for something completely different – obliging them to supply a cake iced with a message with which they profoundly disagreed. In my view they would be entitled to refuse to do that whatever the message conveyed by the icing on the cake – support for living in sin, support for a particular political party, support for a particular religious denomination. The fact that this particular message had to do with sexual orientation is irrelevant to the FETO claim.[1]

The Court found in favor of the bakery, and ruled that the legislation should not be "read or given effect in such a way as to compel providers of goods, facilities, and services to express a message with which they disagree unless justification is shown for doing so."[2]

Just before the *Ashers' Bakery* judgment, the US Supreme Court dealt with a similar case concerning conflicting claims. In the *Masterpiece Cakeshop* case, the baker refused to design and bake a wedding cake for a same-sex wedding ceremony. Here, Mr. Philips promised to sell anything in his bakery but refused to design and bake a wedding cake celebrating same-sex marriage. The US Supreme Court found in favor of the baker, arguing that:

> The Commission's[3] treatment of Phillips' case violated the State's duty under the First Amendment not to base laws or regulations on hostility to a religion or religious viewpoint … Factors relevant to the assessment of governmental neutrality include "the historical background of the decision under challenge, the specific series of events leading to the enactment or official policy in question, and the legislative or administrative history, including contemporaneous statements made by members of the decision-making body." In view of these factors the record here demonstrates that the Commission's consideration of Phillips' case was neither tolerant nor respectful of Phillips'

1 *Lee v. Ashers' Baking Company Ltd & Ors* [2018] UKSC 49, [55] (appeal taken from Scot.).
2 *Id.*, 56.
3 The Colorado Civil Rights Commission (the Commission).

> religious beliefs. The Commission gave "every appearance," of adjudicating Phillips' religious objection based on a negative normative "evaluation of the particular justification" for his objection and the religious grounds for it. It hardly requires restating that government has no role in deciding or even suggesting whether the religious ground for Phillips' conscience-based objection is legitimate or illegitimate. On these facts, the Court must draw the inference that Phillips' religious objection was not considered with the neutrality that the Free Exercise Clause requires.[4]

The overriding consideration in the case was the hostility expressed by the Commission. The judgment considered the different treatment afforded by the Commission to Mr. Phillips refusing to design and bake a wedding cake celebrating same-sex marriage (that was contrary to his honestly held religious beliefs) and other bakers refusing to design and bake cakes with messages disapproving same-sex marriage on religious grounds (that were contrary to their beliefs).

In his concurring judgment, Justice Gorsuch noted that "the Commission failed to act neutrally by applying a consistent legal rule."[5] Just as courts are (or should be) unwilling to force bakers to bake a cake condemning same-sex marriage, they should be unwilling to force bakers to bake a cake endorsing same-sex marriage.[6] In contrast, when a vendor is selling off-the-shelf products, denying service to someone who wanted to use them as part of a same-sex-marriage celebration (or to communicate a message of disapproval of same-sex-marriage) would much more likely be unlawful discrimination.

Nevertheless, there can be real conflicts, such as when there is a law prohibiting discrimination in housing and a private religiously-affiliated university with a doctrinal objection to same-sex marriage wishes to reserve eligibility for its housing to couples in heterosexual marriages. Without an exception to the non-discrimination rule, the religious university could be deemed to violate the non-discrimination rule if it does not make its married student housing available to married same-sex couples. Recognizing the human dignity of everyone involved will help facilitate reaching reasonable compromises that can provide non-discrimination provisions in housing and employment while recognizing the rights of religiously-affiliated schools and universities to be allowed to follow their religious tenets. For example, the dignity of same-sex couples can be recognized by the general prohibition on discrimination in housing, and the dignity of the members of the religious

4 *Masterpiece Cakeshop v. Colo. Civil Rights Comm'n*, 138 S.Ct. 1719, 1745 (2018) (US) (Kennedy J., Opinion). Internal references omitted.

5 *Id.* (Gorsuch J concurring).

6 "'States cannot put individuals to the choice of "be[ing] compelled to affirm someone else's belief" or "be[ing] forced to speak when [they] would prefer to remain silent."'" *Id.* (Thomas, J., concurring) (citing *Pruneyard Shopping Ctr. v. Robin,* 447 U.S. 74, 99, 100 (1980)).

community can be recognized by an exception to the non-discrimination rule for its university.[7]

Ordinary exceptions to non-discrimination provisions

Rules prohibiting discrimination often include exceptions that are designed to recognize such needs. For example, laws prohibiting housing discrimination typically include exceptions for roommates, people sharing a house, or small housing units such as duplexes and four-plexes.[8] This enables someone who is looking for a "single white female" roommate to discriminate based on marital status, race, and sex.[9] We can pursue social policies that seek to address problems of discrimination in housing without turning it into an absolute rule that does not take into account the important dignitary and privacy interests of people to live with whom they choose to live. Thus, non-discrimination can be the rule for apartment complexes above a certain size, while choice can be the exception to the rule concerning more intimate living arrangements.

Laws prohibiting discriminating in hiring employees often include exceptions for small businesses,[10] in recognition of the fact that some small businesses appeal to small affinity groups (such as a hair salon that serves a particular minority group, or a gym that wants to serve just women customers). Small businesses are also often family-owned and operated, in which case the owner who favors their child might be accused of discriminating based on race, nationality, or even religion. Similarly, accommodations can be made for religious convictions as well. A Christian bookshop should be able to hire Christians without being accused of religious discrimination. A bar that appeals to an LGBTQ clientele should not be required to hire someone who insists on wearing t-shirts with anti-gay messages (even if this could be construed as discrimination on the basis of religion). Such accommodations also recognize that small businesses often do not have the resources to comply with stringent non-discrimination claims.

Because we live in a time when non-discrimination norms have such powerful political and moral valence, it is easy to forget that not every differentiation is

7 S.B. 296, 2015 Leg., Gen. Sess. (Utah 2015) (Antidiscrimination and Religious Freedom Amendments, or Utah Compromise).

8 See Title VIII of the Civil Rights Act of 1968 (Fair Housing Act), 42 U.S.C.A. § 3602 (2019); 42 U.S.C. § 3607(a) (2019); Cal. Gov't Code § 12927(c)(2) (2019).

9 *Fair Hous. Council v. Roommates.com*, 521 F.3d 1157 (9th Cir. 2008). *See* Cal. Gov't Code § 12927(c)(2) (2019).

10 For example, Title VII of the Civil Rights Act says, "'employer' means a person engaged in an industry affecting commerce who has *fifteen or more employees* for each working day in each of twenty or more calendar weeks in the current or preceding calendar year, and any agent of such a person, but such term does not include (1) the United States, a corporation wholly owned by the Government of the United States, an Indian tribe, or any department or agency of the District of Columbia subject by statute to procedures of the competitive service (as defined in section 2102 of Title 5 *[United States Code]*)." Title VII of the Civil Rights Act of 1964, 42 U.S.C. §§ 2000e-2000e-17 (2000) (emphasis added).

discrimination, and not every instance of discrimination is insidious. It is crucial to recognize the many overlapping pluralisms or the societies in which that we live, and to ensure that the human dignity of everyone (including those on both sides of a human rights conflict) is adequately recognized and protected.

b. Focusing on human dignity for everyone everywhere encourages people to move beyond exclusively legal mechanisms for harmonizing, implementing, and mutually vindicating human rights and finding solutions to conflicts

Focusing on human dignity for everyone everywhere encourages us to seek ways to harmonize, implement, and mutually vindicate human rights by finding practical solutions to conflicts that may arise. These accommodations often go beyond, legal mechanisms discussed under section (a).

Informal accommodations of conscience

Outside the formal accommodation of conscience in business scenarios (for example, as in the US under Title VII), there may be other cases where individuals would wish to live following their conscientiously held beliefs. For example, in the US, some states enacted explicit provisions to clarify that religious officials and religious institutions are allowed to determine whose marriages they will solemnize according to their beliefs.[11] As a technical legal matter, explicit provisions in the US should not be needed as religious institutions are protected by the Free Exercise Clause of the First Amendment.[12]

In some places, for example, Texas, accommodation of religious belief is inferred from the existing law. Indeed, after the decision in *Obergefell*, Attorney-General Paxton clarified that "the Supreme Court did not diminish, overrule, or call into question the First Amendment rights to free exercise of religion ... [the] federal constitutional right to same-sex marriage should peaceably coexist alongside longstanding constitutional and statutory rights."[13] It is usually possible to protect people on both sides of important human rights conflicts, rather than creating situations where one side is forced to subordinate their claim.

11 Judges – Marriage – Recusal Act, S.L. 2015–75, 2015 N.C. Sess. Laws 160, 160–63 (West) (an act to allow magistrates, assistant registers of deeds, and deputy registers of deeds to recuse themselves from performing duties related to marriage ceremonies due to sincerely held religious objection). S.B. 297, 2015 Leg., Gen. Sess. (Utah 2015). See Nicholas J. Schilling, Jr., "Analysis of Statutory Religious Accommodations for State-Employed Religious Objectors to Same-Sex Marriage Solemnization" (2017) 31 *Notre Dame Journal of Law, Ethics and Public Policy* 431.

12 For example, the Free Exercise Clause of the First Amendment to the United States Constitution states: "Congress shall make no law respecting an establishment of religion, or prohibiting the free exercise thereof[.]" US Constitution, Amendment I.

13 Op. Att'y Gen. KP-0025 (2015).

In many places where employees issue state licenses, work assignments can be arranged in a way that protects the conscience of an employee who objects to issuing or signing a same-sex marriage license, without denying service (or even the customers being aware that the conscientious objection is being accommodated).[14] While it is not always possible to accommodate conscience through such informal measures, such informal accommodations can often be made in ways that permit the legitimate expectations of both parties to be served, without the need for long and costly litigation that will pronounce a winner and a loser.

In countries where there is no formal legal mechanism requiring businesses to make reasonable accommodations, it may be advisable to consider whether such mechanisms could be adopted, whether formal or informal. For example, in the UK, Ms. Ladele, a registrar of births, deaths, and marriages, was asked to register civil partnerships after the Civil Partnership Act 2004 came into force. Initially, Ms. Ladele was allowed to make informal arrangements so that she did not have to conduct civil partnership ceremonies. However, after a complaint from another employee that her refusal to perform civil partnership ceremonies was discriminatory, Ms. Ladele was requested to comply with such duties under the threat of being in breach of the Code of Conduct and the equality policy.[15] Ms. Ladele refused and requested an accommodation of her religious belief. She was refused, and her case proceeded all way to the ECtHR where the court found that there was no violation of Article 14 taken in conjunction with Article 9 as the "local authority employer which brought the disciplinary proceedings and also the domestic courts which rejected the applicant's discrimination claim" did not exceed the margin of appreciation available to them.

In the joint partly dissenting opinion, Judges Vucinic and De Gaetano disagreed with the analysis in the case of Ms. Ladele and stated their view that "no one should be forced to act against one's conscience or be penalized for refusing to act against one's conscience."[16] They continued:

> We are of the view that once that a *genuine* and *serious* case of conscientious objection is established, the State is obliged to respect the individual's freedom of conscience both positively (by taking reasonable and appropriate measures to protect the rights of the conscientious objector) and negatively (by refraining from actions which punish the objector or discriminate against him or her).[17]

14 For example, maybe an employee gets assigned to issue drivers' licenses if they have a conscience concern about certain wedding licenses. In *Patterson v. Walgreen Co.,* an employee was originally given accommodations to have Saturdays off because he was Seventh-day Adventist. *Patterson v. Walgreen Co.*, 727 Fed. Appx. 581 (11th Cir. 2018), petition for cert. filed, (U.S. Sep. 17, 2018) (no. 18–349). As the employee was promoted, he was asked to work more and more Saturdays; this case is now on petition for certiorari before the United States Supreme Court. *Id.*

15 *Eweida and Others v. the UK*, 2013-IV Eur. Ct. H.R. 7–10.

16 *Id.*, 1 (Joint partly dissenting opinion of Judges Vucinic and De Gaetano).

17 *Id.*, 3.

Finally, they concluded that:

> Given the cogency, seriousness, cohesion and importance of her conscientious objection (which, as noted earlier, was *also* a manifestation of her deep religious convictions) it was incumbent upon the local authority *to treat her differently* from those registrars who had no conscientious objection to officiating at same-sex unions – something which clearly could have been achieved without detriment to the overall services provided by the Borough including those services provided by registrars, as evidenced by the experience of other local authorities. Instead of practising the tolerance and the "dignity for all" it preached, the Borough of Islington pursued the doctrinaire line, the road of obsessive political correctness. It effectively sought to force the applicant to act against her conscience or face the extreme penalty of dismissal – something which, even assuming that the limitations of Article 9 §2 apply to prescriptions of conscience, cannot be deemed necessary in a democratic society.[18]

When the dignity of only some classes of people is valued, it is more likely that those whose conscience compels them to object will be unnecessarily coerced into bending to majoritarian values. As the example of the state employees in the licensing office illustrate, the goal should be to harmonize and mutually vindicate the human dignity of everyone involved – rather than to give one side a victory that comes at the expense of the other. Ultimately, it is crucial to recognize the importance of finding a solution that will allow the rights of both parties to be realized, without enforcing the rights of one party in a way that suppresses the rights of the other party.

In an attempt to do so, in December 2019, the Parliamentary Assembly of the Council of Europe's Committee on Legal Affairs and Human Rights adopted a resolution and recommendations by Davor Stier, Member of the Croatian Parliament, that contained a reference to the mechanism of reasonable accommodation in its draft resolution, stating:

> 8 The Assembly, therefore, calls on Council of Europe member States to:
>
> 8.1 promote a culture of tolerance and "living together" in a religiously pluralist society, in accordance with Articles 9 and 14 of the European Convention on Human Rights and other international legal instruments on human rights protection;
> 8.2 ensure that the right of all individuals under their jurisdiction to freedom of thought, conscience, and religion is respected;
> 8.3 take all necessary measures to combat discrimination based on religion or beliefs in all fields of civil, economic, political, and cultural life.
>
> 9 Given the importance of the right to manifest one's religion or belief in the workplace, the Assembly calls on Council of Europe member States to:

18 *Id.*, at 7.

9.1 adopt effective anti-discrimination legislation which covers the prohibition of discrimination on grounds of religion or belief and establish appropriate monitoring mechanisms to assess its implementation, in case this has not been done yet;
9.2 consider taking legislative or any other appropriate measures, in order to ensure that employees may lodge requests for reasonable accommodation of their religion or belief;
9.3 establish appropriate adjudication or mediation mechanisms in cases of disputes related to the employer's refusal to accommodate an employee's request based on their religion or belief;
9.4 provide training and advice to public and private employers in order to heighten their awareness of the notions of religion and religious diversity, the specific needs of employees belonging to religious groups, and how to accommodate the specific needs of such employees;
9.5 encourage dialogue between employers, religious communities, trade unions, and non-governmental organizations (NGOs) working for the protection of human rights in order to foster co-operation and tolerance;
9.6 promote the work of national human rights institutions (NHRI) on combating discrimination, including indirect discrimination based on religion or belief, and encourage them to develop training activities for both public and private employers."[19]

Similarly, Mr. Davor Stier proposed draft recommendations for the Committee of Ministers to:

1.1 identify and disseminate examples of good practice in respect of religious diversity and ensuring reasonable accommodation of religion or belief in the workplace;
1.2 reflect on the ways in which reasonable accommodation in the workplace can be best introduced in order to ensure everyone's freedom of religion or belief;
1.3 call on those member States which have not yet done so to sign and ratify Protocol No. 12 to the European Convention on Human Rights;
1.4 strengthen co-operation with the European Union, the Organisation for Security and Cooperation in Europe (OSCE) and the United Nations, with a view to promoting coherent interpretations of the freedom of thought, conscience and religion and the implementation of common policies in the field of combating discrimination based on religion or belief in the workplace.[20]

However, once the resolution and recommendations were debated and voted on at the Plenary, the references to reasonable accommodation were removed. The Plenary debates revealed a common misunderstanding on what the mechanism of reasonable accommodation was and many Parliamentarians conflated

19 Committee on Legal Affairs and Human Rights, "The Protection of Freedom of Religion or Belief in the Workplace," December 2019, Doc. 1501517.
20 *Id.*

conscientious objection and reasonable accommodation. This suggests that to find common grounds, comprehensive human rights literacy is key. Understandably, the concept of reasonable accommodation is a very complex concept and one that is "subject to a variety of different conceptions."[21] And ultimately, it will be up to the conceptual framework used whether reasonable accommodation will be possible. A reasonable accommodation could be considered as an "unfortunate exception to general and neutral rules," "an adaptation that individuals must make to the state," or as "a place of refuge and safety," and each conception shapes the way reasonable accommodation is considered and approached.[22]

21 Brett G. Scharffs, "Conceptualising Reasonable Accommodation" in Paul T. Babie, Neville G. Rochow and Brett G. Scharffs (eds.), *Freedom of Religion or Belief: Creating the Constitutional Space for Fundamental Freedoms* (Elgar Publishing, 2020) 182.
22 *Id.*, 182.

9 Article 7
Implementing and realizing human rights in legislation

Article 7 reads as follows:

> Recognition of human dignity for everyone everywhere is a foundational principle of law and is central to developing and protecting human rights in law and policy. The richness of the concept of dignity resists exhaustive definition, but it encourages the pursuit of optimum mutual vindication where conflicting rights and values are involved. It is critical for moving beyond thinking exclusively in terms of balancing and tradeoffs of rights and interests.

The following is an expanded explanation of each part of Article 7, which focuses on human dignity as sometimes recognized in legislation as a right, while at other times it is identified as a foundation for rights rather than as a right itself. It also encourages legislative solutions that seek the mutual vindication of rights.

a. Recognition of human dignity for everyone everywhere is a foundational principle of law and is central to developing and protecting human rights in law and policy

We have discussed at length how human dignity is a foundational principle of law. Here we focus on specific ways that it is useful in the development and protection of human rights, specifically in constitutions and legislation.

Human dignity and the specification of human rights

It is often difficult to know how to implement broadly articulated human rights, such as freedom of speech or freedom of religion or belief, in particular contexts. Focusing on human dignity can remind us of the stakes when implementing human rights, and deciding what a right means or requires in a specific context or situation. This can be facilitated by focusing on what the implications are in the situation for human dignity.

For example, a recurring issue is the scope of legitimate limitations on manifestations or exercise of religious freedom. In weighing the state's interest and the interest of the religious claimant, focusing on human dignity can help differentiate

DOI: 10.4324/9781003207030-10

between core religious needs and interests versus those that are less central, or even peripheral to religious life. An analysis of the right to freedom of religion or belief that is deeply rooted with respect to human dignity will seek to protect individuals wishing to manifest their religious belief from excessive limitations of the right.

Human dignity in law as a response to dictatorship or severe injustice

As Catherine Dupré, associate professor of comparative constitutional law, has observed, human dignity is implemented in law, notwithstanding that it is a difficult and controversial idea, "to introduce change in the law,"[1] in response to dictatorship or severe injustice. "In this context, human dignity can be understood as a solemn constitutional commitment 'never again' to deny people their humanity and to destroy it in a systematic manner."[2] German judge Dieter Grimm agrees stating that:

> Regarding dignity in a German constitution drafted in 1948–9, it is of importance that before the enactment the Nazi regime had committed atrocities unheard of in history, and the Basic Law's underlying motive can be summarized in the words "Never again," meaning never again a self-destruction of democracy as in 1933, and never again a total neglect of human rights and the recognition that every human being deserves as a part of mankind.[3]

Recognizing human dignity for everyone everywhere and protecting it adequately is the only way to keep the promise of "never again." Any law or policy that fails to recognize human dignity for everyone everywhere paves the way for future human rights violations and even mass atrocities. Indeed, as noted by the UN Office of the Special Adviser on the Prevention of Genocide:

1 "The use of human dignity to break away from regimes of indignity and destruction of humanity is a well-known reason for enshrining it in constitutions adopted after a dictatorship, with the 1949 German Basic Law being the emblematic, but certainly not isolated, example." Catherine Dupré, "Constructing the Meaning of Human Dignity" in Christopher McCrudden (ed.), *Understanding Human Dignity* (Oxford University Press: Oxford, 2013) 119. Dupré notes that, "In Europe, the constitutions of Greece, Portugal, Spain, Hungary (1989), Bulgaria, Romania, Slovenia, Estonia, Slovakia, Lithuania, Czech Republic, Latvia, and Poland enshrine dignity to mark a break away from a regime of dictatorship … The South African constitution adopted at the end of the apartheid also enshrined dignity in a similar move away from the racist regime that had prevailed until then." *Id.*

2 *Id.*

3 Dieter Grimm, "Dignity in a Legal Context and as an Absolute Right" in Christopher McCrudden (ed.), *Understanding Human Dignity* (Oxford University Press: Oxford, 2013) 384–385. Thus, it is not surprising that the German Constitutional Court begins its explanation of dignity with a reference to Nazi atrocities. "But this does not mean that the application of dignity is limited to cases of repetition of Nazi atrocities. It shows, however, that in the light of historical events that had been up to then unthinkable, more was at stake than a number of liberties, something that forms the common ground of the various constitutional rights and guides their understanding." *Id.*

> If the root causes of genocide revolve around inequalities between identity groups, preventing genocide begins with ensuring that all groups within society enjoy the rights and dignity of belonging as equal citizens. Early prevention therefore becomes a challenge of good governance and equitable management of diversity. That means eliminating gross political and economic inequalities, and promoting a common sense of belonging on equal footing.[4]

Nonetheless, it is crucial to recognize that human dignity is not limited to post-dictatorial constitution-making, as illustrated by the 1994 Belgian constitution, the 2000 Finnish constitution, and the 2009 Lisbon Treaty (to the extent that it can be considered as founding the new constitutional order of the EU).[5]

Human dignity in the German Basic Law

An example of the use of dignity in legislation is found in Germany. Human dignity is enshrined in Article 1(1) of the German Basic Law (*Grundgesetz*) which states, "(1) Human dignity shall be inviolable. To respect and protect it shall be the duty of all state authority."

Human dignity under the German Basic Law is the most powerful and absolute protection.

> Any violation of human dignity immediately calls for the unconstitutionality of the statute or the administrative action. In contrast to the fundamental rights provisions in the Basic Law, the dignity clause does not allow for a legal limitation … Human dignity, therefore, is a truly sharp weapon in German constitutional law, and it also practically denies the parliament any regulatory action in the respective area. Hence, the Court should use the human dignity clause only as an ultimate remedy.[6]

As German Federal Constitutional Court judge Dieter Grimm has written,

> Interpretation is everywhere. If the term "dignity" appears in a constitutional text, such as in the German Basic Law, more precisely in its Bill of Rights ("Human dignity is inviolable"), the question arises to whom it is addressed. Against who is human dignity constitutionally protected? The text itself does not answer this question. This leaves room for more than one answer. The obvious answer might be that the norm is addressed to everybody. Nobody may violate another's dignity. The widely accepted answer in Germany is,

4 UN Office of the Special Adviser on the Prevention of Genocide, Booklet (July 2010), https://www.un.org/ar/preventgenocide/adviser/pdf/osapg_booklet_eng.pdf

5 *Id.*

6 Oliver Lepsius, "Human Dignity and the Downing of Aircraft: The German Federal Constitutional Court Strikes Down a Prominent Anti-terrorism Provision in the New Air-transport Security Act" (2006) 7 *German Law Journal* 9, 768–769.

> however, that all holders of public authority in Germany or all state agents are the addressees of the norm. They are bound by it. They must not violate it.[7]

This means the constitutional guarantee runs only against state agents. But the legal text goes beyond a mere prohibition. As Grimm explains:

> The Basic Law ... prescribes that the state has to respect and protect dignity. "Respect" means the obligation of the state to refrain from actions that would violate someone's dignity. "Protect" means that the state is under the additional duty to shield the beneficiaries of the guarantee from acts by third parties incompatible with their dignity.[8]

The powerful tool that human dignity is under the German Basic Law is the response to the atrocities perpetrated by the Nazis, that despite adhering to the law at the time, were in severe violation of human dignity.

As Johannes Rau, a German politician, emphasized:

> The most important sentence in the Basic Law will always be Article 1 ... It is an explicit rejection of every ideology which sacrifices human life or life chances to a supposedly higher cause. And it is a rejection, too, of every form of discrimination on grounds of origin, color, creed or conviction. Article 1 does not say: "The dignity of the German people shall be inviolable". Nor does it refer to the dignity of the healthy or wealthy. It is a clear commitment to the inviolability of human dignity. This is not an abstract philosophical concept, but a binding obligation and an enduring mission for all those who bear political responsibility in our democratic and social state under the rule of law.[9]

The German Federal Constitutional Court has, however, addressed the question of who possesses dignity: everyone – referring to each individual, and humanity at large. In the *Evil Dead* case, the German Federal Constitutional Court ruled that a horror film's degrading, gory and brutalizing images was an offense to human dignity even though it was just a movie. Human dignity is not just for the individual dignity of each respective person, but also for humanity as a species.[10] This forms the basis of the argument against cloning and other forms of genetic design.[11]

7 *Id.*, 382.

8 *Id.* Judge Grimm goes on to explain, "But this does not change the previous statement that dignity as formulated in the German Constitution binds exclusively the state. Individuals are not bound by dignity as a constitutional norm, but they are submitted to the laws or acts that the state may issue in order to fulfill its protective duty." *Id.*

9 Johannes Rau, "Foreword by the Federal President" in *Basic Law for the Federal Republic of Germany* (Bundestag: Berlin, 2000) 5–6.

10 Collings, *Dignity Plus*, Unpublished, 8–9.

11 *Id.* at 9.

The German Federal Constitutional Court has also held that dignity neither begins at birth nor ends with death. In 1971, the German Federal Constitutional Court allowed a book by a novelist which affronted the dignity of a late actor to be banned, since the state's duty to protect individuals against attacks on their dignity did not end with death.[12] In 1975, the German Federal Constitutional Court addressed the question of whether a fetus possesses human dignity. It ruled that abortions must remain illegal for the full duration of pregnancy because human dignity is enjoyed where human life exists, even though the bearer of such dignity may be unaware.[13] The German Federal Constitutional Court has also used the Basic Law to ban the instrumentalization of human life.

In 2006, the German Federal Constitutional Court found that the Aerial Security Act was unconstitutional for allowing military officials to shoot down hijacked planes to protect civilians in buildings or on the ground.[14] This is offended human dignity by treating passengers on the planes as "mere objects" in the state's objective to rescue others.[15]

Dignity as an absolute value is necessarily narrow in scope. Justin Collings observes that in most cases, dignity is mediated in three principal ways. One, in operation with another constitutional guarantee by linking dignity to another right, such as the right to religious liberty and the right to asylum. This, Collings suggests, signals the right's importance.[16] Two, in combination with Article 2's promise of freedom of development of one's personality to form a general right of liberty that entitles all right-bearers a proportionality analysis.[17] Three, by deriving new and unenumerated rights from the general rights of liberty and personality. For example, in 1983, the German Federal Constitutional Court "invented" the right to "personal data self-determination," addressing how automatic data processing of data collected by the census would facilitate the production of "partial or virtually complete personality profiles."[18] The German Federal Constitutional Court recognized that technological advances would give rise to unprecedented risks for human dignity.[19]

Human dignity in other legal systems

While the German legal system is the most prominent example of how human dignity can be deeply rooted in the law and flourish in jurisprudence, human dignity is recognized in other legal systems too.[20]

12 *Id.* at 9–10.
13 *Id.* at 11.
14 115 BVerfGE 118 (2006).
15 Collings, *Dignity Plus*, Unpublished, 13.
16 *Id.* at 21.
17 *Id.* at 23.
18 Russell A. Miller, "A Pantomine of Privacy: Terrorism and Investigative Powers in German Constitutional Law," (2017) 58(5) *B.C.L. Rev.* 1545, 1574.
19 Collings, *Dignity Plus*, Unpublished, 26.
20 See below.

For example, the concept of human dignity is very prominent in several constitutions, including the South African Constitution in:

Article 1 of the South African Constitution

> The Republic of South Africa is one, sovereign, democratic state founded on the following values:
>
> (a) Human dignity, the achievement of equality, and the advancement of human rights and freedoms.

Article 7(1) of the South African Constitution

> This Bill of Rights is a cornerstone of democracy in South Africa. It enshrines the rights of all people in our country and arms the democratic values of human dignity, equality and freedom.

Article 10 of the South African Constitution

> Everyone has inherent dignity and the right to have their dignity respected and protected.

The South African Constitutional Court has recognized dignity as both a right, and a value that informs all other rights; it is both an entitlement conferred, and a value that guides the Court's decisions. In *Makwanyane*, Justice O'Regan opined that "recognizing a right to dignity is an acknowledgement of the intrinsic worth of human beings: human beings are entitled to be treated as worthy of respect and concern. The right is therefore the foundation of many of the other rights that are specifically entrenched."[21] This is demonstrated in the *Sodomy Case*, where the Court opined that the criminalization of sodomy interferes with the ability of homosexuals to achieve self-identification and self-fulfillment by limiting the ways they express their sexual orientation.[22]

Dignity is also a value that guides decision-making and helps interpret the meaning of rights, and the justification of their limitations. For example, in *Grootboom v. Government of the Republic of South Africa*,[23] the Court ruled that the government is obligated to provide housing to children when their parents could not, recognizing that "a society must seek to ensure that the basic necessities of life are provided to all if it is to be a society based on human dignity, freedom, and equality."[24]

The quest for dignity guides the Court's equality jurisprudence. It already assumes that equality should be informed by other values, rather than stand alone,

21 Susie Cowen, "Can Dignity Guide South Africa's Equality Jurisprudence?" (2001) 17 *South African Journal on Human Rights* 34, 42–43.

22 *Id.* at 43.

23 2001 (1) SA 46 (CC).

24 *Id.* at ¶44.

and requires focusing on context and pattern of disadvantage. The Court has rejected the "identity of treatment" approach, recognizing that it serves to entrench patterns of disadvantage that already exist.[25] The Court has also rejected that seeking equality is seeking uniformity in the outcome: "Equality should not be confused with uniformity; in fact, uniformity can be the enemy of equality. Equality means equal concern and respect across differences. It does not presuppose the elimination or suppression of difference."[26]

Justice O'Regan in *Dawood v. Minister of Home Affairs* explained that as far as the South African Constitution is concerned:

> dignity is not only a value fundamental to our Constitution, it is a justiciable and enforceable right that must be respected and protected. In many cases, however, where the value of human dignity is offended, the primary constitutional breach occasioned may be of a more specific right such as the right to bodily integrity, the right to equality or the right not to be subjected to slavery, servitude or forced labor.[27]

Article 30 of the Constitution of Poland

While the Polish Constitution before 1997 did not feature human dignity, the Constitutional Tribunal still recognized the principle through Article 1 of the Constitution which guarantees that the principle of a democratic state would be the source of constitutional standards and a guideline for constitutional and legal interpretation.[28] In the judgment of June 24, 1997, the Tribunal ruled that a law entitling tax authorities to publish individual tax information was unconstitutional because such an invasion of privacy contends with personal dignity.[29] This is because a democratic state grants the individual a right to live according to his own will with minimal interference. Publicizing such information may have negative consequences for an individual's personal, economic, and reputational interests, and thus their dignity.

The new Polish Constitution came into force in 1997, and explicitly enshrines human dignity as a source for freedoms and rights in Article 30,[30] enumerating several specific human and civic rights. This includes the legal protection of life,[31]

25 Cowen, *Dignity Plus*, Unpublished, 40.
26 *Id.* at 41.
27 *Dawood v. Minister of Home Affairs* [2000] 5 *Law Reports of the Commonwealth* 147, 2000 (3) SA 936 (CC), 35.
28 Biruta Lewaszkiewicz-Petrykowska, "Principle and Respect for Human Dignity," Polish Constitutional Tribunal, judgment of March 17, 1993, in European Commission for Democracy through Law, at 9.
29 Judgment of June 24, 1997 (K 21/96), OTK 1997/2/23 at ¶23.
30 "The inherent and inalienable dignity of the person shall constitute a source of freedoms and rights of persons and citizens. It shall be inviolable. The respect and protection thereof shall be the obligation of public authorities."
31 Constitution of the Republic of Poland, Article 38.

the right to personal inviolability,[32] the right to legal protection of private life,[33] the freedom of conscience and religion,[34] and the freedom to express opinions.[35]

In the judgment of October 23, 2007,[36] the Constitutional Tribunal found that a regulation granting women the right to receive a retirement pension at 55, but at age 60 for men was unconstitutional on the grounds that it was unfairly discriminatory towards men, violating Articles 32 and 33 of the Constitution. The Tribunal explained that the principle of equality means that all entities that are equally characterized by a given significant feature (in this case, biological sex) should be treated equally. A legislator that makes differentiations based on this significant feature violates the principle of equality. Nevertheless, such a violation is not necessarily a breach of Article 32 if (1) the differentiation is rationally related to the purpose of the regulation, (2) the weight of differentiation is proportional to the weight of the interests violated and the differentiation criteria are related to other constitutional values.[37] Since there was no rational reason, social or economic, that justifies differentiating between men and women, it clearly violates Article 32 and was thus unconstitutional.[38]

In the Judgment of May 19, 1998, the Constitution Tribunal considered the constitutionality of a regulation requiring doctors to enter a reference number that corresponded with a patient's medical conditions on the patient's medical certificate which would then be sent to the patient's employer, to be unconstitutional. Since this regulation was a violation of one's right to private life,[39] and the right not to disclose information,[40] it was unconstitutional.

Other constitutions incorporating provisions on dignity include:

Article 4(2) of the Bulgarian Constitution

> The Republic of Bulgaria shall guarantee the life, dignity and rights of the individual and shall create conditions conducive to the free development of the individual and of civil society.

Article 38 of the Constitution of the Dominican Republic

> The State bases itself on respect for the dignity of the person and organizes itself for the real and effective protection of the fundamental rights that are inherent to it. The dignity of the human being is sacred, innate, and inviolable; its respect and protection constitute an essential responsibility of the public powers.

32 *Id.* at Art. 41.
33 *Id.* at Art. 47.
34 *Id.* at Art. 53.
35 *Id.* at Art. 54.
36 Judgment of the Constitutional Court of October 23, 2007, P10/07, OTK-A 2007/9/107.
37 *Id.* at ¶5.
38 *Id.* at ¶5.1, 5.2.
39 *Id.* at Art. 47.
40 *Id.* at Art. 51.

Article 3 of the Armenian Constitution

> A human being, his/her dignity, fundamental rights, and freedoms are an inalienable and ultimate value …

Article 14 of the Armenian Constitution

> Human dignity shall be respected and protected by the State as an inviolable foundation of human rights and freedoms …

Article 47 of the Armenian Constitution

> Everyone shall be obliged to honor the Constitution and the laws, to respect the rights, freedoms, and dignity of others …

Article 2(1) of the Greek Constitution

> Respect and protection of the value of the human being constitute the primary obligations of the State.

Article 7(2) of the Greek Constitution

> Torture, any bodily maltreatment, impairment of health, or the use of psychological violence, as well as any other offense against human dignity are prohibited and punished as provided by law.

Is dignity too vague to be useful?

In response to the criticism that dignity is a vague term that is not defined by the German Basic Law, Judge Grimm notes, "this is not a peculiarity of dignity. While ordinary laws often define the notions they use, such definitions are rare within bills of rights," leaving the ascertainment of meaning to the implementation of law. "Vagueness does not deprive a norm of its legal nature. Vagueness has to be reduced by way of interpretation."[41]

As Waldron notes:

> Sometimes clarity and determinacy are over-rated. There are an awful lot of legal terms, mostly evaluative terms used in high-flown standards, that are also bereft of clear definition – think of terms like "cruel," in the 8th Amendment, or "inhuman," and "degrading" in constitutions and bills of rights the world over – and in many ways it is a good thing that they are not pinned down in a determinate definition. Such terms are supposed to operate as sites for some

41 Dieter Grimm, "Dignity in a Legal Context and as an Absolute Right" in Christopher McCrudden (ed.), *Understanding Human Dignity* (Oxford University Press: Oxford, 2013) 382–383.

> of the thoughtfulness that the rule of law sponsors. It's a mistake to think that we always want legal norms to be mechanically and applicable in an operationalized way; it is a mistake to think of the demand for clarity as though it were supposed to be a way of implacably ruling out thought and argumentation in the law.[42]

Indeed, most important constitutional provisions – liberty, equality, due process and equal protection of the law, and non-discrimination – are vague and aspirational and usually are not defined in the text. This is to ensure that the provisions can be elaborated and developed over time in ways that are responsive to contemporary challenges.

Dignity as the foundational value of the social order

According to Judge Grimm, dignity plays an important role in the German constitutional order:

> The German Constitution starts with a guarantee of human dignity. Although without impact on the legal validity, the prominent position of dignity helped the Constitutional Court to declare dignity the foundational value of the social order, a basic norm that appears behind the more concrete guarantees in the Bill of Rights, but also behind the structural and organizational provisions of the constitution such as democracy and the rule of law, yet a value that had to be made explicit after the Nazi government had departed from a shared moral consensus. The older rights then appear as more concrete expressions of the overarching idea of dignity and have to be understood and applied in its light.[43]

Similarly, in *Lüth*, a case concerning a question of the Basic Law being an objective order of values for disputes between two private individuals, the German Federal Constitutional Court emphasized that: "this value system, which centers upon the dignity of human personality developing freely within the community, must be looked upon as fundamental constitutional decision affecting all spheres of law."[44]

41 Jeremy Waldron, "What Do Philosophers Have Against Dignity?" (2014) NYU School of Law Public Law Research Paper no. 14-59, 8.

42 Dieter Grimm, "Dignity in a Legal Context and as an Absolute Right" in Christopher McCrudden (ed.), *Understanding Human Dignity* (Oxford University Press: Oxford, 2013) 386.

43 *Lüth*, 7 BVerfGE 198, 205 (1958). In the case, Lüth called for a boycott of a movie directed by Veith Harlan who collaborated with Goebbels on the anti-Semitic propaganda movie *Jud Süß*. Harlan's production company won an injunction against Lüth on grounds that such an incitement to boycott was illegal under the civil code. The case proceeded to the German Federal Constitutional Court where Lüth argued a violation of his freedom of speech.

Arthur Chaskalson, a human rights lawyer writing about the importance of the concept of human dignity to the South African legal system, said that:

> The affirmation of human dignity as a foundational value of the constitutional order places our legal order firmly in line with the development of constitutionalism in the aftermath of the second world war.[45]

Human dignity may have different meanings in different legal systems

Human dignity will not necessarily have the same meaning in each legal system, as each will be responsive to the history and context in which the term is added to the constitution. As Dieter Grimm explains:

> In countries with a racist past, for instance, dignity, if included in the constitution, will have a strong emphasis on equal treatment. Differences exist also with regard to rank and function. Dignity may be regarded as a principle that informs the interpretation and application of rights; it may be regarded as one right among others or count as a preferred right. In a country with a rudimentary bill of rights, such as Israel, the main function of the constitutional guarantee of dignity may be to fill the gaps and to generate new rights based on the argument that they are implied in the notion of dignity.[46]

The recognition of human dignity for everyone everywhere, as a right or as a foundation of rights, is a foundational value that can help define rights. Depending upon legal systems, the details will vary in ways that reflect the constitutional history and structure of rights in the country.

The implications of treating dignity as an absolute right

In the German constitutional system, unlike all other rights in the German Basic Law, which are subject to limitation, dignity is regarded as an absolute right.[47] This means that no restrictions on human dignity are permitted, and dignity is not subject to limitation or balancing. Thus, the usual approach to fundamental rights – determining whether there was an infringement of the right, followed by a determination of whether the infringement was justified – does not apply. Rather, "every infringement is a violation."

45 Arthur Chaskalson, "Human Dignity as a Foundational Value of Our Constitutional Order" (2000) *South African Journal on Human Rights* 16, 196.

46 Dieter Grimm, "Dignity in a Legal Context and as an Absolute Right" in Christopher McCrudden (ed.), *Understanding Human Dignity* (Oxford University Press: Oxford, 2013) 385.

47 Dieter Grimm, "Dignity in a Legal Context and as an Absolute Right" in Christopher McCrudden (ed.), *Understanding Human Dignity* (Oxford University Press: Oxford, 2013) 387.

Judge Grimm notes that there are several implications of this priority of dignity as an absolute right.[48] First, only one right can be treated as absolute; otherwise, conflicts would arise between the two or more absolute rights. "The second consequence is that dignity, if understood as an absolute right, cannot have a broad scope."[49] In the German Federal Constitutional Court, while dignity is often invoked, it is rare for courts to find a violation of Article 1. The jurisprudence of the German Federal Constitutional Court suggests that a violation of human dignity (under Article 1) is reserved for "gross assaults on humanity."[50] Despite this established high-threshold, this does not mean that invocations of dignity are rare because dignity often has "indirect effects when other provisions of the constitution are interpreted and applied."[51] Where human dignity is not the sole basis for a decision, it often informs other rights.[52] Human dignity is reflected in several legal concepts and ideas that are often given legal protection, such as equality[53] and autonomy.[54]

Other uses of dignity as a constitutional principle

Constitutions do not treat dignity as an absolute right. Human dignity is a common feature of many post-World War II domestic constitutions across the world. Apart from placing obligations upon the state to protect human dignity, some constitutions invoke human dignity as the underlying constitutional rights as

48 Similarly, the South African Constitution recognizes human dignity as a non-derogable right.

49 Dieter Grimm, "Dignity in a Legal Context and as an Absolute Right" in Christopher McCrudden (ed.), *Understanding Human Dignity* (Oxford University Press: Oxford, 2013) 388–389.

50 *Id.*

51 *Id.*, 390.

52 *Id.* "The combination of dignity and a more concrete basic right is not limited to certain rights. Every right has a dignity core, and this can become relevant when the principle of proportionality is applied. The closer the restriction of a right comes to its dignity core the higher the weight of the right in the balancing process." *Id.*

53 See, e.g., Denise Réaume, "Dignity, Choice and Circumstances" in Christopher McCrudden (ed.), *Understanding Human Dignity* (Oxford University Press: Oxford, 2013) 541. "Full equality of status at the formal level has been achieved at least since the eradication of slavery and the enfranchisement of all adult citizens. However, as T. H. Marshall so aptly noted long ago, the content of the 'status' of bearer of dignity (Marshall would have said 'citizenship') has been evolving over the modern period, the rights entailed gradually being enriched to achieve a 'fuller measure of equality.'" *Id.* (internal citations omitted).

54 "The extension of legal and civil rights to all is grounded in the value of personal autonomy, and the legal recognition of these rights has been part of the process of constructing the modern conception of dignity. The priority given to these rights reflects one particular aspect of autonomy, and builds it into the idea of moral status. These specific rights protect a range of important choices, and well before they were extended to all they had come to be bound up with what it means to be a full member of society, a bearer of dignity." *Id.*, 542.

an interpretive principle, and as a standard to inform a state's approach to human rights.

Former Israeli Supreme Court Justice Aharon Barak, Professor of Law at the Interdisciplinary Center in Herzliya, has written a thorough analytical study of human dignity as a value and right in international documents and constitutions.[55] He explains that,

> Human dignity as a constitutional value has several functions in the field of human rights. It provides the theoretical foundation for human rights; it assists in the interpretation of human rights at the sub-constitutional level; it is one of the values that every constitutional right is intended to realize; it plays a role in the limitations to constitutional rights and in determining the limits to such limitations; it plays a primary interpretative role in those cases where the constitution does recognize a constitutional right to human dignity.[56]

Dignity as a principle in adjudication

Human dignity has also been used in judicial decision-making. For example, Justice Sopinka, in the Canadian Supreme Court decision *R. v. Butler*, utilized human dignity in his analysis of pornography and Canada's obscenity laws:

> Among other things, degrading or dehumanizing materials place women (and sometimes men) in positions of subordination, servile submission or humiliation. They run against the principles of equality and dignity of all human beings. In the appreciation of whether material is degrading or dehumanizing, the appearance of consent is not *necessarily* determinative. Consent cannot save materials that otherwise contain degrading or dehumanizing scenes. Sometimes the very appearance of consent makes the depicted acts even more degrading or dehumanizing.[57]

The use of human dignity has become more prominent (though perhaps disjointed)[58] following the Canadian Charter of Rights and Freedoms in 1982. In the case of *Hill v. Church of Scientology of Toronto*, the Canadian Supreme Court

55 Aharon Barak, "The Constitutional Value and the Constitutional Right" in Christopher McCrudden (ed.), *Understanding Human Dignity* (Oxford University Press: Oxford, 2013) 34–64.

56 *Id.*, 362–363.

57 *R. v. Butler* [1992] 1 SCR 452, 479.

58 See R. James Fyfe, "Dignity as Theory: Competing Conceptions of Human Dignity at the Supreme Court of Canada," (2007) 70 *Saskatchewan Law Review* 1, 2 ("[The Court's] varied conceptions [of human dignity] reveal the Court's failure to develop a coherent approach to, or understanding of, dignity. Its use is muddled and inconsistent. Furthermore, the Court errs by conflating human dignity with human interest.").

found that human dignity underlies the Charter of Rights and Freedoms and that protecting human dignity requires protection of one's good reputation:

> 107. [...] Although much has very properly been said and written about the importance of freedom of expression, little has been written of the importance of reputation. Yet, to most people, their good reputation is to be cherished above all. A good reputation is closely related to the innate worthiness and dignity of the individual. It is an attribute that must, just as much as freedom of expression, be protected by society's laws. In order to undertake the balancing required by this case, something must be said about the value of reputation ...
>
> 120. Although it is not specifically mentioned in the [Canadian]Charter, the good reputation of the individual represents and reflects the innate dignity of the individual, a concept which underlies all the [Canadian] Charter rights. It follows that the protection of the good reputation of an individual is of fundamental importance to our democratic society.[59]

In the United States, Justice Potter Stewart made similar use of dignity in the case of *Rosenblatt v. Baer*, stating that:

> The right of a man to the protection of his own reputation from unjustified invasion and wrongful hurt reflects no more than our basic concept of the essential dignity and worth of every human being – a concept at the root of any decent system of ordered liberty.[60]

While human dignity is never mentioned in the US Constitution, it has played a background role in the Supreme Court's decisions on a number of issues.[61] For example, Justice Felix Frankfurter in *American Federation of Labor v. American Sash and Door Co.*, a case involving the rights of unions, invoked human dignity to explain the challenges of industrialization:

> The industrial history of the early Nineteenth Century demonstrated the helplessness of the individual employee to achieve human dignity in a society so largely affected by technological advances. Hence, the trade union made itself increasingly felt, not only as an indispensable weapon of self-defense on the part of workers.[62]

Human dignity has become more prominent because of the jurisprudence of Justice Anthony Kennedy, especially surrounding issues of equality and the

59 *Hill v. Church of Scientology of Toronto* [1995] 2 SCR 1130.
60 *Rosenblatt v. Baer*, 383 US 75, 92 (1966).
61 See Maxine D. Goodman, "Human Dignity in Supreme Court Constitutional Jurisprudence" (2005) 84 *Nebraska Law Review* 740.
62 *American Federation of Labor v. American Sash and Door Co*, 335 US 538 (1949) 542.

Fourteenth Amendment. In *Lawrence v. Texas*, for example, Justice Kennedy (writing for the majority) invoked the notion of human dignity multiple times to strike down the state anti-sodomy statutes as unconstitutional.[63] Quoting the Court's prior decision in *Planned Parenthood v. Casey*, Justice Kennedy rooted concerns about dignity in the Fourteenth Amendment: "These matters, involving the most intimate and personal choices a person may make in a lifetime, choices central to personal dignity and autonomy, are central to the liberty protected by the Fourteenth Amendment."[64] Justice Kennedy went even further in *Obergefell v. Hodges*, the 2015 case that struck down state laws defining marriage as between one man and one woman. Writing for the majority, Justice Kennedy invoked dignity (both of marriage and persons) frequently, using it as a centerpiece of the Court's reasoning that state definitions of marriage that exclude same-sex couples violate the Fourteenth Amendment. Justice Kennedy wrote: "There is dignity in the bond between two men or two women who seek to marry,"[65] and that same-sex couples seeking to marry are asking for "equal dignity in the eyes of the law."[66] In the majority's view, "[t]he Constitution grants them that right."[67]

Justice O'Regan in the South African case of *Dawood v. Minister of Home Affairs* found that human dignity informs judicial decision-making in a variety of ways:

> Human dignity … informs constitutional adjudication and interpretation at a range of levels. It is a value that informs the interpretation of many, possibly all, other rights. This court has already acknowledged the importance of the constitutional value of dignity in interpreting rights such as the right to equality, the right not to be punished in a cruel, inhuman or degrading way, and the right to life. Human dignity is also a constitutional value that is of central significance in the limitations analysis.[68]

Even though the European Convention on Human Rights never mentions human dignity, the European Court of Human Rights (ECtHR) has employed dignity in a variety of ways.[69] For example, in *Tyrer v. UK*, the ECtHR found

63 *Lawrence v. Texas*, 539 US 558, 567, 574, 575 (2003).
64 *Id.* at 574.
65 *Obergefell v. Hodges*, 135 S.Ct. 2584, 2599 (2015).
66 *Id.* at 2608.
67 *Id.*; see also *Masterpiece Cakeshop, Ltd v. Colorado Civil Rights Com'n*, 138 S.Ct. 1719 (2018). For criticism of the use of human dignity in US constitutional law, see Neomi Rao, "On the Use and Abuse of Dignity in Constitutional Law" (2008) 14 *Columbia Journal of European Law* 201.
68 *Dawood v. Minister of Home Affairs* [2000] 5 Law Reports of the Commonwealth 147, 2000 (3) SA 936 (CC), 35.
69 In *Christine Goodwin v. the UK*, the ECtHR found that human dignity and human freedom are the "very essence" of the ECHR (see para. 90). The ECtHR considered human dignity as a norm especially where dealing with the right to life, the prohibition of torture and inhuman and degrading treatment, prohibition of slavery (Articles 2, 3, and 4 of the ECHR). For example, in the case of *Jalloh v. Germany*, the ECtHR

that Article 3, which prohibits torture and inhuman or degrading treatment, requires the protection of a person's dignity. The case concerns a teenager, Mr. Tyrer, 15 years of age at the time, who was given three strokes of the birch in 1972 in the Isle of Man, as a punishment for unlawful assault occasioning actual bodily harm, in accordance with the local juvenile court's sentence. The ECtHR found that such punishment constituted a violation of Article 3 of the ECHR, stating that:

> [A]lthough the applicant did not suffer any severe or long-lasting physical effects, his punishment – whereby he was treated as an object in the power of the authorities – constituted an assault on precisely that which it is one of the main purposes of Article 3 [art. 3] to protect, namely a person's dignity and physical integrity.[70]

The ECtHR has continued this logic in various cases surrounding prison conditions, police violence, and protections for disabled persons, holding that Articles 2, 3, and 4 require states to not only respect but also to protect human dignity in its variegated forms.[71] Indeed, as Jean-Paul Costa has observed, "many violations [of human dignity] found by the Court rely on the failure from the state to fulfill its *positive obligations.* Dignity is therefore an objective to be reached by state authorities."[72] While human dignity has played an important role in the thinking of the ECtHR, Costa also noted that "[t]he judicial approach of the Court ... generally appears to use the concept of human dignity to *reinforce* the reasoning leading to a violation of the Convention," rather than using human dignity solely as the ground of its decisions.[73]

Finally, and perhaps most famously, human dignity was essential in the decision of the German Federal Constitutional Court to strike down an anti-terrorism law based on human dignity.[74]

found that "authorities subjected the applicant to a grave interference with his physical and mental integrity against his will ... The manner in which the impugned measure was carried out was liable to arouse in the applicant feelings of fear, anguish and inferiority that were capable of humiliating and debasing him." Id. 82. The ECtHR has also used the concept of human dignity as a tool to be tailored in the context. For example, in *Selmouni v. France*, the ECtHR found that "in respect of a person deprived of his liberty, recourse to physical force which has not been made strictly necessary by his own conduct diminishes human dignity and is in principle an infringement of the right set forth in Article 3." Id. 99.

70 *Tyrer v. United Kingdom*, 2 EHRR 1, at 33.

71 See Jean-Paul Costa, "Human Dignity in the Jurisprudence of the European Court of Human Rights" in Christopher McCrudden (ed.), *Understanding Human Dignity* (Oxford University Press: Oxford, 2013) 393, 396–400.

72 *Id.* at 397.

73 *Id.* at 400.

74 See also Oliver Lespius, "Human Dignity and the Downing of Aircraft: The German Federal Constitutional Court Strikes Down a Prominent Anti-terrorism Provision in the New Air-transport Security Act," (2006) 7 *German L. J.* 761.

b. The richness of the concept of dignity resists exhaustive definition, but it encourages the pursuit of optimum mutual vindication where conflicting rights and values are involved

Human dignity's upward lift

One important feature of human dignity is that it points us upwards rather than downwards as we try to find solutions to situations involving conflicting rights or interests. It lifts our gaze rather than lowering it. It encourages us to look beyond finding winners and losers or finding reasons why human rights cannot be protected. Focusing on human dignity may not generate absolute certainty, but it points us in directions of protecting human beings, valuing them, and regarding them as worthwhile.

Even if we don't agree on the precise definition or parameters of dignity, focusing on it can help orient our minds towards finding solutions to difficult problems. While the definition of human dignity may not be easily agreed upon, human dignity nevertheless serves certain definable aims. For example, Andrew Clapham, Professor of International Law, has identified four important aspects of concern for human dignity:

1. the prohibition of all types of inhuman treatment, humiliation, or degradation by one person over another;
2. the assurance of the possibility for individual choice and the conditions for each individual's self-fulfillment, autonomy, or self-realization;
3. the recognition that the protection of group identity and culture may be essential for the protection of personal dignity; and
4. the creation of the necessary conditions for each individual to have their essential needs satisfied.[75]

Mutual vindication of dignity

The focus on everyone and everywhere will create an impetus to seek ways to vindicate the interests of both sides of a dispute – for example, by extending non-discrimination protections to people on the basis of sexual orientation or gender identity, but also protecting free speech, freedom of association and the dignity rights of those who object to participating in a marriage, for example.

The idea of optimal mutual vindication seeks to find ways to enhance the dignity interests of everyone involved, rather than to elevate the dignity of some over others.

Edward J. Eberle states that human dignity does not only focus on individuals but also has a communitarian dimension. He notes that "by requiring respect for others' claims to dignity, vindication for the human dignity of all is better assured,

75 Andrew Clapham, *Human Rights Obligations of Non-State Actors* (Oxford University Press: Oxford, 2006) 545–546.

and a community of mutual cooperation and solidarity is fostered."[76] Similarly, Eberle states that human rights are most effective when they are exercised within the bounds of community: "freedom can truly exist only with provision for well-being, mutual toleration, and respect. It is in this sense that the 'human person is an autonomous being developing freely within the social community.'[77] Thus, individual self-determination is offset by responsibility, civility, and participation."[78]

c. Human dignity is critical for moving beyond exclusively thinking in terms of balancing and trade-offs of rights and interests

One of the most powerful metaphors of law and justice is the image of a balance. Indeed, artistic depictions of "Lady Justice" often depict her blindfolded (suggesting that justice is blind to differences such as appearance, sex, wealth, race, or religion) and holding "scales" that can be used to weigh in an even-handed fashion important legal values such as evidence, rights, and interests.[79] This image of justice is powerful and important. Judges who are impartial and disinterested are an essential prerequisite of a system of justice that will be just.

Nevertheless, the balancing metaphor has its limitations, and may even distort our thinking about important legal issues. Two primary problems arise with the balancing metaphor. The first is the tendency to think exclusively in terms of tradeoffs, with one side winning and the other side losing. The balancing metaphor, itself, suggests more than "winner-take-all" since that would result in scales that are out of balance, but as a practical matter, balancing seems to incline us towards awarding victory to the side with the heavier weight.

The second problem is more conceptual and involves the fact that balancing reduces everything to a single consideration, "weight," whereas often the values at stake are not so easily reduced to a common metric. This is sometimes called the problem of the incommensurability of value. If, for example, the value of non-discrimination and the value of freedom cannot be reduced to a common weight, say "utility," then the effort to balance may distort or misconstrue the character of the values at stake.

Sometimes determining whether the law has been violated involves applying a rule, rather than balancing rights or interests. For example, in Germany, where human dignity is an inviolable legal norm, balancing is completely inappropriate.

76 Edward J. Eberle, "Observations on the Development of Human Dignity and Personality in German Constitutional Law: An Overview" (2012) 33 *Liverpool Law Review* 206.

77 *Mephisto*, 30 BVerfGE at 193.

78 Edward J. Eberle, "Observations on the Development of Human Dignity and Personality in German Constitutional Law: An Overview" (2012) 33 *Liverpool Law Review* 201.

79 Dennis Edward Curtis and Judith Resnik, *Representing Justice: Invention, Controversy, and Rights in City-states and Democratic Courtrooms* (Yale University Press, 2011). See also Dorothy Harley Eber, *Images of Justice* (McGill-Queen's University Press, 1997).

Fundamental human dignity is an absolute right, protected by a rule, which is not subject to balancing or limitation.

For example, in the *Aviation Security Act* case, the German Federal Constitutional Court concluded that:

> In view of this relation between the right to life and human dignity, the state is prohibited, on the one hand, from encroaching upon the fundamental right to life by measures of its own, thereby violating the ban on the disregard of human dignity. On the other hand, the state is also obliged to protect every human life. This duty of protection demands of the state and its bodies to shield and to promote the life of every individual, which means above all to also protect it from unlawful attacks, and interference, by third parties. Also, this duty of protection has its foundations in Article 1.1 sentence 2 of the Basic Law, which explicitly obliges the state to respect and protect human dignity.[80]

Paul Sourlas, Professor Emeritus of Legal Philosophy at the University of Athens, identifies a way that a right might be considered inviolable and still play a role in balancing analyses:

> Since values are seen as comparative concepts distinguished by their dimension of weight, for a value to be inviolable is to possess such an outstanding importance that it appears quite impossible for it to be outweighed by any other value. That doesn't imply the categorical exclusion of the principles of balancing and of proportionality; it means only that the outcome of the balancing procedure shall most likely be in favor of dignity, because no other value can in *abstracto* be envisaged to possess a comparable degree of importance.[81]

80 *Aviation Security Act*, 1 BvR 357/05 (Feb. 15, 2006), 120 (internal citations omitted).

81 Paul Sourlas, "Human Dignity and the Constitution" (2016) 7 *Jurisprudence* 1, 30–46.

10 Article 8

Reconciliation and adjudication

Article 8 reads as follows:

> Recognition of human dignity for everyone everywhere is an important constitutional and legal principle for reconciling and adjudicating competing human rights claims, as well as claims between human rights and other important national and societal interests. Mutual vindication of rights may be possible in adjudication and may be further facilitated if all involved focus on respecting the human dignity of everyone. When mutual vindication of rights is not possible, dignity for all can help us to delineate the scope of rights, to set the boundaries of permissible restrictions on the exercise of rights and freedoms, and to seek to bring into fair balance competing rights claims. Respect for dignity plays an important role not only in formal adjudication but also in mediation or other forms of alternative dispute resolution.

The following is an expanded explanation of each part of Article 8.

a. Recognition of human dignity for everyone everywhere is an important constitutional and legal principle for reconciling and adjudicating competing human rights claims, as well as claims between human rights and other important national and societal interests

When conflicts between competing human rights arise, the goal should be to try to protect the dignity of all. Sometimes the claims may even be between competing dignitary claims, in which case the goal again should be to protect the dignity of all.

Conflicts between competing human rights claims provide an opportunity to seek solutions that will mutually vindicate the rights and freedoms of everyone involved.

Focusing on the rights and freedoms of everyone encourages us to differentiate between dignity claims that lie at the core of a human right and claims that are less central, or even lie at the periphery of the right. The goal will be to protect the core rights of everyone and to look for compromises or sensible limitations on

DOI: 10.4324/9781003207030-11

rights claims that lie away from the center or at the periphery of the right. In the last 70 years, human dignity has emerged as an important principle in adjudicating rights claims. Some of the best examples are the developments in the jurisprudence of South Africa and Germany.

Human dignity can be misused in adjudicative contexts. For example, sometimes there will be a sweeping conclusion that is reached based on a dignity claim. Very specific rights may not follow of necessity from a general recognition of human dignity. For example, it may be an oversimplification to assert broadly that human dignity requires a minimum wage of a certain amount. But human dignity can be a useful heuristic for framing discussions about what is a reasonable minimum wage in specific social and economic circumstances.

b. Mutual vindication of rights may be possible in adjudication and may be further facilitated if all involved focus on respecting the human dignity of everyone

Human dignity for everyone everywhere is a strategy that moves beyond balancing and towards an ideal of the *mutual vindication* of competing rights claims and other important interests.

Rights claims often exist in competition with each other. For example, non-discrimination rights may conflict with religious freedom rights. Focusing on human dignity for everyone involved may open our horizons to strategies to seek mutual vindication of rights rather than a straightforward victory of one right over another. Other times, reasonable accommodations for conscientious objectors can often be made without subjecting others to undue hardship or discrimination.

For example, in several countries, there are ongoing conflicts about the ability of religiously affiliated adoption services to continue to operate even if they do not facilitate adoptions for same-sex couples. Human dignity for everyone everywhere could focus on the broader dignitary interests at stake, especially those of the children who are awaiting placement. The rights of the religious groups to provide services in a way that is consonant with their conscience can often be accommodated, as can the rights of same-sex couples to adopt children, provided that there are a variety of providers available, so no one is unnecessarily excluded. Focusing on dignity for everyone helps widen the analysis beyond thinking exclusively of the rights claims of one particular group; the reality is that multiple dignitary interests are implicated, including those of the religious service providers, those who desire to adopt a child, and most importantly (and often sacrificed in the crossfire of culture wars), the dignity interests of the children. Human dignity for everyone everywhere encourages us to look for solutions that vindicate as many of the competing rights and interests as possible, rather than solutions that provide complete victory for one side. When conflicts arise between competing dignity claims, the impulse will be to try to find solutions that protect the dignity of all.

One of the best examples where this approach was applied was the Utah Compromise. The Utah Compromise refers to two landmark LGBT non-discrimination bills that were passed by the Utah legislature in March 2015. The Utah Compromise aims to balance LGBT rights and religious freedoms. As Robin Fretwell Wilson, Professor of Law at the University of Illinois College of Law and contributor to the bills, explains:

> The first bill, SB 296, protects LGBT individuals from discrimination in employment or housing based on their gender identity or sexual orientation, but it exempts religious organizations and their affiliates … from the bill's requirements. The second bill, SB 297, permits faith groups to solemnize and host only those weddings and receptions consistent with their faith and to limit religious counseling to those in traditional marriages – without threat of civil suit or government penalty; it also requires county clerk offices to establish a process for solemnizing all legal marriages – not required by Utah law before the Utah Compromise – but the office may outsource the duty to any willing celebrant in the community, avoiding the need to fire "individual local officials who object to same-sex marriage" or force them to quit their jobs.[1]

She adds that "In bypassing religious objectors entirely, the Utah Compromise ensures the dignity of same-sex couples seeking licenses, who receive access to marriage on the same basis as straight couples, and never even know whether someone in the office had a religious objection."[2] Understanding that everyone was afraid and had a reasonable basis for being afraid, it became possible to forge a legislative solution that addressed the fears on both sides. The result was a bill that prohibited discrimination in employment and housing on the basis of both religion and sexual orientation, with special protections for religious institutions including church-owned schools, and workarounds to address conscientious objection issues by public employees who objected to performing same-sex marriages without resulting in embarrassment or denial of service to same-sex couples. To call this a "compromise" is a misnomer since neither side was asked to sacrifice what was most important to them; rather it was a principled mutual vindication of rights while recognizing the rights and interests of others.[3]

1 Robin Fretwell Wilson, "The Politics of Accommodation. The American Experience with Same-Sex Marriage and Religious Freedom" in Timothy Shah, Thomas Farr and Jack Friedman (eds.), *Religious Freedom and Gay Rights: Emerging Conflicts in the United States and Europe* (Oxford University Press: New York, 2016) 144.

2 *Id.*, 144.

3 *Id.*, 144. Senator J. Stuart Adams explained the process behind introducing the Utah Compromise stating that: "We did what legislators should do: get stakeholders across the spectrum to find constructive solutions. We sat down with members of Utah's LGBT community, social conservatives, and business leaders. Many were familiar to us as seasoned advocates at the statehouse, others we had never met, especially from the LGBT community. We listened to stories they shared of feeling like outcasts and second- class citizens. Putting a human face to legislative needs changed the tenor of the discussion. Similarly, those who expressed concerns for religious liberty, as I did,

c. When mutual vindication of rights is not possible, dignity for all can help us to delineate the scope of rights, to set the boundaries of permissible restrictions on the exercise of rights and freedoms, and to seek to bring into fair balance competing rights claims

Human dignity for everyone everywhere reminds us that freedom from discrimination can co-exist with other human rights. It is possible and desirable to prohibit and punish harmful discrimination while at the same time respecting other established individual and institutional rights, including the rights of freedom of expression, freedom of thought, conscience, and religion, and other rights.

Sometimes balancing and limiting rights claims may be necessary, but in many situations, it is possible to pursue strategies and policies that will result in the mutual vindication of those claims.

Human dignity for everyone everywhere suggests that identity-based discrimination is wrong and should be prohibited. All human beings should be treated equally in dignity and rights and should enjoy the exercise of their human rights without identity-based distinctions such as race, color, sex, religion, national or social origin, or another status. Increasingly, extending non-discrimination protections to sexual orientation and gender identity is also recognized as an important dimension of nondiscrimination.

For example, over recent years, we have been witnessing the ever-growing problem of discrimination based on religion or belief. In several countries with a state- or favored religion, religious minorities are subjected to discrimination, marginalization, or even violence. In countries such as Pakistan, religious minorities such as Ahmadis have their rights severely limited because of their religion or

felt listened to and respected, as well. That process was not only best done legislatively, it could only be done legislatively." J. Stuart Adams, "Cultivating Common Ground" in William N. Eskridge, Jr. and Robin Fretwell Wilson (eds.), *Religious Freedom, LGBT Rights, and the Prospects for Common Ground* (Cambridge University Press, 2019) 449. Governor Michael O. Levitt further added that, "A brave gamble took place in 2015 when the LGBT and faith communities mutually worked for passage of what is now known as the Utah Compromise. Representatives of both groups met repeatedly, honestly seeking to understand one another. Though the discussions involved tension and disagreement, the two sides were held together by strong conveners and a commonly defined objective. They sought fairness, not unilateral advantage. All the traditional points of view were present. There were naysayers on both sides who worried about giving an inch in their traditional battle of extreme points of view. In the end, legislation passed in a deeply red state that extended protection against discrimination in housing and employment for LGBT people while also protecting the capacity of churches and critical auxiliary organizations to carry out their essential missions and doctrines. Predictably, the outcome was praised by a large majority of people and criticized by advocates at both extremes who thought the Utah Compromise gave up too much ground. The doubting extremes on both sides said it was not replicable elsewhere." Michael O. Leavitt, "Shared Spaces and Brave Gambles" in William N. Eskridge, Jr. & Robin Fretwell Wilson (eds.), *Religious Freedom, LGBT Rights, and the Prospects for Common Ground* (Cambridge University Press, 2019) 462–463.

belief.[4] This was further exacerbated by the COVID-19 pandemic in 2020 when, in many countries, religious minorities were blamed for the spread of the virus.

More broadly, COVID-19 further exacerbated the challenges faced by individuals and groups with specific characteristics, and this because of their identity. As the UN identified:

> Reports of violence, discrimination, arbitrary denial of services, heightened exclusion or other forms of disparate negative impact in the COVID-19 crisis against minorities are widespread and have affected Roma, people of African Descent, people of Asian Descent, refugees, asylum seekers, migrants and stateless persons, internally displaced persons and religious minorities. Other persons and groups are also exposed to stigma and/or discrimination such as lesbian, gay, bisexual, trans or intersex (LGBTI) people, as well as based on caste.[5]

d. Respect for dignity plays an important role not only in formal adjudication but also in mediation or other forms of alternative dispute resolution

Human dignity for everyone everywhere helps us remember that balancing rights claims should take place when there are genuine conflicts between rights. Here the goal can be to seek fairness for all. Regulatory norms concerned with addressing potentially discriminatory conduct must be based on principles of equity and fairness for all members of the community. The principles of fairness and impartiality for all members of the community are important in conflicts regarding rights, discrimination, and related issues. Failure to achieve a *balance* that will provide equity and fairness for all will simply shift the burden of discrimination from one disadvantaged group to another, instead of finding solutions that optimize the protection of everyone's rights. For example, anti-discrimination protections in education, housing, and employment do not necessarily require a compromise of protections for the rights of conscience and expression of individuals and institutions in the public square.

Human dignity for everyone everywhere reminds us that compromise is essential in pluralistic societies. Confrontations regarding competing rights claims sometimes have a spirit of "all or nothing." To achieve peace and justice in a pluralistic society, groups and individuals may not be able to implement all of their values in legal and social norms. Compromise or accommodations of difference must be encouraged and accepted. A spirit of compromise and accommodation

4 See for example: All Party Parliamentary Group for the Ahmadiyya Muslim Community, "Suffocation of the Faithful: The Persecution of Ahmadi Muslims in Pakistan and the Rise of International Extremism" (2020).

5 OHCHR, "Covid19 and Minority Rights: Overview and Promising Practices" (June 2020). Available at: https://www.ohchr.org/Documents/Issues/Minorities/OHCHRGuidance_COVID19_MinoritiesRights.pdf

will likely result in reciprocal compromises and accommodations and will help promote equal dignity and rights for all.

For example, Alternative Dispute Resolution (ADR) focuses on values such as preserving or restoring relationships resulting in ways that recognize and protect the rights and interests of everyone rather than a "winner takes all" solution. ADR, apart from providing monetary remedies where applicable, can help to promote behaviors, restore relationships, or provide outcomes not otherwise available under the law.[6] Robert Ellickson, Professor of Property and Urban Law at Yale Law School, notes that

> [l]egal instrumentalists have tended to underappreciate the role that nonlegal systems play in achieving social order … State law is the Johnny-come-lately on the scene because the State itself is a relatively recent development. When we look realistically at the way disputes are resolved currently in even the most State-saturated society, it is obvious that State dispute resolution techniques play only a backup role.[7]

Similarly, Jerold S. Auerbach, historian and professor emeritus of history at Wellesley College, noted that,

> In many and varied communities, over the entire sweep of American history, the rule of law was explicitly rejected in favor of alternative means for ordering human relations and for resolving the inevitable disputes that arose between individuals.[8]

This suggests that not all disputes are suitable for courts and that ADR can provide more amicable solutions.

6 John Lande, "Getting the Faith: Why Business Lawyers and Executives Believe in Mediation" (2000) 5 *Harvard Negotiation Law Review* 150. ("Although respondents generally believe that mediation often saves time and money as compared with traditional litigation, their belief in mediation seems to be most strongly related to perceptions that mediation helps preserve relationships and that business' top executives are often satisfied with the results in suits where mediation issued, especially relative to suits where mediation is not used.")

7 Robert Ellickson, *Order Without Law: How Neighbours Settle Disputes* (Harvard University Press, 1991) 137.

8 Jerold S. Auerbach, *Justice Without Law?* (Oxford University Press, 1983) 4.

11 Article 9

Potential difficulties involving competing human rights claims

Article 9 reads as follows:

> Respecting the human dignity of everyone everywhere supports effective human rights advocacy. Recognizing the universal and reciprocal character of human dignity is a corrective to positions claiming rights for some but not for others. It helps to diffuse the hostility that is often associated with human rights controversies and to foster constructive dialogue. It also helps mitigate the distortion, avoidance, and selective recognition of human dignity.

The following is an expanded explanation of each part of Article 9.

a. Respecting the human dignity of everyone everywhere supports effective human rights advocacy

Human dignity for everyone everywhere makes it more difficult for advocates and opponents of human rights to be dogmatic and rigid in their understanding of human rights.

Some human rights advocates can be myopic in their advocacy for a particular right, or rights for a particular group. Human dignity for everyone everywhere is an antidote to both types of myopia. Human dignity is deeply connected to all human rights, so it facilitates thinking of rights questions more broadly than focusing on just one right. The emphasis on everyone and everywhere helps address the problem of special pleading, where advocates for a particular group promote the rights and interests of that group without regard for the rights and interests of others, including those who might be affected by the rights claims of the favored group. For example, advocates for assisted suicide or euthanasia, while attempting to promote the autonomy of the individuals wishing to die, neglect the high risk of vulnerable individuals or their families being left without any protection of the law.[1]

Responsible human rights advocacy will be mindful of not just one right, or one group, but of human rights and responsibilities broadly understood, as these rights

1 R. J. D. George, I. G. Finlay and D. Jeffrey, "Legalized Euthanasia Will Violate the Rights of Vulnerable Patients" (2005) 331 *BMJ (Clinical research ed.)* 684–685.

DOI: 10.4324/9781003207030-12

claims affect all people. "NGOs are playing an increasingly prominent role in setting the agenda in today's globalised world. This places a clear responsibility on us to act with transparency and accountability."[2]

Michael Edwards, Senior Civil Society Specialist in the World Bank's NGO Unit, notes that to be legitimate, an organization must be "lawful, admissible, and justified in its current course of action."[3] Hugo Slim, scholar and policy advisor in international relations, considered that such an organization must further be able to justify their voice and prove their effectiveness.[4] Also, they must be accountable, this includes "loyalty to a mission statement, transparency, good governance, monitoring, reporting, evaluation, and the existence of a mechanism to receive complaints and issue sanctions if an organization is found to be behaving improperly."[5]

Hugo Slim further notes that NGOs must be accountable for their voice:

> This sort of "voice accountability" had to respond to two areas of interrogation: the veracity of what they said and the authority with which they spoke. Although obviously linked, questions of veracity were essentially empirical (can you prove it?) while questions of authority were essentially political (from where do you derive your power to speak?)[6]

The ultimate distinction that must be made is whether they are "speaking as, speaking with, or speaking for the group in concern."[7] The response to these questions will help to identify the risks associated with such advocacy and the unintended consequences.[8]

NGOs are not the only organizations engaged in human rights advocacy. Indeed, as businesses are more and more engaged in the issue, there are certain guidelines for them to follow. The Business and Human Rights Resource Centre established a blueprint for legitimate human rights advocacy for businesses that are

2 Press Release, Amnesty International, "NGOs Lead by Example: World's International NGOs Endorse Accountability Charter" (June 6, 2006). Available at: www.amnesty.org/en/library

3 Michael Edwards, *NGO Rights and Responsibilities: A New Deal for Global Governance* (Foreign Policy Centre, 2000) 20.

4 Hugo Slim, *By What Authority?: The Legitimacy and Accountability of Non-governmental Organizations* (International Council on Human Rights Policy, 2002).

5 Diana Hortsch, "The Paradox of Partnership: Amnesty International, Responsible Advocacy, and NGO Accountability" (2010) 42 *Columbia Human Rights Law Review* 119, 128.

6 Hugo Slim, *By What Authority?: The Legitimacy and Accountability of Non-governmental Organizations* (International Council on Human Rights Policy, 2002) 5.

7 Diana Hortsch, "The Paradox of Partnership: Amnesty International, Responsible Advocacy, and NGO Accountability" (2010) 42 *Columbia Human Rights Law Review* 119, 145.

8 Barbora Bukovská, "Perpetrating Good: Unintended Consequences of International Human Rights Advocacy" (2008) *Revista Internacional de Direitos Humanos* 6.

based, among others, on effectively responding to the concerns, collaborating with others, being transparent and accountable, and being judicious.[9]

b. Recognizing the universal and reciprocal character of human dignity is a corrective to positions claiming rights for some but not for others

The focus on everyone also makes it difficult to focus exclusively on the rights and interests of one particular group, since there will be an ongoing recognition and insistence that the rights of everyone implicated should be taken into account.

Such an approach could address the challenges posed by identity politics and the divisions they create. Mark Lilla, Professor of the Humanities at Columbia University, suggests that "American liberalism has slipped into a kind of moral panic about racial, gender and sexual identity that has distorted liberalism's message and prevented it from becoming a unifying force capable of governing."[10] William Voegele, visiting scholar at Claremont McKenna College's Henry Salvatori Center, explains that the problem with identity politics is that its "polemicists dismiss any consideration that might modify these harsh accusations."[11] He further adds that:

> In its obsession with self-validation, identity politics not only diminishes liberty but thwarts democracy. Its thoroughgoing subjectivity imposes what philosophy professor Cressida Heyes calls "an epistemology of provenance," wherein "political perspectives gain legitimacy by virtue of their articulation by subjects of particular experiences." The danger is that this framework "closes off the possibility of critique of these perspectives by those who don't share the experience, which in turn inhibits political dialogue and coalition-building."[12]

Human dignity for everyone everywhere is a powerful antidote to identity politics, which seeks to emphasize factors that make us different. To be sure, sometimes special needs arise from our differences, but human dignity points us towards

9 Florian Wettstein, "Legitimate Human Rights Advocacy: A Blueprint for Business." Available at: https://www.business-humanrights.org/en/legitimate-human-rights-advocacy-a-blueprint-for-business

10 Mark Lilla, "The End of Identity Liberalism" (Nov. 18, 2006) *New York Times.*

11 William Voegeli, "The Democratic Party's Identity Crisis" (Winter 2016/2017) *Clemont Review of Books.* ("Identity politics proceeds in the complacent assumption that diversity, tolerance, and inclusion mean pretty much the same thing. The reality is far messier. The etymology of 'tolerance,' for example, rests on the Latin word for bearing or enduring, a notion markedly different from encouraging or affirming. The modest demand to put up with people, ideas, or customs you don't like but which do you no harm lubricates greater diversity. By contrast, the idea that true tolerance mandates applauding and welcoming any and all that are alien or disagreeable stokes resentments, which inevitably make getting along more rather than less difficult.")

12 *Id.* (internal citations omitted).

something deeper than our differences – our shared humanity. Thus, despite what divides and differentiates us from each other, at our core we are similar in ways that are important for any conceptualization of human rights.

Human dignity and dignitary harms

Human dignity for everyone everywhere helps us evaluate claims involving dignitary harm, the right not to be offended, and other forms of "identity politics," and is a powerful mechanism for encouraging all making such claims not to forget the dignity of others while pressing individual claims.

In recent years there has been a growing body of thought that would justify limitations on important civil and political rights including freedom of speech and press, freedom of religion or belief, freedom of association, and assembly because speakers are expressing views or engaging in activities that inflict "dignitary harm" on religion, on a group, or even a particular individual.

Claims of dignitary harm are problematic in that they often give the person or group suffering the offense or harm the ability to define the offense in terms of how much offense they take.

Claims of dignitary harm are also problematic when they are designed to protect particular religious groups, or other protected classes, such as ethnic or sexual minorities. One problem is that human rights are designed to protect human beings, not religions or other groups, from criticism.

For example, there have been important controversies about speech that offends religion, including blasphemy and hate speech. On the opposite side of the coin, there have been controversies about religious speech that offends other groups, including sexual minorities.

There is no human right to be free from offensive speech or conduct by others. Some speakers will speak very critically of religion, while other speakers may offend by speaking of their religious beliefs. Both types of offense are generally protected speech under widely accepted principles of the human right to freedom of expression and speech.

Efforts to limit speech that is "intolerant" are especially suspect, since such limits will almost always protect the politically powerful from offensive speech and will not provide reciprocal protections for those who are not politically powerful. Demanding limits on "intolerant" speech will often itself be intolerant. The supposed or actual "intolerance" of a group or individual should not be used as a basis for limiting the human rights of the intolerant.

However, this does not mean that certain types of speech cannot be limited. One of the best examples is speech that incites violence, speech that dehumanizes a certain group because of their characteristics, and justifies the use of violence against them.

Human dignity and identity politics

Human dignity for everyone everywhere is a powerful mechanism for understanding and evaluating "identity politics." Human dignity for everyone everywhere helps address important questions involving human identity. As Francis Fukuyama, political scientist and author, notes, "The rise of identity politics in modern liberal democracies is one of the chief threats that they face unless we can work our way back to more universal understandings of human dignity, we will doom ourselves to continuing conflict."[13]

The Punta del Este Declaration helps us understand that human beings often have multiple sources of identity that are very important to their understanding of who they are. For example, one's race, nationality, sex or sexual orientation, gender or gender identity, as well as one's religion, among many others, are important sources of identity. Human dignity for everyone everywhere helps us understand that these multiple sources of identity are important, and one source of identity should not be treated as being more important than others.

Human dignity for everyone everywhere recognizes that identities are an important part of human dignity, but also that individual identities should not be used as a basis for limiting the human dignity and identity interests of others.

Some identities will be more fundamental and deserving of human rights protection than others. For example, most of us would agree that one's allegiance to a particular sports team is not a type of identity that deserves special protection. But the usual rights of freedom of expression, association, and assembly will be relevant to protecting even identities such as these.

Identity politics seeks to divide us into groups based upon particular characteristics. At its worst, identity politics insists that those who do not share a particular group's features of identity cannot say anything about that group.

Taken to an extreme, identity politics is opposed to the idea of human dignity for everyone everywhere since it seeks to create special treatment for certain "identities" at the expense of others. Focusing on dignity helps us define the scope of identity protections, and focusing on everyone everywhere reminds us of the importance of reciprocity and universality in thinking about issues involving identity.

c. It helps to diffuse the hostility that is often associated with human rights controversies and to foster constructive dialogue. It also helps mitigate the distortion, avoidance, and selective recognition of human dignity

Distortion and avoidance of human rights

Human dignity for everyone everywhere helps avoid the distortion and avoidance of human rights by authoritarian governments or others. Human dignity for everyone everywhere can help states focus on their obligations to all people within their jurisdiction and make it more difficult for authoritarian or oppressive states to

13 Francis Fukuyama, *Identity, The Demand for Dignity and the Politics of Resentment* (Farrar, Straus and Giroux: New York, 2018) xvi.

avoid their obligations to protect the fundamental human rights of all people at all times.

Distortions and abuses of human rights may be subtle or severe. Human rights tragedies such as genocide or mass atrocities are a direct assault on the ideals of human dignity for everyone everywhere.

When minority groups are persecuted, this is a clear violation of the principle of human dignity for everyone everywhere. In our world, religious persecution that rises above simple discrimination or social hostility is a serious problem that seems to be on the rise. Examples are not difficult to identify. Current examples include the plight of Rohingya Muslims in Myanmar, Baha'is in Yemen and Iran, Ahmadis in Pakistan and elsewhere, Yazidis in Iraq during the Daesh occupation, Christians in many parts of the Middle East, and the internment of as many as one to two million Uyghur Muslims in prison camps in China, among others.

Furthermore, regimes routinely violate human rights to distort what human rights are. This is particularly visible in the case of the right to freedom of religion or belief and blasphemy laws. Blasphemy laws aim to protect established or privileged religion from criticism and dissent. However, as such, blasphemy laws are excessively used and abused against religious minorities and violate their rights and human dignity. Despite various glaring concerns surrounding blasphemy laws, such laws often carry the death penalty.

Instrumentalization of human rights

Human dignity for everyone everywhere helps avoid the instrumentalization of human rights. Some governments engage in rhetoric or practices that instrumentalize human rights, as mechanisms for promoting national interest, party interest, or a particular politician's interest.

For example, China has been using the argument of national security and combating extremism to limit the human rights of certain groups of people. Indeed, China has used this line of argument to detain one to two million Uyghur Muslims in the Xinjiang region.[14] The "re-education camps," the world's largest 21st Century mass incarceration of a minority group, reportedly subject the members of this ethno-religious group to months of political indoctrination and deprive them of their religious and ethnic identity. Indeed, in October 2018, the Chinese government introduced a new law aimed at combating extremism that ultimately legalized such re-education camps. Article 3 of the Xinjiang Uyghur Autonomous Region Deradicalization Regulations defines extremism as the "expressions and behaviors that are influenced by extremism, rendering radical religious ideas, and rejecting and intervening in normal production and life."[15]

14 See for example Yuan Yang, "Xinjiang Security Crackdown Sparks Han Chinese Exodus" (December 22, 2019) *Financial Times*. Available at: https://www.ft.com/content/fa6bd0b0-1d87-11ea-9186-7348c2f183af

15 Xinjiang Uyghur Autonomous Region Deradicalization Regulations. Available at: www.sohu.com/a/258631718_115479?g=0

Furthermore, "extremism … refers to the propositions and actions of inciting hatred, inciting discrimination, and advocating violence by distorting religious teachings or by other means." Article 9 of the Xinjiang Uyghur Autonomous Region Deradicalization Regulations prohibits activities that are used to

> "promote and disseminate the idea of extremism," "Intervening in normal cultural and recreational activities, or rejecting public goods and services such as radio and television," "Generalizing the concept of halal, expanding the concept of halal to other fields outside the field of halal food, and rejecting and interfering with the secular life of others by the name of the truth," "Not allowing children to receive national education and hinder the implementation of the national education system," "publishing, printing, distributing, selling, producing, downloading, storing, copying, consulting, exchanging, holding articles, publications, audio and video containing extreme content," "Deliberately interfering with or undermining the implementation of the family planning policy," and "Other extreme speeches and behaviors."[16]

The activities, while they should be protected under international standards in the UDHR (and the ICCPR), are banned as they are allegedly linked to the very dangerous concept of "extremism."

It is noteworthy that Russia is also restricting human rights using the concept of extremism, in its very broad understanding. This, again, has the effect of targeting some religious groups. For example, Article 282.2 of the Russian Criminal Code criminalizes the act of organizing the activity of an extremist community:

1 organizing the activity of a non-governmental or religious association or other organization that due to its extremist activity was liquidated or had its activity banned by a court decision that has entered legal force, with the exception of organizations declared terrorist under Russian Federation legislation
2 participating in the activity of a non-governmental or religious association or other organization that due to its extremist activity was liquidated or had its activity banned by a court decision that has entered legal force, with the exception of organizations declared terrorist under Russian Federation legislation.

Furthermore, Article 282.2, Subsection (1.1.) criminalizes the act of "persuading, recruiting, or otherwise inducing a person to participate in the activity of an extremist organization." The danger of such laws is not only theoretical. Indeed, in 2017, when the Supreme Court of the Russian Federation adopted a ruling that liquidated the Administrative Center of Jehovah's Witnesses in Solnechnoye and 395 Local Religious Organizations (LROs) used by Jehovah's Witnesses throughout Russia, the Russian Supreme Court opened the door to charges under Article 282.2 of the Russian Criminal Code against (virtually) any member of the

16 *Id.*, Article 9.

LROs (used by over 175,000 Jehovah's Witnesses in Russia). This has resulted in hundreds of Jehovah's Witnesses in Russia being arrested and many of them prosecuted.

These examples illustrate how some states use a narrow understanding of human rights or exaggerate arguments for limiting human rights on the grounds of national security, to leave individuals or groups without the protections of human rights. The focus on human rights for everyone everywhere could help to prevent such abuse. The Punta del Este Declaration is a reminder that human dignity and human rights for everyone everywhere is a repudiation of these efforts to marginalize or minimize human rights. Human rights are designed to protect human beings, not governments or ruling parties. For the most part, human rights indicate obligations that states have to those who live within their spheres of jurisdiction.

Depoliticizing human rights

Human dignity for everyone everywhere is an idea that can help depoliticize, or perhaps even more importantly, *de-tribalize*, human rights. One worrisome trend is that human rights are viewed skeptically by many. Specific interest groups often try to capture human rights discourse to advance their own political objectives, often at the expense of others. Identity politics has a primary goal of emphasizing differences and dividing people into groups to seek special treatment for their group. The idea of human dignity for everyone everywhere reminds us that despite our differences, what we share is more important than what divides us. Extreme versions of identity politics descend into tribal identities and divisions that almost inevitably lead to conflict, and claims of victimization are also often made to agitate for special treatment and compensation.

12 Article 10

Most egregious and most feasible

Article 10 reads as follows:

> Human dignity for everyone everywhere reminds us to work toward the elimination of the most egregious abuses of the human rights of individuals and groups, including genocide, crimes against humanity, war crimes, and other atrocities. It also reminds us to protect those human beings most at risk of human rights violations. At the same time, it encourages efforts to respond to problems that may be amenable to practical and feasible solutions.

The following is an expanded explanation of each part of Article 10.

a. Human dignity for everyone everywhere reminds us to work toward the elimination of the most egregious abuses of the human rights of individuals and groups, including genocide, crimes against humanity, war crimes, and other atrocities

Atrocity crimes such as genocide, crimes against humanity, or war crimes, are the ultimate denial of the human dignity of individuals as well as groups or communities. Such atrocities, and especially genocide, do not happen overnight. Genocide is a process, a well-planned and organized crime. It is not spontaneous or committed in the heat of a moment. The first steps committed towards genocide are those denying the human dignity of individuals belonging to the protected groups, whether by way of furthering the "us and them" mentality, symbolization, or discrimination against the group. This groundwork denying the human dignity of members of a protected group is done by the perpetrators to enable mass atrocities and justify them. Only by ensuring human dignity for everyone everywhere will it be possible to prevent atrocity crimes that flourish on the very denial of human dignity.

The ten stages of genocide[1] illustrate how early warning signs of massive violations of human rights also involve a violation of the principle of human dignity for

1 The ten stages are: 1. Classification, 2. Symbolization, 3. Discrimination, 4. Dehumanization, 5. Organization, 6. Polarization, 7. Preparation, 8. Persecution, 9. Extermination, 10. Denial. Gregory Stanton, "Ten Stages of Genocide." Available at: http://genocidewatch.net/genocide-2/8-stages-of-genocide/

DOI: 10.4324/9781003207030-13

everyone everywhere. Indeed, stage four of dehumanization goes to the very core of human dignity. Under stage four:

> One group denies the humanity of the other group. Members of it are equated with animals, vermin, insects, or diseases. Dehumanization overcomes the normal human revulsion against murder. At this stage, hate propaganda in print and on hate radios is used to vilify the victim group. The majority group is taught to regard the other group as less than human, and even alien to their society. They are indoctrinated to believe that "We are better off without them." The powerless group can become so depersonalized that they are actually given numbers rather than names, as Jews were in the death camps. They are equated with filth, impurity, and immorality. Hate speech fills the propaganda of official radio, newspapers, and speeches.[2]

Genocide itself is a blatant example of a violation of the principle of human dignity for everyone everywhere. Each stage involves escalating violations of human rights that easily translate into escalating violations of human dignity and vice-versa.

Egregious abuses of human dignity

Severe violations of human dignity such as genocide warrant special attention and protection and must be high priorities for prevention. Elimination or prevention of atrocity crimes is an aim yet to be fulfilled. Prevention of mass atrocities as genocide is a duty of states under the UN Convention on the Prevention and Punishment of the Crime of Genocide. Nonetheless, despite the promise of "never again" after World War II, the international community and states have been failing to uphold this duty and prevent atrocity crimes from happening.

Human dignity and the road to "final solution"

Atrocity crimes, especially those that are identity-based, begin with the denial of human dignity of those deemed as less worthy of protection or not deserving protection or rights. This is very clear from the atrocities ordered or authorized by the Nazis even before World War II.

Shortly before the war, on August 18, 1939, Adolf Hitler enacted a decree that required all physicians, nurses, and midwives to report children under the age of three suffering from severe physical or mental disabilities.[3] Initially, Hitler introduced a program allowing parents to request the so-called "mercy killings" of their children suffering from severe disabilities.[4] Under the name Tiergarten 4 ("T4"), the program endeavored to destroy life unworthy of living ("*Vernichtung lebensunwerten Lebens*")[5] and was aimed at children with mental and physical disabilities up to the

2 *Id.*
3 Stephen J. Lee, *Hitler and Nazi Germany* (Routledge: London, 2000) 80.
4 *Id.*, 84.

age of three.[6] However, over time, older children and adults were included in the T4 program as well.[7] Subsequently, Hitler signed a decree to provide:

> The authority of certain physicians to be designated by name in such manner that persons who, according to human judgment, are incurable can, upon a most careful diagnosis of their condition of sickness, be accorded a mercy death.[8]

This authority was then extended to mainstream the process:

> Originally, one has taken into consideration to kill the single incurable persons ... by injections or overdosed sleeping pills. Nevertheless, this consideration ... has been called impracticable from the technical point of view..., by the majority of the consulted doctors. Therefore, it was proposed... to kill the persons being eligible simultaneously in a bigger crowd somehow. After many consultations ... hearing the chemist of the *Reichskriminalpolizeiamt* too, one decided to install a room in a number of conveniently located sanatoriums. The room should be filled with carbon monoxide gas then.[9]

In 1939–40 alone, over 70,000 mental health patients were killed in gas chambers.[10] Researchers assess that between 1939 and 1945, over 200,000–250,000 mentally and physically disabled people were killed in pursuance of the program.[11] Additionally, as a result of World War II, 5.6–6.25 million Jews, 3 million Soviet prisoners of war, 3 million Poles, 700,000 Serbians, 222,000 to 250,000 Roma, Sinti, and Lalleri, 80,000 German political and religious prisoners, 12,000 homosexuals, and 2,500 Jehovah's Witnesses (others deemed as unworthy of protection) were killed.[12]

Contemporary genocides

Over the subsequent decades after World War II and the reign of the Nazi regime, mass atrocities that amount to genocide have been perpetrated in Cambodia, Rwanda, Bosnia, Darfur (Sudan), Syria and Iraq, Myanmar, and most recently in

5 Robert J. Lifton, *The Nazi Doctors: Medical Killing and the Psychology of Genocide* (Basic Books, 1986) 142.
6 *Id.*, 46.
7 *Id.*
8 Adolf Hitler, Letter of Appointment (September 1, 1939), Exhibit 330, 630-PS, Nuremberg Military Tribunals, Trials of War Criminals, Vol. 1, 794.
9 Testimony of Dr. Richard von Hegener, Ludwigsburg Archive. Available at: http://deathcamps.org/euthanasia/t4intro.html
10 Benno Muller-Hill, "Eugenics: The Science and Religion of the Nazis" in Arthur L. Caplan (es.) *When Medicine Went Mad: Bioethics and the Holocaust* (Springer: New York, 1992) 47.
11 "Nazi Euthanasia Program: Persecution of the Mentally and Physically Disabled." Available at: https://www.jewishvirtuallibrary.org/jsource/Holocaust/disabled.html
12 *The Holocaust Chronicle*, "Total Deaths from Nazi Genocidal Policies." Available at: www.holocaustchronicle.org/holocaustappendices.html

China, naming only a few. The genocide in Cambodia was the first genocide since the introduction of the UN Convention on the Prevention and Punishment of the Crime of Genocide. From 1975 to 1979, between 1.7 and 2 million people were killed by the Khmer Rouge regime.[13] In 1994, in Rwanda, 800,000 Tutsis were killed. Thousands of people were injured. It is estimated that between 250,000 and 500,000 women were subjected to systematic rape.[14] In 1995, in Bosnia, approximately 100,000 people were killed.[15] In 2003, over 300,000 people were killed and over 3 million people were displaced in Darfur.[16]

The second decade of the 21st Century has seen an escalation of such atrocities with four cases that may meet the legal definition of genocide, namely, the Daesh atrocities against religious minorities in Syria and Iraq, the Burmese military atrocities against the Rohingya Muslims and other religious minorities in Myanmar, the Boko Haram and Fulani militia atrocities in Nigeria and the atrocities perpetrated against the Uyghur Muslims in China.

Despite the duty to prevent such atrocities, states that are under the duty to prevent have acted too little or too late to be able to prevent these atrocities. One of the ongoing challenges is that if the alleged atrocities are ordered or authorized by a state, other states may shy away from responding and fulfilling their duty to protect because of various diplomatic considerations and not wishing to interfere with a state's sovereignty. Focusing on the human dignity of those subjected to atrocity crimes would allow states to look beyond the diplomatic or sovereignty consideration and focus on protecting the endangered communities.

b. Human dignity for everyone everywhere reminds us to protect those human beings most at-risk of human rights violations

Certain human beings, or even groups of people, are more at risk to become victims of human rights violations.

For example, the World Health Organization (WHO) defines vulnerability as the "degree to which a population, individual or organization is unable to anticipate, cope with, resist and recover from the impacts of disasters."[17] The WHO identifies children, pregnant women, elderly people, malnourished people, and people who are ill or immunocompromised as vulnerable individuals in case of a disaster. The UN Office for the Disaster Risk Reduction (the UNISDR) defines vulnerability as "the conditions determined by physical, social, economic, and environmental factors or processes which increase the susceptibility of an

13 "The Cambodian Genocide," http://endgenocide.org/learn/past-genocides/the-cambodian-genocide/

14 "The Rwandan Genocide," http://endgenocide.org/learn/past-genocides/the-rwandan-genocide/.

15 "The Bosnian War and the Srebrenica Genocide," http://endgenocide.org/learn/past-genocides/the-bosnian-war-and-srebrenica-genocide/

16 "The Situation in Darfur," http://endgenocide.org/conflict-areas/sudan-backgrounder/

17 B. Wisner and J. Adams, *Environmental Health in Emergencies and Disasters: A Practical Guide* (WHO, 2002).

individual, a community, assets or systems to the impacts of hazards."[18] The International Federation of Red Cross and Red Crescent Societies defines vulnerability as "the diminished capacity of an individual or group to anticipate, cope with, resist and recover from the impact of a natural or man-made hazard. The concept is relative and dynamic. Vulnerability is most often associated with poverty, but it can also arise when people are isolated, insecure, and defenseless in the face of risk, shock, or stress."[19] This may include, among others,

- displaced populations who leave their habitual residence in collectives, usually due to a sudden impact disaster, such as an earthquake or a flood, threat or conflict, as a coping mechanism and with the intent to return;
- migrants who leave or flee their habitual residence to go to new places, usually abroad to seek better and safer perspectives;
- returnees – former migrants or displaced people returning to their homes;
- specific groups within the local population, such as marginalized, excluded, or destitute people;
- young children, pregnant and nursing women, unaccompanied children, widows, elderly people without family support, disabled persons.[20]

Despite differences, these definitions are similar in focusing on individuals and groups who, because of their characteristics, are more susceptible to human rights violations or more disadvantaged when human rights violations occur.

The phrase used in the Punta del Este Declaration, "at risk of human rights violations," is closely related to the concept of vulnerability as it is defined in the above-discussed definitions. However, the choice of the wording focused on human rights violations rather than the wording focused on the characteristics of the victims aims to provide for more flexibility. It is crucial to note the issue of vulnerability and to consider how the focus on human dignity could help to address the challenges faced by vulnerable individuals or groups.

Those at risk of human rights violations require protection. By way of providing them with such protection, one reaffirms their human dignity which is often violated even before the mass atrocities occur. For example, the UN Convention on Prevention and Punishment of the Crime of Genocide imposes upon states a duty to prevent genocide (namely, forbidden acts perpetrated with the specific intent to destroy, in whole or in part, a protected group, whether national, ethnic, racial or religious). However, as discussed above, as genocide does not occur overnight but with lower-level human rights violations, to be able to prevent genocide it is crucial to protect the groups from human rights violations (rather than from atrocity crimes only).

18 United Nations Office for Disaster Risk Reduction. https://www.unisdr.org/we/inform/terminology

19 International Federation of Red Cross and Red Crescent Societies. https://www.ifrc.org/en/what-we-do/disaster-management/about-disasters/what-is-a-disaster/what-is-vulnerability/

20 *Id.*

c. At the same time, it encourages efforts to respond to problems that may be amenable to practical and feasible solutions

Atrocity crimes like genocide, crimes against humanity, or war crimes require a complex and comprehensive response, including stopping the atrocities, investigating the crimes and prosecuting the perpetrators, providing the survivors with short- and long-term assistance, and much more.

Such a response is time- and resource-consuming. Protecting human dignity for everyone everywhere aims to prevent human rights violations that could escalate to atrocity crimes. Focusing on human dignity for everyone everywhere calls for an early response to human rights violations before these violations turn into atrocity crimes.

An early response to human rights violations should be focused on practical and feasible solutions that would ultimately help to prevent violations escalating to atrocity crimes. The means required to respond to atrocity crimes will always be more complex and more comprehensive than those required to respond to human rights violations.

Among others, the concept of human dignity reminds us not only to be mindful of the most severe violations of human rights but also to be watchful and mindful of opportunities for improvement. As such, human dignity should be used to help to prevent human rights violations from escalating to atrocity crimes and responding to post-atrocity challenges faced by affected communities.

Conclusion

The concept of human dignity can be used to strengthen human rights, focusing on the ten articles of the Punta del Este Declaration that have added to the rich legacy of the UDHR.

Today the UDHR is increasingly being seen as an international legal document, even though that was not the case when it was first adopted. Instead, the UDHR was seen as a worldwide educational tool, with the hope that "every individual and every organ of society, keeping this Declaration constantly in mind, shall strive by teaching and education to promote respect for these rights and freedoms and by progressive measures, national and international, to secure their universal respect and effective recognition and observance, both among the peoples of the Member States and among the peoples of territories under the jurisdiction."[21] However, to ensure that the UDHR can continue to be influential and relevant, it is crucial to ensure that its interpretation is grounded in human dignity and its aim is human dignity for everyone everywhere.

21 Morsink (2009) 150.

13 Conclusions and the way forward

Introduction

The concept of human dignity must be understood and appreciated because the success of the human rights project depends on it. The key to ensuring that the UDHR does not stagnate or lose its significance but continues to empower and allow human rights to flourish, is to go back to basics and affirm human dignity for everyone everywhere. We believe the focus on human dignity for everyone everywhere is the key to creating a world where human rights protect everyone. The UDHR is as important now as it was back in 1948, and the rights enshrined in the UDHR empower us all. Over the past 70 years, significant progress has been made to ensure that the UDHR is universally accepted and recognized as the fundamental document concerning human rights.

However, as the rights affirmed in the UDHR are not fully protected and enforced, it is crucial to look beyond the rights listed in the UDHR and consider how the concept of human dignity, that united the drafters of the UDHR, can be used today to strengthen our commitments towards human rights for everyone everywhere.

The discussions in previous chapters provide an elaboration of how the concept of human dignity can strengthen human rights and ensure that they become truly universal. Indeed, the concept of human dignity should be used as a touchstone for interpreting the UDHR, and for implementing and enforcing human rights.

However, it is equally important to identify the practical ways the Punta del Este Declaration could assist in achieving the goal of strengthening human rights and ensuring human dignity for everyone everywhere. Here we offer a few concluding thoughts about some of the ways the Punta del Este Declaration can and should be used.

How should the Punta del Este Declaration be used?

The Punta del Este Declaration is a guide to understanding the many ways that the concept of human dignity for everyone everywhere can be used to strengthen human rights protections.

DOI: 10.4324/9781003207030-14

The Punta del Este Declaration champions an approach to reading, interpreting, and implementing human rights with an eye continually focused on the goal of human dignity for everyone everywhere. The focus on human dignity for everyone everywhere aims to aid the human rights project in ensuring that it becomes truly universal; it places human dignity at the forefront of any considerations involving human rights. Human dignity is key in assisting the human rights projects of preserving and protecting human rights for all people, as:

- Human dignity is the foundational principle of human rights.
- Human dignity is the telos, goal, or end of human rights.
- Human dignity is a metric that can be used to assess human rights performance.
- Human dignity has played an important role in forming, guiding, and sustaining consensus on core human rights.
- Human dignity remains important in a world that is highly polarized and pluralistic.
- Human dignity was recognized as one of the foundational principles in the Preamble of the Charter of the United Nations.
- Human dignity is recognized in the first sentence of the Preamble of the UDHR.
- Human dignity is also recognized in the first article of the UDHR.
- It was grave violations of human dignity that provided much of the impetus for the nations of the world to adopt the UDHR.
- National and local laws alone are not adequate to protect human dignity; it should be emphasized as a principle of international law as well.
- Despite their differences, the drafters of the UDHR, and the nations they represented, rallied around the idea of human dignity as a basic principle for promoting freedom, justice, and peace in the world.
- The UDHR, in turn, has served as the foundational document for many other important human rights instruments, including international treaties, regional human rights instruments, and constitutions and laws in many parts of the world.
- Human dignity is an extremely generative concept, inviting many different conceptions and understandings.
- Although human dignity is sometimes criticized as being too abstract or general to be useful, in fact like many important fundamental legal principles such as freedom, equality, justice, and nondiscrimination, it has been used in a variety of ways in legal instruments.
- Human dignity as a counterpart to human identity helps us focus on not only the many ways that we are different as human beings but what we have in common as well.
- Human dignity reminds us of the importance for human beings of the right to find and define meaning and purpose in their own lives.
- Human dignity points us towards respecting pluralism and differences among people and groups.

- Human dignity helps us think beyond rights, and beyond ourselves, to focus on others, as well as our obligations to others.
- Violations of human dignity, including severe violations, continue today, including in wars and other armed conflicts, in genocides, crimes against humanity, war crimes, and the global crises concerning refugees, migrants, asylum seekers, and human trafficking.
- Human dignity helps counter the tendency for human rights to be fragmented, eroded, or neglected.
- Human dignity for everyone everywhere reminds us of the problems that arise when the interests or rights of one group or individual are placed ahead of those of other groups or individuals.
- There are many different theories of human dignity, some emphasizing status, other inherent values or worth, and other standards of behavior.
- Violations of human dignity are something important that warrant appropriate redress.
- Human dignity is a concept that can help us find common ground and build bridges.
- Human dignity can help us understand other important legal and moral concepts such as justice, freedom, and equality.
- Human dignity can help with the implementation of human rights.
- Human dignity can help adjudicate conflicts between human rights, or between human rights and other important state interests.
- Human dignity can help reduce the divisiveness of human rights discourse.
- Human dignity reminds us that human rights must be read and realized together.

The Human Dignity for Everyone Everywhere approach

The Punta del Este Declaration can be used by states and regional and international actors as a guide to reading, interpreting, and implementing the UDHR and other human rights documents.

International actors

The Punta del Este Declaration could be adopted by international actors. For example, it could be adopted by the UN General Assembly or the UN Human Rights Council as a resolution and so become an official UN declaration for member states to follow.

States

States could utilize the Punta del Este Declaration as their domestic mechanism to aid with reading, interpreting, and implementing human rights documents. This could be achieved by way of including the Punta del Este Declaration in their human rights policies. The Punta del Este Declaration could also be used in human rights training delivered to all civil servants.

Civil society

The Punta del Este Declaration is not for the exclusive use of states and international actors. Conversely, it is a document that should be used by a broad range of actors. Indeed, as discussed in previous chapters, the UDHR does not only identify the rights but also prescribes the duties of everyone, and not states alone.

Civil society representatives could ensure that they adopt the Punta Del Este Declaration's reading of human rights obligations in all their dealings, putting human dignity first.

Businesses

The issue of businesses having human rights obligations continues to receive more and more attention. The Punta del Este Declaration could assist in guiding businesses to introduce a human rights-based approach in their dealings and ensure that they are human-rights compliant.

Educational institutions

The Punta del Este Declaration could be used by educational institutions in teaching about human rights, their interpretation, implementation, and enforcement. To be able to equip the next human rights-literate generations, it is crucial to ensure that they have a good understanding of the very concept that enabled the adoption of the UDHR, despite the differences between drafters and delegates that had to be overcome for the initiative to succeed. Without this narrative, the human rights project may never become fully universal and inclusive.

Strengthening human rights mechanisms

For the human rights project to succeed, it is crucial to ensure that adequate mechanisms are put in place to monitor human rights, to respond to human rights violations, to assist the victims and survivors, and to work towards preventing similar human rights violations in future. While several such mechanisms already exist, the continuing struggle to ensure human rights for everyone everywhere suggests that new approaches may be needed. Below are proposals for new UN mechanisms that could help to aid the process.

UN Forum on Human Dignity

The UN Human Rights Council could adopt a resolution establishing the UN Forum on Human Dignity to provide a forum for states and a wide range of civil society representatives (and especially those who do not have ECOSOC accreditation who otherwise would not be able to engage with the Human Rights Council). The forum could engage with the different aspects of human dignity and consider how violations of human rights affect human dignity. The forum could work on practical ways to ensure the protection of human rights and human dignity of everyone everywhere.

Monitoring the effects of states' implementation of human rights on human dignity

Within the UN system, several mechanisms are engaged with monitoring treaty obligations (including human rights treaty bodies and special procedures). While they are focused on states' implementation of human rights, they do not measure the effectiveness of such implementation upon human dignity. This is a crucial consideration that would require further attention. Such monitoring could be conducted by a new mechanism specifically established to conduct this function. Alternatively, the role and functions of the existing mechanisms could be amended to include this monitoring function as the means to analyze the implementation of human rights.

UN Special Rapporteur on Human Dignity

The UN Human Rights Council could establish the mandate of a Special Rapporteur on Human Dignity, an independent expert appointed to identify existing and emerging obstacles to the affirmation and protection of human dignity of everyone everywhere and present recommendations to address such obstacles. The mandate could be modeled on, for example, the mandate of the Special Rapporteur on Freedom of Religion or Belief, the Special Rapporteur on Minority Issues, the Special Rapporteur on Freedom of Opinion and Expression, and many more.

As recent years have seen the emergence of new issues affecting human dignity not otherwise covered by other mandates, for example how artificial intelligence and technology affect human dignity, there is a growing need to find ways to better protect human dignity.

Appendix A: The Punta del Este Declaration on Human Dignity for Everyone Everywhere

The following is the final text of the Punta del Este Declaration as adopted in December 2018.

Punta del Este Declaration on Human Dignity for Everyone Everywhere

70 years after the Universal Declaration of Human Rights

December 2018

Preamble

Whereas seventy years ago in the aftermath of World War II, the nations and peoples of the world came together in solidarity and solemnity and without dissent adopted the Universal Declaration of Human Rights (UDHR) as a common standard of achievement for all peoples and all nations;

Whereas the Preamble of the UDHR declares that "recognition of the inherent dignity and of the equal and inalienable rights of all members of the human family is the foundation of freedom, justice, and peace in the world";

Whereas Article 1 of the UDHR proclaims that "All human beings are born free and equal in dignity and rights. They are endowed with reason and conscience and should act towards one another in a spirit of brotherhood";

Whereas the equal human dignity of everyone everywhere is the foundational principle of human rights and reminds us that every person is of value and is worthy of respect;

Whereas it is important to remember, reaffirm, and recommit ourselves to these basic principles;

Recalling that it was grave violations of human dignity during the wars of the twentieth century that preceded and precipitated the UDHR;

Recalling the international consensus that domestic law alone had not been sufficient to safeguard against and avoid the human rights violations of the World Wars;

Recalling that despite all of their differences, nations of the world concurred that the dignity of all people is the basic foundation of human rights and freedom, justice, and peace in the world;

Recalling that human dignity is the wellspring of and underpins all the rights and freedoms recognized in the UDHR as fundamental;

Recalling that the UDHR has served as the inspiration for an array of international and regional covenants and other instruments, as well as numerous national constitutions, bills and charters of rights, and legislation protecting human rights;

Recognizing that human dignity is not a static concept but accommodates respect for diversity and calls for a dynamic approach to its application in the diverse and ever-changing contexts of our pluralistic world;

Recognizing that although the notion of dignity has been criticized by some as being too abstract, it actually has been and remains a powerful organizing force that points humanity towards its highest ideals and has proven itself as an influential heuristic in constitutional and human rights discourse;

Recognizing that the concept of human dignity emphasizes the uniqueness and irreplaceability of every human being; that it implies a right of each individual to find and define the meanings of his or her own life; that it presupposes respect for pluralism and difference; and that it carries with it the responsibility to honor the dignity of everyone;

Recognizing that severe violations and abuses of human dignity continue to this day, including through wars, armed conflicts, genocides, crimes against humanity, war crimes, and the global crises concerning refugees, migrants, asylum seekers, and human trafficking, and that such depredations continue to threaten peace, justice, and the rights of all;

Recognizing that human rights can easily be fragmented, eroded, or neglected and that constant vigilance is necessary for human rights to be implemented, realized, and carried forward in the world;

Recognizing that human dignity for everyone everywhere and at every level is threatened when the needs, interests, and rights of one group or individual are placed ahead of those of other groups and individuals;

Emphasizing that equal human dignity is a status with which all human beings are endowed, but also a value that must be learned, nurtured, and lived;

Emphasizing that violations of human dignity require appropriate redress;

Emphasizing that human dignity is now a time-tested principle that can help find common ground, reconcile competing conceptions of what justice demands, facilitate the implementation of human rights, and guide adjudication in case of conflicts, and that can also help us respond to distortions, abuse, and hostility towards human rights;

Believing that human rights discourse might be less divisive than it often is and greater efforts might be made to find common ground;

Believing that human rights must be read and realized together;

Believing that the concept of human dignity can help us understand, protect, and implement human rights globally; and

Hoping that the present century will be more humane, just, and peaceful than the 20th Century;

We, the undersigned, do solemnly reaffirm:

The Universal Declaration of Human Rights continues to be "a common standard of achievement for all peoples and all nations, to the end that every individual and every organ of society, keeping the Declaration constantly in mind, shall strive by teaching and education to promote respect for these rights and freedoms and by progressive measures, local, national and international, to secure their universal and effective recognition and observance."

We, the undersigned, do solemnly issue the following Declaration on Human Dignity for Everyone Everywhere:

1. *Foundation, objective, and criterion*

The inherent human dignity of all people and the importance of respecting, promoting, and protecting human dignity for everyone everywhere is the foundational principle and the key objective or goal of human rights, as well as an invaluable criterion for evaluating laws, policies, and government actions for how well they accord with human rights standards. Protecting, promoting, and guaranteeing respect for the human dignity of everyone is a fundamental obligation of states, governments, and other public bodies, whether local, regional, national, or international. Promoting human dignity is also a responsibility of all sectors of society, and of each of us as human beings. Doing so is the key to protecting the equal and inalienable rights of all members of the human family, and remains the foundation of freedom, justice, and peace in the world.

2. *Generating agreement and building common understanding*

The inherent dignity of every human being was the key idea that helped generate agreement and a common understanding at the time of the adoption of the UDHR about human rights of all people, in spite of diversity and deep differences, notwithstanding divergent political and legal systems.

Human dignity for everyone everywhere is valuable as a point of departure for exploring and understanding the meaning of human rights, as a basis for finding common ground regarding human rights and consensus about their content and meaning. It provides an approach to building bridges between various normative justifications of human rights, including those with religious and secular theoretical groundings. Respecting human dignity for everyone everywhere facilitates discussions on different conceptions of shared values. Human dignity is a broad concept that nevertheless invites in-depth reflection within differing traditions and perspectives.

Human dignity for all reminds us that human rights are universal, inalienable, indivisible, interdependent, and interrelated.

3. *Defining and specifying human rights*

Dignity is an essential part of what it means to be human. Respect for human dignity for everyone everywhere helps us define and understand the meaning and scope of all human rights. Focusing concretely and in actual situations on human dignity and its implications for particular human rights claims can help identify the specific content of these rights as well as how we understand human dignity itself.

4. Duties and responsibilities

Human dignity for everyone everywhere emphasizes the concept in the UDHR that rights include accompanying obligations and responsibilities, not just of states but also of all human beings with respect to the rights of others. Dignity is a status shared by every human being, and the emphasis on everyone and everywhere makes it clear that rights are characterized by reciprocity and involve corresponding duties. Everyone should be concerned not only with his or her own dignity and rights but with the dignity and rights of every human being. Nonetheless, human dignity is not diminished on the ground that persons are not fulfilling their responsibilities to the state and others.

5. Education

Recognition of human dignity is a vital basis for teaching and education. Human rights education is of importance to promoting respect for the equal dignity of everyone. Such education is essential for sustaining dignity and human rights into the future. Equal access to education is a crucial aspect of respecting human dignity.

6. Seeking common ground

Focusing on human dignity for everyone everywhere encourages people to search for ways to find common ground regarding competing claims and to move beyond exclusively legal mechanisms for harmonizing, implementing, and mutually vindicating human rights and finding solutions to conflicts.

7. Implementing and realizing human rights in legislation

Recognition of human dignity for everyone everywhere is a foundational principle of law and is central to developing and protecting human rights in law and policy. The richness of the concept of dignity resists exhaustive definition, but it encourages the pursuit of optimum mutual vindication where conflicting rights and values are involved. It is critical for moving beyond thinking exclusively in terms of balancing and tradeoffs of rights and interests.

8. Reconciliation and adjudication

Recognition of human dignity for everyone everywhere is an important constitutional and legal principle for reconciling and adjudicating competing human rights claims, as well as claims between human rights and other important national and societal interests. Mutual vindication of rights may be possible in adjudication and may be further facilitated if all involved focus on respecting the human dignity of everyone. When mutual vindication of rights is not possible, dignity for all can help us to delineate the scope of rights, to set the boundaries of permissible restrictions on the exercise of rights and freedoms, and to seek to bring into fair balance competing rights claims. Respect for dignity plays an important role not only in formal adjudication but also in mediation or other forms of alternative dispute resolution.

9. Potential difficulties involving competing human rights claims

Respecting the human dignity of everyone everywhere supports effective human rights advocacy. Recognizing the universal and reciprocal character of human dignity is a corrective to positions claiming rights for some but not for others. It helps to diffuse the hostility that is often associated with human rights controversies and to foster constructive dialogue. It also helps mitigate the distortion, avoidance, and selective recognition of human dignity.

10. Most egregious and most feasible

Human dignity for everyone everywhere reminds us to work toward the elimination of the most egregious abuses of the human rights of individuals and groups, including genocide, crimes against humanity, war crimes, and other atrocities. It also reminds us to protect those human beings most at-risk of human rights violations. At the same time, it encourages efforts to respond to problems that may be amenable to practical and feasible solutions.

Appendix B: African perspectives on human dignity for everyone everywhere

An endorsement and elaboration of the Punta del Este Declaration on Dignity for Everyone Everywhere

By the African Consortium for Law and Religion Studies at its seventh annual Law and Religion in Africa conference, "Law, Religion, and Environment in Africa," Gaborone, Botswana, May 19–21, 2019

Whereas the Seventh Annual Conference on Law and Religion in Africa of the African Consortium for Law and Religion Studies (ACLARS) was held in Gaborone, Botswana, on 19–21 May 2019, with the conference theme, Law, Religion and Environment in Africa;

Whereas the conference participants wish to add their collective voices to the commemoration of the seventieth anniversary of the Universal Declaration of Human Rights by endorsing and elaborating upon the Punta del Este Declaration on Human Dignity for Everyone Everywhere;

Whereas there are many unique and characteristic understandings of human dignity that arise from African perspectives, and it is our hope that these perspectives can enhance and enrich the global and universal appreciation of human dignity as the foundational principle of human rights;

The following statement was drafted and welcomed by delegates and participants at ACLARS' seventh annual Law and Religion in Africa conference

1. African conceptions of human dignity. Human dignity is a foundational societal, religious, cultural, and legal concept in Africa. There is no one single African concept of dignity, but rather many different and often complementary conceptions. Dignity is a concept that has widespread purchase in African cultures, religions, and languages. As with many concepts, there is in Africa an ongoing contestation or negotiation about the meaning of human dignity. Nevertheless, there are African characteristics of the concept that are widespread and widely shared. For example, Sir Seretse Khama, the first President of the Republic of Botswana said, "Human dignity, like justice and freedom, is the common heritage of all men." The legacy of South African president Nelson Mandela is also as a champion of human dignity and freedom. As U.S. President Bill Clinton said upon the passing of Nelson Mandela, "History will remember Nelson Mandela as a champion for human dignity and freedom, for peace and reconciliation." We reiterate the Punta del Este Declaration's emphasis that human rights are interdependent, universal, indivisible and interrelated, and each one is critical for achieving human dignity.

2. Relationships and community. Africans think of dignity not solely as an individual human characteristic or right, but as a concept that implicates our most important relationships, including family, community, tribe, and nation. Human dignity is a concept that is understood as existing in relationships with others. As such dignity implicates understandings of human duties and relationships, not just individual claims against others. There is a natural reciprocal understanding of human dignity. Part of our human dignity is recognizing and respecting the dignity of others. An African perspective on dignity is outward-looking, not just inward reflecting.

For example, in southern Africa, the Nguni Bantu concept of *Ubuntu* (it is *Xhosa/botho* in Setswana) and in Eastern Africa's Kiswahili concept of *Utu* are closely related to human dignity, and clearly involves a relational character of human lives existing in connection and community with others. In some African cultures such as Botswana, the concept of totems is closely related to the idea of familial ties, which extend broadly, creating connections with others. African thinking about dignity necessarily includes the idea of equality; a concern for dignity is a concern for the equal dignity of all.

The meaning of dignity is taught first of all in the home, by parents and grandparents, and should then be reinforced by primary and secondary education, and through social institutions such as mosques and churches.

In some African countries, including Zimbabwe, the idea of dignity is closely associated with the idea of solidarity. This communal ideal of unity and sharing confirms a communal dimension to human dignity.

3. An indigenous concept. While "human rights" is a concept that can be difficult to translate into some African languages, the concept of human dignity is much easier to integrate linguistically. Rights are claims of what someone owes us, whereas dignity is inherent in the human person. For example, in the Yorùbá language rights (*eto*) are assertions of a claim of something owed to you, whereas dignity (*iyi*) lies at the foundation of rights. While the idea of rights resonates with Africans, in African languages such as Yorùbá, dignity (*iyi*) is a noun, a state or quality of being. Even when there is not agreement about the specific definition of human dignity, it is a concept that resonates widely and meaningfully. We believe there is much that can be learned from various African perspectives on dignity that will enrich not only African understandings of this concept, but global understandings as well.

4. Many meanings of dignity. There are many different meanings of dignity in African contexts, including the idea of living a dignified life (which can be related to ceremony and honor), dignity as rank or status (which can be hierarchical), dignity as a moral ideal (reflected in dignified behavior, including dress), dignity as a right, dignity as a personal responsibility (the duty to behave in a dignified manner), as well as dignity as describing the inherent value and worth of the human person. In a fundamental sense, because they are human, all human beings have dignity, even if they behave in ways that are undignified. We can urge others, such as our children, to behave with dignity without questioning the inherent human dignity of all regardless of how they behave.

There are dimensions of dignity that include living a complete and virtuous human life, for example, reflected in the Yorùbá people's concept of *omoluwabi*, which suggests the ideal of someone who has a good character in all dimensions of life, reflecting virtue or good character in every sphere. This idea of being completely trustworthy, courageous, hard-working, humble, and of good character, and of treating others with respect, is also an ideal that is closely related to the ideal of dignity.

Discussions of human dignity, as with discussions of human rights, should take place in a spirit of genuine dialogue, including between the northern and southern hemispheres, rather than in a spirit of instruction or direction. When we focus on one perspective of human dignity, we should not mistake it as an "African" perspective, since there will be many African perspectives. Dignity eludes definition and capture by any one group or viewpoint.

5. Dignity as a right and as a "mother" of rights. In some countries, such as South Africa and Nigeria, human dignity is a recognized fundamental constitutional right, and there are important judgments of these nations' highest courts elaborating the meaning of human dignity and related concepts such as *Ubuntu*. Even in places where human dignity is a recognized constitutional right, there are challenges in definition, scope, and implementation of the right. In other countries, human dignity is a foundational concept, but is not itself a legal right. It can be understood as the "mother" of rights, or lying at the genesis of rights. While dignity is foundational, this is not to understate the importance of rights or of the duty of states to respect and protect rights. Dignity is a common concept in African society, and in the contemporary world, human rights can be seen as a way of operationalizing human dignity. The concept of human dignity can reinforce what we know and have as human rights. Human dignity should not be used as a nebulous concept that governments can invoke to limit or deny rights to people.

6. Concrete concern for basic human needs. African discussions of dignity are less abstract and theoretical than some other discussions of dignity, focusing on basic human needs that must be satisfied in order to be fully human and to enjoy one's basic human dignity, including food, clothing, shelter, gainful employment, and the ability to care for oneself and one's family. Social and economic rights are the cornerstone of human dignity. In many African contexts, including Mozambique, dignity is understood as relating to the basic capacity to fulfill one's human needs, and then to be able to help fulfill the needs of others, including family and extended relations. Thus, discussions of dignity need to focus on basic human needs and capacities, such as the ability to find meaningful and remunerative work that is sufficient to provide for oneself and one's family. Discussions of human dignity will be regarded as too theoretical and abstract if they do not include an emphasis on basic economic and social rights, including not just problems of poverty, but of extreme poverty. The rising generation, including university students, will not have patience with theoretical discussions of human dignity when their education does not empower them with basic capacities to make a decent living.

An African perspective on human dignity is also to be mindful of the most serious violations of human dignity, including genocide, other atrocities, forced migrations and displacements, and extreme poverty. Hence, the saying that, "a person possesses no '*utu*'" among Kiswahili speaking communities. Extreme disparities of wealth and poverty will be viewed as a violation of human dignity.

7. State obligations. An important obligation of states is to enable its people to live lives of dignity, in light of the broad African recognition of the importance of dignity. Former presidents Julius Nyerere and Ian Khama, have respectively stressed its importance. In Julius Nyerere's farewell 1985 speech he recalled that, "The single most important task, which I set out in my inaugural address in December 1962, was that of building a united nation on the basis of human equality and dignity;" and this he reinforced in his socialist concept of *ujamaa*. And for Ian Khama, it formed a part of the 5 Ds Roadmap: Democracy, Discipline, Dignity, Development & Delivery.

In spite of the broad African recognition of the importance of dignity by some governments, there are places in Africa where dignity is often violated and places where governments do not do enough to protect human dignity and ensure it is taken seriously. Occasionally governments in Africa use references to duties in the African Charter on Human and Peoples' Rights as a pretext for not protecting human rights including human dignity.

8. Religious and theistic foundations. African understandings of human dignity are usually based upon a belief in God, a creator who made human beings in God's image. As such, there is an element of reverence and a dimension of humility in understanding human dignity. The idea of human dignity implicates relationships beyond those in this life, including with our creator, and with our ancestors who live in an afterlife beyond the visible world. Thus dignity implicates our treatment of the dead. Dignity implicates the departed as well, recognizing that belonging and being recognized does not just involve the present.

In some parts of Africa, understandings of dignity are inextricably connected to Islam. Muslims in Africa are familiar with the Quranic verse that God honored human beings in creating Adam as God's vice-regent or steward, and that human beings reciprocate this by treating other human beings with dignity. This is evident even in architecture (that is, in the environment), where a room of the house is dedicated to providing hospitality to strangers. This has implications for how we should treat all people, including beggars. While from a Muslim perspective, human rights may seem like a foreign concept, the concept of human dignity is not foreign, but an accepted and intrinsic part of the Muslim faith.

Christian and indigenous religions also have deep and meaningful teachings about human dignity, and each of these perspectives adds depth and flavor to an African understanding of dignity.

In spite of deep reservoirs of reverence and a sense of the sacred that infuse African understandings of dignity, it is not an exclusively religious concept; it is meaningfully significant to those who have no religious beliefs but who are morally righteous and scrupulous.

9. Gender/age dimensions. There may be gender dimensions in discussions of dignity that must be noticed. If dignity is understood primarily as a matter of status (the dignity of the King or of tribal elders), it can have a gender dimension that distorts the universal and inherent value of all human beings that is the hallmark of dignity. We also caution that dignity should not be comprehended mainly as a matter of age, where the dignity of the elder is opposed to that of the young.

Human dignity has deep implications for relationships involving gender difference and age groups, including domestic violence, which is an affront to dignity. If, for example, a man disrespects the woman or the young girl-child acts impolitely towards an elderly person then that person is described as someone who has no ***utu***.

10. Human dignity and our environments. This conference has focused on the relationships between law, religion, and the environment in Africa. An important recurring theme has been the relational character of human rights and human dignity, and that it implicates and impresses upon all of our relationships, not just with other people, but with other animals and with our natural environments. Just as concepts like isiXhosa's ***ubunt***, Shona's ***unhu*** and Kiswahili's ***utu*** extend concern for human beings beyond rights and into relationships, they also extend our concern beyond human relationships and into other relationships, such as with God, with the world, and the various environments in which we live.

Bibliography

Books

Richard Amesbury and George M. Newlands, *Faith and Human Rights: Christianity and the Global Struggle for Human Dignity* (Fortress Press, 2008).

Robert Audi, *Religious Commitment and Secular Reason* (Cambridge University Press: Cambridge, 2000).

John Austin (Robert Campbell, ed.), *Lectures on Jurisprudence, or The Philosophy of Positive Law* (John Murray: London, 1885).

Aharon Barak, *Human Dignity: The Constitutional Value and the Constitutional Right* (Cambridge University Press, 2015).

Gaymon Bennett, *Technicians of Human Dignity: Bodies, Souls, and the Making of Intrinsic Worth* (Fordham University Press, 2016).

Karel Blei, *Freedom of Religion and Belief: Europe's Story* (Van Gorcum Ltd, 2002).

Sabine C. Carey, Mark Gibney, and Steven C. Poe, *The Politics of Human Dignity. The Quest for Human Dignity* (Cambridge University Press, 2010).

Andrew Clapham, *Human Rights Obligations of Non-State Actors* (Oxford University Press: Oxford, 2006).

Dennis Edward Curtis and Judith Resnik, *Representing Justice: Invention, Controversy, and Rights in City-states and Democratic Courtrooms* (Yale University Press, 2011).

Erica-Irene Daes, *Freedom of the Individual Under Law: A Study on the Individual's Duties to the Community and the Limitations on Human Rights and Freedoms under Article 29 of the Universal Declaration of Human Rights (E/CN.4/Sub.2/432/Add.1)* (United Nations, 1980).

Erin Daly, *Dignity Rights: Courts, Constitutions, and the Worth of the Human Person* (University of Pennsylvania Press, 2013).

Robert F. Drinan, *The Mobilization of Shame: A World View of Human Rights* (Yale University Press: New Haven, CT, 2001).

W. Cole Durham and Brett G. Scharffs, *Law and Religion: National, International, and Comparative Perspectives* (Wolters Kluwer: New York, 2019).

Ronald Dworkin, *Law's Empire* (HarperCollins, 1988).

Dorothy Harley Eber, *Images of Justice* (McGill-Queen's University Press, 1997).

Christoph Enders, *Die Menschenwürde in der Verfassungsordnung. Zur Dogmatik des Art. 1 GG* (Mohr Siebeck: Tübingen, 1997).

Amitai Etzioni, *The Spirit of Community: Rights, Responsibilities and the Communitarian Agenda* (Touchstone: New York, 1995).

Pablo Gilabert, *Human Dignity and Human Rights* (Oxford University Press: Oxford, 2018).

Mary Ann Glendon, *A World Made New: Eleanor Roosevelt and the Universal Declaration of Human Rights* (Random House: New York, 2001).

Mary Ann Glendon, *Rights Talk: The Impoverishment of Political Discourse* (Simon & Schuster: New York, 1991).

Jonathan Glover, *Humanity: A Moral History of the Twentieth Century* (Yale University Press: New Haven, CT, 1999).

Ronald H. Graveson, *Status in the Common Law* (Athlone Press: London, 1953).

Louis Henkin, *The Age of Rights* (Columbia University Press: New York, 1990).

Stephen J. Heyman, *Free Speech and Human Dignity* (Yale University Press: New Haven, CT, 2008).

Douglas Hodgson, *Individual Duty within a Human Rights Discourse* (Ashgate Publishing, 2003).

M. Glen Johnson and Janusz Symonides, *The Universal Declaration of Human Rights: A History of Its Creation and Implementation 1948–1998* (UNESCO, 1998).

Mohammad Hashim Kamali, *The Dignity of Man: An Islamic Perspective* (The Islamic Texts Society: Cambridge, 2002).

Immanuel Kant (Paul Guyer and Allen W. Wood, eds.), *Practical Philosophy* (Cambridge University Press: New York, 1999).

Immanuel Kant (Mary Gregor, trans. and ed.), *The Metaphysics of Morals. Metaphysical First Principles of the Doctrine of Virtue* (Cambridge University Press, 1996).

Immanuel Kant (Thomas E. Hill, Jr. and Arnulf Zweig, eds.), *Groundwork for the Metaphysics of Morals* (Oxford University Press, 2002).

George Kateb, *Human Dignity* (Harvard University Press, 2011).

Hans Kelsen (Max Knight, trans.), *Pure Theory of Law* (The Law Book Exchange: New York, 1967).

Martti Koskenniemi, *Fragmentation of International Law: Difficulties Arising from the Diversification and Expansion of International Law* (International Law Commission, Study Group on Fragmentation, 2006).

David Kretzmer and Eckart Klein, *The Concept of Human Dignity in Human Rights Discourse* (Brill, 2002).

Jacqueline Langwith (ed.), *Human Rights* (Greenhaven Press: Detroit, MI, 2008).

Joseph P. Lash, *Eleanor Roosevelt: A Friend's Memoir* (Doubleday, 1964).

Liora Lazarus, Benjamin Goold, Rajendra Desai and Qudsi Rasheed, *The Relationship between Rights and Responsibilities* (Ministry of Justice Research Series, 2009).

Stephen J. Lee, *Hitler and Nazi Germany* (Routledge: London, 2000).

Robert J. Lifton, *The Nazi Doctors: Medical Killing and the Psychology of Genocide* (Basic Books, 1986).

David Luban, *Legal Ethics and Human Dignity* (Cambridge University Press, 2007).

Douglas MacArthur (Vorin E. Whan, Jr., ed.), *A Soldier Speaks: Public Papers and Speeches of General of the Army Douglas MacArthur* (Praeger, 1965).

Alasdair MacIntyre, *After Virtue: A Study in Moral Theory* (University of Notre Dame Press: Notre Dame, IN, 2007).

Jacques Maritain, *Man and the State* (Catholic University of America Press, 1998).

Ann Elizabeth Mayer, *Islam and Human Rights: Tradition and Politics* (Routledge, 1999).

Fred D. Miller, Jr., *Nature, Justice and Rights in Aristotle's 'Politics'* (Oxford University Press, 1997).

Glenn Mitoma, *Human Rights and the Negotiation of American Power* (University of Pennsylvania Press, 2013).

Johannes Morsink, *Inherent Human Rights: Philosophical Roots of the Universal Declaration* (University of Pennsylvania Press: Philadelphia, 2009).

Johannes Morsink, *The Universal Declaration of Human Rights and the Challenge of Religion* (University of Missouri Press: Columbia, MO, 2017).

Johannes Morsink, *The Universal Declaration of Human Rights: Origins, Drafting, and Intent* (University of Pennsylvania Press, 1999).

Chandra Muzaffar, *Rights, Religion and Reform: Enhancing Human Dignity through Spiritual and Moral Transformation* (Routledge, 2002).

Roger Normand and Sarah Zaidi, *Human Rights at the U.N.: The Political History of Universal Justice* (Indiana University Press, 2008).

Robert Nozick, *Anarchy, State and Utopia* (Basic Books: New York, 1974).

Raimundo Panikkar and Arvind Sharma, *Human Rights as a Western Concept?* (DK Print World, 2007).

Jean H. Quataert, *Advocating Dignity: Human Rights Mobilizations in Global Politics* (University of Pennsylvania Press, 2009).

John Rawls, *A Theory of Justice* (Harvard University Press: Cambridge, MA, 1971).

John Rawls, *Political Liberalism* (Columbia University Press: New York, 1993).

Alison Dundes Renteln, *International Human Rights: Universalism versus Relativism* (Sage: Newbury Park, CA, 1990).

Eleanor Roosevelt, *The Autobiography of Eleanor Roosevelt* (Da Capo Press, 1958).

Michael Rosen, *Dignity: Its History and Meaning* (Harvard University Press: 2012).

William D. Ross (Philip Stratton-Lake, ed.), *The Right and the Good* (Clarendon Press: Oxford, 2007).

Hans Ingvar Roth, *P. C. Chang and the Universal Declaration of Human Rights* (University of Pennsylvania Press, 2018).

Rudolph J. Rummel, *Lethal Politics: Soviet Genocide and Mass Murder Since 1917* (Routledge, 1990).

William A. Schabas, *The Abolition of the Death Penalty in International Law* (Cambridge University Press, 2009).

William Schabas, *The Universal Declaration of Human Rights. Thetravaux Préparatoires.* (Cambridge University Press: Cambridge, 2013).

David Selbourne, *The Principle of Duty: An Essay on the Foundations of the Civic Order* (Sinclair-Stevenson: London, 1994).

Arvind Sharma, *Hinduism and Human Rights: A Conceptual Approach* (Oxford University Press, 2004).

Pinghua Sun, *Historic Achievement of a Common Standard: Pengchun Chang and the Universal Declaration of Human Rights* (Springer: Singapore, 2018).

Jeremy Waldron (Meir Dan-Cohen, ed.), *Dignity, Rank and Rights. The Tanner Lectures on Human Values* (Oxford University Press: New York, 2012).

Marjorie M. Whiteman, *Digest of International Law*, Volume 5 (Dept. of State Publication 7873: Washington, DC, 1965).

Jay Winter and Antoine Prost, *René Cassin and Human Rights: From the Great War to the Universal Declaration* (Cambridge University Press: Cambridge, 2013).

B. Wisner and J. Adams, *Environmental Health in Emergencies and Disasters: A Practical Guide* (WHO, 2002).

John Witte, Jr. and M. Christian Green (eds.), *Religion and Human Rights: An Introduction* (Oxford University Press, 2011).

Contributions and chapters in books

J. Stuart Adams, 'Cultivating Common Ground' in William N. Eskridge, Jr. and Robin Fretwell Wilson (eds.), *Religious Freedom, LGBT Rights, and the Prospects for Common Ground* (Cambridge University Press, 2019).

Pentti Arajärvi, 'Article 26' in Gudmundur S. Alfdredsson and Asbjørn Eide (eds.), *The Universal Declaration of Human Rights* (Martinus Nijhoff, 1999).

Yehoshua Arieli, 'On the Necessary and Sufficient Conditions for the Emergence of the Doctrine of the Dignity of Man and His Rights' in David Kretzmer and Eckart Klein, *The Concept of Human Dignity in Human Rights Discourse* (Brill, 2002).

Aharon Barak, 'The Constitutional Value and the Constitutional Right' in Christopher McCrudden (ed.), *Understanding Human Dignity* (Oxford University Press: Oxford, 2013).

Tina Beattie, 'The Vanishing Absolute and the Deconsecrated God: A Theological Reflection on Revelation, Law, and Human Dignity' in Christopher McCrudden (ed.), *Understanding Human Dignity* (Oxford University Press: Oxford, 2013).

Lynda S. Bell, Andrew J. Nathan and Ilan Peleg, 'Introduction: Culture and Rights' in Lynda S. Bell, Andrew J. Nathan and Ilan Peleg (eds.), *Negotiating Culture and Human Rights* (Columbia University Press: New York, 2001).

Nancy Berlinger, 'Conscience Clauses, Health Care Providers, and Parents' in Mary Crowley (ed.), *From Birth to Death and Bench to Clinic: The Hastings Center Bioethics Briefing Book for Journalists, Policymakers, and Campaigns* (The Hastings Center: Garrison, NY, 2008).

Roger Brownsword, 'Human Dignity from a Legal Perspective' in Marcus Düwell, Jens Braarvig, Roger Brownsword and Dietmar Mieth (eds.), *The Cambridge Handbook of Human Dignity: Interdisciplinary Perspectives* (Cambridge University Press, 2014).

Christian Byk, 'Is Human Dignity a Useless Concept? Legal Perspectives' in Marcus Düwell, Jens Braarvig, Roger Brownsword and Dietmar Mieth (eds.), *The Cambridge Handbook of Human Dignity: Interdisciplinary Perspectives* (Cambridge University Press, 2014).

Edwin Cameron, 'Moral Citizenship and Constitutional Protection' in Christopher McCrudden (ed.), *Understanding Human Dignity* (Oxford University Press: Oxford, 2013).

Hubert Cancik, '"Dignity of Man" and "Persona" in Stoic Anthropology: Some Remarks on Cicero, *De Officiis I*' in David Kretzmer and Eckart Klein, *The Concept of Human Dignity in Human Rights Discourse* (Kluwer Law International: The Hague, 2002).

Paolo G. Carozza, 'Human Rights, Human Dignity, and Human Experience' in Christopher McCrudden (ed.), *Understanding Human Dignity* (Oxford University Press: Oxford, 2013).

Andrew Clapham, 'Issues of Complexity, Complicity and Complementarity: From the Nuremberg Trials to the Dawn of the New International Criminal Court' in Philippe Sands, *From Nuremberg to the Hague: The Future of International Criminal Justice* (Cambridge University Press: Cambridge, 2003).

Horst Dreier, 'Human Dignity in German Law' in Marcus Düwell, Jens Braarvig, Roger Brownsword and Dietmar Mieth (eds.), *The Cambridge Handbook of Human Dignity: Interdisciplinary Perspectives* (Cambridge University Press, 2014).

Catherine Dupré, 'Constructing the Meaning of Human Dignity' in Christopher McCrudden (ed.), *Understanding Human Dignity* (Oxford University Press: Oxford, 2013).

Marcus Düwell, 'Concepts, Discussions, Philosophical Perspectives' in Marcus Düwell, Jens Braarvig, Roger Brownsword and Dietmar Mieth (eds.), *The Cambridge Handbook of Human Dignity: Interdisciplinary Perspectives* (Cambridge University Press, 2014).

Asbjørn Eide, 'Article 28' in Gudmundur S. Alfdredsson and Asbjørn Eide (eds.), *The Universal Declaration of Human Rights* (Martinus Nijhoff, 1999).

Asbjørn Eide and Gudmundur Alfredsson, 'Introduction' in Gudmundur S. Alfdredsson and Asbjørn Eide (eds.), *The Universal Declaration of Human Rights* (Martinus Nijhoff, 1999).

Anton Fagan, 'Human Dignity in South African Law' in Marcus Düwell, Jens Braarvig, Roger Brownsword and Dietmar Mieth (eds.), *The Cambridge Handbook of Human Dignity: Interdisciplinary Perspectives* (Cambridge University Press, 2014).

Robin Fretwell Wilson, 'The Politics of Accommodation. The American Experience with Same-sex Marriage and Religious Freedom' in Timothy Shah, Thomas Farr and Jack Friedman (eds.), *Religious Freedom and Gay Rights: Emerging Conflicts in the United States and Europe* (Oxford University Press: New York, 2016).

Bas de Gaay Fortman, 'Equal Dignity in International Human Rights' in Marcus Düwell, Jens Braarvig, Roger Brownsword and Dietmar Mieth (eds.), *The Cambridge Handbook of Human Dignity: Interdisciplinary Perspectives* (Cambridge University Press, 2014).

Robert P. George, 'Response to Tollefsen and Cameron' in Christopher McCrudden (ed.), *Understanding Human Dignity* (Oxford University Press: Oxford, 2013).

Christoph Goos, 'Restoring Human Dignity in Post-Nazi Germany' in Christopher McCrudden (ed.), *Understanding Human Dignity* (Oxford University Press: Oxford, 2013).

Dieter Grimm, 'Dignity in a Legal Context and as an Absolute Right' in Christopher McCrudden (ed.), *Understanding Human Dignity* (Oxford University Press: Oxford, 2013).

Paul Groarke and J. L. A. West, 'Individual Rights and the Common Good' in William Sweet (ed.), *Philosophical Theory and the Universal Declaration of Human Rights* (University of Ottawa Press, 2003).

David P. Gushee, 'A Christian Theological Account of Human Worth' in Christopher McCrudden (ed.), *Understanding Human Dignity* (Oxford University Press: Oxford, 2013).

James Hanvey, 'Dignity, Person, and Imago Trinitatis' in Christopher McCrudden (ed.), *Understanding Human Dignity* (Oxford University Press: Oxford, 2013).

Louis Henkin, 'Human Rights: Ideology and Aspiration, Reality, and Prospect' in Samantha Power and Graham Allison (eds.), *Realizing Human Rights: Moving from Inspiration to Impact* (St. Martin's Press: New York, 2000).

Thomas E. Hill, Jr., 'In Defence of Human Dignity: Comments on Kant and Rosen' in Christopher McCrudden (ed.), *Understanding Human Dignity* (Oxford University Press: Oxford, 2013).

David Hollenbach, 'Experience and History, Practical Reason and Faith' in Christopher McCrudden (ed.), *Understanding Human Dignity* (Oxford University Press: Oxford, 2013).

Nihal Jayawickrama, 'Hong Kong and the International Protection of Human Rights' in Raymond Wicks (ed.), *Human Rights in Hong Kong* (Oxford University Press: Hong Kong, 1992).

David A. Jones, 'Dignity Language in Bioethical Discussions' in Christopher McCrudden (ed.), *Understanding Human Dignity* (Oxford University Press: Oxford, 2013).

Sallie B. King, 'Buddhism and Human Rights' in John Witte, Jr. and M. Christian Green (eds.), *Religion and Human Rights: An Introduction* (Oxford University Press, 2011).

Eckart Klein, 'Should the Binding Effect of the Judgments of the ECtHR be Extended?' in P. Mahoney *et al.* (eds.), *Protecting Human Rights: The European Perspective* (Carl Heymannns: Cologne, 2000).

Aurel Kolnai, 'Dignity' in Robin S. Dillon (ed.), *Dignity, Character, and Self-Respect* (Routledge, 1995).

Martti Koskenniemi, 'Preamble of the Universal Declaration of Human Rights' in Gudmundur S. Alfdredsson and Asbjørn Eide (eds.), *The Universal Declaration of Human Rights* (Martinus Nijhoff, 1999).

H. Kuhse, 'Is There a Tension Between Autonomy and Dignity?' in P. Kemp *et al.* (eds.), *Bioethics and Biolaw* (Rhodos International Science and Art Publishers: Copenhagen, 2000).

H. Lauterpacht, 'The Law of Nations and the Punishment of War Crimes' in Guenael Mettraux (ed.), *Perspectives on the Nuremberg Trial* (Oxford University Press: New York, 2010).

Michael O. Leavitt, 'Shared Spaces and Brave Gambles' in William N. Eskridge, Jr. and Robin Fretwell Wilson (eds.), *Religious Freedom, LGBT Rights, and the Prospects for Common Ground* (Cambridge University Press, 2019).

Joy Liddicoat, 'Dignity Online and Offline' in Edward Sieh and Judy McGregor (eds.), *Human Dignity: Establishing Worth and Seeking Solutions* (Palgrave Macmillan, 2017).

Tore Lindholm, 'Article 1' in Gudmundur Alfredsson and Asbjørn Eide (eds.), *The Universal Declaration of Human Rights: A Common Standard of Achievement* (Martinus Nijhoff, 1999).

Tore Lindholm, 'Philosophical and Religious Justification of Freedom of Religion or Belief' in Tore Lindholm, W. Cole Durham and Bahia Tahzib-Lie (eds.), *Facilitating Freedom of Religion or Belief: A Deskbook* (Martinus Nijhoff, 2004).

David Luban, 'Human Rights Pragmatism and Human Dignity' in Rowan Cruft, S. Matthew Liao and Massimo Renzo (eds.), *Philosophical Foundations of Human Rights* (Oxford University Press: Oxford, 2005).

Christopher McCrudden, 'In Pursuit of Human Dignity: An Introduction to Current Debates' in Christopher McCrudden (ed.), *Understanding Human Dignity* (Oxford University Press: Oxford, 2013).

Jakob Th. Möller, 'The Universal Declaration of Human Rights: How the Process Started' in Gudmundur S. Alfdredsson and Asbjørn Eide (eds.), *The Universal Declaration of Human Rights* (Martinus Nijhoff, 1999).

Benno Muller-Hill, 'Eugenics: The Science and Religion of the Nazis' in Arthur L. Caplan (ed.), *When Medicine Went Mad: Bioethics and the Holocaust* (Springer Science & Business Media: New York, 1992).

Bradley R. Munro, 'The Universal Declaration of Human Rights, Maritain, and the Universality of Human Rights' in William Sweet (ed.), *Philosophical Theory and the Universal Declaration of Human Rights* (University of Ottawa Press, 2003).

Gerald L. Neuman, 'Discourses of Dignity' in Christopher McCrudden (ed.), *Understanding Human Dignity* (Oxford University Press: Oxford, 2013).

Mary E. O'Connell, 'Peace and War' in Bardo Fassbender and Anne Peters (eds.), *The Oxford Handbook of the History of International Law* (Oxford University Press: Oxford, 2012).

Adamantia Pollis and Peter Schwab, 'Human Rights: A Western Construct with Limited Applicability' in Christine M. Koggle (ed.), *Moral and Political Theory* (Broadview Press, 2006).

Francisco O. Ramírez, David Suárez and John W. Meyer, 'The Worldwide Rise of Human Rights Education' in A. Benavot and C. Braslavsky (eds.), *Comparative and Historical Perspective* (Springer Science & Business Media, 2007).

Johannes Rau, 'Foreword by the Federal President' in *Basic Law for the Federal Republic of Germany* (Bundestag: Berlin, 2000).

Denise Réaume, 'Dignity, Choice and Circumstances' in Christopher McCrudden (ed.), *Understanding Human Dignity* (Oxford University Press: Oxford, 2013).

Eleanor Roosevelt, 'On the Adoption of the Universal Declaration of Human Rights' in James Daley (ed.), *Great Speeches by American Women* (Dover: Mineola, NY, 2008).

Michael Rosen, 'Dignity: The Case Against' in Christopher McCrudden (ed.), *Understanding Human Dignity* (Oxford University Press: Oxford, 2013).

Åshild Samnøy, 'The Origins of the Universal Declaration of Human Rights' in Gudmundur S. Alfdredsson and Asbjørn Eide (eds.), *The Universal Declaration of Human Rights* (Martinus Nijhoff, 1999).

Bernhard Schlink, 'The Concept of Human Dignity: Current Usages, Future Discourses' in Christopher McCrudden (ed.), *Understanding Human Dignity* (Oxford University Press: Oxford, 2013).

Elizabeth S. Scott and Ben Chen, 'Fiduciary Principles in Family Law' in Evan Criddle, Paul Miller and Robert Sitkoff (eds.), *Oxford Handbook of Fiduciary Law* (Oxford University Press, 2019).

Janet Soskice, 'Human Dignity and the Image of God' in Christopher McCrudden (ed.), *Understanding Human Dignity* (Oxford University Press: Oxford, 2013).

Martha Tarasco, 'Hinduism and Human Rights' in Joseph Tham *et al.* (eds.), *Religious Perspectives on Bioethics and Human Rights* (Springer: New York, 2017).

John Tasioulas, 'Human Dignity and the Foundations of Human Rights' in Christopher McCrudden (ed.), *Understanding Human Dignity* (Oxford University Press: Oxford, 2013).

Christopher Tollefsen, 'The Dignity of Marriage' in Christopher McCrudden (ed.), *Understanding Human Dignity* (Oxford University Press: Oxford, 2013).

Jeremy Waldron, 'Citizenship and Dignity' in Christopher McCrudden (ed.), *Understanding Human Dignity* (Oxford University Press: Oxford, 2013).

Jeremy Waldron, 'The War on Terror and the Image of God' in John Witte Jr., and Frank S. Alexander (eds.), *Christianity and Human Rights: An Introduction* (Cambridge University Press, 2010).

David Walsh, 'Dignity as an Eschatological Concept' in Christopher McCrudden (ed.), *Understanding Human Dignity* (Oxford University Press: Oxford, 2013).

Micha Werner, 'Individual and Collective Dignity' in Marcus Düwell, Jens Braarvig, Roger Brownsword and Dietmar Mieth (eds.), *The Cambridge Handbook of Human Dignity: Interdisciplinary Perspectives* (Cambridge University Press, 2014).

Journals

Rebecca Adami, 'Intersectional Dialogue: Analyzing Power in Reaching a Universal Declaration of Human Rights in 1948 on Conflicting Grounds' (2018) 17 *Journal of Human Rights* 357–366.

Reza Afshari, 'An Essay on Islamic Cultural Relativism in the Discourse of Human Rights' (1994) 16 *Human Rights Quarterly* 235, 250.

Allen Buchanan, 'Human Rights and the Legitimacy of the International Order' (2008) *Legal Theory* 41.

Grainne de Búrca, 'After the EU Charter of Fundamental Rights: The Court of Justice as a Human Rights Adjudicator?' (2013) 20 *Maastricht Journal of European and Comparative Law* 168–184.

Arthur Chaskalson, 'Human Dignity as a Foundational Value of Our Constitutional Order' (2000) 16 *South African Journal on Human Rights* 196.

Catherine Cisse, 'The International Tribunals for the Former Yugoslavia and Rwanda: Some Elements of Comparison' (1997) 7 *Transnational Law and Contemporary Problems* 103.

Richard Pierre Claude, 'The Right to Education and Human Rights Education' (2005) 2 *Revista Internacional de Direitos Humanos* 36, 63.

Joshua Cohen, 'Minimalism about Human Rights: The Most We Can Hope for?' (2004) 12 *Journal of Political Philosophy* 190–213.

Jeremy Davies, 'The Fire-Raisers: Bentham and Torture' (2012) 19 *Interdisciplinary Studies in the Long Nineteenth Century* 15.

Remy Debes, 'Review of Dignity, Rank, and Rights' (2013) *Notre Dame Philosophical Reviews.*

Surya Deva, 'Guiding Principles on Business and Human Rights: Implications for Companies' (2012) 9 *European Company Law* 106.

Jack Donnelly, 'Human Rights and Human Dignity: An Analytic Critique of Non-Western Conceptions of Human Rights' (1982) 76 *American Political Science Review* 303.

Edward J. Eberle, 'Observations on the Development of Human Dignity and Personality in German Constitutional Law: An Overview' (2012) 33 *Liverpool Law Review* 206.

David Estlund, 'Jeremy Waldron on Law and Disagreement' (2000) 99 *Philosophical Studies* 117.

George P. Fletcher, 'Human Dignity as a Constitutional Value' (1984) 22 *University of Western Ontario Law Review* 171.

Stuart Ford, 'Complexity and Efficiency at International Criminal Courts' (2014) 29 *Emory International Law Review.*

Michael A. Fragoso, 'Taking Conscience Seriously or Seriously Taking Conscience: Obstetricians, Specialty Boards, and the Takings Clause' (2011) 86 *Notre Dame Law Review* 1687.

Francis Fukuyama, 'Asian Values and the Asian crisis' (1998) 105 *Commentary*, 2: 23–27.

W. B. Gallie, 'Essentially Contested Concepts' (1956) *Proceedings of the Aristotelian Society* 167.

Mary Ann Glendon, 'The Rule of Law in the Universal Declaration of Human Rights' (2004) 2 *Northwestern University Journal of International Human Rights* 1.

Erin E. Goodsell, 'Constitution, Custom, and Creed: Balancing Human Rights Concerns with Cultural and Religious Freedom in Today's South Africa' (2007) 21 *BYU Journal of Public Law* 111.

Kent Greenwalt, 'On Public Reason' (1994) 69 *Chicago Kent Law Review* 673.

Emilie M. Hafner-Burton and Kiyoteru Tsutsui, 'Human Rights in a Globalizing World: The Paradox of Empty Promises' (2005) 110 *American Journal of Sociology* 1373.

Hurst Hannum, 'The UDHR in National and International Law' (1995) *Health and Human Rights* 151.

Hurst Hannum, 'The Status of the Universal Declaration of Human Rights in National and International Law' (1998) 3 *Health and Human Rights* 145.

Walter Kasper, 'The Theological Foundations of Human Rights' (1990) 50 *The Jurist* 148.

J. Paul Kelleher, 'Emergency Contraception and Conscientious Objection' (2010) 27 *Journal of Applied Philosophy* 290.

John H. Knox, 'Horizontal Human Rights Law' (2008) 102 *American Journal of International Law.*

Robert Kolb, 'The Relationship between International Humanitarian Law and Human Rights Law: A Brief History of the 1948 Universal Declaration of Human Rights and the 1949 Geneva Conventions' (1998) 324 *International Review of the Red Cross* 409.

Aurel Kolnai, 'Dignity' (1976) 51 *Philosophy* 251.

Tineke Lambooy, 'Corporate Due Diligence as a Tool to Respect Human Rights' (2010) 28 *Netherlands Quarterly of Human Rights* 404.

Mette Lebech, 'What Is Human Dignity?' (2006) *Maynooth Philosophical Papers* 59.

Oliver Lepsius, 'Human Dignity and the Downing of Aircraft: The German Federal Constitutional Court Strikes Down a Prominent Anti-terrorism Provision in the New Air-transport Security Act' (2006) 7 *German Law Journal* 9, 768–769.

Lucas Lixinski, 'Choice of Forum in International Human Rights Adjudication and the Unity/Fragmentation Debate: Is Plurality the Way Forward?' (2008) XVIII *Italian Yearbook of International Law* 183–200.

David Luban, 'Liberalism, Torture, and the Ticking Bomb' (2005) 91 *Virginia Law Review* 1425.

Paweł Łuków, 'A Difficult Legacy: Human Dignity as the Founding Value of Human Rights' (2018) 19 *Human Rights Review* 313.

Ruth Macklin, 'Dignity Is a Useless Concept' (2003) 327 *British Medical Journal* 1419–1420.

Marquette Law Review, 'Legal Philosophers: Aristotle, Aquinas and Kant on Human Rights' (1972) 55 *Marquette Law Review* 64.

Christopher McCrudden, 'Human Dignity and Judicial Interpretation of Human Rights' (2008) 19 *European Journal of International Law* 655.

Ben A. McJunkin, 'Rank Among Equals' (2015) *Michigan Law Review* 856.

I. de Melo-Martin, 'Human Dignity in International Policy Documents: A Useful Criterion for Public Policy?' (2011) 25 *Bioethics* 37–45.

Fred D. Miller, Jr., 'Aristotle and the Origins of Natural Rights' (1996) 49 *The Review of Metaphysics* 873.

Office of the Director of National Intelligence, 'Scenarios: Alternative Futures the IC Could Face' (2004) 4 *Quadrennial Intelligence Community Review* 1.

Joakim Öjendal and Hans Antlöv, 'Asian Values and Its Political Consequences: Is Cambodia the First Domino?' (1998) 11 *The Pacific Review* 4: 525–540.

Conor O'Mahony, 'There Is No Such Thing as a Right to Dignity' (2012) 10 *International Journal of Constitutional Law* 551.

Michael Pakaluk, 'Aristotle on Human Rights' (2012) 10 *Ave Maria Law Review* 379.

Jordan J. Paust, 'Human Rights Responsibilities of Private Corporations' (2002) 35 *Vanderbilt Journal of Transnational Law* 813.

Jordan J. Paust, 'The Other Side of Right: Private Duties under Human Rights Law' (1992) 5 *Harvard Human Rights Journal* 51.

Dietmar von de Pfordten, 'On the Dignity of Man in Kant' (2009) 84 *Philosophy* 372.

Benjamin Porat, 'Rights-based Law v. Duty-based Law: Old Dilemma, New Perspective' (2015) Hebrew University of Jerusalem Legal Research Paper No. 16–04.

Eric Posner, 'Some Skeptical Comments on Beth Simmons's Mobilizing for Human Rights' (2012) 44 *New York University Journal of International Law and Politics* 819.

John Rawls, 'The Idea of an Overlapping Consensus' (1987) 7 *Oxford Journal of Legal Studies* 1.

John Rawls, 'The Idea of Public Reason Revisited' (1997) 64 *University of Chicago Law Review* 766.

Denise G. Réaume, 'Discrimination and Dignity' (2003) 63 *Louisiana Law Review* 645.

Ben Saul, 'In the Shadow of Human Rights: Human Duties, Obligations and Responsibilities' (2000) 32 *Columbia Human Rights Law Review* 566.

Oscar Schacter, 'Editorial Comment: Human Dignity as a Normative Concept' (1983) 77 *American Journal of International Law* 848.

Oscar Schachter, 'Human Dignity as a Normative Concept' (1983) 77 *American Journal of International Law* 848.

Nicholas J. Schilling Jr., 'Analysis of Statutory Religious Accommodations for State-employed Religious Objectors to Same-sex Marriage Solemnization' (2017) 31 *Notre Dame Journal of Law, Ethics and Public Policy* 431.

Perry Schmidt-Leukel, 'Buddhism and the Idea of Human Rights: Resonances and Dissonances' (2006) 26 *Buddhist-Christian Studies* 33.

Dieter Schönecker and Elke E. Schmidt, 'Kant's Ground-Thesis: On Dignity and Value in the Groundwork' (2018) 52 *The Journal of Value Inquiry* 81.

Doron Shultziner, 'A Jewish Conception of Human Dignity. Philosophy and Its Ethical Implications for Israeli Supreme Court Decisions' (2006) 34 *Journal of Religious Ethics* 666.

Robert Mark Simpson, 'Dignity, Harm, and Hate Speech, Law and Philosophy' (2013) 32 *Law and Philosophy* 701.

Paul Sourlas, 'Human Dignity and the Constitution' (2016) 7 *Jurisprudence* 1, 30–46.

Herbert Spiegelberg, 'Human Dignity: A Challenge to Contemporary Philosophy' (1971) 9 *Journal of New Paradigm Research*.

Cass R. Sunstein, 'Commentary: Incompletely Theorized Agreements' (1995) 108 *Harvard Law Review* 1733.

Felisa Tibbets, 'On Human Dignity: The Need for Human Rights Education' (1996) 60 *Social Education* 428.

Jeremy Waldron, 'What Do Philosophers Have against Dignity?' (2014) NYU School of Law, Public Law and Legal Theory Research Paper Series 2014, No. 14-59.

Jeremy Waldron, 'The Image of God: Rights, Reason, and Order' (2010) NYU School of Law, Public Law and Legal Theory Research Paper Series 2010, No. 10-85.

David Wippman, 'The Cost of International Justice' (2006) 100 *American Journal of International Law* 861.

Lee Kuan Yew, 'Asian Values Did Not Cause the Meltdown' (1998) 15 *New Perspectives Quarterly*12: 32–34.

Legislation

International

Additional Protocol to the American Convention on Human Rights in the Area of Economic, Social and Cultural Rights (Protocol of San Salvador) (1988)

African Charter on Human Rights and Peoples' Rights (1981)

African Charter on the Rights and Welfare of the Child (1990)

American Convention on Human Rights (1969)

Convention on the Elimination of All Forms of Discrimination against Women (CEDAW)

Convention against Torture and Other Cruel, Inhuman or Degrading Treatment or Punishment (CAT)

Convention on the Rights of the Child (CRC)

Convention on the Rights of Persons with Disabilities (CRPD)

European Convention for the Protection of Human Rights and Fundamental Freedoms (1950)

European Social Charter (1961)

International Convention on the Elimination of all forms of Racial Discrimination (ICERD)

International Covenant on Civil and Political Rights (ICCPR)

International Covenant on Economic, Social, and Cultural Rights (ICESCR)

International Convention on the Protection of the Rights of All Migrant Workers and Members of Their Families
International Convention for the Protection from Enforced Disappearance (CED)
Protocol to the African Charter on Human and Peoples' Rights on the Rights of Women in Africa (2003)
Revised European Social Charter (1996)
United Nations Declaration on Human Rights Education and Training
Universal Declaration of Human Rights (UDHR)

Domestic

Belgian Penal Code
Cal. Gov't Code §12927(c)(2) (2019)
California Penal Code §3605(c)
Church Amendments 42 U.S.C. §300a-7
Code of Alabama §15–18–82.1(i)
Connecticut Department of Correction Directive Number 6:15.
Free Exercise Clause of the First Amendment to the United States Constitution
Federal Conscience Protection in 18 U.S.C. §3597(b)
German Basic Law
Judges – Marriage – Recusal Act, S.L. 2015–75, 2015 N.C. Sess. Laws 160, 160–163 (West)
Law 194 of the Italian Republic, 1978 (Italy)
Law of 17 December 2014 (Luxemburg)
S.B. 296, 2015 Leg., Gen. Sess. (Utah 2015) (Antidiscrimination and Religious Freedom Amendments, or Utah Compromise)
The Declaration of Independence para. 2 (US 1776)
Title VIII of the Civil Rights Act of 1968 (Fair Housing Act), 42 U.S.C.A. §3602 (2019); 42 U.S.C. §3607(a) (2019); Cal. Gov't Code §12927(c)(2) (2019)
Xinjiang Uyghur Autonomous Region Deradicalization Regulations. Available at: http://www.sohu.com/a/258631718_115479?g=0

Code of Conduct

American Medical Association Code of Medical Ethics
American Medical Association Principles of Medical Ethics (1957)
Code of Conduct for United States Judges, *Canon 3*
New York Lawyers' Code of Professional Responsibility

Cases

Adyan and others v. Armenia
American Federation of Labor v. American Sash and Door Co, 335 US 538 (1949) 542
Aviation Security Act, BVerfG,1 BvR 357/05 (Germany)
Bayatyan v. Armenia
Christian Education in South Africa v.Minister of Education, Case CCT 4/00 (South Africa)
Conseil d'État [CE Ass.] [supreme court of administrative justice], Oct. 27, 1995, *Rec. Lebon* 372

Dawood v. Minister of Home Affairs [2000] 5 Law Reports of the Commonwealth 147, 2000 (3) SA 936 (CC), 35

Eweida and Others v. The UK, 2013-IV Eur. Ct. H.R. 7–10

Fair Hous. Council v. Roommates.com, 521 F.3d 1157 (9th Cir. 2008)

Ghaidan v. Godin-Mendoza [2004] 2 AC (HL) 557, 605

Greater Glasgow Health Board (Appellant) v. Doogan and another (Respondents) (Scotland)

Gütl v. Austria

Hill v. Church of Scientology of Toronto [1995] 2 SCR 1130

Lang v. Austria

Law v. Canada (Minister of Emp't and Immigration) [1999] 1 S.C.R. 497 (Can.)

Lee v. Ashers Baking Company Ltd & Ors [2018] UKSC 49, [55]

Life Imprisonment Case, 45 BVerfGE 187, 227 (1977) (Germany)

Löffelmann v. Austria

Lüth, 7 BVerfGE 198, 205 (1958) (Germany)

Masterpiece Cakeshop v. Colo. Civil Rights Comm'n, 138 S.Ct. 1719, 1745 (2018) (US)

Mephisto, 30 BVerfGE (Germany)

Microcensus Case, BVerfGE 27

Minister of Home Affairs and Another v. Fourie, Case CCT 60/04 (South Africa)

Morr-Fitz, Inc. v. Quinn (Morr-Fitz, Inc. v. Quinn, 2012 IL App (4th) 110398)

Op. Att'y Gen. KP-0025 (2015)

Papavasilakis v. Greece

Patterson v. Walgreen Co., 727 Fed. Appx. 581 (11th Cir. 2018) (US)

Public Committee against Torture in Israel and Palestinian Society for the Protection of Human Rights and the Environment v. The Government of Israel and others [2005] HCJ 769/02 (Israel)

R. v. Butler [1992] 1 SCR 452, 479

R. v. Kapp [2008] 2 S.C.R. 483, 2008 SCC 41 (Canada)

Rosenblatt v. Baer, 383 U.S. 75, 92 (1966)

R.R. v. Poland, no. 27617/04, ECHR 2011

*S. v. Makwanyane*1995 (3) SA 391 (CC) at para. 329 (S. Afr.)

*S. v. Lawrence*1997 (4) SA 1176 (CC) at 128 (S. Afr.)

Savda v. Turkey; Tarhan v. Turkey

Stormans Inc v. John Wiesman, Secretary, Washington State, Department of Health, et al. [2016] 15-862

Tyrer v. United Kingdom, 2 EHRR 1

Online articles

David Brooks, 'In Search of Dignity' (July 6, 2009). *New York Times.*

Ján Figel', 'Freedom of Religion or Belief Is a Litmus Test of Civil and Political Rights' (April 21, 2019). Available at: https://www.janfigel.eu/single-post/2019/04/21/Freedom-of-religion-or-belief-is-a-litmus-test-of-civil-and-political-rights

Ján Figel', 'Freedom of Faith a "Litmus Test" for All Human Rights' (April 28, 2019). Available at: https://europe.upf.org/what-we-do/conferences/ilc/315-2018/vienna-4-2018/session-1/573-freedom-of-faith-a-litmus-test-for-all-human-rights

Mary Ann Glendon and Seth D. Kaplan, 'Renewing Human Rights' (February 2019). *First Things.*

Riffat Hassan, 'Are Human Rights Compatible with Islam? The Issue of the Rights of Women in Muslim Communities'. Available at: https://www.iemed.org/documents/novesrealitats/Strawson/a.pdf

David Littman, 'Universal Human Rights and "Human Rights in Islam"' (1999). *Midstream*.

Hillel Neuer, 'South Africa at the UN: Your Freedom and Mine' (December 9, 2007). *Sunday Times of South Africa*.

Dan Olmstead, 'Did More Russians or Americans Die during WWII?' (September 17, 2018). *The National WWII Museum*.

Fr Michael Perry, Letter to the General Minister of the Order of Friars Minor on the 800th Anniversary of the Encounter between St. Francis and Sultan al-Malik al-Kāmil. Available at: https://ofm.org/blog/letter-of-the-general-minister-on-the-800th-anniversary-of-the-encounter-between-st-francis-and-sultan-al-malik-al-kamil/

Steven Pinker, 'The Stupidity of Dignity' (May 28, 2008). *The New Republic*.

Eric Posner, 'Human Rights Treaties Are Expensive to Follow' (December 28, 2014). *New York Times*.

Eric Posner, 'Human Rights Law Is Too Ambitious and Ambiguous' (December 28, 2014). *New York Times*.

Eric Posner, 'The Case Against Human Rights' (December 4, 2014). *The Guardian*.

Friedrich Schweitzer, 'Human Dignity and Education: A Protestant View'. Available at: https://hts.org.za/index.php/hts/article/view/3436/7806

Gregory Stanton, 'Ten Stages of Genocide'. Available at: http://genocidewatch.net/genocide-2/8-stages-of-genocide/

Yuan Yang, 'Xinjiang Security Crackdown Sparks Han Chinese Exodus' (December 22, 2019). *Financial Times*.

Websites and online resources

Amnesty International, 'Amnesty International's Statute' https://www.amnesty.org/en/about-us/how-were-run/amnesty-internationals-statute/

Amnesty International, *Amnesty International Report 2017/18: The State of the World's Human Rights*' (2018). Available at: https://www.amnesty.org/download/Documents/pol1067002018english.pdf

Amnesty International, 'What We Do' https://www.amnesty.org/en/what-we-do/

Human Rights Watch, 'About Us' https://www.hrw.org/about-us

Human Rights Watch, *World Report 2019* https://www.hrw.org/sites/default/files/world_report_download/hrw_world_report_2019.pdf

International Federation of Red Cross and Red Crescent Societies https://www.ifrc.org/en/what-we-do/disaster-management/about-disasters/what-is-a-disaster/what-is-vulnerability/

'Nazi Euthanasia Program: Persecution of the Mentally and Physically Disabled'. Available at: https://www.jewishvirtuallibrary.org/jsource/Holocaust/disabled.html

Pew Research Center, 'A Closer Look at How Religious Restrictions Have Risen Around the World' (Jul. 15, 2019) *Pew Forum: Religion*. Available at: https://www.pewforum.org/2019/07/15/a-closer-look-at-how-religious-restrictions-have-risen-around-the-world/

'Testimony of Dr Richard von Hegener, Ludwigsburg Archive'. Available at: http://deathcamps.org/euthanasia/t4intro.html

'The Bosnian War and the Srebrenica Genocide' http://endgenocide.org/learn/past-genocides/the-bosnian-war-and-srebrenica-genocide/

'The Cambodian Genocide', http://endgenocide.org/learn/past-genocides/the-cambodian-genocide/

The Holocaust Chronicle, 'Total Deaths from Nazi Genocidal Policies'. Available at: www.holocaustchronicle.org/holocaustappendices.html

'The Rwandan Genocide', http://endgenocide.org/learn/past-genocides/the-rwandan-genocide/

'The Situation in Darfur', http://endgenocide.org/conflict-areas/sudan-backgrounder/

United Nations, 'Growth in United Nations Membership, 1945–Present' https://www.un.org/en/sections/member-states/growth-united-nations-membership-1945-present/index.html

United Nations Office for Disaster Risk Reduction https://www.unisdr.org/we/inform/terminology

UN OHCHR, 'What Are Human Rights?' https://www.ohchr.org/EN/Issues/Pages/WhatareHumanRights.aspx

UN Secretary General, 'Education Greatest Tool to Enhancing Human Dignity, Building Lasting Peace, Secretary-General Says in Message for International Day of Non-Violence'. U.N. Press Release SG/SM/16224-OBV/1380 (Sept. 29, 2014). Available at: https://www.un.org/press/en/2014/sgsm16224.doc.htm

World Health Organization, '2.1 Billion People Lack Safe Drinking Water at Home, More than Twice as Many Lack Safe Sanitation' (July 12, 2017). Available at: https://www.who.int/news-room/detail/12-07-2017-2-1-billion-people-lack-safe-drinking-water-at-home-more-than-twice-as-many-lack-safe-sanitation

Lectures, speeches, etc

John Von Doussa QC, *Incorporating Human Rights Principles into National Security Measures* (Oct. 16–17, 2007), International Conference on Terrorism, Human Security and Development: Human Rights Perspectives, City University of Hong Kong.

Rt. Hon. Lord Falconer, 'The Role of Judges in a Modern Democracy' (Sep. 13, 2006) The Magna Carta Lecture, Sydney.

Eleanor Roosevelt, 'The Great Question' (March 27, 1958) United Nations, New York.

Eleanor Roosevelt, Statements at presentation of In Your Hands: A Guide for Community Action for the Tenth Anniversary of the Universal Declaration of Human Rights (1958).

Michael Rosen, 'Replies to Jeremy Waldron: Dignity, Rank and Rights' (April 21–23, 2009) Tanner Lectures, Berkeley, CA.

UN Records

Summary record of the 65th meeting, 3rd Committee, held on Friday, 7 December 1984, *New York*, General Assembly, 39th session. UN Doc. A/C.3/39/SR.65.

Summary Record of the Ninety-Sixth Meeting for the Third Comm., U.N. Doc. A/C.3/SR.96 (Oct. 7, 1948).

Summary Record of the Ninety-Eighth Meeting for the Third Comm., U.N. Doc. A/C.3/SR.98 (Oct. 9, 1948).

United Nations, Charter of the United Nations, 24 October 1945, 1 UNTS XVI.

United Nations. 'Guiding Principles on Business and Human Rights: Implementing the United Nations "Protect, Respect and Remedy" Framework'. 2011.

UNCHR: 'The UN Refugee Agency, Missing Out: Refugee Education in Crisis' (Sept. 2006), https://www.unhcr.org/57d9d01d0

UN Compilation of General Comments and General Recommendations Adopted by Human Rights Treaty Bodies, U.N. Doc. HRI/GEN/1/Rev.9 (Vol. I), at 71, 77 (May 27, 2008).

UNESCO, 'Education and Disability: Analysis of Data from 49 Countries', Information Paper No. 49 (March 2018), http://uis.unesco.org/sites/default/files/documents/ip49-education-disability-2018-en.pdf

UNESCO, Fact Sheet No. 48 UIS/FS/2018/ED/48 (Feb. 2018), http://uis.unesco.org/sites/default/files/documents/fs48-one-five-children-adolescents-youth-out-school-2018-en.pdf

UNESCO, 4th General Conference, November 1949.

UN Human Rights Council, Human Rights and Transnational Corporations and other Business Enterprises, 16 June 2011, A/HRC/17/4.

UN General Assembly, Basic Principles for the Treatment of Prisoners: Resolution Adopted by the General Assembly, 28 March 1991, A/RES/45/111.

UN General Assembly, Vienna Declaration and Programme of Action, 12 July 1993, A/CONF.157/23.

Other international documents

Council of Europe, Committee of Ministers, Charter on Education for Democratic Citizenship and Human Rights Education. Available at: https://search.coe.int/cm/Pages/result_details.aspx?ObjectID=09000016805cf01f

Council of Europe, Committee of Ministers, Recommendation No. R(85)7. Available at: https://rm.coe.int/16804c2d48

The Congressional Globe, 39th Cong., 1st Sess. 111 (1865).

Film

Neil Halloran, *The Fallen of World War II*. Available at: http://www.fallen.io/ww2/

Index

Note: Page numbers followed by "n" denote footnotes.

Adams, J. Stuart 214n3
Adyan and others v. Armenia 144n45
Aerial Security Act 197
African Charter on Human and Peoples' Rights 23, 245
African conceptions of human dignity 242–243
African Consortium of Law and Religious Studies 26
African Court of Human Rights 23
African Perspectives on Human Dignity for Everyone Everywhere 25–26
Africa of the African Consortium for Law and Religion Studies (ACLARS) 242; African conceptions of human dignity 242–243; basic human needs 244–245; dignity 243–244; gender/age dimensions 246; human dignity and our environments 246; indigenous concept 243; relationships and community 243; religious and theistic foundations 245–246; state obligations 245
Afshari, Reza 14
After Virtue: A Study in Moral Theory (MacIntyre) 15n26
Ali, Begum Hamid 156
Alternative Dispute Resolution (ADR) 217
American Anthropological Commission 65
American Declaration on the Rights and Duties of Man 166
American Federation of Labor v. American Sash and Door Co. (Frankfurter) 206
Amnesty International 78
Andrade, Jorge Carrera 39n5, 85
anti-discrimination protections 216
anti-terrorism law 208
Aquinas, Thomas 151n62
Arajärvi, Pentti 69n78
Arieli, Yehoshua 52n44
Article I of the AMA Code of Medical Ethics 132
Article 1 of the Constitution 199
Article 1 of the Declaration 102n57
Article 1 of the German Basic Law 10n7, 75
Article 1(1) of the German Basic Law 142–143, 195
Article 1 of the Punta del Este Declaration 2, 37, 43, 73–85
Article 1 of the South African Constitution 198
Article 1 of the UDHR 9, 25, 42, 43, 104, 155
Article 2(1) of the Greek Constitution 201
Article 2 of the UN Charter 95n32
Article 2 of the UN Declaration on Human Rights Education and Training 181n19
Article 3 of the Armenian Constitution 201
Article 3 of the ECHR 208
Article 3 of the Xinjiang Uyghur Autonomous Region Deradicalization Regulations 223
Article 4(b) of the UN Declaration on Human Rights Education and Training 181n20
Article 4(2) of the Bulgarian Constitution 200
Article 5 of the Vienna Declaration 124
Article 7(1) of the South African Constitution 198
Article 7(2) of the Greek Constitution 201
Article 9 of the European Convention on Human Rights (ECHR) 144n45, 190
Article 9 of the Punta del Este Declaration 170

Article 9 of the Xinjiang Uyghur Autonomous Region Deradicalization Regulations 223
Article 10 of the South African Constitution 198
Article 10(1) of the ICCPR 135
Article 13 of the ICESCR 176
Article 13(1) of the ICESCR 135
Article 14 of the Armenian Constitution 201
Article 14 of the European Convention on Human Rights 190
Article 22 of the UDHR 81, 151
Article 23(1) of the CRC 137
Article 26 of the UDHR 68n77, 176, 178
Article 26(1) of the UDHR 176
Article 28(2) of the CRC 137
Article 29(1) of the UDHR 82
Article 30 of the UDHR 82
Article 30 of the Constitution of Poland 199
Articles 32 and 33 of the Constitution 200
Article 37(c) of the CRC 137
Article 38 of the Constitution of the Dominican Republic 200
Article 39 of the CRC 138
Article 40(1) of the CRC 138
Article 47 of the Armenian Constitution 201
Article 282.2 of the Russian Criminal Code 224
Article 350 of the Belgian Penal Code 145n47
Asiaín Pereira, Carmen 28
Asian cultures 13
"Asian values" 13
Audi, Robert 113
Auerbach, Jerold S. 217
Aviation Security Act Case 143, 211

Barak, Aharon 47n33, 149, 205
Basic Law 143, 194–197, 202
Bayatyan v. Armenia 144n45
Beaufort 159
Begtrup, Bodil 84
"believing" clauses 62–63
Bennett, Gaymon 40n9, 51n40, 52n42
Bielefeldt, Heiner 28
Bienenfeld 177
Bilbo, Theodore G. 97n40
Bill of Rights 87, 88, 195, 198, 202
blasphemy laws 223
Bogomolov, Alexander 102n56
Brooks, David 130
Buchanan, Allen 16
Byk, Christian 32n105
BYU Conference 27

Cadogan, Sir Alexander 94n28, 96n35
California Penal Code 145n46
Canadian Charter of Rights and Freedoms 205
Carlos Romulo of the Philippines 96
Carozza, Paolo G. 140
Cassin, René 30n100, 39n5, 42, 45n28, 50n38, 67n69, 70n79, 82–84, 92, 94n28, 101, 104n60, 105, 154n9, 156, 158, 163n38
CEU conference 26
Chang, P. C. 34n109, 39n5, 42, 49n38, 69, 87, 88, 98n45, 100, 103n58, 104, 105, 151, 151n62, 156, 168
Charter of Rights and Freedoms 206
Chaskalson, Arthur 203
Churchill, Winston 96n35, 129n8
Cisneros, Guy Pérez 105
Cisneros, Perez 159
Civil Partnership Act 2004 189
Clapham, Andrew 209
Clinton, Bill 242
Code of Alabama 145n46
code of conduct 117n98, 130–132, 189
code of ethics 145n46
Collings, Justin 197
Commission of Inquiry on Human Rights in the Democratic People's Republic of Korea (CoIDPRK) 22–23
Commission on Human Rights 74, 157
constitutional democracy 35n110
Constitutional Tribunal 199–200
contemporary genocides 228–229
The Convention Against Torture and Other Cruel, Inhuman or Degrading Treatment or Punishment (CAT) 137
The Convention on the Elimination of All Forms of Discrimination Against Women (CEDAW) 136
The Convention on the Rights of Persons with Disabilities (CRPD) 138–140
The Convention on the Rights of the Child (CRC) 137–140
Costa, Jean-Paul 208
Council of Europe 180, 190
Court of Justice of the European Union 23
Croce, Benedetto 91n19
Cruz, Hernan Santa 45n28, 101
customary international law 20, 81, 161

Daesh atrocities 229
Daesh genocide 57
Dawood v. Minister of Home Affairs 199, 207

de Burca, Grainne 23
de Chardin, Pierre Teilhard 91n19
de Gaulle, Charles 50n38
de Madariaga, Salvador 91n19
Deva, Surya 83
de Wiar, Carton 85
de Wiart, Henry Carton 39n5
Dicke, Klaus 51n40
"dignitary harm" 221
Dignitatis Humanae 118, 119, 171–172
dignity-based principles 27
"dignity of one's office" 129
"dignity of one's position" 129
"dignity of truth" 124
domestic laws 46, 140
Donnelly, Jack 75
Dulles, John Foster 97n39
Dupré, Catherine 194
duties and responsibilities 168–70, 240; dignity and rights 170–172; human dignity 152–167, 172–174
Düwell, Marcus 33n107
Dworkin, Ronald 123

Eberle, Edward J. 209, 210
Economic and Social Council 74
education: equal access to 182–183; human rights 176–182; teaching and 175–176
Education for Democratic Citizenship 180
Edwards, Michael 219
effective anti-discrimination legislation 191
effective human rights advocacy 218–220
effective human rights education 178
Ellickson, Robert 217
"emphasizing" clauses 60–62
Enders, Christoph 142
enforceable international law 40
"enforcement deficit" 22
"enhanced interrogation" techniques 113, 150
Equality Act 2006 79
Equality and Human Rights Commission 79
equality of resources 123
EU Charter of Fundamental Rights 23
European Convention on Human Rights (ECHR) 146n49, 207
European Court of Human Rights (ECtHR) 23, 144n45, 146n47, 207, 208, 208n68
European Union Charter of Fundamental Rights 20
"Evangelical Declaration against Torture" 113

Fact-Finding Mission on Myanmar 22
Falconer, Lord 58n57
Farley, Margaret 32n105
Figel, Ján 1, 2, 27, 105
"flexible universalism" 154
Fortman, De Gaay 71n83
Foucault, Michel 52n42
foundational principle 2, 74–75
Frankfurter, Felix: *American Federation of Labor v. American Sash and Door Co.* 206
"Free & Equal" campaign 43
Free Exercise Clause of the First Amendment 188
French Declaration of the Rights of Man 32n105
Fukuyama, Francis 222

Gandhi, Mohandas 91n19, 157
genocides 226, 227, 230, 231; in Cambodia 229; contemporary 228–229
German Basic Law 55, 201, 203
German Constitution 51n42
German constitutional order 202
German constitutional system 203
German Federal Constitutional Court 197, 202, 204
German legal system 197
Gewinh 15n26
Ghaidan v. Godin-Mendoza 140
Glendon, Mary Ann 14, 16, 17, 29n98, 30n100, 40, 40n13, 41, 45n27, 46n33, 47n35, 48n36, 48n37, 49n37, 49n38, 50n38, 66, 66n66, 67n69, 68n74, 69n77, 70n81, 71n84, 75, 87, 89n13, 89n15, 91, 91n19, 91n21, 95n31, 95n32, 96n34, 97n38, 97n39, 97n42, 98n45, 100n51, 101n53, 101n56, 102n57, 103n57, 105, 125, 125n123, 126, 127, 151, 154, 154n5, 155, 170, 171; *A World Made New: Eleanor Roosevelt and the Universal Declaration of Human Rights* 11
Glover, Jonathan 56n54, 57
Goldsmith, Jack 20
Goos, Christoph 51n41
Greenawalt, Kent 114
Grimm, Dieter 194–196, 196n8, 202–204
Grootboom v. Government of the Republic of South Africa 198
"gross assaults on humanity" 204
Grumbach, Salymon 10n4
Gutierrez, Gustavo 74

Hannum, Hurst 21
Harlan, Veith 202n43
Heuss, Theodor 51n41
Heyes, Cressida 220
Hill, Thomas E. Jr. 169, 170
Hill v. Church of Scientology of Toronto 205
Hitam, Musa 117n98
Hitler, Adolf 156, 227
Hodgson, William 66n67, 101, 155n9
Hollenbach, David 32n105
Holocaust-type abominations 92
Homer 129n9
"hoping" clause 63–64
Howe, Timothy H. 107
human dignity 1–7, 9, 12, 20, 35n110, 43, 49, 55, 55n52, 58, 60, 73, 104–116, 122–124, 152–153, 174, 212–213, 215, 216, 231, 232, 241, 243; African perspectives on 242–246; balancing and trade-offs 210–211; civil society 235; conceptual connections between rights and duties 156–159; as constitutional principle 204–205; defining and understanding rights of conscience 144–148; definitions of 127–129; different legal systems 203; duty of the state 163–165; educational institutions 235; egregious abuses of 226–229; flexible universalism and different social, political, legal, and economic contexts 151; foundational value of the social order 202–203; in German Basic Law 195–197; implications for rights and duties 162–163; inalienable 125; indivisible 126; informal accommodations of conscience 188–192; interdependent 126; international actors 234; in international and domestic law 134; interrelated 126; is broader than human rights 142–144; in law 194–195; mechanisms 235–236; mutual vindication of 209–210; "of" and "for" everyone everywhere 36–38; ordinary exceptions to non-discrimination provisions 187–188; in other legal systems 197–201; as principle in adjudication 205–208; recognition of 175–176, 240; relationship between rights and duties 166–167; religious freedom and non-discrimination 184–187; and rights 28n97; rights-first (or rights-only) approach to human rights 154; and rights of enemy combatants 149–150; and road to "final solution" 227–228; and specification of human rights 193–194; states 234–235; state's duties regarding human rights 165–166; as status 129–132; in the UDHR 57; UDHR on rights and duties 155–156; universal 125; universal and reciprocal character of 220–222; upward lift 209; as worth 132–134
"human dignity for everyone" 37
Human Dignity for Everyone Everywhere 24–35
human rights 14, 21, 58, 172–174; advocacy 218; aim or end of 75–76; claims 241; controversies 222–225; defining and specifying 239–240; depoliticizing 225; distortion and avoidance of 222–223; implementation and application of 13–16; implementing 16–21; instrumentalization of 223–225; issues 2; justifications of 116–122; monitoring and enforcing 21–24; obligations 81; project 21; promoting 81–85; protections on human dignity 79; revolution 10; standards 76–80; understanding 16; universality of 12–13; violations 22, 62, 79, 229–231
Human Rights Committee 48
Human Rights Watch 77
Humphrey, John 11, 30n100, 39n5, 45n28, 50n38, 74, 81, 85, 98n45, 100, 101n53, 151n62, 154n9
Huxley, Aldous 91n19

identity-based discrimination 215
"identity of treatment" approach 199
identity politics 60, 221–222, 225
Ignatieff, Michael 35n109
inalienable rights 12, 25, 37, 41, 73, 83–85, 125, 135, 139, 237, 239
"incompletely theorized agreement" 33
indivisible 124, 126
Inter-American Court of Human Rights 23
interdependent rights 124, 126
international and domestic law, dignity in 134
international and regional human rights bodies 21
International Bill of Rights 87, 88
The International Convention on the Elimination of All Forms of Racial Discrimination (ICERD) 135–136
The International Covenant on Civil and Political Rights (ICCPR) 17, 53, 82, 126, 135, 162
The International Covenant on Economic, Social and Cultural Rights (ICESCR) 17, 82, 135, 162

International Criminal Tribunal for Rwanda (ICTR) 22
International Criminal Tribunal for the Former Yugoslavia (ICTY) 22
international customary law 12
International Federation of Red Cross 230
International Independent Commission of Inquiry on the Syrian Arab Republic (IICoISAR) 22
"international law" 39n9
International Law Commission 58
international legal institutions 16
international religious freedom 77
interrelated rights 124, 126
Islamic law 13
Islamic Republic of Iran 14
Islamic schemes 14

Jacobs, Irving 74
Jalloh v. Germany 207n68
Japanese imperialism 38
Jayawickrama, Nihal 17
Johnson, M. Glen 38n5, 49n37
John Yoo 150
Jones, David A. 52n43

Kamali, Mohammad Hashim 120
Kant, Immanuel 34n109, 52n44, 121, 122, 128, 134, 169, 170
Kaplan, Seth D. 125, 125n123, 126, 127, 151, 154, 154n5, 155, 170, 171
Kateb, George 37n2
Katz-Suchy 85
Kennedy, Anthony 206
Khama, Ian 245
Khama, Sir Seretse 242
Ki-moon, Ban 176
Kolnai, Aurel 141, 142
Koretsky, Vladimir 101, 101n56
Koskenniemi, Martti 66n66

Lash, Joseph P. 98n44
"laundry list" of rights 4
Lauterpacht, Hersch 74
Lawrence v. Texas 207
Lebech, Mette 128n1
Lee Kuan Yew 13
Lethal Politics (Rummel) 56n54
Levitt, Michael O. 215n3
Life Imprisonment Case 143
Lilla, Mark 220
Lincoln, Abraham 65, 106
Lindholm, Tore 33, 42, 74, 104
Lisbon Treaty 32n105, 194
Local Religious Organizations (LROs) 224, 225
Loutfi, Omar 70n81
Luban, David 21
Łuków, Paweł 104

MacArthur, Douglas 88
MacIntyre, Alasdair 15; *After Virtue: A Study in Moral Theory* 15n26
Mahmood, Tahir 28
Malik, Charles 21, 39n5, 42, 45n27, 48n37, 49n37, 50n38, 83, 88, 90n15, 98n45, 100, 100n50, 102n56, 103n57, 104, 157, 159
Mandela, Nelson 242
Mao 56n54
Maritain, Jacques 125
Marshall, George 84
Mayer, Ann Elizabeth 14
McCrudden, Christopher 27
McNitt, Rollin 74
Melloni, Alberto 27
Menon, Lakshimi 89n14
Microcensus Case 143
moral reasoning 160
Morsink, Johannes 29n98, 30n100, 31n101, 38n5, 45n28, 46, 46n31, 46n32, 47n35, 48n35–48n36, 50n38, 50n39, 53n46, 65, 66n66, 68n77, 69n78, 70n80, 70n81, 71, 71n83, 89n13, 89n14, 90n17, 91n18, 94n28, 101n53, 153; *The Universal Declaration of Human Rights and the Challenge of Religion* 10n6
mutual vindication of rights 212, 213–216, 241

national human rights institutions (NHRI) 79, 191
national security 58, 58n57, 223, 225
Nazi fascism 38
Neuhäuser, Christian 31n103
Neuman, Gerald L. 76n24
non-departmental public body 79
Nuremberg Trials 40
Nyerere, Julius 245

Obergefell v. Hodges 207
O'Connell, Mary Ellen 93n27
Olmstead, Dan 39n8
Ordonneau, Pierre 89n15
Organisation for Security and Cooperation in Europe (OSCE) 191
"overlapping justification" 33

Oxford Conference 26–27
Oxford Journal of Law and Religion 26

Parsons, Wilfred 74
A Path to Dignity: The Power of Human Rights Education 179
Patterson v. Walgreen Co. 189n14
Paust, Jordan J. 82, 164
Pavlov, Alexei 49n37, 102n56, 159
Paxton 188
Perry, Michael 163n37
"personal data self-determination" 197
Planned Parenthood v. Casey 207
Polish Constitution 199
Political Liberalism (Rawls) 112n81
Politis, Nikolas 93n28
Posner, Eric 154, 166
Preamble of the American Declaration 166
prima facie duties 134
Principle 17 of the Guiding Principles 83
Prost, Antoine 93n28
public policy proposals 115
"public reason" 112–116
Punta del Este Declaration 4, 8, 11, 27, 28, 35, 44, 63, 66, 68, 144, 149, 222, 225, 230–232, 242–246; "believing" clauses 62–63; "emphasizing" clauses 60–62; "hoping" clause 63–64; on human dignity 233–241; on Human Dignity for Everyone Everywhere 24–35; human dignity "of" and "for" everyone everywhere 36–38; initial declaration of the UDHR 64–72; rationale for 11–24; "recalling" clauses 44–53; "recognizing" clauses 54–60; "whereas" clauses 38–44

Quataert, Jean H. 40n12

Radovanovic 162n36
Rajaie-Khorassani 13
Rau, Johannes 196
Rawls, John 33, 33n107, 108n77, 110n78, 111n78, 112, 112n82, 113–115, 123; *Political Liberalism* 112n81
"recalling" clauses 44–53
"recognizing" clauses 54–60
Red Crescent Societies 230
"re-education camps" 223
religious freedom 105
religious minorities 57, 215
The Religious Peace of Augsburg (1555) 92n27
Renteln, Alison 15
Rhéaume, Denise 141
rights-first (or rights-only) approach to human rights 154
Rohingya Muslims 57
Romulo, Carlos 95n33
Roosevelt, Eleanor 30n100, 39n5, 45n28, 49n38, 64, 64n62, 68n74, 70, 75, 82, 85, 97, 97n39–97n42, 98n44–98n45, 99, 100, 102n56, 105, 161, 168, 181
Roosevelt, Franklin Delano 45n28, 97, 129n8
Roosevelt, Theodore 129n8
Rosenblatt v. Baer 206
Rosen, Michael 170n56
Ross, William D. 134
Roth, Hans Ingvar 67, 89n14, 98n44, 100n51
Ruggie, John 82
Rule EC 1-7 of the Code 131
"rule of law" 47, 47n34
Rummel, R. J.: *Lethal Politics* 56n54
Russian Federation legislation 224
R. v. Butler 205

Sachs, Albie 142
Samnøy, Åshild 98n44
Schabas, William 70n79, 95n33, 162n36
Schlink, Bernard 52n43, 76n23, 142
Schmidt, Elke Elisabath 121
Schönecker, Dieter 121
Schweitzer, Friedrich 119
Section 1 of the American Medical Association (AMA) 131
Section 4 of the Abortion Act 1967 145n47
Section 15(1) of the Canadian Charter of Rights and Freedoms 141
Selmouni v. France 208n68
Shulzinger, Doron 119, 119n107
Slim, Hugo 219
Sourlas, Paul 211
The South African Constitution 20, 140, 167, 199
South African legal system 203
Special Rapporteur on Human Dignity 236
Stewart, Potter 206
Stier, Davor 190, 191
Sun, Pinghua 45n27, 46n32, 48n36, 49n38, 51n42, 92n22, 100n51, 103n58
Sunstein, Cass R. 33n106, 109n78, 110n78, 111n78
Sustainable Development Goals (SDG) 179–182
Symonides, Janusz 38n5, 49n37

Tasioulas, John 34n109, 76n23, 142, 159n26, 160
Tepliakov, Valentin 30n100, 101n56
Te Water, Charles Theodore 84
Tollefsen, Christopher 10n7
Treaty of Westphalia 92n27
Truman, Harry 49n38, 97, 97n38, 97n41
Trump, Donald 130
Tutsis 56n4, 57n4, 229
Tyrer v. UK 207

Ubuntu 243, 244
Uitz, Renata 27
UN Commission on Human Rights 99
UN Convention on the Prevention and Punishment of the Crime of Genocide 31n102, 227, 229, 230
UN Declaration on Human Rights Education and Training 177–180
UN Forum on Human Dignity 235–236
UN General Assembly 11n9, 41, 100, 101, 124, 161, 177, 234
UN Guiding Principles on Business and Human Rights 82
UN Human Rights Commission 99n49, 101
UN Human Rights Committee 22
UN Human Rights Council 22, 82, 235, 236
United Nations Declaration on the Elimination of All Forms of Racial Discrimination 136
Universal Declaration of Human Rights (UDHR) 1–3, 5, 8, 11, 14, 15, 17, 35, 37, 38, 46, 46n32, 49, 50, 52n44, 53, 56, 65, 70, 71, 75, 78, 80, 101, 117, 127, 136, 160n28, 161, 182, 224, 231, 232, 235, 237–242; "all peoples and all nations" 65; common standard of achievement 64–65; "constantly in mind" 67–68; "every individual and every organ of society" 65–67; human dignity 9–11; Human Dignity for Everyone Everywhere 24–35; local, national, and international 70–71; preamble to 9; progressive measures 69–70; rationale for Punta del Este Declaration 11–24; striving through teaching and education 68–69; universal and effective recognition and observance 71–72
The Universal Declaration of Human Rights and the Challenge of Religion (Morsink) 10n6
Universal Periodic Review (UPR) 79
UN Office for the Disaster Risk Reduction (UNISDR) 229
UN Special Rapporteur on Freedom of Religion or Belief 80
UN Special Rapporteur on Human Dignity 236
UN Universal Periodic Review 22
Utah Compromise 213, 214, 214n3, 215n3

Vienna Conference on Human Rights 1993 17
Vienna Declaration and Program of Action 66n69, 124, 164
Vienna World Conference on Human Rights 1993 124
Vincent, R. J. 47n33
Voegele, William 220
von Doussa, John 60n61, 61n61

Waldron, Jeremy 60n60, 128, 149, 150, 150n56, 152, 156n15, 169, 173, 201
Walsh, David 34n109
Walzer, Michael 154n5
"War on Terror" 113, 150
Washington, George 129, 130
Wells, H. G. 74
"whereas" clauses 38–44
"whole of society" approach 83
Wilson, Geoffrey 89n14, 101
Wilson, Henry 106
Wilson, Robin Fretwell 27, 213
Winter, Jay 93n28
World Conference on Human Rights 164
World Health Organization (WHO) 229
A World Made New: Eleanor Roosevelt and the Universal Declaration of Human Rights (Glendon) 11
World Program for Human Rights Education 179, 180

Yorùbá language rights 243

9781032074580